ERIC WALROND

A Life

in the

Harlem

Renaissance

and the

Transatlantic

Caribbean

ERIC WALROND

JAMES DAVIS

Columbia University Press   New York

COLUMBIA UNIVERSITY PRESS
Publishers Since 1893
New York   Chichester, West Sussex
cup.columbia.edu

Library of Congress Cataloging-in-Publication Data

Davis, James C. (James Cyril)
   Eric Walrond : a life in the Harlem Renaissance and the Transatlantic
Caribbean / James Davis.
      pages cm
   Includes bibliographical references and index.
   ISBN 978-0-231-15784-1 (cloth : alk. paper) —
   ISBN 978-0-231-53861-9 (ebook)
      1. Walrond, Eric, 1898–1966. 2. American literature—Caribbean American
authors—Biography. 3. Harlem Renaissance. I. Title.

   PS3545.A5826Z68 2015
   818'.5209—dc23
   [B]

                                                            2014029768

Cover image: Robert H. Davis Papers, Manuscripts and Archives Division,
The New York Public Library, Astor, Lenox and Tilden Foundations.

Cover and book design: Lisa Hamm

References to Web sites (URLs) were accurate at the time of writing.
Neither the author nor Columbia University Press is responsible for URLs
that may have expired or changed since the manuscript was prepared.

For my father

Eric Walrond is the unknown quantity among Negro authors. None is more ambitious than he, none more possessed of keener observation, poetic insight, or intelligence. There is no place in his consciousness for sentimentality, hypocrisy, or clichés. His prose demonstrates his struggles to escape from conventionalities and become an individual talent. But so far this struggle has not been crowned with any appreciable success.

WALLACE THURMAN, *AUNT HAGAR'S CHILDREN* (1930)

CONTENTS

ACKNOWLEDGMENTS

My greatest debt is to Louis Parascandola and Carl Wade, experts on Eric Walrond and keepers of the flame. They have been unstintingly generous, providing critical documents and deepening my understanding of the value of Walrond's writing and life story to scholars and general readers alike. I am grateful to Joan Stewart, granddaughter of Eric Walrond, who provided access to the family papers in the possession of her late mother, Dorothy Stewart. I also wish to thank Dorothy Bone, whose late husband, Robert Bone, conducted extensive research toward a biography of Eric Walrond thirty years ago, without which this book would not be possible. Many people supported this project with interventions and encouragement, including Imani Wilson, Charles Molesworth, David Killingray, John Cowley, Oneka Labennett, A'Lelia Bundles, Shondel Nero, Katherine Zien, Brent Edwards, Nydia Swaby, Laura Lomas, Amy Cherry, Alice Goheneix, Claire Joubert, Emelienne Baneth, Vanessa Perez-Rosario, Michelle Stephens, Tryon Woods, Aaron Jaffe, Jeffrey Perry, Luis Pulido Ritter, Patrick Scarborough, and my colleagues at *Radical Teacher* magazine and the Professional Staff Congress. For submitting gamely to unannounced interviews in Wiltshire County, UK, I am grateful to John Cottle, Gerald Bodman, and Mary Lane. For their generosity, I wish to thank Melva Lowe de Goodin and Glenroy James of the Society for the Friends of the Afro-Antillean Museum, Panama City. This project benefited from the early support of a National Endowment of the Humanities seminar, led by Carolyn Levander and Rachel Adams, and a fellowship at the Leon Levy Center for Biography, whose founder, Shelby White, deserves thanks. My co-fellows, Ilan Ehrlich, Hyewon Yi, Maryann Weaver, Thulani Davis, and Molly Peacock, were wonderfully supportive, as were the directors David Nasaw and Nancy Milford. I am grateful for the assistance of many archivists: Sara Garrod, George Padmore Institute; Mary Kiffer, Guggenheim Foundation; Lorna Haycock and Bill Perry, Wiltshire Heritage Museum and Library; Claire Skinner and Michael Marshman, Wiltshire and Swindon History Centre; Elspeth Healey, Harry Ransom Research Center, University of Texas; JoEllen El Bashir, Moorland-Spingarn Research Center, Howard University; Andrea Jackson and Kayin Shabazz, Robert W. Woodruff Library, Atlanta University Center; Carol Leadenham, Hoover Institution Archives, Stanford University; Lee Anne Titangos, Bancroft Library, University of California; Christopher Harter, Amistad Research Center, Tulane University; Diana Carey, Schlesinger Library, Radcliffe Institute; and Sherry Warman, Brooklyn College Library. For supporting my research and travel, I thank the Research Foundation of the City University of New York, the Leonard and Claire Tow Faculty Research Fund, and the Brooklyn College School of Humanities and Social Sciences. I would like to acknowledge the encouragement of my colleagues in Brooklyn College's English Department and American Studies Program, too numerous to name here, and I am especially grateful to Joseph Entin, Ellen Tremper, Prudence Cumberbatch, and Martha Nadell. My students are a source of inspiration, and those in Comp Lit 7701 in Spring 2011 deserve particular recognition for helping me refine my thinking. At Columbia University Press, Whitney Johnson has been enormously helpful, and my outside readers, Gary Holcomb and Michelle Stephens, offered incisive suggestions that dramatically improved the book. My editor, Philip Leventhal, has been unflappable and sagacious at every turn, and I am grateful for his guidance. My family has been stalwart in their support and interest; many thanks to Jane and Rob Madell, to my parents, and most of all to Eva, Rose, and Jody, with great affection.

ABBREVIATIONS

ALP	Alain Locke Papers, Moorland-Spingarn Research Center, Howard University
ARC	Amistad Research Center, Tulane University
CJMC	Countee Cullen–Harold Jackman Memorial Collection, Robert W. Woodruff Library, Atlanta University Center
CVV	Carl Van Vechten Papers, New York Public Library, Rare Books and Manuscripts Division
ERN	Ethel Ray Nance Papers, Bancroft Library, University of California at Berkeley
GFP	John Simon Guggenheim Memorial Foundation Papers, New York
HFC	Hoyt Fuller Collection, Robert W. Woodruff Library, Atlanta University Center
HFP	William T. Harmon Foundation Papers, Library of Congress, Washington, DC
HRHRC	Harry Ransom Humanities Research Center, University of Texas, Austin
JFC	Joseph Freeman Collection, Hoover Institution on War, Revolution and Peace, Stanford University
JWJ	James Weldon Johnson Collection, Beinecke Rare Book & Manuscript Library, Yale University

LP	Liveright Publishing Co. Papers, W. W. Norton Co., New York
MSRC	Moorland-Spingarn Research Center, Howard University
NUL	National Urban League Papers, Library of Congress, Washington, DC
RPP	Rosey E. Pool Papers, University of Sussex Library, UK
RWW	Robert W. Woodruff Library, Atlanta University Center
SCNYPL	Schomburg Center for Research in Black Culture, New York Public Library
SGD	Shirley Graham Du Bois Collection, Schlesinger Library, Harvard University
WFP	Walrond Family Papers, possession of Joan Stewart

CHRONOLOGY

1898 (December 18)	Eric Derwent Walrond born to William and Ruth Walrond in British Guiana (Guyana).
1906	Walrond family moves to Barbados. Eric Walrond studies at St. Stephen's School for Boys.
1910	William Walrond moves to Colón, Panama, followed a year later by family.
1911–16	Eric Walrond studies in Canal Zone public schools, then with private tutors.
1916–18	Employed as reporter for Panama's *Star & Herald*.
1918	Moves to Brooklyn, New York.
1918–20	Works multiple jobs, including associate editor of Garveyite newspaper *The Weekly Review*. Moves to Harlem.
1920	Marries Edith Melita Cadogan, a Jamaican immigrant with whom he has three daughters in three years. Moves back to Brooklyn.
1921	Begins contributing to Garvey's *Negro World*, promoted the following year to assistant editor then associate editor.
1922–24	While at *Negro World*, attends the College of the City of New York.

1923	Separates from Edith, who returns to Jamaica with their three children. Moves back to Harlem, helps establish the Writer's Guild, a group of young African Americans.
1924	First reference to anxiety and depression in correspondence. Disillusionment with Garvey and United Negro Improvement Association (UNIA). Begins study of creative writing at Columbia University.
1924	Helps organize event in downtown Manhattan introducing African American writers to publishing establishment, resulting in special Harlem issue of *Survey Magazine*.
1925	Publishes in Alain Locke's groundbreaking anthology *The New Negro*.
1925–27	Employed as business manager at *Opportunity*, journal of the National Urban League.
1926	Publishes *Tropic Death* with Boni & Liveright. Contracts for a second book, *The Big Ditch*, a "romantic history" of Panama.
1926 (November)	Edits special Caribbean issue of *Opportunity*.
1927	Receives Harmon Foundation Award for achievement in literature and Zona Gale Scholarship to study creative writing at the University of Wisconsin. Anthologized in *The American Caravan*.
1928	Receives Guggenheim Fellowship to conduct research in the Caribbean.
1928–29	Travels in the Caribbean, including Panama, Haiti, Dominican Republic, St. Thomas, and Barbados.
1929	Moves to France. Lives one year in Paris, one year in Mediterranean village of Bandol.
1931	Horace Liveright voids contact for *The Big Ditch*. Walrond returns briefly to New York to negotiate.
1931–39	Moves to London. Contributes to several periodicals and joins emergent anticolonial movement. Struggles to place creative writing.
1935	Employed as publicity manager for "negro musical revue" touring UK.

1935–38	Employed by Garvey's journal *The Black Man*. Anticolonial movement galvanized by Italy's invasion of Ethiopia.
1938	Arrested for assault on colleague but acquitted.
1939	Onset of World War II, evacuates London to Bradford-on-Avon, Wiltshire.
1940–44	Contributes to three U.S. periodicals from England, including war reporting.
1944	*Chicago Defender* reports "wireless operator and gunner" Walrond shot down flying air raid over Germany for the Royal Air Force (unconfirmed).
1944–51	Struggles to publish, takes factory position in Avon Rubber Corporation.
1952	Admitted voluntarily to Roundway Psychiatric Hospital, Devizes, England, for treatment of depression. Renews copyright for *Tropic Death*.
1952–57	Cofounds and publishes in *The Roundway Review*, including Caribbean fiction and installments of his Panama history.
1957	Erica Marx of Hand and Flower Press employs Walrond as researcher on a "negro poetry programme" in London. Discharge from Roundway Hospital, return to London.
1958	Amid tensions over Notting Hill riots, "Black and Unknown Bards" performed in London's Royal Court Theatre.
1959–65	In declining health, lives in London suburb of Hornsey, employed by import-export firm in financial district.
1966	Contacted by Liveright Publishing regarding sale of reprint rights to *Tropic Death*.
1966 (August 8)	Dies of pulmonary thrombosis in London. Buried in Abney Park Cemetery, Stoke-Newington, London.
1970	Kenneth Ramchand (University of the West Indies) publishes "Eric Walrond: The Writer Who Ran Away" in Jamaican journal *Savacou*.
1972	Collier Books (Macmillan, Inc.) republishes *Tropic Death*.

1983–85	Robert Bone (Columbia University) begins biography of Walrond.
1998	Publication of *"Winds Can Wake Up the Dead": An Eric Walrond Reader.*
2011	Publication of *In Search of Asylum: The Later Writings of Eric Walrond.*
2012	Publication of *Eric Walrond: The Critical Heritage.*
2013	Liveright Publishing Corporation (W. W. Norton) republishes *Tropic Death.*

ERIC WALROND

INTRODUCTION

A HARLEM STORY, A DIASPORA STORY

Jean Campbell deposited a check for $850 at Barclay's Bank on Barbour Street in Kingston, Jamaica, in 1969. It was an advance on the sale of the reprint rights for a book her father published to great acclaim in 1926, the first tangible benefit she and her sisters received from his writing. Liveright Publishers, a New York firm, had sold Eric Walrond's lugubriously titled short story collection, *Tropic Death*. A check for $150 had been mailed to the author in London in early 1966 and, when he died that August, the balance of his $1,000 advance was made out to his estate. It was a closing scene that Walrond himself could have written, the sort of bitter irony that ends his stories. Finally, the literary labor he performed as a young man was profitable as he was headed for his grave; finally, he was providing for his daughters, from whom he had been estranged for forty years; finally, a West Indian family received royalties for a book by a West Indian about West Indians. Composed in Harlem, set in the Caribbean, and now profitable in London and Kingston, *Tropic Death* had traced a path across generations through the diaspora.

The book was Walrond's calling card and claim to fame, and although he did not live long enough to see its reissue, the knowledge of its impending sale had cheered him immensely. He considered himself a failure, and he was not alone in this opinion. A heralded prose writer and respected journalist of the

Harlem Renaissance, he never published another book-length work. By the mid-1960s, few of his friends and fewer scholars knew of his whereabouts. An immigrant to New York from the Panamanian city of Colón, born in British Guiana (now Guyana) to Barbadian parents, Walrond had made a strong impression in 1920s New York. "Anyone who ever met him remembered him," said one close friend, "as soon as he entered the room you knew he was there."[1] Almost no one knew he was there, however, by the 1960s. The former Guggenheim Fellow had all but vanished into a quiet suburb north of London, working at an export firm near St. Paul's Cathedral. In addition to *Tropic Death*, he had placed roughly 150 publications in nearly 40 periodicals in at least five countries, a record of uneven but compelling work that belies the one-hit wonder label. His tumultuous, peripatetic life and the radical, innovative writing to which it gave rise are this book's subject.

When Robert Bone, the author of two pioneering studies of African American literature, began work on a biography of Walrond in the 1980s, he sought to solve the mystery of why "after so promising a start, he was reduced to silence."[2] In a sense, Bone had the advantage of proximity to important sources, including Walrond's nephew, who contacted family members and conducted extensive research. Their book was not completed, however, extending the obscurity into which Eric Walrond had drifted.[3] But the intervening years have been propitious, not only revealing additional archival materials (thanks principally to Louis Parascandola and Carl Wade) but also because of a paradigm shift in the study of Caribbean "New Negro" writers and transnational black writing broadly. This is therefore a very different book from the one Bone had in mind, despite drawing on some of the same materials.

A HARLEM STORY

Walrond was at the social and institutional center of 1920s Harlem. "I venture to say there isn't another fellow in town anywhere near his age with as wide an acquaintance," said the painter Aaron Douglas.[4] Ethel Ray Nance, Walrond's colleague at *Opportunity* magazine, recalled him as "a person that held our little group together and built the group, because he had the faculty of bringing in interesting people. If Eric walked down the street, someone interesting was bound to show up."⁵ "Suave" and possessed of a "rippling wit," as historian David Levering Lewis notes, Walrond was a regular at Harlem's literary gatherings, often accompanied by the poets Countée Cullen and Langston Hughes; their friends Harold Jackman and Arna Bontemps; Jessie Fauset, literary editor of *The Crisis*; and the artist and poet Gwendolyn Bennett.⁶ He also befriended Shirley Graham, who later married W. E. B. Du Bois; Alain Locke, philosophy professor and "midwife" of the New Negro movement; Casper Holstein, head of the Harlem numbers racket; Charles S. Johnson, editor of *Opportunity*; and Carl Van Vechten, author of *Nigger Heaven*. They thought him a "top-notch writer," Nance said, charismatic, a generous friend, and a hustler with shrewd business sense.

A journalist by training, Walrond worked for two important black periodicals, first as associate editor at *Negro World*, the journal of Marcus Garvey's Universal Negro Improvement Association (UNIA), then as business manager at *Opportunity*, the journal of the National Urban League. At opposite ends of the ideological spectrum, the UNIA advocated a separatist, race-first platform while *Opportunity*, led by the indefatigable Johnson, a Chicago-trained sociologist, championed interracial cooperation. Johnson called Walrond one of the few "Negro writers who can, with complete justice, be styled intellectuals," a remark that is striking when one considers that Walrond never completed college.⁷ Walrond was a more important catalyst for the New Negro movement than has been recognized, including a critical role in a 1924 dinner event at the downtown Civic Club that launched the movement, introducing black writers to New York's publishing establishment. His journalism focused on literature and the arts, but he also covered history and politics. Once his talent became known outside Harlem, he published in *Vanity Fair*, *Current History*, *The New Republic*, and *The Smart Set*, among others. His recent arrival from the Caribbean did not prevent editors from identifying him as an authority on African American culture, from the Charleston dance craze, to the Harlem cabaret scene, to the Great Migration.

But fiction writing was Walrond's passion, publicly recognized first in an *Opportunity* story contest and in Locke's anthology *The New Negro* (1925). The publication of *Tropic Death* the following year with a prominent firm was a major coup for a black writer. The publishers of O'Neill, Dreiser, Pound, and Eliot, Boni & Liveright had a highbrow imprimatur and a number of bestsellers as well. *Tropic Death* exhibited the technical innovation and aversion to sentimentality prized among American modernists, and its fidelity to Caribbean speech and folk culture was unprecedented. The book drew frequent comparisons to Jean Toomer's *Cane*, and Sterling Brown recalled these two books as the era's "brilliant high marks in fiction" and Walrond's talent as "tremendous."[8] Even genteel critics, such as Benjamin Brawley and Du Bois, were impressed with *Tropic Death* despite its many disreputable characters and fatalistic tone. Du Bois called it "a distinct contribution to Negro American literature," "a human document of deep significance and great promise."[9]

On the heels of *Tropic Death*, Walrond placed a story in the inaugural issue of *The American Caravan*, obtained a $1,000 advance for a second book, and won three prestigious awards: a Harmon Foundation Award "for Excellence in Literary Achievement by a Negro," a Zona Gale Scholarship to study at the University of Wisconsin, and a Guggenheim Fellowship to conduct research in the Caribbean. Donald Friede, vice president of Boni & Liveright, wrote, "I believe him to be the outstanding Negro prose writer of this country, and [. . .] I believe that his work will in time place him among the important writers in America—both Negro and white."[10] These were major accolades for someone just a few years removed from his job as a clerk in a Manhattan hospital, living with his aunt in Brooklyn. Given these achievements and the praise that followed, why is so little known about him?

One reason is that he left New York and never published another book. He failed to fulfill expectations. By leaving Harlem at the height of his fame and the movement he helped invigorate, he sabotaged his promising career, publishing sporadically and never moving back to the United States. His departure is often cited as his downfall. But why did he leave? Where did he go, and why? What *did* he go on to write? In 1979, David

Levering Lewis noted that another Harlem writer saw Walrond "in a London railway station in late 1929," and "that was about the last heard of him."[11] But since then, Harlem Renaissance scholarship has broadened its scope beyond the United States, and the Caribbean diaspora has been the subject of extensive research. Both developments have encouraged extranational modes of inquiry. In these contexts—a transnational understanding of the Harlem Renaissance and a diaspora approach to Caribbean writing—Walrond's significance takes on a different cast.

Born on the Caribbean coast of South America, Walrond was raised in a village near Bridgetown, the capital of Barbados, by middle-class parents. He received an English education at St. Stephen's School for Boys, then spent his adolescence in Panama, where many West Indians, including Walrond's father, moved to find work. William Walrond was "caught up inexorably in the stream of history," his son wrote, "like the migrants of every race, colour and nationality then flocking to the country through which Uncle Sam was cutting a canal" ("From" 1). After completing his schooling, he began writing for an English-language newspaper, Panama's *Star & Herald*. When the opportunity arose in 1918, he left for New York. Ten years later, he packed his bags again and left for Europe. Walrond's peripatetic career has impeded examination of his life and work. He defies categorization as a conventional immigrant writer or Harlem writer. This book tells a different sort of story, a diaspora story in which Walrond's restless itinerary is an inducement to inquiry rather than an obstacle.

A DIASPORA STORY

Although we begin with Walrond's youth in a Caribbean region in the throes of upheaval, the richness of his diaspora story is best suggested by considering England, most of whose black residents before World War II were students and seamen. This was a generation before the SS *Empire Windrush* deposited nearly five hundred Caribbean passengers at Tilbury docks in 1948, inaugurating a new phase in black British history. Walrond shared common experiences with other pre-*Windrush* intellectuals, such as C. L. R. James, George Padmore, and Una Marson, forerunners to the West Indian writers who established a full-fledged literary movement after World War II. London's small but active black community galvanized anticolonial sentiment through a vibrant transnational periodical culture. Walrond wrote for Garvey's journal *The Black Man*, publishing trenchant critiques of imperialism and English "liberality" and contributing articles to mainstream papers such as London's *Spectator* and *The Evening Standard* and New York papers such as *The People's Voice* and the *Amsterdam News*. This book considers Walrond's career in England in relation to the anticolonial movement and the resistance black Britons mounted against the "colour bar" at home.

But Walrond differed in many respects from his contemporaries, not least because he did not remain long in London, moving in 1939 to Bradford-on-Avon in rural Wiltshire County. During his twelve years there, he was from all accounts the town's only black resident, and among the perplexing questions about Walrond's life is why he stayed as long as he did. Though it was only a ninety-minute train ride from Paddington Station, life in Bradford-on-Avon was a far cry from London. Interviews with his neighbors shed light on this period about which little was previously known. Walrond took a job at the Avon Rubber Company and quietly went about his writing, sending articles to London, New York, and even Nashville, Tennessee, interminably revising a manuscript about the history of Panama.

Were it not for the war and the onset of severe bouts of depression, Walrond may have been more adept at advancing his career. Instead, he was admitted to the Roundway Psychiatric Hospital in 1952 as a voluntary patient. At Roundway, with 1,300 residents, he found a sense of support he had been lacking. The hospital engaged patients in activities rather than subjecting them to confinement, and Walrond helped establish *The Roundway Review*, a literary journal. A fortunate reference in 1957 from Nancy Cunard resulted in an extensive research assignment. The first performance of "Negro poetry" was to be staged in London, and Walrond's involvement encouraged him to apply for a discharge from the hospital. The London to which he returned was changed considerably. Within months, the Notting Hill riots of 1958 expressed white working-class resentment toward the former colonials who had made England their home. The violence yielded an ambivalent response: an affirmation of Afro-Caribbean culture, on one hand, represented in the inception of Carnival, and on the other hand, the restriction of immigration through the Commonwealth Immigrants Act. Walrond lived just long enough to witness these birth pangs of modern black Britain, to see the rise and fall of the West Indian Federation movement in the 1960s, and to glimpse, in the founding of the Caribbean Artists Movement, the stirrings of postcolonial literature. Living modestly in a North London suburb, he suffered a series of heart attacks, including a fatal one in 1966.

CHOMBO, NEGRO, COLOURED: NEGOTIATING RACE ACROSS BORDERS

Walrond was more disappointed than anyone that he did not publish another book after *Tropic Death*. *The Big Ditch*, his history of Panama, was advertised in Boni & Liveright's fall 1928 catalog. It never appeared. He was reduced to serializing some of it in the 1950s in *The Roundway Review*. The obscure publication failed to right his career or mitigate his disappointment, but a close reading of its fifteen installments reveals a work of tremendous potential, much of it realized. Walrond's research was prodigious, and his vision of Panama's centrality to the black Atlantic was prescient. Just as James's famous history of the Haitian Revolution, *The Black Jacobins* (1938), traced the tensions French imperialism generated among classes, races, nations, and stakeholders in Haiti, all mediated by the figure of Toussaint L'Ouverture, *The Big Ditch* reframed Panama's role in the Caribbean and beyond, casting the maneuvers of the French and Americans as a pivotal transition in colonial history and placing the revolutionary Pedro Prestán at the narrative's center. Walrond was keenly aware of Panama's place in the "El Dorado" myth. From the conquistador Hernán Cortes, to the U.S. diplomat John Lloyd Stephens, to Ferdinand de Lesseps and Theodore Roosevelt, the prospect of putting a canal through the wasp waist of the Americas signaled the irresistible promise of commerce and national glory. Walrond's history, though uneven, is a document of startling scope and analysis. Had it found a capable editor it may well be cited as a pioneering study.

The remnants of the Panama book dispel a rumor that Walrond spent his time in France in dissolution.[12] Like many expatriates, he passed his share of Paris evenings (and early mornings) carousing. But he was also immersed in the archives, as evidenced by his research into Panama-related developments in France and elsewhere. If Walrond was not prolific there, he was far from idle. The heterogeneity of Paris' black community represented a departure from Harlem. There, Walrond had translated the Caribbean for North American readers, not only in *Tropic Death* but also by editing a Caribbean issue of *Opportunity* and bringing a Caribbean perspective to his essays. In France and England, his Caribbeanness signified differently, and his decade in the United States distinguished him from the colonial intellectuals in the metropole.

Two tensions that were central to Walrond's career emerge from his Caribbean background. Above all, the Caribbean instilled a thoroughgoing skepticism toward monolithic notions of race. The differences in ethnicity, religion, language, class, and culture that were conventionally subsumed under the designations "Negro" or "Coloured" fuel much of his work. But the Caribbean also fostered a race radicalism, a desire to identify and challenge white supremacy. Despite his Anglophilic education, Walrond developed an early awareness that the racism he encountered derived from colonial relations. Nowhere was this clearer than in Panama, where locals called him a *chombo*, a racial slur, and Jim Crow segregation was imposed by the United States. Hence the ongoing tension for Walrond between his desire to affiliate with other people of color, drawing him to Pan-Africanism and anticolonialism, and a competing desire to deconstruct the category of blackness as itself an expression and instrument of white supremacy. The Caribbean also cultivated in Walrond a discerning analysis of the region's colonial history, from the "liberal" English, to the "business imperialism" of the French and Dutch, to

U.S. "colonialism without colonies." He was alert to nationalist rivalries, cultural paternalism, and the capitalist quest for larger markets, cheaper materials, and flexible labor. Nonetheless, although he found these features of Caribbean colonialism pernicious, the resulting arrangements of people and cultures intrigued him. He was fascinated by linguistic polyphony, intercultural contact, political alliances, and emancipatory social movements. Hence another recurring tension—he abhorred state practices of colonialism, but the complexity of the resulting societies fired his political and aesthetic imagination.

We begin, then, in the Caribbean, where the indigenous people of the hemisphere first encountered Europeans, where enslaved Africans first landed, and where the plantation system and its triangle trade yielded the heterogeneous societies that animated Walrond's writing. The descendant of a Scottish planter and an African woman he freed from slavery, Walrond was a living testament to the convoluted history of the Caribbean and the age in which he was born.

1

GUYANA AND BARBADOS (1898–1911)

Like many writers whose lives are defined by itinerancy, Eric Walrond was concerned with place, or more accurately with the relation between places. "The facts about me are puny enough," he said self-effacingly, "I was born in British Guiana, December 18, 1898, and at the age of eight, my parents went to live in Barbados."[1] "I remember boarding a sailing vessel bound for the West Indies. [. . .] We were the only passengers on the vessel, I think, and it was a voyage that was not without its exciting moments. I slept on a bed that was always damp with the water of the sea" ("Godless" 32). In this way, Walrond introduced himself in 1924 to readers of *Success* magazine, emphasizing passages between places as much as the places themselves. "I remember, five years later, being on another ship—a giant ocean liner. At St. Thomas, the Virgin Islands, we had to transship to another larger steamer going to the Isthmus of Panama. It was the most exciting moment of my life" ("Godless" 32). Finally, on arriving in New York, he could not believe his good fortune: "I go into the most amazing of places. Sometimes, I meet rebuffs; other times, I have had [. . .] to pinch myself and say: '*I must be dreaming. This surely is not you, Eric.*' Eric, the black boy from a race once in slavery!" ("Godless" 32). He would always think of himself this way: as a black man, and one whose relocations profoundly shaped his views, especially his views on race. Today, such a person might be called cosmopolitan but that suggests a privileged mobility. Walrond's itinerary was often set by material concerns, and although he was a transnational intellectual, it is not in the same sense as cosmopolitan writers with whom we are familiar today.

The collapse of Barbadian sugar had propelled his parents to the coast of South America, and protracted labor unrest in British Guiana drove them back. Ruth and William Walrond were not poor; William was a tailor and Ruth a devout churchgoer and missionary for the Plymouth Brethren. But they depended on the vitality of the local economy and as a result, Eric, his two brothers, and two sisters were—like many Caribbean families—moved in pursuit of opportunity. Ruth's desire for middle-class respectability is apparent in *Tropic Death*'s title story, whose protagonist resembles the author. He stands with his mother at the waterfront in Bridgetown, Barbados, waiting for the boat to Panama.

> He was a dainty little boy, about eight years of age. He wore a stiff jumper jacket, the starch on it so hard and shiny it was ready to squeak; shiny blue-velvet pants, very tight and very short—a little above his carefully oiled knees; a brownish green bow tie, bright as a cluster of dewy crotons; an Eton collar, an English sailor hat, with an elastic band so tight it threatened to dig a gutter in the lad's bright brown cheeks. (161)

The very picture of propriety, the boy is at once black and English. This combination was no paradox for Barbadians, but Walrond's description puts the two qualities in tension, raising the question of whether the ill-fitting attire is a costume, a performance of Englishness. Beneath the watchful eye of Lord Nelson's statue, residents clamor about.

> City urchins, who thrived on pilfering sewers or ridding the streets of cow dung which they marketed as manure; beggars, black street corner fixtures, their bodies limp and juicy with the scourge of elephantiasis; cork-legged wayfarers, straw hats on their bowed crinkly heads; one-legged old black women vending cane juice and hot sauce. It was noon and they had come, like camels to an oasis, to guzzle Maube or rummage the bags of coppers,

untie their handkerchiefs, arrange their toilet and sprawl, snore, till the sun spent its crystal wrath and dropped behind the dark hulk of the sugar refineries to the western tip of the sky. (162)

This was life at the wharf in turn-of-the-century Bridgetown. But Walrond differentiated himself from the other boys, those defiant ruffians who sneaked "on the wharves at sundown and bored big holes in the wet sacks of brown sugar" or shot "popguns at the black, cork-hatted police" (162). Irreverent and daring, they dived after coins thrown by tourists while he was forbidden even from touching the water: "Keep yo' hands inside, sah," the mother of his character worries on the ferryboat, "shark will get you, too." The scene distills a number of features of Walrond's childhood, from his mother's doting care to the sharp tension between his respectability and the Barbadian peasantry. Despite their shared complexion, he felt different from the "ragged" boys, the "wharf rats" whose activity he envied as sensual and transgressive. In fact, this dual sense of being proudly black yet different from others would characterize his entire life's experience, and it had a long family history.

It began with his mother's grandfather. Dodo, as he was called, was the child of Benjamin Joseph Prout, a white planter, and an enslaved woman, a Coromantee from the west coast of Africa. Known as Baba in her youth, she was christened Matilda by her owner, the father of her seven children. A Scotsman born in 1786, Prout came to Barbados as a young man to seek his fortune in sugar and, although he did not grow extravagantly wealthy or ascend to the plantocracy, by the time of Dodo's birth he managed two modest estates: Arise, a ten-acre estate in the parish of St. Thomas, and Mess House, a twelve-acre estate in the parish of St. George.[2] It is clear that Matilda, Eric Walrond's great-great-grandmother, was Joseph Prout's "lifelong companion and the chief beneficiary of his will." He not only acknowledged paternity of Dodo, whose given name was Joseph Benjamin Prout, he set him up to run the family business and to enjoy the comforts of planter life, sending him to a school for mulatto children. Dodo grew up at Mess House, in the district of Flat Rock, inheriting Arise upon his mother's death.[3]

For Walrond, whose nutmeg complexion and kinky hair marked him unmistakably, it was less his white ancestry than his middle-class respectability that fostered a certain aloofness, a pride accentuated by the stern religiosity of his mother, Ruth Ellen Ambrozine Prout, granddaughter of Dodo. Ruth and her sister Julia were raised in their grandfather's home, and Julia's grandson, Brown University professor Charles Nichols, remembered them as "statuesque beauties."[4] They converted from Anglicanism to the Plymouth Brethren, a Calvinist sect that required righteous behavior and regular participation in services to affirm their souls' salvation. It required missionary work, and many evangelicals including Ruth and Julia traveled to "pagan lands," Julia to Trinidad, where thousands of South Asians worked the sugar estates, and Ruth to British Guiana on the northeast coast of South America. Here she not only found souls to save, she also met William Walrond, a Barbadian tailor who had moved to Georgetown in the mid-1890s. "According to family legend," notes Robert Bone, "Ruth made several sea voyages back and forth from Barbados in the course of her courtship," and after marrying William in 1898, she gave birth to Eric, the first of five children, in a house on New Market Street a week before Christmas.[5]

Turn-of-the-century Georgetown was extraordinarily diverse yet highly stratified. The novelist Anthony Trollope called British Guiana's administration "a despotism tempered by sugar," though as one magistrate said in 1903, "It seemed to me more like a despotism *of* sugar."[6] Unlike Barbados, where a middle class developed after emancipation and people of African descent constituted a majority, Guiana consisted of a small, powerful minority of European officials and planters, large populations of Afro-Caribbeans and South Asians working on the sugar estates, some Portuguese and East Asians, and a native population living principally in inland villages.[7] The latter represented utter backwardness for Ruth Walrond, a reminder of the civilizing properties of European culture.[8] The Walrond family lived on stilts. Anyone of means moved into the houses the Dutch had built on tall pilings during colonization. Perched fifteen feet high, the Walronds conducted their domestic lives above the mud, for mud was everywhere in turn-of-the-century Georgetown—along the banks of the many canals, in yards that flooded with alarming regularity, situated just above sea level. Wealth and status were reflected in residential elevation. Derelict tenements housed laborers along the canals, their barefoot children scrambling after paper boats set adrift on the brackish watercourse. Indian "coolies," indentured workers, gathered manure from the streets to sell or burn. Wooden planks traversed the ubiquitous sewers, precarious passage for respectable West Indian women, dressed primly in taffeta. The year Walrond was born, an English magistrate and sheriff of Demerara wrote of Georgetown's deplorable conditions: "Let anyone walk through the yards [. . .], and let him ask himself how he could expect respectable, law-abiding citizens to be raised therein."[9] Walrond was kept indoors as much as possible, and when his mother was not around, a West Indian maid kept a watchful eye, warning him of *duppies*, the ghosts beneath the toadstools in the yard, and shielding him from the dangers beyond.

His father's position as "head cutter" at Hendricks, a tailor on Water Street, allowed them to move into a well-appointed home full of "dark gleams of polished wood and the sparkle of glass." On pleasant days, the maid brought him to the sea wall, where he delighted in catching "the small iridescent fish that came twinkling over on to the esplanade" ("Servant" 9).[10] He attended Robb Street School in the Sixth Ward, near his father's shop, and with his mother attended the services of the Plymouth Brethren ("Two Sisters" ii, 25). But he was kept from playing with the neighborhood boys, the rough children from the Ruimveldt estate whose games he observed from the veranda. They teased and tormented each other, splashing mud and catching eels and crayfish. "*Ah Chichi lay, Ah Chichi lay*," they sang, "*Chichi's the washer, the July washer.*" Walrond "wondered what the song meant. Who was Chichi? And what was a 'July washer'"? ("Servant" 12). He resolved to ask the maid, who belonged to a lower class, thus beginning a career in idiomatic translation that would come to comprise his life's work.

His earliest memories of Georgetown were of his eagerness to escape the smothering respectability of home. He was "too small to take more than one step at a time" but "could not get down the stairs fast enough."

He was in flight from the monotony and boredom of going from window to window on the gallery and flicking the shutters up and down. He'd escaped from the prison—4 ft wide, enclosed with lattice work of a light shade of green and extending along the front of the house—in which he had been condemned to spend the long mornings and the hot, drowsy afternoons. An occasional descent upon the Lamaha . . . tadpole fishing in the Canal? That was for boys in rags and tatters or with no clothes at all and often with the midwife's cord hanging from their navels. Not for a boy in a blue and white outfit, his knees well coconut-oiled and with shoes on his feet ("Coolie's" 20).

Impatient, "arms folded on the window sill," he watched the boys from a distance, straining to hear the pitched cadence of their struggle. Their squabbles rang in profane counterpoint to his mother's Christian hymns. "[O]n Sunday evenings, lying face down across her swaying knees," she "would sing and pat him to sleep." Despite the comforts of his childhood home, Walrond felt suffocated, attempting "truant-like escapes." He was afraid of what lay beyond the front gate, including the other boys, but in staying aloof he risked their contempt: "You little big-eyed, poor great, hot-house brat," he imagined them saying, "wha' all-yo' lookin' down here for?" ("Servant" 9, 11).

The young boy could not have known it, but the community in which his parents had settled was combustible. At the turn of the century, relations between residents of African and South Asian descent were poisoned by colonial relations of severe domination. Sugar profits had been falling across the Caribbean, and with Europe weaning itself off cane, the renowned Demerara industry suffered. By the turn of the century, the value of British Guiana's sugar exports to the mother country plummeted to less than one-third of its value in 1884.[11] As landowners reeled from the decline and the colonial administration introduced new crops, wages stagnated and living conditions deteriorated. "When the rains fell," wrote historian Walter Rodney, "Georgetown residents waded among floating feces; when casual laborers obtained two days' work per week, the entire earnings could barely cover the rent and keep away the bailiff's cart."[12]

In this context, tensions between "Negroes" and "Hindus" were aggravated by their shared deprivation. The "Hindus" felt the "Negroes" were lazy, while the "Negroes" resented the "Hindus" for driving down wages, as estate owners continued to recruit indentured Indian labor despite rising unemployment. The colonial administration ran Georgetown like a police state, with criminal convictions averaging between ten and thirteen thousand annually in the years leading up to 1905.[13]

This was a fateful year, as labor actions escalated and brutal retaliation ensued in December. The stevedores, truckers, and clerks on the Georgetown docks led a strike that spread quickly to allied industries and to the interior, where miners demanded better wages. One morning, police opened fire on a crowd that refused to disperse, grievously injuring four men; riots erupted. At Ruimveldt, the largest estate near the Walrond's house, people were assaulted and fired upon as they left to join the strike.[14] Thousands of workers filled the streets, occupying public buildings and chasing the governor into hiding; the local newspaper declared that three-fourths of the population had "gone stark staring mad."[15] By the day's end seven were dead and seventeen critically wounded. Because the colonial administration's authority was virtually unchecked and wedded to the interests of the estate owners, and because laborers could not afford to strike, the uprising was soon suppressed. The arrival in the harbor of two British naval ships fortified the ruling elite. But the conflict alarmed the middle class, which largely sat the matter out, letting the workers—male and female alike—challenge vigilante police patrols and a militia comprised of white men. It is unclear whether William Walrond's shop was harmed in the conflict, but they were among the middle-class families shaken by what transpired.[16] They now had four children—the eldest of whom, Eric, turned seven soon after these events—and they left the country.

Within the Caribbean, the economic prospects looked best in Cuba, where sugar and tobacco were thriving, and in Panama, where work had begun on a "trans-isthmian" canal. An experienced tailor might have done well, but both countries were far from British Guiana. More importantly they were Latin American, and the Walronds identified with Great Britain, proud citizens of the oldest Caribbean island in her empire. The prevailing tale of West Indians in Panama at that point was a cautionary one—thousands of Jamaicans had perished in the failed French canal attempt in the 1880s, their deaths the stuff of legend, replete with black vomit and errant dynamite blasts. Ruth's grandfather, Dodo, now in his mid-seventies, still lived at Mess House in Barbados, where a village bore his name.[17] They decided to return and place themselves in the care of the patriarch. Barbados had a formative influence on Walrond's life and imagination, furnishing material for nearly half the stories in *Tropic Death*. It became his muse, color palette, and mental grammar, cultivating an exuberant and promiscuous lexicon, a knowledge of formal and folk speech, and a Victorian sensibility toward public and professional life. David Levering Lewis has described Walrond as "debonair and superior" but he may as well have said "Bajan," for it was Barbados that taught him to be fiercely independent and to conduct himself as a gentleman.[18]

A transplant from "away," he was teased as a "mud-head," a derisive term for the Guianese, who lived at sea level on the soggy coast. He felt like an oddity. "At school he was like something cast up from the Sargasso Sea, a newcomer from Demerara," Walrond wrote in the autobiographical story "Two Sisters," "and the fact that his classmates drew a line between him and themselves added to his feeling of isolation" ("Two Sisters" iii, 19). He described an incident that mirrored his own experience.

"Hey, hear the 'Mud-Head' spouting!"

One boy tugged at the collar of [his] sailor jacket. Another crept up behind him, made a circle of his thumb and forefinger and released it against his ear. A third boy spotted a tiny blue square in [his] white short trousers.

Patch in the crutch

Is nothing much

But patch in the knee

Is poverty.

"What school in Demerara did you go to?" asked one boy, continuing the Inquisition.

"Robb Street School," [he] answered.

"What they teach you there, bo?"

"Latin and Greek."

"Oh!"

The bell rang for the end of recess and the boys, full of ugly suspicions, walked with him in silence into the crush of the schoolhouse
steps. Running up the steps, [he] stumbled and fell. The boys burst out
laughing.

"That ought to knock the Latin and Greek out of your head!" ("Two
Sisters" ii, 25)

Compounding his disorientation were unfamiliar surroundings, far more
rural than Georgetown. Walrond found himself at age eight amid the
vestiges of a bygone era, when sugar was king. Cane fields surrounded
Mess House, and the ruins of an old windmill and an abandoned barracks that housed the estate's laborers lay nearby.[19] When Dodo Prout was
Eric Walrond's age, the sugar industry boomed, producing nearly twenty
thousand tons in 1834, the year slavery was abolished and Dodo turned
five. This was achieved on the backs of eighty-two thousand slaves who
comprised 80 percent of the island's population. Barbados did not have
the largest slave population in the Caribbean, but its place was established early in the triangle trade, the destination of more than sixteen
thousand Africans in one decade alone.[20] Thus Walrond came "home" to
a contradictory yet quintessentially New World inheritance, the descen-
dent of master and slave.

Schooling finessed the contradiction, for everything pointed away from
local history toward the seat of the empire in which the island played a
privileged part. Barbados was "the oldest and purest of England's children," the novelist George Lamming recalls learning, "The other islands
had changed hands. Now they were French, now they were Spanish. But
Little England remained steadfast and constant to Big England." Even his
elementary school "wore a uniform of flags: doors, windows and parti-
tions on all sides carried the colours of the school's king. [. . .] In every
corner of the school the tricolor Union Jack flew its message." The total

effect, Lamming said, was to render any question of the arrangement unaskable, indeed unthinkable. The notion of slavery was foreign and preposterous.[21] One wonders what Dodo Prout and his great-grandson discussed as they walked the estate grounds. Whatever it was, whatever St. Stephen's School instructed about the eternal link between Big and Little England, he would identify himself to New York readers in 1924 as a "black boy from a race once in slavery!"

He had fond memories of his great-grandfather, the gray eminence who was his mother's "idol in the golden days of her childhood there." He recalled Dodo in "Two Sisters."

> [A]n early riser, clad in spotless white drill and so tall that he had to stoop to come through the front door of "Mess House"... with a silvery goatee and a lean, ochre-brown face beneath a cork helmet; his boots caked with mud and shining with dew from the morning's turn around the estate grounds; his big coat pockets filled with okras plucked from the vegetable patch behind the crumbling walls of the old sugar mill; unloading the okras on the big dining room table and slowly ascending the stairs to occupy himself in the seclusion of the room above with the affairs of the Vestry Board of which he'd been a member for forty years and the Burial Society which he'd founded and the large family of which he was the head. (i, 21)

Dodo also appears (as Bellon Prout) in the *Tropic Death* story "The Vampire Bat." He returns from fighting with the British in the Boer War to survey the deteriorating grounds of Arise, "a garden of lustrous desolation." He fetches his "old shaggy mare, a relic from the refining era," and astride her "plodded through the dead, thick marl," "wearing a cork hat and a cricketer's white flannel shirt, open at the throat" (146). The sympathetic portrait of the benevolent Creole planter is undercut by Walrond's ironic critique of the man's paternalism toward the island's black residents and his smug sense of mastery over history and nature. When an old woman warns him that "fire hags" are burning the cane brake "down in de gully to-night," Prout bursts "into a fit of ridiculing laughter" at her superstition. She challenges him: "Ent yo' got a piece o' de ve'y cane in yo' mout' suckin'?" But he is too certain of the rational order of things to believe in such "tommyrot" as duppies and fire hags. "Orright den, go 'long," she replies, "All yo' buckras t'ink unna know mo' dan we neygahs. Go 'long down de gully 'bout yo' business, bo" (150). By the story's end both horse and master are dead, and the island's spirits figure a kind of retributive violence for the sins of the "buckra."

After a year at Mess House, the Walronds moved to a two-room cottage on a half-acre that Dodo left them in the parish of St. Michael. Called Black Rock, the area was within walking distance of Bridgetown. From their lane, Jackman's Gap, Ruth brought her children to the Walmer Lodge, where the Plymouth Brethren worshipped, took the produce of her garden to market in Bridgetown, and visited her sister Julia in Eagle Hall Corner ("Two Sisters" iii, 22). The Cave Hill quarry lay nearby, a big operation whose workers lived in the cabins in Jackman's Gap. A breadfruit tree graced the backyard, beyond which lay a stream that in the dry season became a parched bed of rocks—a playground for lizards, centipedes, and mischievous children ("Two Sisters" ii, 21). The place had long been vacant and was in disrepair, the roof missing shingles, the yard lacking a fence. Walrond spent long hours working outdoors with his family, and when he paused "the silence all around him was broken by the song of a bird overhead ('Kiss-kiss-ka-dee!') and the clink of steel on stone from afar: the quarrymen's drills" ("Two Sisters" ii, 23).²² When the workers returned for lunch, he eavesdropped as they drank at the standpipe, talking volubly, sweat drenching the "stiff tails of their blue denim coats" (TD 21). Some lived well in Black Rock, but mainly they were poor, putting coucou on the table when saltfish was too dear, the bare feet of the children calloused by the marl roads and ravaged by "chiggers," fleas that burrowed mercilessly into their exposed flesh.

It was not only the Jackman's Gap residents who were suffering in 1908 but all of Barbados. An infernal drought plagued the island, deepening the troubles that a long depression had induced. Despair and anxiety were common as the land ceased to yield produce, livestock fell ill or perished, and prices climbed. This is the setting of the story that opens *Tropic*

Death, "Drought." It is also the context in which the young mother of four "squabbling" children in "The Black Pin" feuds with her neighbor, who steals her rack-ribbed goat when the unfortunate creature wanders off. William Walrond had resisted the call to Panama, but he found upon returning to Barbados that unemployment was rampant and men were leaving in droves. Now with the punishing drought, the appeal was stronger still. Testimonials of "Panama men" invariably cite "economic problems in the islands" as their reason for leaving; "the opportunity seemed to be a get-rich-quick proposition, with a daily rate of pay that was much higher than could be had in the islands."[23] Contrary to the conventional view that the Panama migrants were unskilled laborers and vagabonds, "the offered rate of eighty cents per day's work brought schoolteachers, barbers, shoemakers, dry goods clerks" and other artisans, including in this case a tailor.[24]

1.1 Photograph of laborers preparing to depart from Barbados for the Panama Canal.

Nowhere was the Isthmian Canal Commission (ICC) recruitment more vigorous or effective than Barbados. There was a preference for West Indians, who as one canal commissioner wrote were "fairly industrious; not addicted to drink; can speak English, [were] willing to work, and not deficient in intelligence," while the "native Isthmian will not work," being "naturally indolent," and the "Chinese coolie," whose labor built the U.S. railroads, was "industrious" and "easy to manage" but hopeless with English and invariably desirous of owning "a store as soon as he gets a few dollars."[25] Transportation of European laborers was costly and West Indians came cheap; wages and conditions were so poor that the promise of a paid passage and a salary was almost irresistible. When subsidized housing, meals, and health care were added, it sounded to struggling West Indians something like salvation. The ICC met with resistance in Jamaica, where colonial officials resented the spectacular tragedy of the French effort, which had killed and injured so many. Barbados was more receptive to recruitment, which began in earnest in 1905, and people left by the boatload. Soon everyone in the Caribbean had seen or heard of the "Colón Man," a legendary figure of folktales and calypsos who made his fortune and returned to the islands, his crisp Panama hat, gold teeth, and watch fob glinting in the sun like a living advertisement. Sometimes these men were actually on the ICC payroll, others just wanted to flaunt their possessions, status symbols that few who stayed home could afford.[26] For every worker who signed an ICC contract and shipped off to Colón, another booked passage without a job, just a dream that "money grows on trees in Panama" as a popular song said. In one decade alone, between forty and sixty thousand Barbadians made the trip.[27]

William made it by himself in 1909, like many men who left families behind to follow. In the Walronds' case this was 1911, and the two intervening years were terribly trying. Ruth's sister Julia and family emigrated to Brooklyn, and the Barbados stories Walrond wrote tend to feature unmarried or widowed women, some childless, some with families, all struggling for self-sufficiency and dignity in the gorgeous but recalcitrant countryside. Ruth's half-brother helped them during her husband's absence; while she and the children coaxed peas, corn, and okra from the garden, he delivered potatoes and an occasional pot of crab soup with dumplings. Thus they managed to stave off hunger while awaiting William's invitation, Ruth placing her faith in the Lord and her community of saved souls, and her children, now five in number, receiving a sound English education at St. Stephen's. When the letter finally arrived, she gathered what she could, starched the children's collars, and with liberal applications of coconut oil to the knees, assembled them on the Bridgetown dock. There under the stern countenance of Admiral Nelson's statue, the Walronds bid farewell to Little England.

2

PANAMA (1911–1918)

> Only forty-eight miles of swampland at Panama separate the two great-
> est bodies of water on the earth's surface. Nature has done so much
> that there is little left for man to do, but it will have to be some other
> man than a native-born Central-American who is to do it.
>
> RICHARD HARDING DAVIS, *THREE GRINGOES IN VENEZUELA & CENTRAL AMERICA* (1896)

Panama has a singular place in the El Dorado myth, the fantasy of lucrative discovery that fired the imaginations of conquistadors and expansionists. It has been one of the hemisphere's most volatile sites of political positioning and a crucible of transnational communities. By the time Richard Harding Davis wrote the aforementioned opinions, North Americans had been operating the interoceanic Panama Railroad for forty years and the French had spent most of the 1880s digging their way through the jungle, exhausting their laborers and funds in the process. For U.S. observers such as Davis, it was as if nature had presented them with a circuit that was nearly closed; all that was left was to throw the switch. In one sense, he was right— the Americans succeeded where the French failed, and credit and glory redounded to them when the first ship passed through the locks in 1914. But he could not have been more wrong in claiming there was "little left for man to do." Despite its propitious location, Panama's topography was no kinder than any of the other contemplated routes, and the land did not cleave easily. The French attempt was by all accounts a cataclys-mic disaster, involving shady financing, engineering miscues on a massive scale, illness, injury, and the death of twenty thousand laborers. The sub-sequent American effort, although successful in the strictest sense, was only slightly less lethal and took ten years. When Davis remarked that it would "have to be some other man than a native-born Central-American" to undertake a canal, his suggestion was that only North American ingenuity could get the thing done right. But the fact is, the "other man" was not just the North American but also the West Indian, thirty thousand of whom contracted with the Isthmian Canal Commission. They found that neither the land nor its residents welcomed the transformation their presence occasioned.

William Walrond was not a ditchdigger, a dynamiter, or a fumigator (positions most West Indians held) but the factors that brought him were similar—a collapsing economy at home and the promise of decent wages. For Eric Walrond, Panama became the place with which he most closely identified, declaring himself in 1924 "spiritually a native of Panama. I owe the sincerest kind of allegiance to it."

> I grew up there.
>> I went to school there.
>> I began working there.
>> I had my first struggles there.
>> I had my first—and possibly my only—love affair there.
>> I studied and played truant—I rambled and roamed and
> adventured—all there. ("Godless" 32)

The experience of Panama's Afro-Caribbean community is well documented, and Walrond wrote a great deal about Panama after he left. A clear picture emerges of its decisive impact on his life and intellectual development. He came to see Panama as his ticket out of the West Indies, a springboard to the United States, but the area in which he lived was in an important sense a satellite of the United States, the Canal Zone a colony in the tropics.

Walrond was among the first Afro-Caribbeans to transmute the Isthmian experience into imaginative fiction. Caribbean journalists covered the region, as did some African Americans, and a vibrant, extensive oral folk culture arose, from calypso to schoolyard rhymes to legends retold throughout the islands. But not until later did a specifically literary

Afro-Caribbean tradition take shape, treating Panama in Spanish and English. In Walrond's time, Panama literature took two main forms: Hispanophone writing, which was belletristic with European pretensions, and travel writing, which relied on tropes and conventions that were sensational and exoticizing. Neither offered much to a writer who wished to engage in earnest with the questions of culture, nation, language, gender, and race confronting Panama's Afro-Caribbeans. Neither called into question the premises of colonialist discourse, most importantly its denial of complex subjectivity to people of the global south. But no writer simply invents a genre, and Walrond's debt to the popular discourse of "tropicality," as some call it, is abundantly clear and exceedingly complex.[1]

Calling his book *Tropic Death* and dwelling with morbid fascination on the ways in which residents of the isthmus suffer and expire, Walrond seems to have drawn on the most sensational elements of writing about Panama. Particularly in writing about Colón, references to disease and decay had abounded since the mid-nineteenth century, when Panama Railroad builders gave the director of the Pacific Mail Steamship Company, William Henry Aspinwall, the dubious honor of naming its Caribbean terminus after him. Travelers took delight in describing its unrivaled offensiveness. "Searching for the specialty in which Aspinwall excelled, we found it in her carrion birds, which cannot be surpassed in size or smell," wrote a 1855 visitor. "The very ground on which one trod was pregnant with disease, and death was distilled in every breath of air. Glued furniture falls to pieces, leather molds, and iron oxidizes in twenty-four hours."[2]

In this tradition, the people of the Isthmus were inseparable from the geography of putrefaction.

The palefaced sailor and the melancholy convalescent negro, sitting smoking their pipes on the steps, remind us that the ugly whitewashed buildings are hospitals, and soon passing by some outlying huts with half naked negresses and pot-bellied children sunning themselves in front, we make our way into the thicker part of the settlement over marshy pools corrupt with decaying matter.[3]

The residents join in the rhetoric of disease and death, symptoms of Colón's virulent strain of tropicality. The writer who would tell these people's stories faced the challenge of extricating them from established positions on the palette of Anglo-American travel writing. Walrond would make recourse to the tropes of the Anglo-American tradition, but he did so to subvert it, to remove the residents of the Isthmus from the amber of primitivism, passion, and perversity. He too would write about Colón's hucksters and clerks, its shopkeepers and laborers, its indigenous people, *mestizos*, and Asians, but he would cast them as historical agents, struggling with modernity rather than sitting inertly in its way, creating communities with all the exuberance and conflict that entails.

It is hard to overstate the Canal Zone's role as a contact zone, a point of convergence of different races, ethnicities, social classes, and linguistic and religious backgrounds. A part of the former colony of *Nueva Granada*, Panama was Hispanophone and Catholic, gaining independence from Colombia in 1903. Panama City and Colón consisted of a small number of elites from Spanish-identified families, many European creoles, descendents of Asian indentured laborers, and a number of West Indians and *mestizos*.[4] Contact between Afro-Caribbeans and indigenous people dated back to slavery, when marronage and emancipation led to rural Afro-Panamanian villages. Over time, indigenous people and *mestizos* came increasingly to the cities. As complex as the resulting society became, it was not unique in Latin America, but what distinguished Panama was the peculiar presence of North Americans. They had not come simply to impose a military occupation; Panama was technically a sovereign state and a republic. But it had only gained independence through U.S. intervention, the compensation for which was the Canal Zone, a band twelve miles wide that bisected the Isthmus and determined conduct throughout the country. The treaty signed two weeks after Panama's independence stipulated that the United States controlled the Zone and the surrounding waters, and did so *in perpetuity*.

Thus, as Walrond's work reminds us, Panama's significance as a contact zone derives not only from its startling diversity but also from the relations of power informing and deforming this diversity. Uncle Sam was not the *buckra* with whom West Indians were acquainted—the planter or landlord—though he shared their pigmentation. He was the Q.M., the quartermaster who supervised work and wages. General Goethals, head of U.S. operations, was clear about the mission: They were to carry out what they had begun in Guam, the Philippines, Hawaii, and Cuba, a neocolonial project that would secure U.S. dominance in the Western Hemisphere. As Theodore Roosevelt told the British Foreign Office:

> It was a good thing for Egypt and the Sudan, and for the world, when England took Egypt and the Sudan. It is a good thing for India that England should control it. And so it is a good thing, a very good thing, for Cuba and for Panama and for the world that the United States has acted as it has actually done during the last six years. The people of the United States and the people of the Isthmus and the rest of mankind will all be the better because we dig the Panama Canal and keep order in its neighborhood. And the politicians and revolutionists at Bogota are entitled to precisely the amount of sympathy we extend to other inefficient bandits.[5]

The anti-imperialists caviled, but there was really no question of the official position. As the assistant secretary of state said, "No picture of our future is complete which does not comprehend the United States as the dominant power in the Caribbean Sea."[6]

The Walrond family lived in an apartment in a six-story tenement— the Ant's Nest, he called it—through whose back door lay Bottle Alley, a dirt street that took its name from the layers of discarded bottles embedded below the unpaved surface. This was a red-light district neglected by the authorities rapidly modernizing the city's infrastructure. Originally built on a mangrove swamp, Colón had never been a welcoming place, and whatever development it enjoyed prior to the Canal resulted from its location as the terminus of the railroad completed during the California gold rush. It was little more than a collection of rudely constructed edifices destined to burn and burn again. It remained for years a terrifically unpleasant, even dangerous, place to live. Cholera and dysentery flourished, open sewers emitted "pestilential vapors," and the rains averaged eleven feet per year. Improvements in Colón were limited until 1912, a year after Walrond's arrival. "The public works created in the city of Colón between 1903 and 1912 could be counted on the fingers of one hand," notes a local historian, but with the arrival of North Americans and their families came modernization of the two port cities, an effort to approximate *el estilo de vida estadounidense* (the U.S. lifestyle).[7] The "Yanks" lived in Cristóbal, separated from the rest of Colón by the railroad and docks, and the majority of resources went there. But even in Colón, streets were paved, sewers installed, and a battalion of mosquito-fumigation crews staffed largely by West Indian men were deployed to eradicate blood-borne diseases. A central refrigerated depository adjoined Colón's train depot, and merchants established laundries, bakeries, even ice cream parlors. By 1912, the Isthmian Canal Commission (ICC) had built twenty-two commissaries to feed employees and twenty-four schools to educate their children, hung telephone lines between Panama City and Colón, and established modern hospitals.[8]

Amid this modernization, Walrond's neighborhood remained a notorious slum, trying his mother's commitment to raise her children as proper Christians. The title story of *Tropic Death* depicts her character dragging her reluctant son to Plymouth Brethren meetings each night. "There, he'd meet the dredge-digging, Lord-loving peasants of the West Indies on the sore knees of atonement asking the Lord to bring salvation to their perfidious souls" (186). No fewer than thirteen Anglican churches with "Negro congregations" sprang up, thanks largely to Barbadian immigrants.[9] Their function was not confined to worship but included cultural and social welfare activities. Nevertheless, challenges to the faithful abounded. Prostitution flourished, and the disproportion of men in the Canal workforce meant that women with whom they might engage in noneconomic relationships were scarce. British and American officers and ICC employees also patronized the brothels, one of which, located on the top floor of the Walronds' building, received florid depiction in *Tropic Death*'s story "Subjection." On the ground floor was a "canteen," one of the many in Bottle Alley where Canal workers slaked their considerable thirst with rum and Cerveza Balboa, and gambling was rampant.

The West Indian men lived in close quarters, severed from the homes and communities in which their values had been rooted.[10]

Because canal labor was difficult and dangerous, physical and mental health were tenuous luxuries. "What the rigors of nature spared West Indian workers, the hazardous strain of the construction of the Panama Canal demanded from them," writes George Westerman. "Particularly during the construction era, hosts of them died violent deaths or sustained permanent physical or mental injuries, by premature or delayed explosions of dynamite, asphyxiation in pits, falling from high places, train wrecks, landslides and falling rocks in the Canal Cut, and other hazards of their work."[11] Readers are often taken aback by *Tropic Death*'s spectacular morbidity. It has been attributed to the author's peculiarity, the influence of European naturalism and the gothic, or a modernist aversion to sentimentality. What each of these compelling ideas misses is the extent to which suffering and death were endemic to the Canal Zone.[12] The reverence with which historians celebrate the engineers who vanquished the Panamanian wilderness is matched only by their admiration for the ICC medical staff, led by William Gorgas. It is an article of faith that the Americans succeeded not because they possessed superior technology (though they did) but because they realized something the French neglected: pursuing the work of the canal meant first caring for the workers themselves. Although West Indians were often the beneficiaries of U.S. medical care, the ICC was capable of terrible exploitation of their injuries and illnesses. Julie Greene has argued that "Gorgas' determination to study pneumonia while doing little to treat it reflects the concerns of an ambitious young medical establishment eager to analyze and tame the tropics in order to make them safe and comfortable—for whites." In the area of mental health, West Indians were institutionalized for insanity at alarming rates.[13]

Perhaps it is not surprising that many West Indians struggled with isolation and despair.[14] Their relationship to the place was provisional, economic. The West Indian community proved that piety and religious practice were not impossible to maintain, but the challenges were acute. This was the environment of Walrond's adolescence. Of course, for a boy of his age, it also offered plenty of amusement and excitement. The character who is his surrogate in *Tropic Death* pursues "secret escapades to the alley below, and spin gigs and pitch taws with the boys who gathered there." But he "had to be careful of the *pacos*," the police, and "careful of the boys he played with. Some of them used bad words; some had fly-dotted sores on their legs. A city of sores. Some of them had boils around their mouths. Some were pirates—they made bloody raids on the marbles" (179). When Walrond writes "a city of sores," he invokes not only the disfiguration of the children's legs but all of Colón. It was not without intrigue and appeal, but it was a far cry from the St. Stephen's churchyard in Barbados.

JIM CROW IN PANAMA

Above all, the defining feature of Panama's transnationalism was the institution of Jim Crow. Imported by the Americans, segregation was neither native to Panama nor familiar to many West Indians. The Caribbean had codes of color, to be sure, but the Canal Zone practices were U.S. innovations. The most infamous was the differential payment of ICC employees, black workers in silver, white in gold. Gold and Silver workers were distinguished not only by their currencies but also by the establishments that accepted them and the locations that disbursed them. Segregation was not limited to employment but extended into almost every arena of public life, including housing, health care, education, and recreation.

Even as Jim Crow subordinated Panama's "Negroes," it masked their differences from one another. Caribbean immigrants spoke French, Dutch, English, and varieties of Creole. Newcomers shared a common background of rural life, agricultural labor, and a history of colonial rule, but many professed loyalty to the mother country, an allegiance that militated against pan-Caribbean consciousness and persisted long after their arrival in Panama.[15] Such expressions caution against assuming race as the primary mode of identification among Caribbean migrants to Panama. The majority came from Barbados and Jamaica, but a striking diversity flourished even within the British islands. Coming together in Colón, West Indians found that their differences were uninteresting and immaterial to the Americans and Panamanians. For Walrond, Panama's racial regime generated a critical tension that he never fully resolved. The experience of the "Silver People" underscored for him the necessity of collective action against oppression, galvanizing his interest in Garveyism and expressions of racial militancy. At the same time, he felt the very category of the "Negro" under whose sign the struggle was waged had to be deconstructed, retrieving the differences it collapsed.

Walrond received as extensive an education as a black child in the Canal Zone could, first attending "a Spanish boys' school, then a school conducted by the Wesleyan Mission," he said.[16] The instructor was a graduate of Wolmer's College, Jamaica, and class met in the vestry of the Wesleyan Chapel. Surrounded by Panamanian children, he learned Spanish, a skill that proved beneficial, but he must not have stayed long at the Wesleyan Mission because he graduated from the Canal Zone Public Schools in 1913 at age fourteen. This was a segregated system and, at the time the Walronds arrived, black children were only admitted through fifth grade. Barbados was highly literate, so it was jarring to have arrived someplace in which only half the children could read and write. The ICC expanded the school system to keep pace with the arrival of laborers' families. In the summer of 1906 alone, the number of students and schools doubled.[17] But an equal education was not provided to all students. Four ICC schools were white-only in 1906, while 26 others admitted both white and "colored" children (though in practice 90 percent were nonwhite). The following year, ten schools served white children and thirteen served "colored" children. Although "schools were provided for the children of all United States citizen employees," no such provision was made for the children of noncitizens. Only those who lived in the Canal Zone proper were guaranteed access, and just "a small percentage of the non-citizen employees lived there." In short, "the funds made available for education could provide for only a small portion of the children requiring education" during the construction era. The year the canal was completed, the student-teacher ratio in the white schools was 30:1, in the "colored" schools 65:1. From the start, white children could attend through twelfth grade, while "colored" students were limited to lower levels that rose incrementally, eventually extending to twelfth grade in 1946. Thus, when Walrond says he graduated in 1913 from the Canal Zone Public Schools, we should understand that he probably completed seven grades. Given these circumstances, it was a privilege to continue one's studies, but Walrond's family sent him to private tutors. "I studied for three years under two private masters—Allan Thomas and W. C. Parker. Here, under these two men, graduates of Wolmer's College in Jamaica, I did supplementary work in Latin, French, and higher mathematics."[18] He met his tutors at the Sixth Street Mission, near Bottle Alley, and Parker was well-known in the West Indian community, a friend of Marcus Garvey and his fiancée, Amy Ashwood, Walrond's neighbor in Colón.[19]

THE ISTHMIAN CANAL COMMISSION

After concluding his schooling in 1916, Walrond continued his informal education in the streets, which offered an eighteen-year-old abundant opportunities for mischief. "I was thrust among a gang of boys whose ideal diversion was to hop moving trains, and I unquestioningly fell in. I don't know how many times I've been chastised, in the most delicate manner, I assure you, for wanting to 'get my legs cut off.'"[20] His first job was as a messenger in the Quartermaster's Department (QMD), which coordinated the construction and maintenance of Canal Zone buildings, painting, carpentry, sanitation, and the dismantling of old French-era machinery. The QMD requisitioned construction supplies, arranging delivery and storage throughout the Canal Zone, and as a messenger Walrond entered an elaborate traffic in invoices and receipts. With transactions of $11 million annually, the QMD was among the largest ICC departments, employing at the height of the construction 221 "Gold" and 3,113 "Silver" workers.[21]

Through this position, Walrond learned of a clerkship in the health department, across the train tracks in Cristóbal. He fictionalized his

experience acquiring this job in "Wind in the Palms." The young protagonist is ambitious, cunning, and linguistically precocious. Upon learning
of the position he approaches the director, addressing him in a different
idiom from his West Indian peers.

> "Beg pardon, sir," he said, "I would like to speak to you. Now that
> you've moved from the old Panama Railroad building on 3rd Street to
> new quarters in Cristobal, I understand you have been getting in a lot
> of new equipment." [. . .] "I also understand," he went on, "that you're
> looking for someone to help out with the work in the office. Do you
> think, Sir, that you could give me the job?" ("Wind in the Palms" 238)

The director bristles at having been accosted in the courtyard, but he
gives the young man the job, admiring his pluck. If the story may be read
autobiographically, Walrond did not do much more than "check and file
the day's sanitary reports," but it put him in close proximity with white
employees and at the "nerve center" of the ICC health operations, legendary for its eradication of malaria and yellow fever.[22] He listened as the
chief clerk bellowed into the telephone, "Fumigate every outdoor sink,
WC and garbage can in the alleys of Colon; flood the G Street sewage
canal with all the oil and tar the budget can stand; tear down and set
fire to anything that looks like an invitation to pestilence!" ("Wind in
the Palms" 236). Professional connections allow Walrond's character to
transcend the squalid conditions of his Bottle Alley flat, a leap attributed
to his aquiline nose, his bronze skin (not too dark), and his facility with
standard English.

Interacting with Americans does not prevent him from code switching, however, once he is back in the company of West Indians. His friend
in the story is the director's chauffeur and an unrepentant roustabout:
"No ten-cent dance on the dim, moonlight, balconied edges of the *bar-
rio* at the lower end of Cash Street was complete without him; waxing
and winding to the rhythm of a Jamaican *mento* was with him a nightly
diversion" ("Wind in the Palms" 239). "The Major say you can go home
now," he tells Charleroy, "Him don't need you any more today" (239).

He slips easily back into the local vernacular: "Lahd, but you lazy, me son," he teases, and he employs a characteristic Caribbean double construction, slyly accusing Charleroy of scrubbing the color from his skin: "Tell me something, is bleach you been bleachin' again?" (239).²³ In addition to code switching, Walrond's character demonstrates shrewdness in managing his knowledge of the U.S. occupation of Haiti and incarceration of Haitian rebels, suppressing it during his impromptu interview with the health department director. If the story is to be credited, he understood as a young man the broader role his ICC bosses played in political maneuverings in the Caribbean.²⁴

THE *STAR & HERALD*

During his stint at the Health Department, Walrond became a working reporter. "I began to write news stories for the daily press on the side. I wrote accounts of cricket matches, baseball games, and 'rounders' among the West Indian colony for the *Star & Herald*," a Panama City English-language daily. "Eventually I met an editor who said he'd give me a regular reporter's job, which he did."²⁵ Walrond made his beat sound romantic and hard-boiled: "I used to write up brawls, murders, political scandals, voodoo rituals, labor confabs, campaigns, concerts, dramatic affairs, shipping intelligence" ("Godless" 33). He held this position until his departure for New York two years later. The *Star & Herald* was an unusual newspaper and Walrond an unusual hire. It was transnational from its inception, the brainchild of three enterprising U.S. gold rushers who found themselves waylaid in Panama en route to California in 1849.²⁶ When Walrond arrived on staff in 1916, the *Star & Herald* was one of Latin America's premier dailies, with offices in Panama City and Manhattan. It published in Spanish and English, covered local and world affairs, and advocated a Pan-American vision: "We want to make the peoples of both continents more and more conscious of their common interest, their mutual dependence, their united destiny."²⁷ Its core readership remained the expatriates, but as this community evolved and adopted a Creole identity, so did the newspaper. Although its editorial orientation was decidedly North American, neither the editors nor the contributors wholly endorsed the U.S. occupation. Editorials differentiated between "the beneficial development" of Panama and its "harmful exploitation by foreign capital." This vision of sustainable development allied the newspaper with Panamanians rather than North Americans and the shareholders of corporations such as United Fruit. This may have been one reason the *Star & Herald* hired a reporter like Walrond—it was not merely an arm of the ICC and recognized the benefits of a transnational perspective on Panamanian affairs. Another reason was the opening in the summer of 1916 of a Colón office. The Colón office may not have been intended to promote West Indian coverage, but because of their concentration on the Caribbean coast this was the effect, one that likely resulted in Walrond's employment.

A column entitled "West Indian Circles" ran almost daily in 1916–1918, some of which was Walrond's handiwork. "More than 3,000 West Indian Youths Attend Celebration of Emancipation Day Fete," for example, and "Cricket Match Date Wanted: Silence Over Intercolonial Tournament Excites Curiosity."[28] Often "West Indian Circles" contained local interest blurbs which, despite their brevity, convey the texture of West Indian life in the Canal Zone and the newspaper's role in consolidating that community. Results of cricket and boxing matches appeared with breathless accounts of upcoming contests, and notices ran for films at the Silver clubhouses. Myriad meeting announcements indicate the institutions West Indian residents established, including fraternal lodges, prayer groups, mutual aid societies, literary societies at the Silver branches of the YMCA, and the West Indian Democratic Club, a forum that facilitated organizing by Garvey's Universal Negro Improvement Organization.[29] The coverage reflected a desire to celebrate initiatives seeking to "uplift the race," and the *Star & Herald* signaled an interest in Afro-Caribbeans not only as a subject to cover but also an audience to reach.

RACE AND NATION IN PANAMA

Walrond dramatized the relationship between Panamanians and West Indians in all of his writing about the Canal Zone. It was fraught with conflict, he suggested, yet inspired some of the most fascinating cultural action in the black Atlantic. He wrote about the prejudice Panamanians harbored toward West Indians in an essay published in England and reprinted in Jamaica, viewing that prejudice as primarily national and only secondarily racial.

> In Panama, where thousands of British West Indians had settled, I got my first taste of prejudice—prejudice on the grounds of my British nationality! The natives were a mongrelized race of Latins with a strong feeling of antipathy toward British Negroes. But their hatred of us, curiously enough, had been engendered by our love of England. [. . .] Emigrants from the British West Indies had settled in large numbers on the Isthmus. They kept sternly aloof. This, to the sensitive and explosive Latins, was regarded as a slight. It was interpreted as an affront to *las costumbres del pais* [customs of the land]. Reprisals took the shape of epithets such as *chombos negros* and occasional armed incursions into the West Indian colony. ("White Man" 562)

His autobiographical stories register his awareness of the tension even as a boy. Before it became a subject of intellectual reflection it induced an acute sense of vulnerability.

> Suddenly a gang of boys came up, Spanish boys. One of them, seeing his top, circling and spinning, measured it; then winding up, drew back and hauled away. The velocity released made a singing sound. [He] stood back, awed. The top descended on the head of his with astounding accuracy and smashed it into a thousand pieces. The boys laughed and wandered on. At marbles some of the boys would cheat, and say, "if you don't like it, then lump it! *Chombo! Perro!*" Some of them'd seize his taw or the marbles he had put up and walk away, daring him to follow. In the presence of all this, he'd draw back, far back, brooding. (*Tropic Death* 180)

The withdrawal and brooding of Walrond's youth reflected his resentment toward West Indians' marginalization, and he struggled to reconcile it with his acculturation to Panama and his emerging vision of common political cause among the country's nonwhite residents, many of whom were vulnerable to the vicissitudes of the U.S. occupation.

Walrond grew keenly aware of the corrosive nature of colonialism, its erosion of the humanity of both oppressor and oppressed. He wrote about the intimidation of laborers and their efforts to resist. The short story "Subjection" dramatizes this struggle explicitly. An American Marine heading a West Indian canal crew knocks one of them down and kicks him in the head for talking back. The injured fellow lies bleeding on the ground but the others decline to help—all but Ballet, a valiant Barbadian who alone is willing to risk a confrontation.

> "Hey, you!" shouted Ballet at last loud enough for the Marine to hear, "Why—wha' you doin'? Yo' don' know yo' killin' dat boy, ni'?"
>
> "Le' all we giv' he a han' boys—"

But his coworkers are unwilling to risk angering the boss. Each demurs. "Wha' yo' got fi' do wit' it?" asks one, "De boy ain't got no business talkin' back to de marinah man." Another agrees, "Now he mek up he bed, let 'im lie down in it" (*Tropic Death* 100). The exchange suggests the divide-and-conquer strategy through which the Marines subdue the workforce. Only Ballet refuses the rationalization that the offending worker must "sleep in the bed he's made" mouthing off to the Marine. He "staggers up to the Marine" and says, "Yo' gwine kill dat boy." To which the Marine replies, "You mind yer own goddamn business, Smarty, and go back to work. . . . Or else" (*Tropic Death* 101). The next day the Marine chases Ballet off the worksite and shoots him, muttering "I'll teach you niggers down here how to mouth off to a white man" (*Tropic Death* 111).

"Subjection" is unusual because Walrond's Panama writing generally relinquishes binary oppositions, white/black, exploiter/exploited. His work tends to emphasize differences of class, race, ethnicity, gender, and language. It is not that the dominant culture vanishes or that colonialism and racism dissolve, but their force is mediated through relationships among subaltern characters. The Panama stories that highlight this point revolve around sites of commercial exchange. Walrond was always drawn to the dramatic possibilities of commercial activity, setting stories in brothels and bodegas, beauty parlors and market squares, restaurants and import-export firms. They ask how the volatile proximity into which the canal project has thrown people of various nationalities will work itself out. These stories are discussed here in relation to their publication, but together they form an extended meditation on what the future may hold for Panama's West Indians, the canal having been completed and the region's social fabric altered fundamentally.

DEPARTURE

Like many ambitious intellectuals of his generation, Walrond realized that opportunities in the Caribbean were limited. H. N. Walrond was the owner and editor of an English-language weekly, *The Panama Work-man*. It has been asserted that Eric Walrond was his nephew and assisted on the *Workman*—a Garveyite newspaper. Although it is possible Eric Walrond was involved, no extant evidence confirms it, nor does Walrond refer to the *Workman* or his uncle in any surviving documents.[30] He was a reporter for the *Star & Herald* up until his departure, which he represented matter-of-factly: "Eventually, I got to the point where I thought I must be moving out into a bigger world of endeavor. So before I knew it *I was on my way to America*!" Among his regular beats was the popular boxing circuit. Covering a bout between two African American fighters, Walrond wound up in discussion with one of their managers, a white Bostonian who encouraged him to come north. "[He] drew for me after the rest had gone home graphic pictures of work and opportunity 'up the States.' It edged its way into me slowly, uprootingly [. . .] and in a month I packed up, and was on my way to New York."[31]

3

NEW YORK (1918–1923)

Arriving in New York in June 1918, Walrond was six months shy of age twenty. He showed the Ellis Island officials $160, told them he was a journalist, and moved into the Brooklyn home of his aunt, Julia King Nichols.[1] A middle-class black community had formed in Brooklyn in the late 1800s, and Bedford Stuyvesant, the Nichols's neighborhood, had become an enclave for West Indians, nine thousand of whom resided in Brooklyn in 1920.[2] Local markets carried saltfish, callaloo, and other Caribbean staples. Italians, Poles, and Jews had supplanted the Dutch and English who gave the neighborhood its name, but now Caribbean sounds emanated from the stoops that adorned the brownstone row houses. Overhearing the conversations about Kingston and Bridgetown, the hum of calypso, or a discussion of the spice buns on Nostrand Avenue, a West Indian could fool himself into believing he had never left home.[3]

But this was New York, as the rattle of the elevated train reminded its residents. The crack of the bat Walrond heard from the street came from children playing baseball, not cricket. In one autobiographical tale, "Success Story," young Jim Prout is newly arrived in Brooklyn. He devours a ball of coucou prepared by his aunt in the familiar Barbadian manner. But she cautions, "You must remember that in America everything is different, even sleeping."

"Sleep?" asked Jim.

"Yes, bo. You mustn't think you does sleep in America the same way as in the West Indies. No, bo."

She proceeded to show him. "You must not lay down '*pon* the sheets, but betwixt them. That is the secret. And you just not forget to do that wherever you da-go. You must not let anybody think you just come" ("Success" 113).

Walrond seems to have been disoriented by the transition. In his story, Jim lapses into a gloomy reverie from which his cousin tries to rouse him.

After tramping the streets all day in search of work Jim had found the armchair by the window in Aunt Josephine's living room, easily the most restful spot in the flat. [. . .]

An "El" train, pulling out of the Grand Avenue Station, swung up high on to the horizon. Swiftly the view of the heavens was obliterated. As the screeching and grinding of the long curving line of coaches mounted to a crescendo Jim felt someone clap him on the shoulder. He turned just as the soft grey haze of the Northern twilight had begun to flow back into the room and saw Timothy Cumberbatch standing there beside him.

"What do you say there, fellah? I ain't seen you in a monkey's age. Where you been keeping yourself?"

"Hello, Timothy. I didn't hear you come in."

Timothy was tall, slim and black. He wore horn-rimmed glasses and a blue serge suit. He had been born in Barbados but the outward manifestations of his powers of adaptation were so impressive Jim had found it difficult to believe Timothy had spent only ten of his twenty-one years in Brooklyn.

"For crying out loud, fellah!" grinned Timothy, shaking Jim by the shoulder, "Don't let it throw you! Buck up, boy, you ain't down in the jungles now. You can't git nowheres going all moony like-a so." (160)

Marked as American through his idiom and affect, Timothy is a foil for Walrond's character, whose adjustment is incremental and painful.

Walrond tried to get his bearings and establish himself by moving to a nearby apartment, but he struggled to find satisfying work. He entered a shorthand contest at the Stenographer's Association, earning an honorable mention.[4] He took odd jobs: "salesman—porter—dish slinger—secretary—elevator operator—editor—longshoreman—stenographer—switchboard operator—janitor—advertising solicitor—houseman—free lance" ("Godless" 32). Soon his family obligations increased, his mother and siblings arriving from Colón in September 1919. The officials who received them dutifully recorded their nationality ("British"), race ("Afn-Black"), and show money ($100). Having satisfied them that she was neither a polygamist nor an anarchist, Ruth said she intended to move her family in with her son in Brooklyn. Her husband would soon join them. Walrond now had two brothers, Claude (age 14) and Carol (7), and two sisters, Annette (17) and Eunice (4), to help look after. After a brief stint as a stenographer, he became a secretary at an architectural firm, and although the job did not last long, his supervisor was sufficiently impressed that he recommended Walrond to a friend who hired him as a clerk at the Broad Street Hospital.[5] It was new but within two years had grown from a 35-bed facility to one of nine stories and more than two hundred beds.[6] Walrond earned $140 per month, slightly above the median family income for New York City.

It was during this time that Walrond wrote his way into New York journalism. Within four years, he would be dining downtown with Alfred and Blanche Knopf, James Weldon Johnson, Carl Van Vechten, Zora Neale Hurston, Countée Cullen, Langston Hughes, Alain Locke, and other literati. He would take them to A'Lelia Walker's parties, heir to the fortune of the first African American millionaire, and dance the Charleston until the early morning in the gin-soaked cabarets of Prohibition-era Harlem. It was a vertiginous ascent from which he would not soon recover.

TONGUE-TIED RAGE

Walrond recounted his difficulty finding work, attributing it to a racial prejudice that continually surprised him. In *The New Republic*, he wrote of having done "battle with anaemic youngsters and giggling flappers" in the employment agencies.

I am ignorantly optimistic. America is a big place; I feel it is only a question of time and perseverance. Encouraged, I go into the tall office buildings of Lower Broadway. I try every one of them. Not a firm is missed. I walk in and offer my services. I am black, foreign-looking, and a curio. My name is taken. I shall be sent for, certainly, in case of need. "Oh, don't mention it, sir. . . . Glad you came in. . . . Good morning." I am smiled out. I never hear from them again. ("On Being Black" 245)

An implicit code made itself felt with unerring consistency. At a Brooklyn optician, the salesman assumed he wanted the style favored by "all the colored chauffeurs."

"But I'm not a chauffeur" I reply softly. Were it a Negro store, I might have said it with a great deal of emphasis, of vehemence. But being what it is, and knowing that the moment I raise my voice I am accused of "uppishness," I take pains—oh such pains, to be discreet. I wanted to bellow in his ears, "Don't think every Negro you see is a chauffeur." ("On Being Black" 244)

The pains Walrond took to be civil—avoiding accusations of "uppishness," refusing to "bellow"—become a recurring trope in these sketches. He gave expression to a common experience among West Indian immigrants, who were often directed into menial labor and predominantly black neighborhoods. Many suffered downward social mobility.[7] When Walrond grew exasperated in print at the narrow horizon of opportunity for black New Yorkers, he was of course expressing the injustices of Jim Crow but more specifically voicing a sense of outrage among West Indian immigrants.

The key question in "Success Story" is whether Walrond's character, Jim, will beat the odds and find work outside the service sector. He is either too ambitious or too naïve to settle for menial work. He declines a job as an elevator operator: "No, I'm sorry Timothy, I don't know anything about running an elevator. [. . .] I shouldn't like to risk it. I might get stuck between floors or something." When Timothy presses him—"You don't seem to realize that you is in America. Don't nobody wait for jobs in

America. You goes out arter 'em and grabs 'em"—he responds, "There are lots of places I haven't tackled yet" (163). But he will not grab if it means manual labor or joining the servant class, whom he derides as "ebony flunkeys, resplendent in blue uniforms trimmed with gold braid [who] moved with stately pomp" through the halls of Manhattan offices (162). "That guy takes the cake," says Timothy, "Why he must be nuts to think he can get the kind of job he had in Panama in this country. Running an elevator ain't good enough for him, huh? Well, you wait till the cold weather sets in. He will come crawling, you wait and see" (164). Thus, the question the story frames is whether the young professional will succumb to the racial logic his cousin expresses so peremptorily, whether he will assume his place as a "Negro" and accept a job he feels is beneath him.

As the title suggests, "Success Story" rejects the proposition that Walrond's character must accede to the inexorable logic of racialization. Interviewing at one firm, he fantasizes, "If he should get the job he would give up sleeping on the bug-stained cot in Aunt Josephine's living room and move into proper lodgings (189)." All goes well: he is hired at eighteen dollars a week, introduced as *Mister* Prout to the secretary, Miss Guzman, and begins training with a Venezuelan émigré. Although the position is clerical—consular invoices, bills of lading—it confers prestige and dignity. He will address secretaries in pink blouses and corduroy skirts with snappy lines, like "Step on it, Sally. I'm in a hurry," as the Venezuelan does. His colleagues are immigrants whose backgrounds help rather than hinder their advancement, such as John Gonzaga, "son of a pushcart pedlar in Little Italy," and Carlos Jimenez, who manages shipments to Chile (193). Jim conducts business with far-flung foreign offices, and rather than operate an elevator he rides one every morning to his nineteenth-floor office. We are meant to see that his persistence paid off, that he was not "nuts to think he can get the kind of job he had in Panama" after all. The story ends with an ironic flourish that underscores the delicate operation he has performed, persuading those in power to see beyond his blackness. His boss, reproached for having hired "a nigger in your department," growls through his cigar, "He is not a nigger, he is a foreigner" (194). Still, the story's ending seems bitterly ironic. In what sense is it a success that Jim circumvents this racial logic? His triumph merely illustrates the false opposition: either black or an immigrant, a "nigger" or a "foreigner." Even after making a successful writing career, Walrond remained militant on this subject.[8] He anticipated what scholars would later observe about the force of racialization and the strategies West Indians developed to negotiate it.

A tacit but unwavering prejudice among white editors forestalled his entry into New York journalism. "Young, black—the city rolling above me—I was seized by the sober aspect of work," he wrote in a 1926 essay, "New York! America! Very logically, the newspapers dominated my vision" ("Adventures" 110). He tried "freely and spontaneously" at several papers, which is to say unencumbered by race consciousness. At one newspaper, a receptionist "became so inflamed at the colossal audacity of me that she did not feel the need to conceal outwardly the horror which seared her. 'Why no!' she cried, 'there are no vacancies here—and you can't see the city editor'" ("Adventures" 110). Trying another, his luck appeared to improve. The managing editor "bristled with the emotion of an idea. *I was the very man for it!*" But the offer turned out to be just as insulting, writing captions for a comic strip about "cullud folks."

> I examined some of it. It was neither truthful nor realistic, but like most comic strips, broad, lewd, and vulgar. [. . .] The managing editor said it would bring the "cullud folks" galloping to the paper if these strips had nice peppy darky titles to them. Would I not like to do them? All I would be required to do was go through the "black belt"—the pool rooms, honky tonks, cabarets, and court rooms—and dig up the stuff. ("Adventures" 110)

He considered accepting, but in an "unconscious fury, my instincts began to quake and with a feeling of self-righteousness I failed to return with samples of the stuff." All the rejection and misdirection left him livid, "the salt of the tropic sea ravaging the blood in my veins." Finally, "adrift on an angry sea," he was reduced to writing "two disgusting darky stories" for a popular magazine. An important tension had emerged in Walrond's career: anger and disbelief, on one hand, at the white establishment's refusal to see past his color, and adaptation, on the other, to the codes that compelled him to perform blackness in print. Negotiating this tension became vital to Walrond's career. For the moment, he complied with "disgusting darky stories," but alternate performances became available. As the extraordinary pressure that flattened intraracial differences became clear, he would devise strategies to manipulate the codes of representation.

But why was Walrond so struck by segregation and prejudice? After all, he spent his adolescence in Panama, where "the race problem, as it is known and understood in the United States, was first introduced on a large scale into the Caribbean."[9] Given his prior exposure, what should be made of his self-presentation as a credulous greenhorn, naïve to the ways of racial discrimination? What appears to be a faithful record of his struggle with racism may also be understood as a rhetorical device. It is not that he fabricated his distress or that his humiliations were baseless, but in depicting the experience he adopted a persona: the innocent who "doesn't know any better," assumes the best of white folks, and believes merit will prevail. This was a powerful rhetorical choice, making a virtue of guilelessness. Winston James notes how "ignorance of the racial mores of the society, naiveté, can sometimes redound to the benefit of the ignorant and the foolhardy."[10]

> Black people from the South who had come to New York during the Great Migration, were, perforce, fully aware of the racial codes and, therefore, would not as readily have taken the risk of violating those codes by knocking down the Jim Crow sign and marching into a factory demanding employment. It took "over-confident," "aggressive," "arrogant" [. . .] foreigners to do that sort of thing. Black people who knew better would have kept away from the place. But by the same token, people who knew better would not have gained jobs in the trades. Ignorance is, at times, a blessing.[11]

Walrond employed the trope of the disillusioned greenhorn to enlist his reader's identification and outrage, not only on behalf of West Indians suffering downward social mobility but any "Negro" whose professional qualifications were disregarded.

Walrond's first *Opportunity* sketch was about his experience as a hotel "houseman" and, like much of his early work, a litany of vituperative exchanges forms a pattern of mistreatment.

> Up to 301 the elevator shot me. On the door I rapt.
>
> "Who is it?"
>
> "Houseman."
>
> "Come back in about an hour. I'm not ready for you yet."
>
> I went to 303. I swept and dusted and mopt and scrubbed and threw at times a misty eye at the poet at the sun-baked window, tugging at his unruly brain. Surreptitiously I sipt of the atmospheric wine. At least he would let me stay—and live. So unlike that other place on the top floor where I had forgot my pail. I went back for it. The lady [. . .] on opening the door and depriving me of the aesthetic privilege of at least hearing her voice, poised on the threshold like an icily petrified thing— and pointed Joan-of-Arc like fingers at it—my pail—nestling under the writing table. Audibly, loudly her fingers articulated, "There it is! Come and get it—you coon!"
>
> In bewilderment I groped my way back to earth—and reason. ("On Being a Domestic" 234)

On returning to clean Room 301 he finds its occupant "cross, crimson, belligerent." "I'm going out for lunch now," she sniffs, "and I won't be back for an hour, so you'll have plenty of time to clean up. I don't want to be alone in the room with you while you're cleaning up." As in many sketches, Walrond's disorientation and injury prevent him from making a rejoinder.

> I am tongue-tied. I drop the broom and the pail and out of eyes white with the dust of emotion, watch the figure chastely going down the steps. Aeons of time creep by me. It is years before I come to. But when I do it is with gargantuan violence. There rises up within me, drowning

all sense of reason and pacification, a passionate feeling of revolt—
revolt against domestic service—against that damnable social heirloom
of my race. (234)

The repressed rejoinder is again the key trope. His inchoate fury begins
as disoriented silence and transmutes into something violent, passionate. He describes a similar encounter with a clerk who refuses, because
of race, to give him the advertised price of a ticket. "I am not truculent.
Everything I strive to say softly, unoffensively—especially when in the
midst of a color ordeal." Managing the anger from such confrontations
becomes the black person's principal challenge, he suggests. "I am out on
the street again. From across the Hudson a gurgling wind brings dust to
my nostrils. I am limp, static, emotionless" ("On Being Black" 146).

Thus, Walrond's early writing about racism represents two kinds of
violence. It conveys the absurdity of qualified candidates systematically
passed over. It also meditates on the psychological effects of routine racial
slurs and relegation to service. "It is low, mean, degrading—this domestic
serving. It thrives on chicanery. By its eternal spirit-wounds, it is responsible for the Negro's enigmatic character. It dams up his fountains of feeling and expression. It is always a question of showering on him fistfuls
of sweets, nothings, tips" ("On Being a Domestic" 234). The repressed
rejoinder, damming up feeling and expression—this is Walrond's figure for
the damage of casual racism. It constitutes racism's affective dimension,
its manifestation in grief rather than grievance. In this sense, Walrond
anticipated James Baldwin's account of "the rage of the disesteemed," a
sensation he called "personally fruitless, but also absolutely inevitable."

Rage can only with difficulty, and never entirely, be brought under the
domination of the intelligence and is therefore not susceptible to any arguments whatever. . . . Also, rage cannot be hidden, it can only be dissembled.
This dissembling deludes the thoughtless, and strengthens rage and adds,
to rage, contempt. There are, no doubt, as many ways of coping with the
resulting complex of tensions as there are black men in the world, but no
black man can hope ever to be entirely liberated from this internal warfare.[12]

What Baldwin is really describing are the *material effects* of affect, for he adds, "This rage, so generally discounted, so little understood even among the people whose daily bread it is, is one of the things that makes history." This is a more radical claim than it appears, and it is crucial to understanding Walrond's life and work. One tends to think of history-making rage as articulate, politicized. Baldwin says something different. He is describing an affective register—the coping strategies of those who may not realize they are coping—and translating these into material effects, unspectacular but profoundly significant. This is the turn Walrond made during his early New York years, away from a sense of history as constituted by political forces to a poetics and politics of affect, a genealogy of rage.

For this reason, Countée Cullen dedicated "Incident," one of his most celebrated poems, to Walrond. Exhibiting Cullen's signature economy of expression, it recalls a distressing moment from the speaker's youth. The poem is often read as a condemnation of racism, specifically its corrosive effect on young people. It is about the ease with which a white boy hurls the epithet "nigger" and its impact on the speaker. But it is as much about the aftereffects as the incident. Despite having stayed eight months in Baltimore, the speaker only remembers having been called "nigger." The poem is not only about hateful speech, in other words, it is about the affective dimension, how the slur punctures and drains his memory. Cullen's dedication acknowledged his friend's effort to articulate these ineffable matters. Just as Cullen's incident constitutes "all that I remember" about Baltimore, so Walrond depicted casual prejudice as generating an unforgettable rage—unforgettable because unutterable, its repression formed the contours of what he called "the Negro's enigmatic character."

MARRIAGE

In 1920, Walrond moved to an apartment at the corner of 137th Street and Seventh Avenue, the heart of Harlem. With two hundred thousand "Negro" residents in two square miles, in less than fifteen years, it had become the most densely populated black community on earth and a "Mecca for the sightseer, the pleasure-seeker, the curious, the adventurous, the enterprising, the ambitious, and the talented of the entire Negro world."[13] But Walrond's connection to Brooklyn was alive and well. His fiancée, Edith Cadogan, was a Jamaican who, prior to their wedding in November 1920, lived a few blocks from him in Bedford Stuyvesant. The ceremony took place at Walrond's Harlem apartment with his parents and Edith's mother as witnesses. Eric was twenty-one, Edith nineteen and possibly pregnant with the first of their daughters. Two more daughters followed in as many years, but the marriage was short-lived: Edith, pregnant with Lucille, boarded a ship to Kingston in 1923 with their daughters Jean and Dorothy.

An unpublished autobiographical novel entitled *Brine*, begun for Walrond's "Technique of the Novel" course at Columbia University, sheds light on the relationship.[14] As in "Success Story," his surrogate is named Jim, and the novel excerpt follows the couple on the emotional day on which he put his two infant children and his pregnant wife on a ship to Kingston. It is a disheartening tale, carefully composed but withering in its depiction of marital discord. Edith's character, Nora, is dependent, pliant, a willing target for Jim's verbal abuse; she is forever sobbing, her frame shaking. Jim is sullen and unsympathetic, though Walrond makes him three-dimensional, unlike Nora. Begun in 1924, *Brine* was Walrond's effort to make sense of his marriage's failure, perhaps to assuage his guilt after his family left. The opening scene establishes the conflict between the couple, though beyond a vague suggestion that Jim feels henpecked, the source of the conflict is unclear. Although Jim seems fond of his children, calling one a "cherub" and comparing the other to "a bed of yellow tulips," he does not engage them. He displays only aggravation, and "Nora hadn't had time in her strenuous life in America as a married woman to know her husband that well" (2). Perpetually cross, Jim replies to few of Nora's entreaties, spitting his answers.

Within this melodramatic account, however, Walrond's painterly sensibility also reveals itself, a quality that soon distinguished him among his peers.

Facing the pier there stretched a queue of trucks, swollen to the ribs, waiting for the signal from the gateman before they bolted in. The drivers, white
men with faces black and limned with dust and dirt of rain and sun, snow
and hail, toil and murk; horses and mules ridden with the brunt of age and
suffering; the tarpaulins shielding the rich, unwieldy cargoes. [. . .] Wharf
hands swarmed about the mouth of the pier. Their lips red and greasy with
victuals they were clad in overalls and dungarees, and were smoking and
carrying on hilariously. One of them, a prizefighter, with sunken, scarlet
eyes and large, high, swollen cheekbones, was shadow boxing. (5)

Such tableaux propelled Walrond's later success in fiction, even as he
struggled with exposition. The chapter ends with Jim telling an Irishman
patrolling the pier, "wife's sick; sent her 'way for a change. She'll be back
in a little while." But he never saw her again.

The pier may have evoked the memory of the more joyful departure of
another ship bound for the West Indies a few years earlier, one he almost
certainly witnessed. William Ferris recalled it in messianic terms.

On a Sunday in the latter part of November, 1919, we stood on a pile
of logs and watched hundreds of people jump up and down, throw hats
and handkerchiefs and cheer while the *Yarmouth*, the first steamship
of the Black Star Line, backed from the wharf at West 135th Street and
slowly glided down the North River. It was sturdily built, but it was not
a large, speedy, modern-equipped boat. But the news that black men
had actually purchased a steamship, manned by a Negro captain and
crew and sent her out into the briny deep electrified the Negro peoples
of the world as no other event since the Emancipation Proclamation of
Abraham Lincoln did. [. . .] A commercial venture ended as an uplift of
the spirit. It was sown a natural body, it was raised a spiritual body. And
that was something of a miracle.[15]

Garvey would declare of this occasion:

"The Eternal has happened. For centuries the black man has been
taught by his ancient overlords that he was 'nothing,' is 'nothing,' and

shall never be 'anything'. . . . Five years ago the Negro [. . .] was sleeping upon his bale of cotton in the South of America; he was steeped in mud in the banana fields of the West Indies and Central America, seeing no possible way of extricating himself from the environments; he smarted under the lash of the new taskmaster in Africa; but alas! Today he is the new man."[16]

GARVEYISM AND *NEGRO WORLD*

Based in Harlem but originally from Jamaica, Marcus Garvey inspired millennial pronouncements of the kind William Ferris expressed. In his organization's principles and in his very bearing, he advocated dignity and self-respect for people of African descent. That link to a place derided by white supremacist cultures across the diaspora was critical to Universal Negro Improvement Association (UNIA) principles. Not only was there nothing inferior about Africanness, Garvey countered, but a rich history of African accomplishment had been obscured by the contemporary racial hierarchy. The control exercised by people of European descent over world affairs was neither inevitable nor irreversible, he maintained. "Why should we be discouraged because somebody laughs at us today? We see and have changes every day, so pray, work, be steadfast, and be not dismayed."[17] Through self-discipline, pride, self-determination, and unstinting resistance to white supremacy, African-descended people could revive their noble past in modernity, establishing a "Negro Empire" on the ashes of those subjugating them. Unlike the National Association for the Advancement of Colored People (NAACP), which advocated integration, the UNIA pursued "Negro" enterprises and institutions, including the "Back to Africa" colonization plan and the Black Star shipping line. Resplendent in martial attire, Garvey and the UNIA burst on the New York scene in 1917 as World War I ended. African American soldiers returned from fighting for democracy to a country riven by segregation, and nation building was the political order of the day. By 1920, the UNIA had a devoted membership in the United States and the Caribbean and held its annual convention that year in Madison Square Garden.

It has been alleged that Walrond "turned to the radical black national-ism" of Garvey out of "anger and frustration" with his poor job pros-pects.[18] But the relationship among Walrond's anger, political militancy, and employment by the UNIA is far more interesting. A common mis-conception is that Garvey, a charlatan and demagogue, was only able to dupe the witless, the white hating, and the West Indian. To be sure, Gar-vey was imperious, suspicious to the point of paranoia, and ruthless in his persecution of detractors. His indictment on mail fraud charges and subsequent deportation vindicated his critics and cast an ignominious pall over his legacy. But he built the largest mass movement among people of African descent to date. If he was a charlatan, there was something extraordinarily compelling in his call for racial pride, his intransigence, and his international campaign. Observers often claim that the UNIA's broad appeal indicates how bitter even northern blacks had become, but what is missed by emphasizing bitterness and resentment is the utopian desire for autonomy and self-respect, a balm for the psychic wounds modernity had inflicted on people of African descent.[19] Garvey's notori-ous African colonization scheme expressed a keenly felt desire to secure a place New World blacks could call their own. If the prospect of a new African empire populated by a reversal of the baleful Middle Passage seems fanciful today, the UNIA's ascendance reflected a widespread long-ing for relief from New World racism.

The "Red Summer" of 1919 punctuated this history and enhanced Garvey's appeal. This was the "summer when the stoutest-hearted Negroes felt terror and dismay," wrote James Weldon Johnson, when the Klan flourished and race riots erupted in Chicago, Omaha, Texas, and the nation's capital, where "an anti-Negro mob held sway for three days, six persons were killed, and scores severely beaten."[20] An irate Claude McKay penned his famous sonnet exhorting, "If we must die—oh, let us nobly die/So that our precious blood shall not be shed/In vain." Johnson, who was generally critical of Garvey, conceded, "He had energy and dar-ing and the Napoleonic personality, the personality that draws masses of followers. He stirred the imagination of the Negro masses as no Negro ever had."[21] It is not hard to imagine why an ambitious black journalist

such as Walrond affiliated with the UNIA. Beyond the bombast of its
leader lay an organization of active adherents in pursuit of a bold collective purpose. Working at its journal, *Negro World*, were two of the finest
minds in black America: William Ferris, who earned degrees from Yale
and Harvard, and Hubert Harrison, a self-taught polymath known as
the "Black Socrates." Walrond's UNIA journalism cannot be attributed
to his susceptibility to the blandishments of a demagogue, the residual
nationalism of a West Indian expatriate, or to the mercenary impulse
of a writer in need of a byline. Nor is it the case that West Indian immigrants such as Walrond were politically conservative prior to their arrival
and only radicalized by confrontations with U.S. racism. The virulence of
prejudice in post-war America made the UNIA appealing, but the West
Indians who swelled its ranks had not, by and large, been a quiet lot of
Tories back home.[22]

When Walrond started as associate editor for the Garveyite newspaper,
The Weekly Review, in December 1919, it was not his first encounter with
the UNIA. Although New York became the hub of Garvey's activity, he
started the UNIA in Jamaica, and the organization's principles were drawn
from his experience there and in Costa Rica, Cuba, and Panama. In Panama, Walrond knew at least two people, Amy Ashwood and W. C. Parker,
who were close to Garvey, and he was aware of the UNIA-led unioniza-
tion drives among "silver" workers, prompting Isthmian Canal Commission crackdowns and strikes.[23] Walrond's departure preceded the largest
of these, but the UNIA was well under way during his tenure at the *Star
& Herald*.[24] During this period, notes Colin Grant, "The traffic between
Harlem and the Caribbean and the West Indian enclaves in Costa Rica and
Panama was non-stop." In fact, Walrond's tutor W. C. Parker facilitated.

It was through the advocacy of men such as the Panamanian-based
teacher Mr. Parker that word of Garvey's movement spread [. . .]. Garvey [also] relied on the willingness of merchant seamen to act as informal agents for the *Negro World*, carrying bundles of the paper from
port to port. By such means the *Negro World* had been successfully
distributed throughout the Panama Canal zone.[25]

Covering "commerce, politics, news, industry, and economics," the New York–based *Weekly Review* was short-lived, but an excerpt from the first issue suggests its fervent anti-colonialism:

> [W]e must make it unprofitable for England to hold her colonies. At the same time we must embarrass her by political agitation and propaganda in foreign countries. In our upward struggle we cannot afford to let any nation or race stand in our paths, and no nation stands so much in our path today as England. Therefore, we must do all in our power to discredit her, disrupt her empire and attain our ends at all costs. And it is not so difficult an attainment as some think.[26]

Sentiments like these were enough to get the attention of British intelligence officials during Walrond's tenure as associate editor.[27] They also indicate the UNIA's departure from narrow nationalism. Walrond's experience at the *Star & Herald* and *The Weekly Review* surely recommended him to *Negro World*. The journal was barely two years old when he was hired, but its circulation soon rose dramatically and it became a platform for the era's most controversial movement.[28]

Within a few weeks of his first contribution in December 1921, Walrond won first prize in the journal's literary competition, and the following week he was on the masthead as assistant editor. He was soon promoted to associate editor, and his contributions appeared regularly throughout 1922.[29] These were turbulent years in the organization, in Harlem, and in Walrond's life. He would leave *Negro World* almost as abruptly as he arrived, accepting a demotion in the spring of 1923 and dissolving all ties to the UNIA that summer. Walrond and Garvey would eventually find one another again in London in 1935 on better terms, but their reconciliation could not have been predicted from their falling out.

Among those who have attended to this stage of Walrond's career, one has condemned him as the worst sort of opportunist, a traitor who deserted the cause in the time of its leader's greatest need; another dismisses the *Negro World* writing as "apprentice work [that] consisted of romantic effusions and naïve hero-worship—hardly the stuff of which tough minded journalists are made."[30] It is true that his *Negro World* material—essays, reviews, and short fiction—is unseasoned work and bears the stamp of its ideological constraints, but a great deal is missed by assessing it strictly in terms of literary quality or fidelity to Garveyism. Walrond was negotiating in print his relationship to UNIA doctrine. On one hand, he chronicled the achievements of black people in order to promote self-esteem and group solidarity; on the other hand, he routinely ran afoul of Garveyite principles and risked alternatives. He was experimenting with voices, including but not limited to the strident assertion Garvey expected, and he put to the test his considerable appetite for polemics. Key tensions that inspired and shaped Walrond's later work appear in incipient form in the *Negro World* material.

Walrond leapt into the fray with the three articles preceding his prizewinning story and staff appointment. As was expected of fledgling contributors, he trained his sights on rival movements, inveighing against Socialists and the NAACP. In "The Failure of the Pan-African Congress" in late 1921, he admonished W. E. B. Du Bois for courting white support. Du Bois and his NAACP colleagues were regular targets of UNIA vitriol. Garveyites such as Walrond cast themselves in opposition as an authentically black organization with a definitive program. The war of words flew in both directions, characterized as often by ad hominem attacks on the class and color of the adversary as by differences of opinion or strategy. Beyond the NAACP, the UNIA battled for the hearts and minds of African Americans with the Socialists and Communists, who also enjoyed black support and leadership from Cyril Briggs, Richard B. Moore, A. Philip Randolph, and Chandler Owen. Hubert Harrison was a renowned Socialist speaker before joining the UNIA, and Claude McKay worked for Communist journals in London and New York before traveling in 1922 to Moscow for the Third Communist International. If the NAACP was considered dangerous because of its elitism and ties to white America, Socialists and Communists were taken to task for being insufficiently race conscious. Walrond played the UNIA rivals against each other in late 1921 in "Between Two Mountains," calling Du Bois "the sphinx of Fifth Avenue," a "sneering god of intellect" who "folds his white gloved hands and gazes at the sublime prospect of life in a warless world," while the "dyed-in-the-wool Leninists" "wave a blood-red flag" but are merely "parading their intelligence" (4). This last point was an implicit defense of Garvey, who was impugned for being uneducated and courting the ignorant masses.[31]

Despite some lively turns of phrase, these first *Negro World* essays were fairly scripted. Less predictable was his next effort, "Discouraging the Negro," which exhibited Walrond's familiarity with the Caribbean and the UNIA's internationalism. The editor of *The Paramaribo Times* (Dutch Guiana) had castigated Garvey's anticolonialism as "vicious and dangerous," destined to "end in disaster and ruin." He warned "the black people of the world" not to "forget the benefits they have enjoyed and still are enjoying under the rulers to whom they owe allegiance" (4). Discerning an apologist for colonialism, Walrond reproved the editor, calling his remarks "typical of colonial propaganda to keep the Negro 'feeling right,'" another instance of the "crocodile sincerity" that persuaded colonial subjects of their "good fortune to be governed by the best, most humane government in the world" (4). Moreover, he added, the horrors of American racism were always trotted out to claim the relative benevolence of colonial rule. But the only difference between Americans and Europeans, he wrote, "is that the latter are veritable past masters in the art of smiling in a man's face and at the same time sticking a dagger in his side, whereas the former are frank and less hypocritical in their domination of the Negro." Thus, to secure "a square deal to the Negro peoples the world over," he concluded, "a mighty republic must spring up on the shores of Africa. Only by the realization of this ideal can we hope to abolish slavery in the Congo, peonage in Hayti, and lynching in Texas" (4).

In an article about the white American novelist T. S. Stribling, Walrond again drew on his Caribbean background to engage questions of racial representation. Stribling praised Trinidadian women in the *Saturday Evening Post* for raising a generation of black professionals. Amplifying Stribling's contention, Walrond said the story of the "Negro mother's heroic part in the evolution of the race" had yet to be written. "One of these days a Negro Dickens will come along and, in his realist sweep, take

in the whole panorama of irony, tragedy, heroism, sacrifice and achievement, and then the women of the race will come into their own" (4).
His remarks indicate his faith in the difference a novel could make and
his feelings about his own Caribbean mother. "I owe everything to the
encouragement of my mother and her determination, a determination
that *just won't down*," he wrote a year later ("Godless" 33).

Walrond won first prize in *Negro World*'s annual literary competition in December 1921 with a bit of fanciful fiction, and it is easy to see
why. "A Senator's Memoirs" featured Garvey as its hero, "the prince of
men." Set twenty years hence, the story's conceit is that the UNIA has
triumphed over adversity and established a sovereign black state capable
of competing with Europe and North America culturally, economically,
and militarily. It projects readers into an idyllic future in which the narrator, a senator from the Congo, marvels at the UNIA's success, framed as
the realization of God's will.

> Thanks to Jehovah, I am a free man—free to traverse the surface of
> the earth—free to stop and dine at any hostelry I wish—free! As I sit
> here and dash off these notes I cannot but think it all a massive dream.
> Twenty years ago, as a stranded emigrant on the shores of Egypt, if
> I had been told that I'd be out here, on my own estate, drinking of
> the transcendent beauty of the Congo, a master of my people, to be
> honored and respected, I'd have discounted it as an overworking of the
> imagination. (6)

As the senator explains, the race's "fate and future" are glorious. Celebrating ten years of independence, "myriad brown-faced people"
gathered in an expansive Liberty Square, "a huge park" named after
Harlem's UNIA headquarters. "From the banks of the Zambesi, from
across the Nile, from South Africa, Liberia, Hayti, America—they
stood, a free and redeemed people!" (6). The sketch turns from the senator's reminiscence to a projection of Garvey himself, "a little man in a
white tunic" who takes the podium to "a chorus of deafening cheers."
Walrond's Garvey, president of "Africa Redeemed," delivers a speech

like those he delivered throughout the early 1920s but with the utopian ideals now fulfilled. Clumsily executed, "A Senator's Memoirs" is
a transparent attempt to demonstrate the writer's fidelity to the cause
and leader, but it is also a clever thought experiment, suspending the
material conditions of the present.

As Walrond continued at *Negro World*, he sought to discredit stereotypes and celebrate black achievement, but he grew increasingly interested in literary matters. Over the next year, he wrote a series of prose
poems, sketches, and reviews that engaged the issues of aesthetics and
politics increasingly occupying the New Negro movement. Elements of
Walrond's later fiction appear here—an alertness to standard and nonstandard language use, a concern with aesthetics, and a struggle to reconcile what were thought to be the conflicting demands of art and politics.
Students of African American literature will recognize these as familiar
questions, but at no previous point and few since did they possess the
urgency of the 1920s. Walrond's *Negro World* meditations may be understood in relation to the debates about representation that intensified over
the decade, punctuated by polemics such as Langston Hughes's "The
Negro Artist and the Racial Mountain," George Schuyler's "Negro Art
Hokum," W. E. B. Du Bois's "Criteria of Negro Art," and Zora Neale
Hurston's "Characteristics of Negro Expression." Walrond was among
those engaging these questions in print and at salons and forums. In
fact, his interest in aesthetic matters isolated him at *Negro World*, which
became hostile toward the arts.

"Art and Propaganda," the terms around which much contemporary
debate was waged, furnished the title for an article Walrond wrote in
December 1921. The Martinican writer René Maran had been awarded
the Prix Goncourt, the prestigious French literary prize, for his novel
Batouala. It caused a stir because he was the first "Negro" winner, and
the novel posed a critique of French colonialism in Africa.[32] Among
those scoffing at the selection was Ernest Boyd, editor of the *Literary
Review*, whom Walrond proceeded to excoriate. Walrond marked out a
position on the relationship between aesthetics and politics that would
be taken up by proponents of New Negro literature. Ironically, it was

a position from which Walrond himself would soon retreat. The lines along which Walrond assailed Maran's detractors were not explicitly racial, but his impatience with the inherited presuppositions of European forms was evident. He conveyed his impatience with his signature wit and linguistic verve.

> Tied to the conventions of literature, Boyd found too many African words in the book; it is replete with crotchets and quavers and demi semi-quavers. [. . .] Also, he sniffs at the introduction to the work, which is a carping, merciless indictment of the brutal colonial system of France. As far as Mr. Boyd can see, what on earth has all this to do with a work of art, a penetrating study of a savage chieftain?

Shifting the discussion closer to home, Walrond compared Boyd's "sniffs" to recent observations made by James Weldon Johnson, NAACP Secretary. In advocating that African Americans write literature free of propaganda, Johnson had misunderstood the basis from which that literature necessarily springs.

> Mr. Johnson tells us there is a tendency on the part of Negro poets to be propagandic. For this reason it is going to be very difficult for the American Negro poet to create a lasting work of art. He must first purge himself of the feelings and sufferings and emotions of an outraged being, and think and write along colorless, sectionless lines. Hate, rancor, vituperation—all of these things he must cleanse himself of. But is this possible? The Negro, for centuries to come, will never be able to divorce himself from the feeling that he has not had a square deal from the rest of mankind. His music is a piercing, yelping cry against his cruel enslavement. What little he has accomplished in the field of literature is confined to the life he knows best—the life of the underdog in revolt. So far he has ignored the most potent form of literary expression, the form that brought Maran the Goncourt award. When he does take it up, it is not going to be in any half-hearted, wishy-washy manner, but straight from the shoulder, slashing, murdering, disemboweling! (4)

These questions gained urgency in subsequent years. Can the "Negro" write from a perspective beyond race? If not, must that perspective express the frustrations of the "underdog in revolt," or is "Negro" experience more expansive?

Another rejoinder to a well-known white journalist followed, as Walrond challenged Heywood Broun of the *New York World* over the use of the word "nigger." Broun endorsed it, arguing that it conveyed in sound and sense the "energy" of a people. "From the standpoint of language there is much to be said for 'nigger,'" he contended. "'Colored man' is hopelessly ornate and 'Negro' is tainted with ethnology. More than that, it is a literary word. 'Nigger' is a live word. There is a ring to it like that of a true coin on a pavement" (4). The former sportswriter Broun located the word's virtue in its evocative masculinity, solid where other words were "namby-pamby." It was time for African Americans to embrace "nigger" and by claiming it transform its meaning. He conceded "the word had its origin in contempt, but acceptance itself would rob 'Nigger' of all its sting." Although Walrond would soon use "Nigger" liberally in his fiction and defend others who did so, in *Negro World* he challenged Broun's glorification of an epithet still freighted with pain.

> Five years ago it was a common thing to speak of an Italian as a "Wop," a Jew as a "Sheeney," a Pole as a "Kike." Today the Negro, to a vast portion of the American public, is yet a "Nigger." The word is a stigma of inferiority and its users know it. Ever since its origin it was used to label the Negro as a member of an inferior race. The Russians and Poles and Lithuanians who came to America and were called "names" strenuously objected to it and the result is, being white, they have managed to grow far beyond the reaches of objectionable cognomens. But "Nigger" lingers. (4)

Walrond's response echoed the UNIA party line: "We deprecate the use of the term 'nigger,'" read the group's 1920 Declaration of Rights, "and demand that the word Negro will be written with a capital N." But his reaction reflected a broader suspicion African Americans harbored toward the self-styled white champions of their race. The "Negro vogue," as Hughes called it, may have been preferable to indifference or hostility, but many felt that stereotypes were simply being revalued, not revised. The question was whether heightened attention from whites could be directed to the race's advantage. During Walrond's tenure at *Negro World*, New York's biggest theatrical hit was the Miller and Lyles musical *Shuffle Along*, the tenor Roland Hayes and dancer Florence Mills became household names, and jazz and blues musicians gained white audiences. Uptown cabarets became destinations for pleasure-seekers eager to see the Charleston and the Black Bottom danced with "primitive" abandon, and major writers in the Greenwich Village scene produced "Negro-themed" work. It is not surprising that Walrond initially met these developments with the circumspect sneer that closes his article about Broun. "Among themselves, Harlem's intellectuals had serious doubts about this new wave of white discovery," notes David Levering Lewis.[33] Broun might locate in "nigger" "the terrific contribution of physical energy which the Negro has made to America," but it would be years before the more irreverent writers, such as Hurston, McKay, Wallace Thurman, Rudolph Fisher, and Walrond, felt confident using it in their own work.

After three months at *Negro World*, Walrond was promoted to associate editor. His attention turned, however, to matters that made him unsuited to continue there: the arts. His response to the apparent conflict between art and propaganda had been to claim that great "Negro" writing necessarily sprang from "the feeling that he has not had a square deal," but soon he began cultivating what he called "the soul of a poet," a lyrical sensibility at odds with orthodox Garveyism. He began to sense the limitations, professional and personal, of the life he had made in New York. His marriage was deteriorating, and he enrolled in college, left *Negro World*, and involved himself in the literary activities of the 135th Street branch of the public library and the National Urban League. Portents of this transition are evident in the two kinds of writing he pursued in *Negro World*: sentimental prose poems and tributes to black artists.

"I WISH I WERE AN ARTIST"

Walrond's *Negro World* prose poems are saccharine and formulaic, but their appearance in this journal is remarkable. Garvey fashioned himself a poet, peppering his journal with paeans to manly race pride in leaden verse. Walrond's effusions were quite different. At the time he wrote them, *Negro World* did not have an official policy for contributors, but the editors' literary values were enumerated in an unsigned 1922 editorial. Contributors were advised not to send poetry "unless they are familiar with the rules of versification. Most that is sent is faulty because the authors are ignorant of the rules. Poetry is the highest form of expression, and no satisfactory impression will be got if the rules governing the expression are not understood and adhered to."[34] One need only recall that this was the moment *The Waste Land*, *Cane*, *Harmonium*, and *Spring and All* appeared to grasp *Negro World*'s aesthetic conservatism by contrast. Walrond split the difference by writing prose that employed poetic devices, indulging in florid metaphors and projecting as his persona a tormented poet manqué. Given the doctrinaire quality of most *Negro World* writing, Walrond's accounts of ethereal encounters with his muse are jarringly lyrical and lachrymose.

"Yesterday I strode into the library and had a glimpse of her," begins "A Black Virgin." "Her eyelids are long—and fluttering. Entranced, I gaze, not impudently, as becomes a street urchin, but penetratingly, studying the features of this exquisite black virgin." The speaker is almost too eager to deny the prurience of his gaze.

> For a long time I sit there dreaming—dreaming—dreaming. Of what? Of the fortunes of the flower of youth? Of the curse of bringing a girl of her color into the world? Of fight, of agitation, of propaganda? No. Clearly separating my art from my propaganda, I sit and prop my chin on my palm and wish I were an artist. On my canvas I'd etch the lines of her fleeting figure. [. . .] Her voice. I wonder what it is like? I go to her. "Will—will—you please tell me where I can find a copy of "Who's Who in America?" I startle her. Like a hounded hare she glances at me.

Shy, self-conscious, I think of my unshaven neck and my baggy trouser knees. I fumble at the buckles of my portfolio. Those eyes! I never saw anything so intensely mythical. [. . .] "Why yes, I think there is one over there." Her voice falls on my ear as the ripple of a running stream. Her face I love—her voice I adore. It is so young, so burdened with life and feeling. I follow the swish-swish of her skirt. I get the book and she is gone—gone out of my life! (4)

Artful skirt chasing formed the subject of half the writing published that spring by the soon-to-be-unmarried author. This writing sounded a discordant note in *Negro World*. Where else in UNIA literature does an author confess to feeling shy, self-conscious, and slovenly? A Garveyite wishing he were an artist instead of an agitator?

Subsequent contributions find the speaker in a similar reverie, the spell of which is broken when the female object of beauty returns his voyeuristic gaze. "A Vision" employs the gothic tropes found in Walrond's later fiction.

I am on a high precipice at the edge of the sea. At my feet its gushing waves slash up against the mouth of a medieval cave. Out on the pearl-like waters of the Caribbean a brigantine drops anchor. It is night. A light tropical breeze tickles my lungs. The sky is scarlet. There is a fire on a sugar plantation five miles away. It does not disturb me. It only adds lustre to the night. (4)

A fire on a sugar plantation and it fails to disturb the speaker? What kind of Garveyite is this? Anywhere else in *Negro World*, a plantation fire signals rebellion, marronage, the demise of the buckra. Not for our speaker, for whom it merely "adds lustre to the night." The political has been superseded by the picturesque. A liminal state of Romantic consciousness conjures his muse, "garbed in a gown of flimsy silk." "She is dark. Her hair is long and flowing. There are chrysanthemum buds in it." Her dance sends the speaker into a reverie that is only broken when "her eyes fly open. She sees my terrible face, and is afraid." (4). Thus the conceit was replayed in weekly installments in the spring of 1922: the forlorn lover, the ideal of female perfection, the furtive gaze first satisfied and then subverted. "A Desert Fantasy" finds the speaker "a wanderer in a vast tree-less Sahara," another "dusky figure hovering about me," administering to his "parched lips" and "flaming forehead" (4). The next week it was a kimono-clad girl, "a pitiful look in her virgin eyes," caressing a rose until, "with a petulant grasp she lifts the rose to her blood red lips and crushes the very life out of it" ("Rose" 5). In another, as his muse recedes into a "paradise of clouds," he notes "a narcissus [at] her lips, and Baudelaire under her arm" ("Geisha" 4). The tortured lament of the poet manqué!

The only justification one can imagine for such effusions in *Negro World* is the darkness of Walrond's heroines, his muses. He is always care-ful to make them "dusky"—if not black then at least not white. All but once. "The Castle D'Or," published in March 1922 contributed, one has to think, to his departure from *Negro World*. If it were not bad enough to be perpetually mooning over maidens draped in gauzy gossamer, the object of affection here was an elusive *white* maiden. Again approaches our "sorry looking poet," "thin, hungry, dreamy eyed," knocking at castle gates only to find them locked. Turning to the flower garden, "the queen, the beautiful queen of old, arose and stretched her ivory white hands out to him." "Her nymph-like arms, soft, baby pink arms" complete the "vision of loveliness!"(6). It seems our poet has finally learned his les-son, for now merely "to gaze at the exquisite face and form was all that mattered." The poet "threw his hat in the grass, took out his pad and pencil, and scribbled sonnets of love to her. That was all he wished" (6). The scandal was not the celebration of poetry, nor the turgid prose in which poetry was exalted (the journal was forgiving in this regard), but the speaker's infatuation with the white queen. Consider Garvey's posi-tion on interracial marriage: "To ignore the opposite sex of his race and intermarry with another race is to commit this crime or this sin for which he should never be pardoned by his race. [. . .] For a Negro man to marry someone who does not look like his mother or not a member of his race is to insult his mother, insult nature and insult God who made his father."[35] At least one alert reader objected to Walrond's transgression, declaring

the tale "at variance with the aims and objects of the UNIA." "Should a
queen necessarily have 'white hands' or 'pink skin'?" he asked. "O shades
of white mania! Mr. Editor, you are under its hypnotic spell."[36] Walrond's
prose poems—tame doggerel in another context—were thus doubly scan-
dalous here. They indulged in escapist fantasies of poetic melancholy and
strayed from the established path of racialized desire.

Walrond was far from alone in feeling the pull of poetry in 1922,
arguably the most pivotal year in the history of African American verse.
McKay's *Harlem Shadows* was published to acclaim; Toomer put the
final touches on *Cane*; Georgia Douglas Johnson published *Bronze*; and
James Weldon Johnson published *The Book of American Negro Poetry*,
the preface to which linked race progress to the arts. The tide was shifting
as *The Crisis* began emphasizing the arts and the Urban League founded
Opportunity in 1922. The transformation prompted one budding poet,
a Columbia dropout, to begin thinking in terms of a movement. Writing
Alain Locke, Langston Hughes said, "You are right that we have enough
talent now to begin a movement. I wish we had some gathering place for
our artists—some little Greenwich Village of our own."[37] In Greenwich
Village at that moment was another poet who would help realize their
vision, the New York University student Countée Cullen, a Harlem product with several publications already to his name.

Walrond began writing regularly in *Negro World* about black artists,
writers, and performers, many of whom were relatively unknown. These
accounts expressed his struggle to reconcile aesthetic pleasure with prag-
matic concerns and political engagement. Walrond expressed his desire
to become an artist differently here than in his prose poems but no less
audibly. His admiration for black artists registered in discussions of the
artists Augusta Savage and Cecil Gaylord, the performers Florence Mills
and Bert Williams, the poets Claude McKay and Georgia Douglas Johnson, and the novelists Vladimir Pushkin and Alexandre Dumas, whose
African ancestry he celebrated.[38] The thrill of bringing black artistic
achievement to public view is especially evident in two articles he published in April 1922. One was a review of the *Book of American Negro
Poetry*, the other an account of his visit to the private library of Arthur

Schomburg, the donation of which later created the New York Public Library's Research Center in Black Culture. His reviews addressed readers casually and intimately.

> Not so very long ago I heard a man—one of the "stalwart intellectuals" of Harlem—say with a flare of braggadocio that he had "searched all through it" and could find nothing "new" or "distinctive" in Negro poetry; that, like Negro music, it was the victim of monotony and "oneness of beauty." What was the man talking about? After reading James Weldon Johnson's "Essay on the Negro's Creative Genius," which is a preface to the present volume, I am tempted to drop everything and collar this know-it-all apostle and bellow in his ears: "Here, read this!" (4)

It was unusual for *Negro World* to endorse an NAACP officer without qualification, but Johnson's analysis of dialect and idiom struck a chord with Walrond, who was sensitive to the paternalistic representation of stock "Negro" characters. Beyond the curatorial service Johnson's volume performed, Walrond was inspired by his engagement with the matter of language itself, which loomed larger as he fashioned himself a fiction writer.

A sense of wonder at the history of "Negro" achievement also characterized his account of Schomburg's library. Schomburg grew up in Puerto Rico, and as a Brooklyn resident and Garvey supporter he had likely met Walrond previously. When Walrond visited Schomburg's "unpretentious little dusty brown house on Kosciusko Street" in March 1922, his companion was another ambitious *Negro World* contributor, Zora Neale Hurston. A Southerner by birth, she had come to New York on a scholarship to Barnard College, where she studied with anthropologist Franz Boas and launched her legendary career. In 1922, however, she was still a novice, thirty-one passing for twenty-one. Her reputation as an exacting judge of character who did not suffer fools was already established, and Walrond was anxious that even before a figure as venerable as Schomburg she might make a scene.

The young lady in our party [. . .] abominates what she contemptuously calls "form" and "useless ceremony." [. . .] As we put our feet on the hallowed ground and the warm glitter of Mr. Schomburg's brown-black eyes shone down upon us, she gave way to a characteristic weakness—whispering—whispering out of the corner of her beautiful mouth. "Well, I declare," stamping a petulant foot. "Why, I am flabbergasted. I expected to find a terribly austere giant who looked at me out of withering eyes. But the man is human, ponderously, overwhelmingly human, a genuine eighteen karat." ("Visit" 6)

Hurston and Walrond were so impressed that both published accounts of the visit. Hurston called it "a marvelous collection when one considers that every volume on his extensive shelves is either by a Negro or about Negroes."[39] Concurring, Walrond said many of Schomburg's materials "unsettled our universe": the first book of African folklore "run off by Negro printers in Springvale, Natal, in 1868"; the slave narrative of Olaudah Equiano; a three-volume *History of Hayti*—in total "about 2,000 books by Negro writers, and they cover every imaginable subject under the sun." All in the modest home of the "chief of the mailing department of the Bankers Trust Company" ("Visit" 6).

For Hurston and Walrond, the trip challenged the conventional wisdom about black inferiority and white civilization. More importantly, the voracious genealogical impulse behind Schomburg's undertaking, the very mode of education his collection embodied, stood in stark contrast to the education that "Negroes" received in formal settings. Schomburg told Walrond of a great poet from his native country, a Guianese "Negro" who "attracted the attention of the world when he took first place in a prize poem contest run by *Truth*, a newspaper in England. Oh, that brought the world to its feet, and he became a great friend of Tennyson" (6). As useful as Schomburg's library was for disarming opponents, Walrond also recognized its intimation of a fundamental rearticulation of history, a "counterculture of modernity," in Paul Gilroy's phrase.

Certainly, it offered Walrond a different view of Western civilization than he received at the College of the City of New York, where he enrolled in the fall of 1921. A short walk from the *Negro World* office, City College was free, and Walrond took courses in education, English, philosophy, and government. With a family, a full-time job, and a full course load in the evenings, his first semester ended with an undistinguished record. One of his instructors was Blanche Colton Williams, author of *A Handbook on Story Writing* and editor of that year's *O. Henry Memorial Award Prize Stories*. Her convictions about the craft of fiction would have encouraged Walrond. "I not only believe that one can 'learn to write,'" she observed, "I know, because more than once I have watched growth and tended effort from failure to success. [. . .] Some students need only an encouraging word and sympathetic criticism."⁴⁰ Walrond took time off in 1922, and although he returned the following fall, he did not complete his three courses and never finished his degree.⁴¹ But his training undoubtedly improved his application in 1924 to study creative writing at Columbia.

Formal schooling was now only a part of Walrond's education, which he also pursued at the 135th Street branch of the public library. Here a Book Lovers Club and an association for the Study of Negro History were convened by chief librarian Ernestine Rose, a white woman assisted by her African American colleagues Sadie Peterson, Regina Andrews, and later Nella Larsen, each of whom contributed signally to the New Negro movement. A group of Harlem-based artists and writers, the Eclectic Club, began hosting readings and public forums in early 1922 at the library and other venues. A "peripatetic group" meeting monthly, the Eclectics "provided an important forum in which poets, politicians, and patrons socialized and discussed future projects."⁴² Walrond involved himself in the activity of the Eclectics, recruiting Hurston and *Negro World* colleagues to their events. The UNIA opened a hotel and a teashop intended as "literary forums and social centers of Harlem."⁴³ Located on 135th Street, "The White Peacock" was briefly "Harlem's Greenwich Village," said Walrond, "Musicians and flappers, students and professional people" sat amid "futurist paintings [. . .] until far into the night talking about love and death, sculpture and literature, socialism and psychoanalysis" ("Books" 4).

At one of Walrond's earliest Eclectic Club meetings, he was so moved by Claude McKay's reading from *Harlem Shadows* that he claimed, "Every poem is a gem—there is not a mediocre one in the entire batch" ("Harlem Shadows" 4). McKay described the event as an obligation rather than a pleasure, claiming to have felt uncomfortable with his status. "I had to sit on a platform and pretend to enjoy being introduced and praised. I had to respond pleasantly. Hubert Harrison said that I owed it to my race."

> The Eclectic Club turned out in rich array to hear me: ladies and gentlemen in *tenue de rigueur*. I had no dress suit to wear, and so, a little nervous, I stood on the platform and humbly said my pieces. What the Eclectics thought of my poems I never heard. But what they thought of me I did. They were affronted that I did not put on a dress suit to appear before them. They thought I intended to insult their elegance because I was a radical.[44]

If Walrond was among those disturbed by McKay's attire, it did not affect his review. "After swallowing these poems (as I did), one is able to appreciate why Claude McKay is idolized by lovers of the beautiful in poetry." Yet what distinguished McKay's work, Walrond observed, was his wedding of the beautiful to the ordinary. Concerned to identify "the life and character of the artist," Walrond approvingly cited "Baptism," in which the speaker enters a furnace boldly and alone, while others remain terrified without. In the galvanizing process inside Walrond discerned "the poet-artist's philosophy": "One may be with the mob and yet not be of it!" he concluded, a reflection on his own predicament ("Harlem Shadows" 4).

The artist's technique, the artist's sensibility—these became Walrond's chief concerns. He paid tribute to black visual artists such as Augusta Savage, a sculptor who wrote poetry for *Negro World*. A Florida native who moved to New York to study art at Cooper Union, Savage became a central figure in the New Negro movement because of her own work and her support of others. Walrond recounted her improbable journey to art school and Harlem, where he visited her "poorly lighted room" to see her "put the finishing touches to a bust of Marcus Garvey" (3). Performing artists, too, became his subjects, and he covered two Broadway openings that exploited the popularity of *Shuffle Along*. *Strut Miss Lizzie* he panned as hackneyed vaudeville fare depicting the "Negro" as a "buffoon" and "curio." About *The*

Plantation Revue he was more enthusiastic, noting that it "palpitates with the spirit of Florence Mills," whose "grace and refinement [. . .] dominated the entire production" ("Florence"). In short, the voice Walrond developed in 1922 was not only an artist in the making—a critic of crude propagandists and champion of technique—but also a particular kind of erudition and authority. Consider what it meant for him to make claims about the quality of Broadway shows, about the ingenuity—or lack thereof—of a vaudeville performance, about the current state of sculpture and classical music, and about African American culture. It is worth recalling that he was still a young man, just 23, and less than four years removed from Panama. His training had given him journalistic practice, but much of the knowledge on which he now drew was specific to African American traditions. It is unlikely that he knew much about these subjects prior to arriving in New York. All of which suggests he was either a quick study or a good mimic.

The truth is that he was both. He was excited by the interest black New Yorkers were taking in the history and accomplishments of their race, especially insofar as this interest translated into greater self-determination, and in this excitement, he was acquiring a wealth of information. More importantly, he was fashioning himself as a diaspora intellectual who drew with equal facility on knowledge of the Caribbean and the United States. This was a challenge, but he was not the first and had models close at hand.[45] If it seems unfair to call Walrond a mimic, I mean to distinguish him from those who were less interested or effective in appropriating forms of African American identity. Putting it this way emphasizes two elements of the *intra*-racial dynamics of black New York. The first is the critical strategy of imitation and masquerade among Caribbean immigrants. There were times at which it was advantageous to be taken for an American Negro rather than a West Indian and times when it was not. Code switching was a critical skill. The second element is the tacit assumption that in the United States "Negro" meant African *American*. Louis Chude-Sokei has referred to this as a form of cultural hegemony, compelling Caribbean immigrants to navigate "a cultural realm dominated by African-American writing, cultural sensibilities, and political concerns."[46] This would prove to be the most significant contribution Walrond made to the Harlem Renaissance, negotiating the unevenly articulated worlds of West Indian and African American New York and writing about it, code switching in subject matter and lexicon.

One of the great ironies of Walrond's Harlem career is that his transition to mainstream periodicals was predicated on his knowledge of African American vernacular culture and speech. He became a preferred writer for white editors seeking an inside story on Harlem, the Great Migration, or the Charleston dance craze. What is extraordinary is not their willingness to rely on a West Indian for an "authentic Negro perspective" but the dexterity with which he executed this work while also writing about the Caribbean. The first of his articles to appear in a white periodical illustrates this point, "Developed and Undeveloped Negro Literature," which ran in the *Dearborn Independent* in 1922.[47] "One reason why the Negro has not made any sort of headway in fiction is due to the effects of color prejudice," he wrote. "It is difficult for a Negro to write stories without bringing in the race question. As soon as a writer demonstrates skill along imaginative lines he is bound to succumb to the temptations of reform and propaganda" (12). The pattern of oppositions is familiar—art versus propaganda, fiction versus race writing—but his position was changing. His article about Maran and the Prix Goncourt had challenged the view that a "Negro" artist "must first purge himself of the feelings and sufferings and emotions of an outraged being, and think and write along colorless, sectionless lines." "Is this possible?" was his rhetorical response; "Negro" fiction would of necessity express "the life of the underdog in revolt." In the *Dearborn Independent*, however, he cast race consciousness as antithetical to the enterprise of fiction, an obstacle to the race's "headway" in that field.

"Developed and Undeveloped Negro Literature" is remarkable not only for this revision of the relationship between art and society but also for the evidence Walrond cited. He based his discussion on a comparison of Paul Laurence Dunbar to Charles Chesnutt, turn-of-the-century African American writers. What Walrond admired in Dunbar was his deft anticipation of audience and his code-switching facility. "In his dialect poems, irresistible in humor and pathos, and his short stories of southern Negro life, Dunbar depicted the Negro as he is. Yet that does not mean he was not capable of

3.1 Photograph of Eric Walrond by Robert H. Davis, 1922.

Robert H. Davis Papers, Manuscripts and Archives Division,
The New York Public Library, Astor, Lenox and Tilden Foundations.

classic prose. Realizing that a Negro poet is expected to sing the songs of the cotton fields in the language of the cotton fields, Dunbar wrote dialect" (12). Intentionally or not, Walrond was allegorizing his own experience, the conditions of his own article's production. A West Indian with just a few years in New York, he was fashioning a voice and a version of authority that were deliberately chosen. He represented himself as expert in matters of African American literature and was persuasive in doing so.

The strategies of mimicry and masking Walrond began to develop were responses to two intersecting pressures. One was the pressure he identified with Dunbar, the expectation to conform to stereotypical modes of "Negro" expression. The other was the pressure on West Indians to become African Americans and suppress signs of intraracial difference in the process. It is not surprising, then, that one figure with whom Walrond identified was Bert Williams, the black actor whose starring roles in the Ziegfield Follies and in the musical comedy *In Dahomey* capped a career of minstrel performances.[48] A black in blackface, Williams was assailed by progressives for pandering to white prejudices, embodying caricatures the New Negro sought to transcend. Walrond's tribute to Williams, published a year after his death, was nominally a review of a biography, but the terms in which it praised Williams, who grew up in the Bahamas, speak to dilemmas Walrond himself confronted. For one thing, Walrond refused to see Williams as the advocates of racial uplift did, the last vestige of a shameful, self-commodifying past. Instead, he claimed him for the current generation of artists, despite their differences, situating him in modernity and extolling him as a forerunner.

> To us, to whom he meant so much as an ambassador across the border of color, his memory will grow richer and more glorious as time goes on. For Bert Williams blazed the path to Broadway for the Negro actor. [. . .] [He] bore the brunt of ridicule—of ridicule from the Negro press—and fought his noble fight. Today the results are just coming to light. The demand for Negro shows on Broadway is taking a number of Negro girls and men out of the kitchens and poolrooms and janitor service. Bert Williams's tree—to him one of gall—is already beginning to bear fruit, and there is no telling how long the harvest will last. ("Bert Williams" 4)

Importantly, Walrond identified with Williams's desire to remove the minstrel mask, a frustration he saw manifest in *melancholia*. Throughout Williams's life "runs a poignant strain—a strain of melancholy," he wrote, "a nostalgia of the soul—of the blackface comedian who wanted to follow in the footsteps of celebrated Negro actors like Ira Aldridge, who wanted to play 'Othello' and other non-comical pieces" (4). The outrage Walrond recounted at having to write two "disgusting darky stories" resonates here. So does his diagnosis of the resulting condition—melancholia—on which Walrond meditated at length.

> Some day one of our budding storywriters ought to sit down and write a novel with a Negro protagonist with melancholia as the central idea. Bert Williams had it. Although it was his business to make people laugh, there were times when he would go into his shell-like cave of a mind and reflect—and fight it out. "Is it worth it?" One side of him would ask, "Is it worth it—the applause, the financial rewards, the fame? Is it really worth it—lynching one's soul in blackface twaddle?" "But it is the only way you can break in," protests the other side of the man. "It is the only way. That is what the white man expects of you—comedy—blackface comedy. In time, you know, they'll learn to expect serious things from you. In time." (4)

Staging this debate, Walrond may appear simply to offer a tears-of-the-clown platitude about the heartbreak behind a stage smile. Or perhaps we hear a reference to Dunbar's poem "We Wear the Mask." But it is worth emphasizing that neither Walrond nor Williams were African Americans by birth, and the question of wearing the "darky" mask is an intricate one. Louis Chude-Sokei reminds us that as a West Indian immigrant,

> [Williams] was self-consciously performing not as a "black man" but as the white racist representation of an *African American*, which he may have phenotypically resembled, but which—as he emphasized—was also culturally other to him. This cross-cultural, intra-racial masquerade constituted a form of dialogue at a time when tensions between the multiple and distinct black groups in New York City were often seething despite various attempts at pan-African solidarity. The process by which Bert Williams learned to both be and play an African American is not only a unique narrative of modernism; it is in fact an experience of assimilation unique to non-American blacks. (5)

It is worth listening with similar alertness to Walrond's writing for the interplay between assimilation and difference, the process by which he "learned to both be and play an African American." "I am a listening post," Walrond asserted in 1924, "I am anchored in the middle of life's gurgling stream. It is a stream that is anthropologically exotic. Up in the Negro belt [. . .] on Lenox Avenue" ("Vignettes" 19). However effectively he assumed an African American identity, he remained an outsider; his sense of Harlem as "anthropologically exotic" speaks to the peculiar conditions he and other West Indians confronted, but it also indicates the deliberateness with which he wielded his difference.

Walrond's tribute to Bert Williams suggests his sensitivity to the frustrations and humiliations of "blacking up," performing a white projection. But the silencing Walrond became aware of was not just the minstrel mask suppressing an oppositional or virtuoso black performance; it was also the elision of West Indian difference from "the Negro" to whom the minstrel performance putatively referred. "It is possible," writes Chude-Sokei, "to hear the sadness and melancholy" that Walrond mentioned "as resulting not only from the limitations of racism but also from the black polyphony itself."[49] Writing in the 1920s, Walrond dealt with fewer constraints than Williams; he could "revel," Chude-Sokei writes, in a "transnational polyphony; his work certainly does." But like the entertainer he admired, Walrond would "experiment with multiple black dialects and modes of register," and he too would masquerade in narrative blackface, struggling with "the burden of too many dialects."[50] This experimentation reached its formal apotheosis in *Tropic Death* but is evident throughout the fiction-writing career gestating at the time of this tribute.

Finally, in hearing Williams's "poignant strain of melancholia," Walrond identified psychological struggles he soon confronted himself. Although his first reference to depression appears in a 1924 letter to Locke, Walrond's early journalism continually described excruciating foreclosures of feeling, sensations of silencing and disorientation attending experiences of racialization. If the fallout was for Walrond, as for Williams, a racial melancholia, his primary coping strategy also resembled Williams: not to deny the thrall in which blackness held him—to suppose that the mask could be casually discarded—but to wear it and in so doing insist nevertheless on his difference, inflecting blackness with multiple dialects and valences. In some respects, *Negro World* was precisely the venue in which to do so because its agenda was international, and it welcomed multiple voices provided they harmonized to support the UNIA. However, Walrond's article on Bert Williams was his last for *Negro World*. It was April 1923, and his relationship to the UNIA had become untenable.

DEPARTURE FROM *NEGRO WORLD*

As Walrond's assertion of the value and autonomy of art put him out of step with *Negro World*, its office became an intolerable environment. This was true despite its success but also because of it. The UNIA's growth created a backlash of hostility and factionalism. Its finances were never soundly overseen save by Garvey, whose concentration of power opened him to the allegations of corruption that led to his conviction for mail fraud in 1923. An acrimonious divorce from Amy Ashwood—precipitated by his affair with Amy Jacques, who worked as his secretary—did not help matters. The UNIA, targeted from its inception by the U.S. Bureau of Investigation as a radical, seditious organization and by the British government as subversive of colonial governments, was infiltrated and investigated.[51] Garvey was masterful at turning accusations to his advantage, casting them as evidence of his effectiveness as the black Moses delivering the race from oppression. But at the office things were under continual siege and in disarray. Hundreds of small investors donated to the Black Star Line, which was undermined when the federal government, after years of pursuing Garvey, determined that the UNIA did not own one of the ships featured in its promotion. A thwarted UNIA Commission to Liberia planned for 1920 furnishes another illustration. Harrison wrote in his diary that delegates were denied passports, "mainly due to Marcus Garvey's prime defect, bombastic blabbing. He talks too much and too foolishly."[52] Harrison's radicalism also drew the Bureau's attention. An agent reported him "holding a series of meetings at 138th St. and Lenox Ave. every night" in the summer of 1920, calling him "a pronounced Negro agitator of the rabid type."[53] Internal struggles were waged around the desks of the *Negro World* editorial staff. The indomitable populist Harrison rarely saw eye to eye with Walrond's supervisor, William Ferris. Perhaps Harrison suppressed his opinion of Ferris more effectively at work than in his diary, where he called him "a mere pseudo-intellectual flunky with no more personality than a painted stick."[54] Harrison scoffed at Ferris's relaxed standards for literary submissions: "The general idea seemed to be that if each line began with a capital letter, if grammar's neck was wrung and rhymes like 'boat' and 'joke' were occasionally interspersed, 'poetry' was achieved. I had to stop all this."[55] Their acrimony was the hornet's nest in which the editorial staff worked.

As word spread in 1922 of Garvey's dismissal of "disloyal" officers, Walrond initially moved to quell the outrage in "Marcus Garvey—a Defense," justifying Garvey's expectation of unwavering loyalty and his "czar-like methods" for expelling "rogues and traitors" (4). Like Garvey, Walrond framed criticism of the UNIA as evidence of its soundness for "the Negro."

> [W]henever a white man opposes a movement started by black people in the interest of black people, it is the best proof of that movement's virtue and timeliness. And when a white employer vents his spleen, he unconsciously betrays fear of the awful potentialities of such a movement. White-like, he thinks of self-preservation, and the easiest way to gratify that is to "take it out of" his Negro help. But this ought to be a scorching lesson to the Negro. It ought to fortify him, to bring to his mind's eye the tragedy of what it is to be black, and upstanding. It ought to send him out in the world with the film torn from his eyes, seeing the red monster labeled race prejudice in all its grizzly colors. ("Dice" 4)

It is no coincidence that Walrond was promoted from assistant to associate editor, a post vacated by Harrison, immediately following these professions of loyalty.

However, that loyalty was tested as the feud between the UNIA and other organizations escalated. Although Ferris maintained *Negro World*'s interest in the arts, Garvey ceded the ground of culture to his rivals, casting the arts as peripheral to the struggle for dignity and equality. For this reason, Tony Martin errs in calling Walrond a "defector" from Garveyism; the UNIA abandoned Walrond as much as he abandoned it. Only by ignoring the extent to which Garvey sought to associate literature with pretension and sybaritic leisure could Walrond be considered an "opportunist," a traitor to the cause.[56] The suggestion is that Walrond's commitment was either disingenuous or easily corruptible by white editors. But Garvey had cast the arts as impractical and elitist: only "when we can provide employment for ourselves, when we can feed ourselves," he declared, "then we can . . . find time to indulge in the fine arts."[57]

Garvey was arrested in 1922 and charged with using the mails to solicit fraudulent investments. Demands for unpaid wages poured in, and lawsuits followed. Along with Garvey's infamous meeting with a Ku Klux Klan leader in Atlanta that year, the arrest and scandal fueled a vituperative campaign, "Garvey Must Go!" Spearheaded by Randolph and Owen at *The Messenger*, others including *The Crusader*, *Opportunity*, and *The Crisis* closed ranks and piled on. The NAACP brought out its big guns for what Garvey biographer Colin Grant calls a "farrago of shrieking malevolence" and "literary assassination."[58] None was more influential than Du Bois, whose criticism grew more frequent and arch. He published a brilliant piece of polemic in *The Crisis*, tracing Garvey's rise and diagnosing the troubles that befell him, chief among which, he alleged, was Garvey's failure to heed the difference between Jamaican and U.S. race relations.[59] Beyond having squandered an estimated $800,000 of "the savings of West-Indians and a few American negroes," Garvey threatened an enlightenment narrative Du Bois held dear, the uniting of humanity after "a thousand years" of atrocity and antagonism. Du Bois would ratchet up the rhetoric soon thereafter with the article "A Lunatic or a Traitor," calling Garvey "the most dangerous enemy of the Negro race in America and in the world."[60]

Though he remained on staff at *Negro World*, Walrond's distance from Garvey was discernible in December 1922, when his coverage of a lecture by Professor Carl Van Doren suggested his affiliation with Harlem's emergent artists. The gadfly persona Walrond adopted reveals more about his self-positioning in this social milieu than about Van Doren's address. It was just "a retracing of the ground covered in his two recent books," Walrond wrote, training his society column ear on the audience instead ("Junk" 4). His voice, knowing and sardonic, evinced a smug assurance about his place in this world and the conversations animating it. Wry and playful, Walrond's account reveals the pleasure he took in such gatherings, not only for their substance but also as rituals of posturing and performance. When he notes having whispered and pinched Countée Cullen's leg during the event, for example, Walrond consolidates for his readers a special sort of intimacy, an exclusive realm of sotto voce exchanges. To those of us reading retrospectively, the article indicates just how rapidly his social milieu was changing. That Cullen had become a close friend is suggested by his proximity to Walrond and the intimate snark with which Walrond conveyed his professional advice. He had formed friendships and professional ties outside the *Negro World* community that would support his transition from journalism to fiction writing, from modest acclaim to a wider audience.

The break from Garveyism was not complete, however. First Walrond began writing things that got him demoted from associate to contributing editor, presaging his departure from the journal. One did not stick around long denouncing Garvey as "a megalomaniac" committing "preposterous mistakes" and acting "for theatrical effect," as Walrond did in the *New York Times* magazine *Current History* ("New Negro" 787–88). But his falling out with Garvey was not so severe as to prevent its repair years later in London. Nor had Walrond's West Indian identification or political militancy diminished. In the same article, he claimed that the majority of black New Yorkers "cannot see beyond the shores of the Hudson. They haven't any international vision." He insisted, "When the epic of the negro in America is written, it will show the West Indian as the stokesman of the furnace of negro ideals" (787).

William Ferris wrote approvingly about Walrond's forays outside *Negro World* in November 1922, claiming him as a UNIA product but anticipating his departure. He sounded like a proud parent. Placing Walrond in the tradition of Chesnutt, Du Bois, and James Weldon Johnson, "molding public sentiment" through "the medium of the story," Ferris predicted that Walrond would propel this effort. "We are glad that Mr. Walrond has joined the circle of storytellers," and he concludes, "He is keen and wide-awake, has the gift of expression, and we expect great things from him in the future."[61] Ferris may not have known it, but for the reasons he cited, his colleague's days at *Negro World* were numbered.

4

THE NEW NEGRO (1923–1926)

"**Y**ou are perfectly correct about Eric Walrond," Robert Davis told Edna Worthley Underwood, "He is quite the most promising young man I have seen in a long time." An esteemed translator and author, Underwood had forwarded four stories to the editor of *Munsey's*. Davis acknowledged Walrond's talent but rejected the stories.

> He has [a] genius for color; I never saw better atmosphere in anything. Of course he is violently irreverent. I can use nothing of the manuscripts enclosed. He has let down the barriers without reserve. It grieves me to let these manuscripts go back to you. In spite of which I am much concerned about his future. [. . .] Nobody understands so well as he the people about whom he writes. I await with eagerness your consent to help. I have no doubt there are many magazines that would publish these stories without changing a syllable. However, I cannot with safety present these bald though brilliant descriptions of men and women and manners—or the lack of manners, whichever you choose.[1]

When they met, Davis persuaded Walrond to write two stories for his other publication, a pulp weekly, *Argosy's All Story*. They were likely the "disgusting darky stories" to which Walrond referred in "Adventures in

Misunderstanding." But it was not the last effort Underwood made on his behalf, broadening his contacts beyond the black community. She was one of three people Walrond had the good fortune to impress in 1923. The others were Casper Holstein, a Harlem real estate baron, and William McFee, an English writer and ship's engineer. Each helped redirect Walrond's career as his disillusionment with Garveyism deepened.

Unhappy in the Garvey movement and his marriage, Walrond had deserted both in the late spring of 1923, signing on to work aboard a ship bound for the Caribbean. "I went to sea," he said, "It is the easiest way to—to forget things" ("Godless" 33). With McFee as chief engineer and Walrond a cook's helper, the ship made port calls from New Orleans to Cartagena. Walrond's voyage profoundly influenced the fledgling writer's development. The settings of several early stories are traceable to this journey, and McFee was a valuable mentor. He discussed Lafcadio Hearn and Pierre Loti as models for writing about tropical places, and he suggested Walrond acquire an agent, recommending Underwood.[2] "I lived!" Walrond declared, "I saw life lived!" ("Godless" 33). Nevertheless, Underwood claimed he was disconsolate when they first met. It is difficult to trust her account, which, despite being among the fullest recollections of Walrond's early career, is riddled with inaccuracies.

> One day he phoned my secretary and asked to come out. He told me he was sad, homesick for the south, and miserable here in the north where he did not know which way to turn for the work he needed. [. . .] He asked me to suggest something that would help him get steady work, a living of sorts, telling me that he had tried newspaper work a little both in Panama and in Harlem. [. . .] I told him he talked unusually well and I believed if he wrote some stories of the tropic home he missed so, with all the homesick eloquence with which he related his memories to me, they might have success. But he had no place in which to write, and he had nothing to live on. Then he called up Caspar Holstein, rich man of Harlem, who had been born in the Virgin Islands and now was owner of a fleet of ships and was noted for his generosity, his unstinted help to his race. I assured him that Walrond had unusual talent and that all

he needed was a little chance to unfold that talent. Holstein [. . .] was his usual greathearted self. He offered him a place to live in his own home, provided him with a finely furnished room, and an allowance. Here young Walrond set about writing his stories—many stories—all of which I had him rewrite again and again; things of charm usually, all of them pulsing with the life of his sensitive responsive youth then at its height. He wrote diligently for months just as I had suggested, bringing the stories to me one after the other. I sent him with a letter of introduction to Bob Davis, whose judgment in the short story art has a certain amount of finality.[3]

Without her intervention, Underwood suggests, Walrond would have toiled away in penury and obscurity. Instead, "over-night he became famous. Praise and social honours were his, together with a secure and considerable income." But a candid assessment reveals the significance of other factors—a 1924 Civic Club dinner at which Walrond and others met New York's publishing establishment; his work with Charles Johnson at *Opportunity*; Alain Locke's *The New Negro* (1925), featuring a story by Walrond; and the collection of what Underwood calls "the stories" into *Tropic Death*. Far from having "tried newspaper work a little," Walrond's journalism was a bridge to his fiction writing, a point made as early as 1928, when the *Annals of the American Academy of Political and Social Sciences* named him among the journalists who midwifed "the birth of the so-called New Negro" in literature.[4] Overstating her role as his savior, Underwood neglected the role of the community in which Walrond was immersed; she omitted the New Negro movement.

White patronage has a thorny legacy in Harlem Renaissance historiography, and Walrond's relationship with Underwood was unconventional.[5] A wealthy white woman twenty-five years his senior, she was not his social equal, but assistance did not flow in one direction alone. In Underwood's view, African American writing infused vitality into a Western tradition that could no longer rely simply on white writers. Casting the deficiencies of Anglo-America in explicitly racial terms, she announced at the first *Opportunity* banquet, "Joy—its mainspring—is dying in the Great

Caucasian race."[6] She was not alone in prescribing black "vitality" and "joy" as remedies for the overcivilization of Anglo-America. "The Negro" figured centrally in the critique of Anglo-America from white bohemians and other detractors of genteel values. If she saw in Walrond a glimmer of the joy "Negroes" could contribute, it may have been a projection, but it also registered her dissent from the exaltation of the "Great Caucasian race" enjoying pernicious currency at the time.

Walrond credited Underwood for encouraging him, reading drafts, and contacting friends on his behalf. She sent him an excerpt from her latest book on translation, and he sent her his "Developed and Undeveloped Negro Literature" essay. "I am also taking the liberty of sending you a short story of mine," he added, "which, I think, is illustrative of the sort of writing I would some day like to do."[7] When Underwood offered to send his story to a fellow writer and critic, he wrote to say he was "deeply indebted."

> I think your plan is excellent, flattering to say the least, and I don't know how to thank you for your wonderful interest and generosity. I think I've done about ten stories already. [. . .] Were it not for the fact that I hate to overload you with my literary troubles, I'd put them in shape and send them to you, and if you think them worthwhile, then we could get together and see about sending them to the publisher of whom you spoke.

In the next two months Walrond wrote "The Consul's Clerk," "The Godless City," "Voodoo Vengeance," and "The Wharf Rats." "I have tried to put my best foot forward in these stories of Panama," he told her, "and I earnestly hope they will measure up to the standard required for admission to Mr. Bob Davis' 'Munsey's.'"[8]

They did not measure up, but Walrond and Underwood had other irons in the fire. He introduced her to *Negro World* readers through his review of her novel *The Penitent*.[9] Three consecutive issues included her translations of Alexander Pushkin's reflections on his African ancestry. She helped him place "On Being Black" in *The New Republic*, where she knew the editor Robert Herrick. Much of what Walrond published the following year was facilitated by Underwood, including pieces in *Current History*, *The Smart Set*, and *The International Interpreter*, a highbrow weekly. This work, in conjunction with his *New Republic* reviews, shifted Walrond's audience and authorial status. In the subsequent two years, his readership expanded to the *New York Herald Tribune*, *Forbes*, *Vanity Fair*, *The Independent*, *Brentano's Book Chat*, and the *Saturday Review of Literature*. Underwood and McFee were invaluable as Walrond crossed into the mainstream, among the first African American writers of his generation to do so.

But the crossover was neither linear nor complete. Like most African American journalists who achieved a measure of mainstream success, Walrond continued to publish primarily in black periodicals. It was the black community that sustained him, even when paychecks came from elsewhere. Walrond left *Negro World* in the spring of 1923, but it was not a transition from black to white, as he placed work in *The Crisis*, *The Messenger*, and *Opportunity*, the last of which offered him a staff position. Nor do McFee and Underwood deserve all the credit; Alain Locke and Charles Johnson advocated for Walrond and his peers, launching careers that straddled the color line. Finally, Walrond's own gift as a pitchman for his work should not be underestimated. "He made his own contacts," said Ethel Ray Nance.

> He would go out and seek editors and publishers, show them his work rather than rely on friends or agents or other people, other sources. [. . .] He had a newsman's sense of timing. He would know when an article should be written and what the subject should be, and he'd busy himself and write a whole evening and go downtown the next day and usually would find a market for his article.[10]

A point about Walrond's transition to mainstream publications bears emphasis. Walrond's break with Garveyism could be seen as an expression of Americanization and an increasing identification with African Americans.[11] The Universal Negro Improvement Association (UNIA), with its foreign-born officers and militant ideology, was widely under-stood as anti-American. Breaking with Garvey and writing for rival publications, Walrond embraced different literary values and a different cultural agenda. But the transition did not constitute a disavowal. The trappings of the greenhorn may appear to be cast off: a foreign-born social movement repudiated, a foreign-born wife returned home, an inter-est in the immigrant experience succeeded by an interest in African Amer-ican experience. But this narrative suppresses many features of Walrond's career as he maintained multiple affiliations, troubling a linear narra-tive of acculturation. Even as his expressions of Americanness became explicit and his fondness for Harlem grew, he maintained a West Indian identity, experimenting on the page with a range of voices and deepening his analysis of the African diaspora in the plural Americas.

CASPER HOLSTEIN AND CRITICAL INTERNATIONALISM

In early 1922, *Negro World* published an unsigned editorial condemning the U.S. government's conduct in the Virgin Islands. Its author was one of Harlem's Virgin Islanders. "When I was on the staff of *Negro World*," Walrond recalled, "Casper Holstein came to me with an article he had written" in rejoinder to sketches T. S. Stribling had published.

> Mr. Holstein, who had just returned from six months' trip to the islands [. . .] felt that the author of *Birthright* had not told the whole truth in regard to the actual labor, racial, and political conditions there. I had the "temerity" to publish the article, which was the first of a series of blows Casper Holstein struck and is still continuing to strike in defense of the manhood of the Virgin Islanders. ("Says" 1)

Walrond's account of Holstein as an astute political actor departs from established histories that depict him as a crooked philanthropist. Hol-stein infamously operated the Harlem numbers racket, an underground lottery, but his shrewd political analysis and commitment to Caribbean

4.1 Photograph of Casper Holstein, 1926, photographer unknown.

Photographs and Prints Division, Schomburg Center for Research in Black Culture,
The New York Public Library, Astor, Lenox and Tilden Foundations.
Courtesy of the National Urban League, *Opportunity: Journal of Negro Life.*

self-determination impressed Walrond. His critique of U.S. imperialism demonstrated a racial militancy that aligned him with the UNIA.[12]
Conditions under U.S. occupation were not well-known, but Holstein
and Harrison exposed the U.S. agenda, seeking representation for Virgin Islanders in local government and in Washington. A tidy narrative of
Walrond's conversion from Garveyite to aesthete, West Indian to American, separatist to integrationist, misses the investment he maintained in
Caribbean struggles.

As Walrond's faith in Garvey wavered, Holstein inspired him.
He emphasized Holstein's modesty, implying a contrast to Garvey's
arrogance.

When it comes to spending money for a cause, to doing things for people without hoping for reward, when it comes to being the receiver of
ungratefulness of the most disillusioning kind, of shouldering a burden
that is growing larger and larger with the rising of each sun, you have to

go to hand it to Casper Holstein. [. . .] And, much to his credit, Casper
Holstein is the poorest, the rottenest self-advertiser in the world. [. . .]
He is contemptuous of the limelight. ("Says" 1)

Holstein represented a different sort of leader, and if Walrond's account
tended toward hyperbole, it underscored his dilemma in 1922.[13] Disillusioned with the UNIA, he was wary of all race leaders, not just Garvey.
His friendship with Holstein developed in the context of this perceived
crisis of leadership, which he discussed in *Current History* in 1923.

"The New Negro Faces America" excoriated Garvey, the first time
Walrond did so in print. But he was no kinder to other race leaders. The
article seemed at first to follow a formula: establish the urgency of the
race problem, identify the deficiencies of Du Bois, Washington, and others, then recommend Garvey as the solution. But Walrond flipped the
script. "The negro is at the crossroads of American life," he began, "He
is, probably more than any other group within our borders, the most vig-
orously 'led.'" Garvey was preferable, he conceded, to Du Bois or Booker
T. Washington's successors. But after enumerating Garvey's improbable success, Walrond went off-script, accusing him of "preposterous
mistakes." As a result, "a reaction set in. The crowds who once flocked
to hear how he was going to redeem Africa have begun to dwindle."
The hard fact was, "the Negroes of America do not want to go back
to Africa." Africa may "mean something racial, if not spiritual" to "the
thinking ones" among them, but most are indifferent to the colonization
scheme, "the salient feature of Garvey's propaganda." "To them Africa
is a dream—an unrealizable dream. In America, despite its 'Jim-Crow'
laws, they see something beautiful" (788). Most damning of all, he called
Garvey a "megalomaniac" (787). The gauntlet had been thrown down.

Where did this leave African Americans? Walrond pinned his hopes on
a distributed model of progress, the gains ordinary African Americans
made in the professions, industry, and the arts, not on a charismatic
individual or vanguard program. He documented sharp increases in
the amount and value of property owned by African Americans but
argued that the truest indicator of "the outlook for the negro" was his

"mental state." In valuing disposition over data, Walrond expressed as much about his own mental state as about the "new negro" for whom he claimed to speak.

> Though there are thousands of college-bred negroes working as janitors and bricklayers and railroad car porters, there are still more thousands in colleges and universities who are fitting themselves well to become architects, engineers, chemists, manufacturers. The new negro, who does not want to go back to Africa, is fondly cherishing an ideal—and that is, that the time will come when America will look upon the negro not as a savage with an inferior mentality, but as a civilized man. The American negro of today believes intensely in America. [. . .] He is pinning everything on the hope, illusion or not, that America will someday find its soul, forget the negro's black skin, and recognize him as one of the nation's most loyal sons and defenders. (788)

This was a dramatic break with Garveyism, the formulation of a "new negro" sensibility drawn from his own tentative embrace of integration and cultural pluralism.

As Walrond's reference to the "new negro" indicates, the phrase had entered the popular lexicon before Locke made it the title of his anthology.[14] It had a nationalist connotation, but Walrond was among those who insisted on the term's critical internationalism. A. Philip Randolph and Chandler Owen called the New Negro "the product of the same world wide forces that have brought into being the great liberal and radical movements that are now seizing the reins of political, economic, and social power in all of the civilized countries of the world."[15] For Walrond, the task was to represent the challenges and opportunities facing people of African descent, remaining alert to the specificity of African American experience without obscuring the common threads of the black Atlantic: relocation and enslavement, colonialism, violence and exploitation, resistance and rebellion, cultural and linguistic syncretism. His vision was no longer grounded in an immutable antagonism between white and black, the UNIA's binary construct. The struggle of the "Negro" in Babylon yielded to an account in which ethnicity, nation, language, class, and culture constituted a field whose complexity was not apprehended by race alone. Walrond's hope that "America will some day find its soul" and recognize the "Negro" as "one of its most loyal sons and defenders" did not prevent him from upbraiding the United States, which was engaged in neocolonial projects in the Caribbean and beyond.

In fact, in another *Current History* essay, Walrond argued that U.S. rule resembled the English administration of Crown Colonies and was in some ways worse for the islands' residents. "From a strategic point of view," Walrond wrote, "the Virgin Islands are necessary to the safety and protection of the Panama Canal and also to American interests in the Antilles" (221). But its "temporary Government" had come to resemble Haiti and the Dominican Republic, both under U.S. Navy occupation.[16] Three deleterious results followed: racism was "aggravated" by the imposition of Jim Crow, local industry was undercut by Prohibition policies, and democracy was thwarted at every turn. This essay, "Autocracy in the Virgin Islands," politicized a region North Americans associated with palm trees and azure skies. Although it resembled Walrond's work in *Negro World*, the tone diverged sharply, trading incendiary rhetoric for dispassionate analysis. His approach abided by *Current History*'s mission, to provide "a survey of the important events of the world, told by those most competent to present them; the FACTS of today's history impartially related, without bias, criticism, or editorial comment." The other mainstream venue in which Walrond began publishing, *The International Interpreter*, professed a similar commitment to impartiality and geographic scope.[17] Neither the *Interpreter* nor *Current History* indulged in special pleading on behalf of "Negroes," about whom articles were scarce. But because of Walrond's adept framing of race in relation to national and international matters, he succeeded in placing five investigative reports in the *Interpreter* in one year. Several shared the theme of migration—two on Caribbean migration to the United States, two on African American migration—while another, "Inter-Racial Cooperation in the South," developed the proposition that mutual understanding across the color line was possible and desirable; it could be engineered to benefit the nation as a whole.

Despite the platform the *Interpreter* and *Current History* provided, their injunction for objectivity did not satisfy his political militancy or his interest in linguistic innovation and narrative form. These found expression in his final publications in *Negro World*, stylized accounts of conversations he had in Guatemala and Havana. Both decried race prejudice in the United States by contrasting it with amicable race relations in other parts of the world. But what stands out is the subordination of argument to characterization and atmospherics.

> Along el Avenida Italia old ragged brown women smoking Ghanga weed—"it mek you smaht lek a flea"—huddled up against picturesque dwellings. Taxis filled with carnivalling crowds sped by. Foreign seamen staggered half-drunk out of Casas Francesas. Doggoning the heat, Babbitt and silk-sweatered Myra clung desperately to flasks of honest-to-goodness Bacardi. Bewitching senoritas in opera wraps of white and orange and scintillating brown stept out of gorgeous limousines.[18]

The ostensible focus of the essay is an encounter with an expatriate African American, an elderly man from Georgia who, after eight years in Havana, renounced the land of Jim Crow. Competing with the overt subject is Walrond's irrepressible narrative voice, for the sketch is also about himself. "Nostalgically I dug into the bowels of the dingy callecitas. Something, I don't know what drew me, led me on. Was it the glamour of the tropical sky, the hot, voluptuous night, the nectar of Felipe's cebada? Or maybe the intriguing echo of Mademoiselle's 'Martinique! Hola, Martinique!' as the taxi skidaddled around the corner? It was all of these and more."[19] The real subject is Walrond's persistent romance with the Caribbean port city. However awkwardly, these sketches wed the political militancy that drew Walrond to *Negro World* with a romantic attachment to "the folk" and a propensity for formal experimentation that unfit him to continue there. The sketches also speak to Walrond's ongoing concern with the varieties of black experience in Latin America. Walrond's work in early 1923 all points to the importance of a critical internationalism in understanding race relations in the United States.

Eager to embrace New York, Walrond nevertheless remained proud of his Caribbeanness and convinced of its value to a movement that often assumed nationalist lines. He began to see the United States as the proverbial land of opportunity, evincing unprecedented enthusiasm, but his transnational sensibility was at odds with the prevailing rhetoric of race.[20] With a hemispheric perspective, "Walrond understood as early as the 1920s what it meant to say that the Caribbean was, in modernity, an American sea," notes Michelle Stephens, "The presence of the U.S. as an economic force in the Caribbean, and a political force in the world at the beginning of the twentieth century, meant a story of economic and cultural integration."[21] His effort to maintain both sides of his cultural identity—the British West Indian and the American "Negro"—is evident in his work throughout this period. One manifestation was his ambivalence about becoming a U.S. citizen; he applied for "first papers" in 1923 but never completed the process. From the perspective of literary history, however, the significant expressions of his attempt to hold Americanness and Caribbeanness in tension occur in his work. A tight-knit community sustained Walrond during this period of dawning recognition of both his extraordinary talent and his psychological fragility.

OUR LITTLE GROUP

Gwendolyn Bennett was an early friend of Walrond's in New York, and a visual artist, poet, and prose writer. Remembered for artwork in *Opportunity* and *The Crisis* and her column "The Ebony Flute," she also taught at Howard University and published in *The New Negro* and *Fire!!* She was raised in Bedford-Stuyvesant, where she and Walrond grew close in the early 1920s, supporting each other's endeavors and working together at *Opportunity*. They were kindred spirits with immense mutual admiration. Walrond called her Gwennie and said in 1946 that she was "the closest approximation to a favourite sister I have ever had."[22] One of his first sketches for *Opportunity* was inspired by a scandal she and her friends provoked at Girls' High School by integrating their prom, an event Bennett memorialized by clipping coverage from local papers.

4.2 Photograph of Gwendolyn Bennett, c. 1920, photographer unknown.

Photographs and Prints Division, Schomburg Center for Research in Black Culture,
The New York Public Library, Astor, Lenox and Tilden Foundations.

Walrond wrote "Cynthia Goes to the Prom" in late 1923, illustrating a
Brooklyn girl's discovery of race consciousness. Before the prom, Cynthia
never felt her color was an impediment. Blessed with "nerve," she was
popular at a school "where Irish, Jew, Italian, and Anglo-Saxon mixed,"
she "always came out at or very near the top" academically, and the
boys, who "first stared askance at the ebony locks that adorn her bronze
temples [. . .] before you knew it, 'took' completely to her" (342). When
our chivalrous narrator offers to accompany her to the prom, he acciden-
tally initiates her into the ways of white prejudice. The eight "Negroes"
stay "silently composed," frustrating the three hundred guests who "all
trotted out to see what we looked like." "Nobody stumbled over the car-
pet. Nobody tripped. In fact, I think I saw a look of disappointment on
some of our spectators' faces. Some of them had come for a good hearty

lung-expanding laugh. But they didn't get it" (343). A showdown ensues at the cloakroom, where the clerk "hasn't any more hooks left," says Cynthia, "so she says she'd have to put our coats on the floor." "I looked at the lady in charge," Walrond writes, "Her face barked at me. Her green eyes spat fire. She was ready to fight, to fly at our throats" (343). The same classmates whose favor Cynthia enjoys at school now snub her, and the narrator poses a loaded question at the evening's end: "What do you think of social equality now?" "Not much," she replies, "I tell you one thing, though—whenever I get a chance I'm going to these affairs. They've got to get used to us! They must!" The sketch concludes with the narrator marveling that such conviction had come from a former "disciple of passivism" (343). Walrond does not declare the futility of changing white folks' views, as he might have earlier, he instead admires Cynthia's resolve to pursue integration and equality. By late 1923, he had determined that the United States would be an ideal place if color were not such a universal preoccupation, not just among whites but also African Americans.

His satire of American color consciousness, "Vignettes of the Dusk," laments that someplace so wonderful could be so afflicted with a debilitating color fixation. Set in Wall Street, "the heart of America's financial seraglio," the sketch has Walrond contemplating lunch at an inexpensive diner and "the most democratic eating place I know. There is no class prejudice; no discrimination; newsboys, bootblacks, factory slaves, all eat at Max's" (19). But it is payday and he feels "flush," entertaining romantic notions of America's promise: "Rich, I am extravagant today. I rub elbows with bankers and millionaires and comely office girls. Of seraphs and madrigals I dream—nut that I am. I look up at the sparkling gems of architecture and marvel at the beauty that is America. America!" (19). He chooses someplace swanky, resplendent with "swinging doors and chocolate puffs in the show case," "mirrors, flowers, paintings, candelabra; waiters in gowns as white as alabaster," and two delicacies on the menu: oyster salad and a dessert suggestively named "vanilla temptation." But the reverie is broken by a racial incident, something amiss when the waiter brings his order. "Couldn't he just hand it to me over there instead of having to come all the way round the counter to make sure it gets into my hands? Couldn't he

have saved himself all that trouble?" But the waiter is not accommodating
Walrond, he is ensuring that a signal of opprobrium is delivered discreetly.

> He is at my side. Stern and white-lipped he hands me a nice brown paper
> bag with dusky flowers on it. He holds it off with the tips of his fingers as
> if its contents were leprous. "Careful," he warns farsightedly, "else you'll
> spill the temptation." I do not argue. Sepulchrally I pay the check and
> waltz out. It is the equivalent of being shooed out. And, listen folks, he
> was careful not to say, "No, we don't serve no colored here." (19)

If this were its only episode, "Vignettes of the Dusk" would resemble Walrond's early journalism: fulminating against racial slights, denials of the
"vanilla temptation." But it is distinguished by its celebration of American
promise, opportunity qualified only by its fixation with color.

With mainstream publications, Walrond found his reputation enhanced
and began thinking of himself in 1923 as a writer of real promise. This
affirmation was nourished by his association with the 135th Street public
library. Bennett saved a report of one event in which they shared space
on the bill. Entitled "Poet's Evening: A Real Library Treat," the article
conveys the frisson of a movement emerging from its chrysalis.[23] And
although Bennett had her own reasons for saving the article—it said she
stole the show—Walrond memorialized the evening differently. Employing the sardonic voice he adopted to cover the Van Doren lecture, his
article bore a portentous, defensive title, "My Version of It." "'Of what?'
you ask, bewildered. Of the to-do at the young writers' evening at the
library Wednesday night" (4). Audience members objected to his risqué
treatment of women.

> After the poets [. . .] got through with their "poetical effusions"—
> Arthur Schomburg's words—it devolved on us to read a story of Negro
> life. In the first place, the title had a tendency to prejudice those who
> heard it against the author. "Woman." Woman, woman, woman—
> Well, for the first two pages it went off all right. Then, tip-toeing, one,
> two, three ladies crept out. On we read. In turning a page we caught

Dorothy Friedman's violet eyes. "Louder," her lips pantomimed; "I can't hear you." On we read. On, on, on . . . Until the end came. Arthur Schomburg, at the behest of the chairlady, was the first to illude us. "I didn't know that fellow Walrond had such a keen pair of eyes. Now, the point about the purple chemise—"The point about the purple chemise is the point they won't let us print. (4)

The grumbling that ensued was audible, prompting the chief librarian to come to his defense.

In the breaking up of the crowd we got a glimpse of the way they reacted to "Woman." "Is he really as bad as all that, Miss Rose?"

"I don't think so," Miss Rose responded spiritedly.

"Well," she condescended to come over to us, "Well, I enjoyed yours too."

"Shake!" cried Joe Gould. "I'll buy you a cup of black coffee, so help me! I sure envy you your courage."

"And to think—that ending—wasn't it awful? And there was a minister in the audience besides! Wasn't that terrible—to think—to think—"

"Lewd! Licentious! Full of passion! Terrible!"

"And that ending! My gawd! I almost blushed!"

"I don't know what's come over our men. Story about white men and colored women—and white men in the audience! Didn't you see how that white man turned and whispered to the girl with him?" (4)

As the article chronicles his contentious reception, it engages in a peculiar sort of performance, reveling in the terms in which the audience applauded or clucked. It celebrates his self-fashioning as someone willing to offend moralistic listeners.

This posture of irreverence aligned Walrond with those who would soon mount the short-lived journal *Fire!!* They frankly addressed sexuality, interracial relationships, and vulgarity, matters that were still taboo among those anxious to improve white opinion of African Americans. Walrond saw a new generation resisting this "vigilantly censorious" impulse: "They are writing of the Negro multitude [. . .] in such a style that people will stop and remark, Why, I thought I knew Negroes, but if I am to credit this story here I guess I don't." In a wonderful flourish, Walrond advocated "going into the lives of typical folks—people who don't have to wait till the pig knuckly parson says good-bye and goes out the gate before they can be themselves" ("Negro Literati" 32–33). If he did not wait for the departure of the "pig knuckly parson" to read suggestive passages about purple chemises, Walrond did feel compelled to subject the tut-tutting of his detractors to satirical treatment. He was sensitive, took insults to heart, and could be aggressive in print.

The 135th Street library was a proving ground, and Walrond made an indelible impression. The discussions did not stop at the door nor was a clear line drawn between socializing and developing one's craft. Regina Anderson, a librarian and writer, shared an apartment at 580 St. Nicholas Avenue with Louella Tucker and Ethel Ray Nance, hosting salons and extending hospitality to many aspiring artists who were moving to New York or passing through. Walrond became a fixture. "The 580 trio was excited by Walrond," writes David Levering Lewis, by "his accented, rippling wit, his urbanity and fearless independence."[24] Among a group of regulars that included Cullen, Bennett, Hughes, and Harold Jackman, a Harlem schoolteacher, Walrond was a charismatic presence. Nance recalled, "You would think of him as being tall," but "he may not have been six feet. [H]e was of slight build, had flashing eyes, his face was very alert and very alive." She described his vitality and magnetism.

> He was very pleasant, but as soon as he entered a room, you knew he was there. He moved very quickly, he couldn't stay still and in one place, especially if he was excited, and he was excited most of the time. Either he had met someone or else he had a new idea about something and he would have to walk up and down when he described it or when he talked to you. He had quite a way of meeting strangers, anyone who ever met him remembered him.[25]

It was due as much to these personal qualities as to his talent that Walrond gained a wide acquaintance, in Harlem and downtown. He became a catalyst for the New Negro movement, "A person that held our little group together and built it," said Nance, "because he had the faculty of bringing in interesting people and meeting interesting people. If Eric walked down the street, someone interesting was bound to show up."[26]

Among the most interesting of Walrond's acquaintances was Holstein, who was unwelcome at 580.[27] The banker for Harlem's illicit numbers racket, he "combined the prosaic traits of a financier with the dizzy imaginative flights of a fingerless Midas."[28] Holstein financed *Opportunity* contests and supported Walrond so generously that he dedicated *Tropic Death* to him.[29] If Holstein was too disreputable for the 580 set, Walrond's other close friend, Countée Cullen, was a pillar of respectability. Cullen was not wealthy, the adopted son of a Baptist minister in Harlem, but he was exceedingly proper. He was candid about his elitism: "I am not at all a democratic person," he wrote Jackman in 1923, "I believe in an aristocracy of the soul."[30] Jackman was handsome, bright, and popular, and his relationship with Cullen was intimate, leading to jealousy among their peers, especially Walrond. Cullen expressed concern to Jackman: "So Walrond feels jealous of our friendship? Well, other people do too. I am wondering whether Walrond received the letter I sent him nearly two weeks ago. He has not answered. [. . .] When you see him mention it to him, and if he did not receive the letter, secure me his address that I may write to him. I don't want him to feel slighted."[31] His kind concern for Walrond's feelings was matched by his admiration for his talent. "When the August [1923] *Crisis* comes out, be sure to get it," he told Jackman, "The issue will be devoted to the younger Negro literati, and [. . .] I wonder if Walrond will be represented. He ought to be." In fact, Walrond was represented, and although his contribution took the modest form of an article on an Afro-Spanish painter, Cullen's sense that his friend belonged in any showcase of "younger Negro literati" was now widely held.

The clearest illustration was the arrival in 1923 of the most prolific period in his career to date, with eight publications: a short story and two sketches, four articles, and a review essay. His sketches were the first works of fiction to appear in *Opportunity*. "On Being a Domestic" recounts the trials and tribulations of a hotel service worker at whom white patrons hurl epithets, glower, even expectorate "a cataract of saliva" (234). It was among Walrond's efforts to highlight the plight of servitude and express the attending "passionate feeling of revolt." Published in the next issue of *Opportunity*, "The Stone Rebounds" was equally fatalistic: "It is useless trying to run up against a stonewall—a Gibraltar of prejudice. Useless!" (277). Walrond's bitterness during this period is even more pronounced in "Miss Kenny's Marriage," a satirical story without one sympathetic character. This may have recommended it to Mencken, the acerbic editor of *The Smart Set*. It was a fable eviscerating social pretensions in Brooklyn's African American community, inviting readers to join him in a laugh at his characters' expense. These are Miss Kenny, a beautician with a propensity for self-aggrandizing prevarications, and her suitor, the young lawyer Elias Ramsey. The story is a ribald portrait of 1920s black Brooklyn. But as the tale unfolds and it becomes clear that the quiet but unscrupulous Ramsey is fleecing Miss Kenny of all ten thousand of her hard-earned dollars, one wonders what exactly the author is after. Is it the pleasure of seeing the pretentious Miss Kenny brought low? Is it a cautionary tale about the perils of entering lightly into the pecuniary arrangement of marriage, a subject that was on the mind of its recently separated author? Neither interpretation rings quite true, for Ramsey is no more virtuous than Miss Kenny, whose fall is thus difficult to relish. Nor does the story offer an alternative to conventional marriage, making the cautionary tale incomplete. Instead, it might be understood as a trickster narrative.

From the outset, Miss Kenny is established as fatuous and haughty, an easy mark for the trickster. We are made to understand that she lies routinely and effectively. "Not that Miss Kenny was a four-flusher in the ordinary sense of the word. Heavens, no! She simply delighted in beating around the bush and misleading folks as to her personal affairs" (150).[32] On "the matter of money" she was given to fabrication. "Yes, Miss Kenny had money. Of course she could never admit it. She always made it a point to impress strangers (and friends alike) with her utter destitution" (151). And though she was not "a member of the olive-skinned aristocracy of Brooklyn, there was evidence abundant to testify to the esteem in which she was held by, as she pertly expressed it, 'gangs and gangs of folks'" (158). She is contemptuous of "niggers," though of course she uses this term to refer strictly to a certain class, those whose coarseness reflects poorly on the race. "There ain't none of the nigger in me, honey," she tells a customer (153). When she hears that people are asking why she is still "doing heads" since she has married and can afford to retire, she declares, "That is just like us cullud folks. I tell you, girlie, I am not like a lot of these new niggers you see floating around here. A few hundred dollars don't frighten me. Only we used-to-nothing cullud folks lose our heads and stick out our chests at sight of a few red pennies" (159). Thus, it is not surprising that the trickster who ruins her comes in the guise of a refined gentleman. "Miss Kenny's Marriage" probably appealed to *The Smart Set* because of its jaundiced tone but also because it departed from the well-worn paths of propagandistic and sentimental fiction. Willingness to air the race's dirty laundry was taken by many as the sign of mature confidence, a repudiation of the "inferiority complex," and a commitment to authenticity over public relations. Miss Kenny, apparently a recent arrival from the South, calls her customers "honey," "girlie, and "chile," and Walrond orchestrates diction and syntax to suggest fidelity to "Negro" speech. But to read the story for its realism—its warts-and-all treatment of black New Yorkers—is to miss its affinity with other trickster tales, from Chesnutt's "conjure stories," to the tales of Br'er Goat and Anansi the Spider recited in the West Indian communities of Walrond's youth.

Putting it this way reveals continuities that characterize Walrond's early fiction, which otherwise seems to divide neatly between stories about New York and about the Caribbean. In subsequent months, five of his Caribbean stories appeared. Informed by his recent sea voyage, they included three in mainstream weeklies and two in *Opportunity*. All invoke obeah, voodoo, or another form of conjure, and three involve tricksters who steal the show.

CARIBBEAN STORIES

Composed in 1923, these five stories were a dress rehearsal for *Tropic Death*, anticipating that book's tremendous vitality as well as its weaknesses. They are transnational and multilingual—representing the region's startling diversity to an audience largely unacquainted—and generically hybrid, blending travel narrative conventions with pulp fiction and Afro-Caribbean folklore. Like *Tropic Death*, they drew on Walrond's experiences in Panama and suggest the profound impact of the United States in the Caribbean, more often through ironic gestures than overt arguments. The concern for narrative detail that *Tropic Death* exhibits is evident in these stories, but above all they dramatize the tension between the natural and the supernatural, reason and unreason, that *Tropic Death* would treat as distinctively Caribbean. Walrond could not afford to write literary fiction and, unlike *Tropic Death*, these stories—two of which appeared in *Opportunity*, two in *Argosy All-Story Weekly*, and one in *Success Magazine*—were not intended to challenge readers but to entertain them and earn their author a paycheck. The circumstances of his departure from the UNIA are unclear, but he was no longer writing for *Negro World* and not yet on staff at *Opportunity*. The stories sought to appeal to U.S. readers despite esoteric cultural references and unflattering depictions of white Americans. For this reason, they exhibit a jarring double discourse: a discourse of tropicality, structured by oppositions between civilization and barbarism, culture and nature; and a discourse of coloniality, the insider's perspective that renders real Caribbean lives, subverting the exoticizing gaze of the outsider.[33] It was not until *Tropic Death* that Walrond coordinated these discourses with sufficient skill that they became mutually transformative rather than discordant.

These stories' protagonists are all Afro-Caribbean. In "The Godless City," Ezekiel Yates is a Jamaican who arrived in Panama in the 1880s and worked as captain's assistant on an American gunboat. In "The Silver King," Salambo is Puerto Rican, an aspiring poet whose fiancée lives in Guatemala, where his ship is headed. "The Voodoo's Revenge" features Salambo's anagram, Sambola, a St. Lucian, servant to the manager of the West Indian Telegraph Company, and another Afro-Caribbean, Nestor Villaine, editor of a Panamanian newspaper. In "The Stolen Necklace" Santiago is a Barbadian whose six years in Colón "duly Latinized" him and landed him a job at the Isthmian Canal Commission. Finally, the character most closely modeled on the author is Enrique, protagonist of the only first-person story, "A Cholo Romance." A resident of Bottle Alley, Walrond's own street, Enrique is a Colón businessman with political connections and a West Indian whose blackness makes him a despised *chombo* in the eyes of his mother-in-law to be.

These stories all undertake a generic masquerade. Walrond depicts the folkways and geography of Panama and the Caribbean, but his narrative voice and plot conventions come from hard-boiled pulp fiction. Men match wits and exploit one another's vulnerability, which is almost invariably occasioned by too fervent an attachment to a woman. Salambo, Santiago, and Enrique are all blinded by their love for Latina damsels, while Nestor Villaine is blinded by his desire for revenge. In this vulnerable state, they are targets for the tricksters and agents of deception who populate the tales. Santiago tries to bamboozle a U.S. Marine eager to make some quick cash but finds in the end that he has gained a wife and lost a fortune. Sambola also winds up betrothed and missing a trunk of silver that he thought was his wedding gift. Enrique calls in a debt from a friend to help him outwit Br'er Goat, only to find himself engaged to Br'er Goat's daughter at the story's end. And Nestor Villaine, who enlists the services of an obeah expert to thwart his nemesis the governor, ends up a meal for the sharks in Limón Bay. In this genre, plot development could be finessed with melodrama and meaning could be retrofitted onto clumsily executed plots through ironic conclusions, preposterous epiphanies that resolve the narratives that precede them and excuse their deficiencies.

Walrond employed these dime story conventions in part because they were expected in magazines such as *Argosy* and *Success* but also because he grew up reading them. Enrique of "A Cholo Romance" is an avid reader of *Dick Turpin*, an English pulp series, and he speaks like one:

> After getting as much fun as it is possible to get out of watching a wet canary dry itself in the sun, I stuck my head between the leaves of a Dick Turpin yarn. Black Bess had just jumped off one of London's tallest skyscrapers, and Dick, eluding his captors, was Johnny-on-the-spot as the shining steed landed on its feet. With his usual dash he leaped into the saddle and in a jiffy was lost from view! (178)

Walrond illustrated his youthful enthusiasm for dime novels in "The Voodoo's Revenge," where he credits such reading with firing the imagination. Mr. Newbold, the story's least sympathetic character, takes his "office boy," Sambola, for a "faithful and obedient servant" because unlike his other employees Sambola "never smoked or whistled or stayed out late at nights or read 'Old Sleuth,' 'Dick Turpin,' or 'Dead Wood Dick.' He hadn't any imagination. That, Mr. Newbold felt, was good for him" (212).

The minstrel figure was another feature of pulp magazines, where nonwhite characters rarely escaped the broad brushstrokes of caricature. "The Silver King" makes overt recourse to this convention. The title character, an African American southerner whose job is to care for the ship's silverware, is ostentatiously proud of his work, which is, after all, quite mundane.

> Chest thrown back, tall, black, majestic, the Silver King, a Mississippi roustabout, walked with the dignity befitting a man of his nautical station. More than any other member of the crew [. . .] he was physically and metaphysically best suited for his treasure hoarding job. As guardian of the ship's silver and basking in the sunlight of the grandiloquent title of "Silver King," it devolved on him to hand out to the waiters and stewards at mealtime the sterling cups and dishes and knives and forks and sheeny platters. In this he ruled like a tyrant. (291)

When Silver King opens his mouth, out pour malapropisms, mispronunciations, and other deformations of standard English. "Say, where dat spoon come from at? [. . .] Well, lissen, pardner, dis joint shets down at six—six sharp—and lissen, pardner, I gots orders from de boss not to recept nothin' from nobody no time atter that. So gwan!" (291–92). His retorts are floridly metaphorical. "Say, lissen, tie dat bull outside. You can't hand me none o' dat gaff. Ma name ain't Green. Wha' do ya think I bin gwine ter sea all dese years fo'? I ain't no monkey chaser" (294).

Insisting he is no "monkey chaser," Silver King uses a pejorative term for West Indians. But in an ironic inversion, it is Silver King's speech that

Walrond marks, while Salambo, who is not only Caribbean but also a native Spanish speaker, somehow delivers lines in impeccable English. "I am going to get married," he tells Silver King. "Zat so? Well, wouldn't dat kill ya?" replies Silver King, "Marry! Wha' fo'?" "You don't understand, Silver King. Elisa is a lady—a nice Spanish lady—and I love her. She has consented to marry me" (294). It is an interesting choice for a West Indian writing in a mainstream publication. Walrond establishes Salambo as a "Negro" (one crewmember calls him the "laziest coon I evah seen in mah whole life"), but his unmarked speech distinguishes him from his African American shipmates. What did it mean for Walrond, a West Indian immigrant, to write vernacular for his African American character and standard English for his Caribbean character? As an author, this was a cross-cultural, intraracial masquerade. Caricaturing African American speech, it illustrates Walrond's experimentation with polyphony and masking, a process Chude-Sokei has called "learning to both be and play an African American."[34] Employing the time-honored American trope of the "happy darky," the story exhibits a supposed authenticity of character. But its artifice is revealed in the very different speech of Salambo, a Sambo on the lam.

But the story is a trickster tale, and just as Silver King gets the best of Salambo in the end, so Walrond engages in a form of narrative tricksterism, his "disgusting darky story" exhibiting popular stereotypes yet subverting them. It turns out that Silver King is only apparently ridiculous; he is sophisticated beyond his modest station. When Salambo reads samples of the verse he composed on the moonlit deck, Silver King calls it mere "mought-water" and lectures him about Paul Laurence Dunbar. In contrast to Salambo's limpid doggerel, Silver King belts out Delta blues in a "golden *basso profundissimo.*" Just as Silver King generates certain expectations only to subvert them, Walrond deploys then deforms the minstrel mask, subverting the expectations generated by Silver King's ostentation and palavering.

If there is more at work formally in "The Silver King" than appears at first glance, it makes no literary pretensions and is really just a lark. Although literariness was not necessarily prized in pulp fiction, these stories are significant for their polyphony and their colonial sensibility. These elements distinguished them from most everything being written at the time. The implicit question Walrond asked was: How could cross-cultural, transnational knowledge be represented in literature? The dominant models were Anglo-American travel and romance narratives. He knew their conventions well, but he was aware of their limitations and distortions. In 1924, he assessed the tradition against which he would define his own practice: "Usually a Melville or a Stevenson can get into a portrait of the tropics an idea of the beauty of nature—the emerald sea, the golden sands, the pearly lakes and teeming forests. It is when they come to the problem of delving into the complex nature of the natives that most of our writers [. . .] slip and make asses of themselves" ("Our" 219). Nowhere was Walrond's break from the Anglo-American tradition more pronounced than in his depiction of Panama. North American readers were familiar with the region because the canal was such a productive site of American national sentiment, generating a certain kind of knowledge. Articles, books, and photo essays issued forth, a mythology of U.S. technology, ingenuity, and determination. However, just as Caribbean labor was all but excised from this narrative, so too was the impact of the occupation and the complexity of the resulting society. Despite their eccentricities, Walrond's pulp stories examined the region's cultural hybridity, its legacy of creolization, and its challenge to Anglo-American powers of discernment.

There is not one Panama story, for example, in which Walrond fails to address the Canal Zone's racial segregation, which effectively sorted residents by wealth and privilege. White Isthmian Canal Commission (ICC) employees lived in Cristóbal, across the bay from the Caribbean workers and families in Colón, cheek by jowl alongside Panamanians, Asians, and others drawn to the region. A frontier sensibility and an entrepreneurial culture suffused the area, compelling interaction across language, ethnicity, class, and nation. The failure of Anglo-Americans to conceive Caribbean complexities also registers at the level of plot and character. Whites do not come in for satirical or overtly critical treatment, but they embody a peculiar paradox: possessed of extraordinary power and privilege in the

Canal Zone, they are blissfully ignorant of and vulnerable to the knowledge and modes of expression of the nonwhite residents. The nonwhite Panamanians in these stories share a counterknowledge set at a subversive angle to North American mythology. As in the trickster tradition, official power and privilege are always susceptible to reversal.

Walrond pursued an equivocal project in these Caribbean stories, invoking Conradian tropes of civilization fraying at the edges into barbarism, yet insisting on an intricacy and counterknowledge inherent in coloniality. Anxious not to "pollute" art with propaganda, he had been pursuing separate projects in his journalism and fiction. Clever and vibrant, the Caribbean stories were innovative without being poignant, saleable but flawed. His investigative reports on migrations demonstrated his grasp of their implications but did not stray from empiricism and reasoned argument. To reach the achievement *Tropic Death* represented, he needed to hone his craft but also to blur the line between art and politics. A fiction equal to the transformations he witnessed would not stop at dialect, folktale, and tropical sunsets; it would incorporate his recognition that the Afro-Caribbean diaspora was nothing less than a decisive convulsion of modernity. Had he followed established paths, he would have continued writing lively but disposable sketches and perhaps advanced as a journalist. That he did not is a testament to his self-willed transformation as a writer and to the influence of *Opportunity*'s quietly ambitious editor.

OPPORTUNITY KNOCKS

Opportunity was arguably the single most important periodical to the New Negro literary movement. Others had higher circulations and featured writers and artists prominently, but they were drawn into the arts in part by the initiative and success of *Opportunity*, founded in January 1923.[35] As a forum for the finest talent of the era, *Opportunity* was exceptional; few New Negro writers published there first, but none escaped its notice. Hughes and Hurston credited editor Charles Johnson with launching their careers. He "did more to encourage and develop Negro writers during the 1920s than anyone else in America," Hughes wrote.[36] Hurston said she "came to New York through *Opportunity*, and through *Opportunity* to Barnard," calling Johnson the "root" of the movement.[37] When Walrond became business manager in 1925, he had been publishing there since its inception.

The defining document of the Harlem Renaissance is widely held to be *The New Negro*, conceived at the downtown Civic Club in March 1924, where a group known as the Writers Guild was introduced to New York's publishing establishment. Locke and Du Bois are credited with orchestrating the Harlem Renaissance, but the impact of Charles Johnson, a sociologist trained at the University of Chicago and recruited to the New York headquarters of the Urban League, was equally decisive. For someone so prolific, "written evidence of his vast influence on the Harlem of the New Negro is curiously spotty," notes David Levering Lewis. "It seems to have been his nature to work behind the scenes, recruiting and guiding others into the spotlight."[38] Johnson's self-effacement belied his true impact. Attending to Walrond's career not only reveals a hidden transcript of Johnson's activity, it suggests that Walrond himself provided more impetus than is generally thought.

In summer 1923, Walrond and Countée Cullen were estranged and managing vexatious personal and professional problems. Both struggled in their intimate relationships—Walrond looking to exit a marriage, Cullen looking to get into one. Walrond's relationship with Edith was further strained when they conceived a third child in August 1923. That fall, his family left for Kingston without him. Cullen was engaged in some soul-searching of his own, convincing himself that the right woman could cure him of homosexuality. He wrote frequently of this "problem" to Locke, whose homosexuality was an open secret. However, soon the reticent preacher's son was cavorting with Yolande Du Bois, whom he recently met. He was smitten, as he told Locke: "I believe I am near the solution of my problem. But I shall proceed warily."[39] Cullen's cryptic phrasing is illuminated by his other correspondence, which expressed alternately and with equal desperation his need to overcome his homosexuality and his

4.3 Photograph of Countée Cullen, 1932, photographer unknown.

Courtesy of the New York *Daily News*.

need to find a discreet, compatible male partner. Locke disapproved of the relationship with Yolande as "a solution." "I can forgive you for refusing my advice," he fulminated, "but I cannot forgive you for transgressing a law of your own nature—because nature herself will not forgive you."[40]

Just as Walrond and Cullen both struggled with their personal lives, they imposed similarly stringent demands upon their artistic development. Each sought to reconcile a desire to transcend sentiment and propaganda in art with a desire to address urgent issues of race. Walrond inveighed against efforts to disguise sociological narratives as good fiction, and Cullen, an admirer of Keats and Millay, took the occasion of receiving the Witter Bynner undergraduate poetry prize to lament the traces of race consciousness in his poetry.[41] Walrond began talking seriously with friends in late 1923 about bold collective steps to publicize their work, and Cullen was among the first he approached. Walrond wrote breezily from Atlanta, where *The International Interpreter* sent him on assignment. Enjoying his most prolific period to date—eight publications in one four-month stretch—his Caribbean stories were placed, and *Success* declared him in a bit of puffery a "new, young master of vivid narrative" with "the making of one the greatest novelists and short story writers of our day" (32). Walrond was thrilled about his role in Harlem's artistic ferment but self-conscious that his talent was surpassed by peers such as Cullen.

> My dear Countée: Well, old fellow, it is Saturday night and I thought I'd drop you a line. I arrived here Monday, after a terrifying experience (which is not going to be without its literary effects, no matter how feeble) on the Jim Crow Car from Washington. I really cannot understand how folks travel that way year in and year out. I can't.
>
> I read Lucien White's write up of you in the "Age." It was fine. That is the sort of recognition that is going to help us put our ideas over. I think if everything goes well we ought to be thinking keenly on that score very soon. What with my success as a hack writer and your growing popularity as a poet of the first rank we ought to be able to do most anything, from seducing Sadie Peterson to conquering Joe Gould's prejudices against the bath tub. [. . .]
>
> I ought to tell you something of the life and my work and experiences here. Atlanta, Countée, is alright for anybody who wants to be a Babbitt, but for a poet or one who is sensitive to the finer things in life it is a pig sty.
>
> Of course I am on a Babbitt-wooing mission, and in that capacity I stand ready willing and able to the gums to resist the emoluments of any of you poets and liberals and neo-liberals and backwoods yankees and nigger upstarts and [. . .] fundamentalists and apostles of culture and idealism and beauty and all such rot.[42]

Despite the wry self-deprecation, Walrond's ambition is clear; he felt the time was right to "put our ideas over" and enlisted Cullen's help in "thinking keenly on that score." The "Babbitt-wooing mission" was a campaign to publicize the Commission on Interracial Cooperation, a federal initiative, but as his ironic closing suggests, he preferred poets, apostles of culture, and others "sensitive to the finer things in life" to the businessmen he was sent to meet.

Walrond's eagerness to take bolder steps found a sympathetic ear with Charles Johnson. Trained by the eminent sociologist Robert Park, Johnson's analysis of the 1919 race riots led to a directorship of the Urban League's Division of Research and Investigations. His empiricism was tempered by a faith in the arts as transformative of public opinion and a conviction that "black artists should be free, not merely to express anything they feel, but to feel the pulsations and rhythms of their own life." Some have cast Johnson as a cunning opportunist, exploiting the "Negro vogue," but this neglects his commitment to publicizing and theorizing the arts.[43] As George Hutchinson has shown, his intellectual orientation was shaped by pragmatist philosophy, in which cultural self-expression was as highly prized as dispassionate analysis (176).[44] He saw the present group of writers as "the legitimate successors of the voices that first sang the Spirituals." The audacity of his vision is difficult to grasp in retrospect, but for its time Johnson's approach to the arts as at once beautiful and useful to the cause of interracial understanding was exceptional.

By February 1924, the group had hatched a plan and Johnson resolved to recruit Locke. He wrote about a "matter which is being planned by Walrond, Cullen, Gwendolyn Bennett, myself and some others, which hopes to interest and include you."

> I may have spoken to you about a little group which meets here, with some degree of regularity, to talk informally about "books and things." Most of the persons interested you know: Walrond, Cullen, Langston Hughes, Gwendolyn Bennett, Jessie Fauset, Eloise Bibb Thompson, Regina Anderson, Harold Jackman, and myself. There have been some very interesting sessions and at the last one it was proposed that something be done to mark the growing self-consciousness of this newer school of writers and as a desirable time the date of the appearance of

4.4 Photograph of Charles S. Johnson, 1948, by Carl Van Vechten.

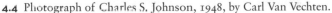

James Weldon Johnson Collection, Beinecke Rare Book and Manuscript Library,
Yale University. Courtesy of the Van Vechten Trust.

Jessie Fauset's book was selected, that is, around the twentieth of March.
The idea has grown somewhat and it is the present purpose to include
as many of the new school of writers as possible. [. . .] But our plans
for you were a bit more complicated. We want you to take a certain role
in the movement. We are working up a dinner meeting, probably at the
Civic Club, to which about fifty persons will be invited. [. . .] You were
thought of as a sort of Master of Ceremonies for the "movement."[45]

Like Walrond and Johnson, Locke saw this generation's work as a threshold. "We have enough talent now to begin to have a movement—and
express a school of thought," he wrote Hughes.[46]

Fauset had gone to great lengths to solicit contributions to *The Crisis*
and to cultivate an audience for creative writing, setting to work in 1922
on a novel of her own. At the same time, Toomer gathered his writings

into a manuscript, and the resulting books, *There Is Confusion* and *Cane*, were published by Boni & Liveright within seven months of each other. Walter White signed with Knopf for *Fire in the Flint*, and work by African Americans appeared in "little magazines" and mainstream venues alike. But the cultural terrain truly shifted with a classical music performance, the American debut of Roland Hayes, an African American tenor who had electrified European audiences. First appearing with the Boston Symphony Orchestra, then at New York's Town Hall, "Hayes promptly became a national symbol, if not a legend," recalled Arna Bontemps, "the first of his color to invade the closed precincts of top-level concert music in this nation." And "Charles Johnson did not fail to put it all in context."[47] It was a propitious time, Johnson realized, to stage a publicity stunt. Walrond and the others meeting at Regina Anderson's apartment found an enthusiastic champion in the staid sociologist.

Johnson's position and tact helped him pull off something unprecedented in African American letters. By enlisting the help of Locke and Fauset, yet keeping Fauset's boss and the folks at *The Messenger* out of the planning, he and the Writers Guild recruited an extraordinary range of white publishers and editors for the Civic Club event, a dinner that featured presentations from Locke, Van Doren, and Liveright and readings by Cullen and Bennett, among others.[48] Johnson benefited from Walrond's assistance because he "made his own contacts" and "would go out and seek editors and publishers [. . .] rather than rely on friends or agents or other people."[49] Their plan was not self-evidently promising, and some thought it inadvisable. Was it not the height of folly, while lynching and intimidation prevailed in the South and discrimination was rampant in public life in the North, to neglect questions of power and politics and expect literature to advance material progress? But Johnson was a shrewd promoter, articulating his convictions about the arts in advance of the event: "There has been manifest recently a most amazing change in the public mind on the question of the Negro," he editorialized. "There is a healthy hunger for more information—a demand for a new interpretation of characters long and admittedly misunderstood." Although "formal inter-racial bodies" deserved some credit for effecting this change, Johnson held "the new group of young Negro writers" primarily responsible.

> [They] have dragged themselves out of the deadening slough of the race's historical inferiority complex, and with an unconquerable audacity are beginning to make this group interesting. They are leaving to the old school its labored lamentations and protests, read only by those who agree with them, and are writing about life. And it may be said to the credit of literary America that where these bold strokes emancipate their message from the miasma of race they are being accepted as literature.[50]

His examples were Toomer, "author of the exotic 'Cane,'" and Walrond, whose "quite unqualified appraisal" by *Success* he cited.

The guest list was long and luminous, including Eugene O'Neill, H. L. Mencken, Oswald Garrison Villard, Zona Gale, Ridgely Torrence, "and about twenty more of this type," Johnson's invitation said. "This type" included Arthur Spingarn of the National Association for the Advancement of Colored People (NAACP); American Civil Liberties Union (ACLU) founder Roger Baldwin; art collector and philanthropist Albert Barnes; philosopher John Dewey; editors from *The Nation*, *Harper's*, *Scribner's*, and *Survey*; columnists Heywood Broun and Konrad Bercovici; and novelists Rebecca West, Gertrude Sanborn, and T. S. Stribling. Among the celebrated African Americans were Robeson, James Weldon Johnson, Walter White, J. A. Rogers, and Montgomery Gregory, along with the Writers Guild members: Walrond, Cullen, Anderson, Hughes, Fauset, Bennett, Jackman, and Eloise Bibb Thompson. As he opened the responses, Johnson realized the scale of the thing. "No accidents can afford to happen now," he told Locke, "The idea has gone 'big.'"[51]

By any measure, the event was a huge success. That Friday evening in March, the Greenwich Village venue was abuzz with more than one hundred revelers. *Opportunity* claimed, "There was no formal, prearranged program," just "a surprising spontaneity of expression both from the members of the writers' group and the distinguished visitors."[52]

But in fact, Charles Johnson, ever the impresario, carefully orchestrated the proceedings, directing Locke to meet him that morning to review plans. Several speakers prepared remarks, Cullen and Bennett were asked to read a poem each, and Van Doren and Barnes were asked to deliver keynote addresses. Thus, if anyone exhibited "spontaneity of expression" it was probably only Liveright, who was notorious for relying principally on liquid courage. No record survives of Walrond's response, but one can imagine the satisfaction he felt. "Our little group," as Nance called it, had engineered a stunning publicity coup. After Charles Johnson welcomed the guests, offering "a brief interpretation of the object of the Writers Guild," Locke, Du Bois, and James Weldon Johnson delivered speeches, striking a common theme: the younger writers' refusal to indulge in apologies or "inferiority complexes." This was also, Liveright said, the chief virtue of *Cane*, whose merits he affirmed despite poor sales. For Walrond, it must have been gratifying to hear Liveright challenge the audience to "test the waters of black talent with a few publishing contracts," and exhilarating to hear poems from his friends Cullen and Bennett, who concluded the evening with "To Usward," likening the new generation to ginger jars gathering dust on a shelf, "sealed/ By nature's heritage." They were ready, Bennett declared, "to break the seal of years/ With pungent thrusts of song."[53]

"A big plug was bitten off," Johnson declared, "Now it's a question of living up to the reputation."[54] Walrond's behind-the-scenes effort ensured that the event yielded results. "When the dinner ended, Paul Kellogg, editor of the *Survey Graphic*, stayed on to talk to Countée Cullen, Eric Walrond, Jessie Fauset, and the others and then approached Charles Johnson with an unprecedented offer. He wanted to 'devote an entire issue to the similar subjects as treated by the representatives of the group.'"[55] This would be the *Survey* issue "Harlem: Mecca of the New Negro," which was guest-edited by Locke and sold 42,000 copies, double the usual. In turn, the *Survey* issue became *The New Negro,* published in 1925. As important as Kellogg's opening gambit, Du Bois announced a *Crisis* literary contest, as did Johnson later that year for *Opportunity,* and he and Liveright mobilized their publicity apparatus. Boni & Liveright advertised in the *New*

York Times Book Review, announcing Fauset's novel and trumpeting the event at which "the intellectual leaders of the metropolis celebrated the birth of a new sort of book about colored people."[56] Walrond was tasked with writing up the event for the *New York World* and sought Locke's assistance gathering transcripts of the speakers' remarks.[57] News of the event spread, and Johnson reported that "a stream of manuscripts has started into my office." It is no exaggeration to say that after March 1924, African American literature would never be the same.

The most tangible benefit for Walrond was the appearance in *The New Negro* of his story "The Palm Porch," a lurid tale set in a Panama brothel. The story's inclusion returns us to a recurring tension in Walrond's career, for although he enjoyed the fruits of his labor with the Writer's Guild, it came at a cost. The movement defined itself as an *American* phenomenon despite the contrapuntal accents of Caribbean immigrants. One in five black Harlemites was foreign-born by the late 1920s, but the movement bearing its name was framed in national terms, with the New Negro representing at once the inheritance and the proleptic overcoming of a spiritual legacy begun with the sorrow songs, sermons, and blues rhythms of the southern black belt. However, recent scholars remind us "just how seminal was the West Indian presence in the Harlem of the 1920s."[58]

To some extent Locke, Du Bois, and Johnson were responsible for the nationalist contours of the movement. Their interests, although not unified, determined much of what was published and how it circulated. Du Bois and Locke were interested in the broader diaspora, but Johnson cut his professional teeth on the social problems of the Great Migration, and the consensus among interested whites was that "Negro" voices were a vital contribution to the chorus of American literature. To the extent that African American writers succeeded at chipping away at publishers' prejudices, they did so because of the era's push toward pluralism, a belief that American literature could only *become* American by emphasizing what made the United States distinctive, drawing on multiple ethnic traditions. Versions of this claim appeared regularly in the progressive journals. Van Doren's remarks at the Civic Club expressed his "genuine faith in the future of imaginative writing among Negroes in the United States," a "feeling" that they were "in a remarkably strategic position with reference to the new literary age." His endorsement was representative of the effort to define New Negro literature as a tributary to the widening stream of American modernism. "What American literature decidedly needs at the moment is color, music, gusto, the free expression of gay or desperate moods. If the Negroes are not in a position to contribute these items, I do not know what Americans are." He invoked novelty of expression and contrasted the "fresh and fierce sense of reality" issuing from African American pens with the "bland optimism of the majority." Finally, he delineated the territory on which African American writers would base their "vision of human life": "this continent." When we understand the Harlem Renaissance as a pivotal era for African American literature we should also understand how *American* its framing was.[59]

How, then, did foreignness figure? One might note the prominence accorded Schomburg, McKay, Walrond, W. A. Domingo, and J. A. Rogers in *The New Negro* and conclude that this was a big tent, including non-Americans (at least males) and fostering *intra*racial understanding. However, differences of ethnicity, language, and nation were often elided in discussions of the movement, as bichromatic U.S. race relations assumed priority. On or about March 1924, as Walrond heard Carl Van Doren incorporate him into the grand unfolding of a distinctive American tradition, there were at least two reasons he and other West Indians were making tacit peace with their internal marginalization: the Johnson-Reed Immigration Act and the campaign against Garvey. As Locke departed Washington to join Johnson in planning the Civic Club event, Congress was crafting the most restrictive immigration legislation of the century, the Johnson-Reed Act. The immediate effect was to cut the number of immigrants arriving each year almost in half, with the heaviest contraction upon southern and eastern Europe. Immigration from the Caribbean was sharply curtailed, and nativism infused urban communities where Afro-Caribbeans lived in large numbers. Garvey was a lightning rod, his ethnicity and alien status regularly impugned. The "foreigner" angle gained virulence, and the terms "West Indian" and "ignorant" were frequently joined in close syntactic proximity. *The Messenger* conceded the existence of many "splendid," "intelligent" Caribbean people but urged ministers, editors, and lecturers to "gird up their courage . . . and drive the menace of Garveyism out of this country."⁶⁰ This was opportunism, but it would not have been possible absent the nativism that delivered the Johnson-Reed Act.

Walrond was not immune to these pressures, and he sought to rescue West Indians from the nativist assault. Paradoxically, he did so through classic American values such as industry and thrift and through a ritualistic disavowal of Garvey. At the height of the "Garvey Must Go" campaign in 1923, he published two articles attacking the presumption "that Garvey, crude, blatant, egocentric, a mental Lilliputian, is the typical West Indian intellectual," claiming instead that "Garvey by virtue of his upbringing, training, and early environment, is not representative of the best the West Indian Negroes have to offer." Walrond called West Indians "the Hebrews of the black race," a model minority for whom "America is the fulfillment of a golden dream" ("Hebrews" 468). To understand the West Indians' promise, he pointed to other parts of the Americas, where they had been welcomed from Cuba to Panama to the banana fields of Guatemala and Honduras ("West Indian Labor" 240).

At this point, Walrond added a breathtaking bit of sophistry. "Endowed with the spirit of conquest of the Puritan settlers of the isles of the Caribbean, he goes to the ends of the earth, building, erecting, assimilating." U.S. readers were to understand, in other words, that despite being black and foreign, perhaps West Indian Negroes most resembled Anglo-Americans, sharing a common Puritanism, an ethic of industry and "spirit of conquest" that took them around the world. If this were not enough to establish the affinity, Walrond distinguished West Indians from other Caribbean peoples on the basis of their Englishness. The "Negroes from Guadeloupe and Martinique" the French hired in Panama, "were not of the sturdy pioneering stock who were willing to weather the storms of malaria and disease and dig the ditch. [. . .] The West Indians stuck to their guns, steeled their jaws, and fought the good fight" (241). It is a measure of the xenophobia of the times that Walrond, who was well aware of the imperialist dimensions of the U.S. role in Panama and its exploitation of black labor, would resort to this effort to establish the West Indian's "sturdy pioneering stock."

Under Locke's direction, *The New Negro* included five foreign-born writers, but the book exudes cultural nationalism. Only Walrond and Domingo addressed non-U.S. subjects in a sustained fashion, and Domingo's essay "The Gift of the Tropics" is fundamentally about black New York, despite encouraging sensitivity toward ethnic differences. For J. A. Rogers in "Jazz at Home," *home* is emphatically the United States though he grew up in Jamaica, and his aim is to trace the cabarets and juke joints back to the Mississippi Delta. McKay could be said to challenge the national frame, but of his six poems only "The Tropics in New York" implies his foreignness, and no poem in *The New Negro* could be more classically American than his "White Houses." Schomburg nowhere betrays his ethnic difference, and although his essay "The Negro Digs Up His Past" takes readers far beyond the borders of the United States, it is finally the *American* Negro whose past Schomburg aims to dig up. To hear the transnational strains of *The New Negro*, one must read against its American grain. Locke set it at the outset in his extraordinary introduction, where he argues that "in the process of being transplanted the Negro is being transformed, [. . .] the migrant masses shifting from countryside to city, hurdl[ing] several generations of experience at a leap." He nodded to a racial cosmopolitanism, but his American exceptionalism was emphatic: African Americans were "the advance-guard" of the diaspora, and here, "The Negro mind reaches out as yet to nothing but American wants, American ideas."[61]

How incongruous Walrond's "The Palm Porch" seems in this context. It appears in a section of fiction following two texts with "America" in their titles. It shares space with stories by Rudolph Fisher, whose protagonist is a North Carolina transplant; John Matheus, whose setting is West Virginia; Toomer, whose "Fern" and "Carma" take place on Georgia's "Dixie Pike"; Bruce Nugent, whose "Sahdji" is ostensibly an African princess but is really an American projection of Africa; and Hurston, whose "Spunk" takes place in a Florida village where men wear "big black Stetson" hats and women drink "sasp'rilluh." Walrond's setting diverges sharply, as does his entire frame of reference. The migration behind Walrond's story is the West Indian's to Panama, not the African American's north.

> East of the Palm Porch roared the city of Colon. Hudson Alley, "G" Street . . . coolies, natives, Island blacks swarming to the Canal. All about, nothing but tenements . . . city word for cabins . . . low, soggy, toppling. Near the sky rose the Ant's Nest. Six stories high and it took up half a city block. One rickety staircase . . . in the rear. No two of its rooms connected. Each sheltered a family of eight or nine. A balcony ringed each floor. [. . .] Sorry lot. Tugging at the apron strings of life, scabrous, sore-footed natives, spouting saliva into unisolated cisterns. Naked on the floors of Chinese rum shops and chow-stands. Nigger-loving Chinks unmoved and unafraid of the consequences of a breed of untarnished . . . seemingly . . . Asiatics growing up around the breasts of West Indian maidens. Pious English peasant blacks . . . perforating the picture . . . going to church, to lodge meetings, to hear fiery orations. (116–17)

"The Palm Porch" is shot through with intraracial and interracial dynamics that exceed the bichromatic North American frame: "Chinks" loving "Niggers," Panamanians living with "Coolies," Caribbean laborers and respectable church-going peasants, an English ship's captain at the brothel. Perhaps in its superficial resemblance to Harlem, this Colón did not strike *The New Negro* readers as foreign. Perhaps the stylized prose affiliated it with experimental New Negro writers such as Toomer. Perhaps its folk speech allied it with Hurston, Hughes, and others who employed African American vernacular.

But to domesticate "The Palm Porch" in this way, to round off its strange corners, involves no small degree of misrecognition and muting. Louis Chude-Sokei has said of Bert Williams, "His was a heteroglossia cursed to be continually recuperated by the 'centripetal' forces of America's racial polarities, which either sifted out the accents of Caribbean crossings or employed them as signifiers of an 'elsewhere' marginal to a primary discursive formation."[62] It would overstate the matter to call

Walrond's heteroglossia cursed to the point of continual recuperation, but the accents of his Caribbean crossings are only audible if we suspend the axiomatic nationalism of the New Negro movement. What if we suppose instead, as Walrond did, that Afro-Caribbean speech, location, and experience were, like their African American counterparts, constitutive of a black Atlantic formation?

Miss Buckner, the protagonist of "The Palm Porch," is Jamaican by birth, descended from "a union of white and Negro, French or Spanish, English or Maroon . . . no one knew. And her daughters, sculptural marvels of gold and yellow, were enshrined in a similar mystery (119). Opening her mouth, she might utter the King's English, as in, "O! Captain, in dear old Kingston, none of this sort of thing ever occurred . . . None! And of course it *constrains me profusely*!" (124). But it might be salty patois: "It a dam' pity shame," she indicts her daughter's relations with a "shiny-armed black" man, "It a dam' pity shame." When another daughter takes up with a mulatto man, she disapproves in heavily marked vernacular. "Oh, Gahd," she cries, "To tink dat a handsome gal like dat would-ah tek up with a dam' black neygah man like him, he? Now, wa' you tink o' dat? H'answer me, no!" (120) Miss Buckner's voice is distinct from the southern U.S. dialects, such as Fisher's Carolinians, Matheus's West Virginians, and Hurston's Floridians, who say things like, "He ain't skeered of nothin' on God's green footstool—nothin'! He rides that log down at the sawmill jus' like he struts 'round wid another man's wife" (105). Nevertheless, the orthographic marks and the characters' blackness conspired to obscure the specificity of Walrond's effort.

DEAR LOCKUS AND ALL THE WITCHES IN CREATION

Walrond should have been elated; the movement was anointed with full-throated praise. The *Opportunity* and *Crisis* awards were generously funded, and a sense of finally having arrived possessed Harlem writers. He sat for the artist Winold Reiss, whose portraits adorned the special issue of *Survey*. Reiss drew Walrond in the style of the others—rich color,

4.5 Portrait of Eric Walrond by Winold Reiss, c. 1925, pastel on board.

Courtesy of Fisk University Galleries, Nashville, Tennessee.

texture, and detail for the face and head atop the sparest outline of shirt and coat—but the others appear at an angle or with eyes averted, while Walrond's portrait stares directly at viewers, fixing us in his gaze. His shoulders squared, jaw set, he appears poised, calm, and confident, every bit as "smooth as long staple cotton," as David Levering Lewis describes him.[63] Inside, however, he was struggling mightily, his profound unease belying the portrait's placid demeanor.

Signs of depression emerged in his letters to Locke, whom he addressed with casual familiarity, calling him "my dear Lockus." The correspondence also reveals an imbalance of power and an anxiety on Walrond's part to impress the exacting professor. A month after the Civic Club event he wrote,

> I hope you do not consider the time we spent together Saturday wasted. [. . .] When I started this letter I wanted to say something about my seeming inability to do justice to you whenever I am with you, but for some reason I can not get my thoughts together this morning to really put them down as I would like to. Some time, say when I take advantage of your kind invitation and come to Washington, I shall try and get it all out. In the meantime, I shall run along—chased by all the witches in creation as to the utter inadequacy of this note.[64]

These were the first of many self-deprecations and apologies. Walrond was not alone in feeling daunted by the austere Locke, whose fastidious refinement made many people insecure. But Walrond was particularly susceptible. He first wrote of depression in May 1924, apologizing for having missed an opportunity to discuss business with Locke, including his work for the *Survey*. Walrond confessed that he had misplaced a letter of reference Locke had written; "I guess you will say I am 'fumbling the balls again.' I am sorry." Although he was delighted that "Countee and I were initiated into Alpha Phi Alpha fraternity last Saturday night," the "rollicking affair" did little to lift his spirits. "Things have not been so very well with me and I have been in a pretty melancholy state for the past week. [. . .] I am not doing very much work at present, but I think I am due for a let up. I am in one of my old shifting, restless, nervous moods." This was clearly not a new condition. He was familiar with its symptoms and rhythms. Perhaps it explains his failure to complete his City College courses that term. A remedy came to mind—"I think what I need is a sea voyage somewhere"—but he promised to visit Locke in Washington soon.[65]

His depression worsened. Anxious about his place in the *Survey*, Walrond visited the magazine's office, inquiring about his contributor's letter.[66] He spent time in New York with Locke, en route to Europe, and they attended a party that ended badly ("I was glad to know that the flat did not burn down," he wrote.) Walrond's letter indicates the depth of his anxiety and the intimacy of his relationship with Locke. Although he had been publishing widely, his work on a novel, *Tiger Lilly*, was frustrating.[67] The tone suggests the two may have had an affair, but no evidence exists. Locke's affairs with other men are a matter of record, and although Walrond is never mentioned, Locke may have counted him among what he called his "spiritual children."[68] Walrond professed anguish that his depression prevented him from traveling to visit Locke.

I have put off writing you until this morning because I had hoped and prayed that my plans would make it possible for me to be with you tomorrow. I find, to my deepest regret, that I will not be able to come down. And here is why. All the winter I have spent in a rather profitless manner—indeed, all I have to show for it is a loosely constructed, badly unadorned novel. And it is on that account I planned to get on my feet again either by going away on a boat or to the mountains where I should have a chance to bolster myself up again and, chiefly, to get away from the sterile environment in Harlem. Then again, as I intimated to you, I must get to Columbia in the Fall, and there is a multitude of little things here that I must get straightened out before I shall be able to do that.

So far I have not been able to get away—and the result is a state of anxiety, melancholy, and depression. In other words, I do not think it would be fair to you, nor would I be doing myself justice, to come down to Washington in this high-strung, unnatural, morbid, discontented state of mind. For it seems strange, yet it is true, that ever since I have known you I have not been really myself. There is really a self, a side of me, I think, that is not bad, not undesirable, but as fate would have it, this side has been for some time submerged by the harsh rulings of life.

You ask me to write you regarding my plans. I hasten to do so. First, of course, is to get away. In the fall I *must* be at school. As regards writing, I am not going to look at that novel until I get back to the city. Perhaps (I don't know) conditions out in the country may make it possible for me to go back to it and try to get it into shape. However, since it has got itself out of my system, I am not really worried about the problem of revision—that I know is something I must do leisurely and in conjunction with my rising (I hope you'll pardon the epithet) powers. Again, I find that another story of similar length is popping up—and I am such a furiously emotional creature I wonder if I ought not to get at that, regardless of my hostile mind, and get that off, too. I really believe that in this raw, briny, floundering state I ought to shoot ahead and get the writing over with—and hope for a day of placid distraction when I shall be able to go over every line with the care and concern of a mothering bird. [. . .]

Despite my fears and disillusions I am doing a lot of reading . . . and I am plumbing the depths of that glowing sahara you pointed out to me the evening we were at Glenn's. . . . Believe me, it is with the utmost regret and pain that I cannot be with you tomorrow.

Among the elusive references here, the most enigmatic is his remark about "that glowing sahara." But his self-image as "a furiously emotional creature" possessed of a "hostile mind" is stark and unambiguous. Characterizing himself as "high-strung, unnatural, morbid, discontented," he attributes his condition to "the harsh rulings of life," circumstances that suppress his better "side."

It was likely this state of mind that led to the most hostile, churlish book review of his career. Reviewing Jessie Fauset's *There Is Confusion* in *The New Republic*, he panned it, barely touching on the book and disparaging Fauset. Some of her peers found her writing fussy and her characters too proper, but none expressed this view as intemperately as Walrond. The novel, he conceded, was "significant," but it was "not really 'younger generation Negro' stuff." "Mediocre, a work of puny, painstaking labor, 'There Is Confusion' is not meant for people who know anything about the Negro and his problems. It is aimed with unpardonable naiveté at the very young or the pertinently old" (192). It is hard to imagine a more divisive statement, and to what end? Perhaps Walrond sought to impress Locke, who dismissed Fauset's talent.[69] He may have firmly believed what he wrote, that the "esoteric" school was the vanguard, that

Fauset, depicting upper-class African Americans, was in the thrall of an "inferiority complex," anxious to prove "Negro" respectability. Nevertheless, even a cursory glance over his shoulder would have revealed the bridges he was burning.

Recklessly uncharitable, the review upset Fauset's friends. "Your review of Jessie Fauset's 'There Is Confusion' is really not worthy of the New Republic," Du Bois wrote, "It is not a review or even a comment, but a quite gratuitous slur upon a work which, whatever its merits, is at least a sincere and unusual product."[70] Jackman and Hughes expressed their outrage to Cullen, but he defended Walrond: "I think you are all too harsh with Eric. Surely a reviewer has a right to his opinion without being dubbed an ass, a numbskull, a jealous prig, and other equally delightful appellations."[71] Hughes was traveling with Locke in Paris, and in an otherwise upbeat letter he expressed his disapproval, calling Walrond's review "ugly," "childish," and "just about as worthless a thing as that publication ever contained. Eric ought to be ashamed of himself."[72]

In fact, Walrond was thoroughly ashamed of himself. Not about the review, but constitutionally so. Shame became a nagging burden he sought continually to exorcise. His ambitions, he felt, were always exceeding his abilities. The intended contribution to the *Survey*, an essay entitled "The Mirrors of Harlem," left him exasperated, much like his "badly unadorned" novel.

> I'm afraid I haven't been able to execute the assignment to the satisfaction of either you or Mr. Kellogg—but [. . .] after all a thing of this sort, conceived and done by someone with a more or less eccentric way of looking at things, which, to me is the only way it ought to be done—in order to be effective must take a quite independent attitude and avoid all this Christian prattle that has been heaped upon the Negro.[73]

The note was handwritten, but its contents were formal. Alternately contrite and defiant but terse throughout, it was addressed "Dear Dr. Locke" and signed, "Yours sincerely, Eric D. Walrond." As late as June 1925 Walrond was still revising "The Mirrors of Harlem," but the essay never appeared. Locke included "The Palm Porch" in *The New Negro* but nothing in the *Survey*.[74]

Walrond's insecurities extended to his social milieu. Despite being someone to whom people were drawn "because he was very friendly," as Nance said, Walrond could agonize over a faux pas and worry himself sick. At a party in 1925 he mistook someone for the wife of Alfred Knopf, an error for which he berated himself in a letter to Carl Van Vechten. Calling himself "a proper, pitiable object for a Freudian psychologist," Walrond took this trivial breach of etiquette as a referendum on his character.

> I am such a terrible searcher after things that are not always clear to me that I myself half of the time do not know what I am going to say or do next. It is a sorry condition to be in, I suppose, but it will probably mean that half of the people whom I care about most in the world will sooner or later pass me up entirely or graciously and charitably let it go at that. . . . All of which is sometimes quite distressing to me.[75]

His present instability and despondency were at odds with his reputation as capable and self-assured, "smooth as long-staple cotton."

THE NIGHT SIDE OF THE SOUL: CABARET WRITING AND THE POLITICS OF RESPECTABILITY

Another way to explain the severity of Walrond's uncharitable review of Fauset's novel is to see it not as a manifestation of psychological distress but as an exhaustion of patience with uplift ideology. The terms in which he criticized it demonstrate the place the book and its author held in the discourse of respectability informing the New Negro project: It lacked the "beauty and passion" of the "insouciant, strident neophytes." Although he would soon work for a paragon of uplift, the Urban League, the premise that "the worst elements of the race" required reform on a model of middle-class respectability smacked of elitism and relegated a great deal of expressive black culture to the realm of the shameful, abject, and

socially deviant. Walrond was fed up, he said, with "all this Christian prat-
tle." In the face of the normative ideals coming to characterize the New
Negro movement, "a more or less eccentric way of looking at things" was
required, and late 1924 and 1925 found Walrond chafing under the stric-
tures of respectability and formulating an "eccentric" perspective. Less a
coherent political or aesthetic platform, it was cosmopolitan, queer, and
transnational, forged primarily in Harlem's cabarets and performed in
prose. At its center was an affirmation of pleasure—pleasure as a challenge to bourgeois respectability, as an affective index of liberated black
writing, and as a remedy for the depression that threatened to undo him.

To be sure, Walrond tried to stay the course of sober self-discipline.
He enrolled in Columbia, taking three classes, one of which was taught
by the author of a study of the supernatural in modern fiction. Dorothy
Scarborough's enthusiasm for the supernatural as "an ever-present force
in literature," "the night side of the soul that attracts us all," influenced
Tropic Death, which is populated by ghosts, spells, and the return of
various forms of the repressed.[76] Unlike his previous term at City College,
Walrond passed his Columbia courses with flying colors.[77] He continued
his involvement with West Indian political affairs, publicizing and attending events organized by Casper Holstein and the Virgin Islands Congressional Council.[78] And he got his longed-for escape from New York, not
with a sea voyage but a trip to Kansas City.

His account of the trip was not published in the Urban League's journal, which sent him there, but in *The Messenger*, detailing his effort to
interview "the richest colored sister in the world." It bore no resemblance
to traditional journalism, as its title, "Romance of a Reporter," indicated.
The romance refers to his attempts—thwarted, then fulfilled—to meet
the reclusive "millionairess" and to discover the source of her wealth.
Departing flagrantly from reporting, Walrond cast himself as an intrepid
gallant who cracks the social codes of the black upper crust. "Mrs. Rector
Campbell, the richest colored girl in the world, whom the black folks in
Kansas City refer to as a 'snitcher,' hates school, hates books, hates to be
'colored,' hates above all to be 'written up'" (382). Walrond boasted of
his success at getting a tough interview where others had failed, including

local editors and even Du Bois. He adapted the percussive prose of bou-doir melodrama to "Negro" society, recounting having "bowed very pret-tily before" Mrs. Campbell, "a silent, black, apple faced girl, reclining Cleopatraly on a rich leopard-spotted couch" (382).

More than "Romance of a Reporter," two essays he published that winter in mainstream journals announced him as an authoritative critic, someone to whom African Americans looked to represent them and to whom whites looked for insight into black culture. Both journals gave him more space than he was accustomed to, and Walrond developed his observations with detail and vigor. "Imperator Africanus," an analysis of the Garvey move-ment, appeared in *The Independent*. Although it cast Garvey as a "roof-raising propagandist" who created "a fairy dream world" with "all the technique of delusion," he was not a cartoonish villain (123).[79] He moved people as Du Bois never could, Walrond maintained, because although Du Bois was "undoubtedly the most brilliant Negro in the United States," he was "proud, haughty, [and] an incurable snob" (126). Walrond offered a transnational account of the first stirrings of the New Negro movement:

> Fresh from the war, from the bloodstained fields of France and Mesopo-tamia, the black troops, bitter, broken, disillusioned, stormed the gates of the whites—pleaded for a share of that liberty and democracy which they were led to believe were the things for which they had fought. [. . .] It was the first mass contact of the negro from the Old and the New Worlds. Here something which the white warlords had not bargained on resulted. The negroes met and exchanged and compounded their views on the whites, their civilization, and their masters. Here the policies of France and Britain and Belgium and the United States with regard to their black wards were put in the scales. And when the blacks rose from the resulting pyre of disillusionment a new light shone in their eyes—a new spirit, a burning ideal, to be men, to fight and conquer and actually wrest their heritage, their destiny from those who controlled it. (121–22)

Historians trace the New Negro movement to the return of black sol-diers from World War I, but the frame is seldom extended, as here, to the experience of people of African descent outside the United States and the political analysis they advanced, putting Western nations "in the scales." The war served in Walrond's view to throw the engine of diaspora into reverse, figuring not a sentimental return to the motherland but the recognition of common interests across new borders.

A similar emphasis on the diversity of black experience characterized "The Negro Literati," an essay that winter in *Brentano's Book Chat*. Walrond addressed his predominantly white audience with a challenge to bichromatic ways of seeing.

> Haven't you ever been to Harlem, New York's black ghetto, on a Sunday afternoon and seen the gay throngs of folk parading along Seventh Avenue? There is nothing like it—this amazing metamorphosis . . . All the colors of the rainbow do not suffice to do them justice. It is like a human mardi gras: Yellow and gold and brown—of Latin and Dutch origin—Indians, creoles, jet blacks . . . What a heterogeneous people! And there is something about the life the Negro lives not only in the United States but everywhere that is immensely enthralling. [. . .] He traverses the seven seas. He is everything from captain to cabin boy. [. . .] He is the roamer, the boulevardier of the universe. (31)

Calling Harlem "a human mardi gras" Walrond underscored the range of color, class, and nationality subsumed by New York's "black belt." Calling the Negro "the boulevardier of the universe," he conferred agency and mobility on people widely supposed to be constrained by circumstance, the products of history rather than its producers.

But the force of "The Negro Literati" is its call for writers to free themselves spiritually. "At present he is free politically and socially, but spiritually he is still enslaved. He is unable to let himself go" (31). Here Walrond launched one of the most remarkable, impassioned series of claims in his entire body of work. In early 1925—before McKay's *Home to Harlem*, Hughes' "The Negro Artist and the Racial Mountain," and *Nigger Heaven*, before *The New Negro* itself—Walrond challenged the respectability brigade, implicating it in the racism its authors sought to contest. What is more, he attributed his perspective to his position as an immigrant.

> As a foreigner, I think I can understand the reason for this [spiritual enslavement]. Always conscious of the color problem, the Negro writer in the United States is vigilantly censorious of anything in his work or expression which may put the black race in a disparaging light. Thinking of the prejudiced white who'd take up his book and contemptuously review it, he writes with that preconceived bias in mind. And of course when he begins to write about his own people he lies miserably. He doesn't paint pictures of people—of tantalizing black people—he knows. No. He dishes up yarns about aristocratic blacks who go to Harvard. He goes down to Wall Street and hires a skyscraper and puts a Negro bank president in it. He goes up to the Adirondacks and buys an estate and puts a black seamstress upon it. He then takes a trip back south. There he takes malicious delight in poking hot irons in the ribs of the "po' white trash." Every white man his hero meets is a "nigger hater." Every yellow girl is a virgin who's got a devil of a time fighting off the white, lustful pack. And if the story doesn't wind up with a lynching or a race riot it is bound to do so with bloodhounds on the scent of the daring black who'd had the guts to go get a gun and shoot up that horrid "cracker" town . . . On occasion these Negro tales deal with what is known about town as "high society." And by God if there is a society that is more stilted, more snobbish, that is harder to break into, than the Negro society these tales depict, then I've yet to hear about it. (32–33)

Among those to whom Walrond looked to refute the emerging orthodoxy, "this negative manner of looking at life," was Hughes, whose manifesto on "The Negro Artist" appeared the following year. American literature would soon be transformed "by the exploits of these gallant youngsters," Walrond predicted, and "that time is not very far off."

> These swashbuckling neophytes are not going in for Charity or Uplift work. They don't give two hurrahs in hell for the sort of writing that

attempts to put the Negro on a lofty pedestal. In fact they don't think of the Negro as a distinct racial type at all. They only write about him because they know more about him than anyone else. He is closer to them. His is part of them. As such they see him. (33)

Walrond cast writing about "respectable" African Americans as willful distortion—public relations without artistry—and writing about the "masses" as realistic and morally courageous. The champions of respectability included elders such as Benjamin Brawley and Allison Davis, who in 1928 rebuked writers who "for nearly ten years [. . .] have been 'confessing' the distinctive sordidness and triviality of Negro life, and making an exhibition of their own unhealthy imagination, in the name of frankness and sincerity."[80] Even some of Walrond's friends advocated respectability. Cullen put it starkly in 1928: "Whether they relish the situation or not, Negroes should be concerned with making good impressions." He frankly admitted the dissembling it required. "Decency demands that some things be kept secret. [. . .] Let[ing] art portray things as they are, no matter who is hurt, is a blind bit of philosophy."[81]

Cullen was more accustomed than most to such compartmentalizing because of his homosexuality, and he was familiar with the cognitive dissonance it occasioned. He confided his desires to Locke, lamenting the difficulty of finding a suitable partner. This was not, he felt, fit for public disclosure. In this context, Walrond's fleeting pursuit of a romance with Cullen appears somewhat incongruously. Most of Walrond's romantic relationships were with women, and his relationship with Cullen seems otherwise platonic. But as Henry Louis Gates observed, the Harlem Renaissance was "surely as gay as it was black, not that it was exclusively either of these."[82] Hughes, McKay, Locke, Nugent, Thurman, and other prominent writers had same-sex relationships, some more public than others, despite also having female partners, and scholars have addressed same-sex relationships among New Negro women.[83] Sexual practices in 1920s Harlem defy our contemporary straight/gay binary.[84] Expressions of love and affection among Harlem Renaissance figures, whatever their sexual preferences, resist our present taxonomies, and we cannot assume that the absence of definitive evidence of homosexuality means that Walrond or his peers were strictly heterosexual. Nor, conversely, can we treat references to homosexual activity or desire as proof of gay "identity" in today's sense. The events of September 1924, when Cullen said Walrond made sexual advances, are instructively indeterminate.[85]

Just as Walrond took Locke into his confidence, so Cullen confided in him a torpor into which he had sunk, an expression of unfulfilled desire. "[M]y days are alike and my need deepens," he wrote, using coded terms for his wish for "an adjustment" to avoid mentioning homosexuality. Cullen wrote to Jackman proposing they borrow his father's car for a weekend trip with Walrond.[86] Upon returning, Cullen wrote Locke, "The trip was a revelation as far as Eric is concerned. He was most surprisingly sympathetic and aggressive, but I am afraid he offers no lasting solution; he is too exacting (I almost said abandoned) and there are some concessions I shall never make."[87] What transpired is uncertain, but it was Cullen's impression that Walrond made overtures. When Locke responded by suggesting a more "lasting solution," Llewellyn Ransom, Cullen reiterated his wish for a discreet alternative.

> How long will it be before you see L.R. again? If it will be over a week, you might enclose a sealed note to him in your next letter to me, with instructions for him to read and destroy in my presence. Please pardon my urgency, but I must have an *adjustment* as soon as possible, or I shall be driven to recourse with E.W. and that I fear. You are busy I know, but if you will answer this soon.[88]

If Cullen's refusal of Walrond's apparent advances troubled their relationship, it did not last long. He found in Ransom an appealing partner, and Walrond evidently did not begrudge Cullen that happiness, accompanying him to dinner with Van Vechten soon thereafter.[89]

Van Vechten's involvement in the subcultures of Harlem and Greenwich Village is well established, and his journals furnish an important record of Walrond's participation in what Shane Vogel has called "the scene of Harlem cabaret." This scene was not only gay-friendly but queer in the sense that its participants forged communities that transgressed the norms of gender, class, race, and sexuality through which respectable culture constituted and disciplined itself. Some of Walrond's work in 1925 might be dismissed as decadent and sensational. His work for *Vanity Fair* particularly invites this criticism: "Enter, the New Negro . . . Exit the Colored Crooner," "The Adventures of Kit Skyhead and Mistah Beauty," "Black Bohemia," and "Charleston, Hey! Hey!" But his accounts of Harlem nightlife and illicit behavior, which depicted spectacular black expressive culture—African Americans performing and enjoying themselves—posed a challenge to the moralistic, class-inflected spirit of reform underpinning the New Negro movement's progressivism. Walrond and others rejected the "normative racial uplift and sexual respectability that guided the Harlem Renaissance," turning "instead to the contested space of the cabaret as material to compose alternative narratives of race and sex."[90] Those who repudiated "the values of the black middle class and the patriarchal order of the family in their prose and poetry—not to mention in their personal lives—[were] grouped together disparagingly as the 'Cabaret School.'"[91]

Indictments of the Cabaret School for "providing maps to guide pleasure-seeking white slummers on their journeys toward greater exoticism and eroticism" have implicated Walrond.[92] Certainly, Harlem fascinated many of his companions but the notion that Walrond was a tour guide for slumming whites, or worse still a sort of pimp, is inaccurate. Though they depicted decadence and dissolution, these writers mobilized a form of class politics that had subsided as the New Negro movement was politely wrested away from leftist radicals by Locke, Du Bois, and other champions of respectability.[93] The Cabaret School's critical impulse is easy to miss because the writing seems to render Harlem a consumable commodity. For Walrond, the cabaret forged "an interclass intimacy between two groups positioned in opposition to each other by uplift sociology: the black working class [. . .] and what Du Bois called the 'submerged tenth,' the morally disgraceful fraction of the race."[94] This interclass dynamic was central to Walrond's writing, especially in connection to Van Vechten. His relationship with Van Vechten is usually couched in terms of patronage: the charismatic "Negro" falling in with the sybaritic white novelist. Elided in this account is the drama of *intra*racial difference and solidarity that both writers felt was the real story of their time. They shared a desire to redraw the racial lines that proscribed personal affairs, an interest in vernacular expressive forms, and a disdain for sanctimony.

Above all, this meant a shared fascination with Harlem nightlife. By the time they met, Walrond was a regular at the cabarets. These establishments, which mixed music, song, and dance with dining, socializing, and illicit alcohol, gained notoriety with Van Vechten's 1926 novel *Nigger Heaven* and the "slumming" trend. Their association with vice and hedonism derived in part from their patrons' behavior but also from their poverty, for many postwar cabarets bore little resemblance to the Cotton Club or other opulent venues. Writers affirming the pleasures of the cabaret were accused of stereotyping and hastening the demise of an already beleaguered community. Hubert Harrison deplored their confusion of "the language of the gutter" with "the language of the common people," a practice they acquired, he said, from white bohemians. "Since 'spice' rhymes with 'nice,' they sometimes think that they are nifty when they are only being nasty [. . .] giving the whole race a bad name."[95] However, what was compelling about the cabaret scene for Walrond and others was precisely the break it signaled from shopworn Negro "types," expanding the representational palette they inherited.

"Enter, the New Negro, a Distinctive Type Recently Created by the Coloured Cabaret Belt in New York" was a collaboration between the artist Miguel Covarrubias and Walrond, who provided delirious captions for the Mexican prodigy's stylized drawings.[96] It is not hard to imagine why "Enter, the New Negro" might cause offense. Adorned with exaggerated lips, distended smiles, and ostentatious garb, the figures verge on parody, stock types given a Jazz Age makeover. However, for Frank Crowninshield, *Vanity Fair* editor, they suggested something new and closer to reality. The subtitle read, "Exit, the Coloured Crooner of Lullabys, the Cotton-Picker, the Mammy-Singer and the Darky Banjo-Player, for so Long Over-Exploited Figures on the American Stage." Crowninshield explained: "Out of the welter of sentimentality [. . .], the Negro now emerges as an individual, an individual as brisk and actual as your next-door neighbour. He no longer has to be a Pullman-car porter, or over-fond of watermelons, in order to be a successful type on our stage. He is a personality, always, and frequently an artist." The tension between Crowninshield's claims and Covarrubias' drawings raises questions. Are these really individuals or merely types? Have the images, in catching the "exotic spirit of the new Negro," simply reinscribed the "Negro" *as* exotic?

Walrond's text stood uneasily astride this ambivalence. Each caption began with a suggestive title, a Harlem slang phrase. A couple clasping hands at a table is "'The Last Jump' Cabaret on a Saturday Night"; two blasé and sartorially resplendent figures, "That Teasin' Yalla Gal" and "The Sheik of Dahomey," flank the first page; and a diffident man seated alone is "Kind O' Melancholy Like." Walrond's text underscored an important dimension of "the scene of Harlem cabaret": the blurred line between performer and spectator. Just as "That Teasin' Yalla Gal" occupied both positions at different times of night, so this cast of characters failed to distinguish patrons from performers. Not only were one venue's performers the spectators in another, their physical proximity and modes of mutual address made the boundary porous. As the Covarrubias–Walrond collaboration insisted, the audience was no less spectacular than anyone onstage. Most of the captions are reported speech, marked by nonstandard orthography and gently sending up each character. The "melancholy" loner is "jess natchely a quiet sort of fellow, dat boy is. Bin at dat table all night, sittin' down, waitin' for somebody, it seem. Don't nevah dance or sing or cut up, Nothin'. Jess sits over there, kind o' melancholy like." The couple "On a Spree" looks anything but, their languid expressions at odds with their natty dress. The discrepancy prompts Walrond's streetwise speaker to warn us against judging a Harlem book by its cover, for their reticence belies their talent on the dance floor. "Looks as if dese folks has got the blues, don't it? Well, that ain't it, prezactly. Ah wants to tell you that dey's a gwine 'out' to a party, that's what. That boy swings a mean wheel-barrow; and de gal, she ain't so bad neither. She sure can shake a wicked soap sud."

These were the voices, Walrond asserted, of "a distinctive type": unselfconscious, unflinching, unashamed of their pleasures. Dark skin need not be thin skin, he suggested; a community that acquired the self-assurance to satirize itself had overcome its "inferiority complex." The Covarrubias–Walrond collaboration was susceptible to being read as a lampoon sketch of the very sort it meant to displace. Compounding this ambivalence, the project hinged on the status of the artists as insiders, its authenticity secured by a tacit understanding that they were "of" the cabaret scene. In a sense they were, but neither was African American, and Covarrubias had just left Mexico the previous year. "Enter, the New Negro" thus involved strategies of mimicry that were obscured by the presumption of intimacy with the community they depicted. Walrond's fidelity to the sounds of Harlem concealed the extent to which he threw his voice. The conceit persisted in Crowninshield's preface to Walrond's next *Vanity Fair* effort: "This article, on the cabarets of Harlem, is written by a Negro writer, Eric Walrond, who knows the scene he writes of intimately" ("Kit" 52). Like many endorsements whites have furnished to authorize African American writing, this gesture concealed as much as it revealed, certifying Walrond's authenticity and obscuring his linguistic and ethnic difference, the very difference that would soon be invoked to authenticate *Tropic Death*.

Extending the *Vanity Fair* collaboration, Covarrubias illustrated Walrond's story "The Adventures of Kit Skyhead and Mistah Beauty: An All-Negro Evening in the Coloured Cabarets of New York." He drew a crowded dance floor, black bodies clothed in white, conjoined in postures of embrace and ecstasy, their heads barely clearing the smoky ceiling and the darkness of the dance floor crosscut by the spotlight's sharp beam. Just as "Enter, the New Negro" offered an ersatz typology of the cabaret, so "Kit Skyhead" played on sociological discourse, the protagonists surveying the gradations of Harlem venues from the swanky to the skanky. The scene of Harlem cabaret was multiform and heterogeneous, the story suggested, only partly revealing itself to the outsider. But Kit and Mistah are established as true Harlemites, possessed of keen powers of apperception despite their accents. They begin the evening seeking "a real big time" spot, but Kit cautions, "I don't want to disembarras nobody's pocket-book" (52). Arriving at the Cotton Club's "illumined façade," Kit scowls at "the pompous anterior of the Negro doorman," asking, "Who's dat nigger all dressed up like Mrs. Astor's horse?" Kit and Mistah grease palms to access the Cotton Club, which was notorious for barring black patrons. "After the mystic ritual of transferring a billet of high dimensions to the snowy paw" of the doorman, Kit and Mistah "ascended the richly carpeted stairs to the jangling throne of Bandannaland." Inside, the black patrons, few and far between, were effectively hidden although black performers occupied center stage. The spectacle is fantastic—"Dawggone," cries Kit, "if this ain't the cat's kanittens" but he realizes "there ain't another nigger in this place but you and me and the waiters" (52). The sketch can be read as pandering to stereotypes; Kit and Mistah act wild, obey their appetites, and utter malapropisms. But it is very self-aware, and its critique of the Cotton Club's practice of packaging blackness for white consumption is shrewdly delivered.

Their "adventures" lead to the Bamville Nest, where guests are enjoying themselves because they have money to spend and white folks are not much in evidence.

> Boys the colour of chocolate pudding, hair black and sleek; tall, slender youths, a bored, brother-there-ain't-a-doggone-thing-you-can-tell-me look in their eyes. Night hawks. Big timers. Niggers with "plenty money." Racehorse touts. Bolita men. California jacks. Two storey guys. Women, the shimmer of pearls, slippers of gold, the yellow ombre, tell you what it is all about. High lifers, laughing, agreeable, hilarious folks. Here to this cabaret come the black stars of the city's revues [. . .] to sing and dance and sup and say hello to the folks. Here every man is a sheik and every girl is willing to go fifty-fifty with you on a proposition. (52)

But to truly be themselves Kit and Mistah head to Sonny Decent's, the "openest" cabaret in Harlem, a joint that looks "as if it were hewn out of a tree trunk." The lack of pretense extends to the patrons, who address the proprietor by his first name, "lie prostrate" about the place, and exude a tawdry charisma. The men take seats near "a primitive coal stove," the patrons dark enough to be called "blue." "Hordes of blue people. Blue girls stunning in tomato reds . . . one of them, a dainty brown elf, wearing a dress of rich henna with a basket weave. Hats to match. Cup hats. Blinker-effect. High yellows of the Spanish type, exhilarating in peacock blue. Girls, dainty, somber, cynical-eyed, passion-mouthed" (100). The sketch tilts perilously toward primitivism, the women objects of a salacious gaze, the music "an incessant boom-booming, tom-tom-ing" that evokes "Africa undraped!" (100). "All Sonny asks of his heterogeneous patrons is that they be nice," Walrond writes. "They may fight and cut each other's throats, but boys, for God's sake, be nice!" (100). Guests talk back to the stage and play the dozens, hurling pungent insults. One patron, told he should "to go to church," retorts, "Nigger, you're a policeman and I'm a gambler. What you want me to go to church fo'. Go yo' self" (100).

If the scene is lewd, Walrond nevertheless affirms its vitality and importance to the community. "You've got to be part of the underworld pattern to fit in" at Sonny Decent's, but that pattern was nothing less than the obverse of the image respectable Harlem sought to showcase. It was a place where "the family feeling runs high" and "a sort of laboratory for song and dance," a creative cauldron where "the jazz steps you see on Broadway [. . .] are first tried out." The songs are shamelessly suggestive, as in "The American woman eats her chicken and rice/ And thinks she's eatin' somethin' nice/ But she ain't eat nuthin' till she tries/ Some monkey hips and dumplin'" (100). This was the blues before it was captured on vinyl, dance before it was codified for Broadway, jazz before Duke Ellington took it to radio. Was it a romantic view of the folk? Perhaps. But it was also an assertion of the integrity of expressive forms whose source lay in an impoverished class, the "degraded tenth" disparaged in the rhetoric of respectability. It is no surprise that perusing the crowd at Sonny Decent's, Kit and Mistah spot none other than Miguel Covarrubias and Eric Walrond. The author wished to be understood as "part of the underworld pattern" even as he enjoyed access to finer establishments.

To be clear, the prevailing discourse of respectability did not simply reflect the privilege or priggishness of its advocates. It was strategically responsive to popular notions about African American inferiority that had attained quasi-scientific status. Many felt that references to violence, sexuality, and deficiencies of intellect and ambition ought to be, if not scrubbed from African American texts, then handled with extreme delicacy. However, Walrond's cabaret writing celebrated the lower class by depicting it as imaginative, resourceful, and most importantly, engaged in interclass dynamics that did not entail being shamed or uplifted.

The Charleston "craze" was central to these class dynamics as Walrond addressed them in *Vanity Fair*. It was preposterous, he felt, that this dance was identified with Broadway or imagined to have its source with any choreographer. He sought the origins of this "dance which is exciting the mineral, animal, emotional, and vegetable life of the United States" ("Charleston" 73). The absurdity, for Walrond, was not just the zealous appropriation of black forms, it was the proliferation of claims to having originated something that was "an integrally triumphant part of every show and musical comedy of consequence in New York," a figure for black expressiveness itself (73). He satirized the eagerness among whites to locate racial authenticity in an urban, black middle class. A "new profession" had arisen in Harlem: "Charleston instructor."

> The mulatto maids of white actresses, in addition to their traditional chores of teaching their principals how to sing darky songs or talk "nigger" talk, are now engaged with an eye to their dexterity at dancing the Charleston. Coloured men [. . .] are engaged to conduct classes in the Charleston to which come the smart folk of Park Avenue. And in Greenwich Village the new symbol of revolt is for some flame-eyed, dusk-faced Shelley [. . .] to jump up and down [. . .] yelling "Charleston, Hey! Hey!" (73)

The irony was that none of them possessed an uncomplicated claim to the Charleston, whose source, Walrond contended, was the black belt of the American South. Cabaret dancers and "Negro theatres" adapted it, devising "new projections in rhythm." Black performers, "freed from the trappings of character" at the end of long nights onstage, repaired to Lenox Avenue's Capitol Club and "invented most of the steps and

4.6 Photograph of Carl Van Vechten, self-portrait, 1934.

defended *Nigger Heaven* against criticism. Van Vechten's journals and correspondence convey the depth of their devotion. Harold Jackman confessed, "You are the first white man with whom I have felt perfectly at ease. You are just like a colored man! I don't know if you will consider this a compliment or not, but that's the only way I can put it."[102] Hughes wished "I could write you every day if it meant getting your delightful notes in return."[103] Cynics may say Hughes had every reason to charm the man who was at that moment helping place *The Weary Blues* with Knopf, but the evidence does not support simplistic accounts of these relationships.

Admittedly, Walrond made use of Van Vechten's interest. When they met, Van Vechten was contemplating a proposal from George Gershwin to collaborate on a "Negro" themed opera.[104] Four days later, however, he was contemplating a solo project instead. "I've been thinking more about the opera & I have more ideas," he told his wife, "but I'm sure Gershwin wants something different, and nothing will come of it. In that case I think I'll write a Negro novel."[105] It would be another year before he began *Nigger Heaven*, but Walrond clearly met him at its germinal stage. He gave Van Vechten some of his work to read, most likely the cabaret writing, which Crowninshield published in the following year. One November afternoon found Van Vechten "reading Eric Walrond's manuscripts" between perusal of "some extraordinary pornographic Japanese prints" and dinner with Edna Kenton.[106] He responded eagerly, "You are, I think, one of the three most promising younger talents that I have run into during the past three years. I am particularly delighted that you write as an artist and not as a defender of the faith. You do not apologize or explain or exhort—you set down the truth as you see it. More than that —you can write!"[107]

Walrond saw Van Vechten regularly that winter. Although much of their activity involved "respectable" events, they had many queer companions and disreputable destinations. Queer Harlem was as much a draw for Van Vechten as black Harlem, and he frequented speakeasies and buffet flats such as Buddie Baker's and Cecil Fields' catering to a gay crowd. At the home of Lewis Baer, an editor at Albert & Charles Boni, they joined parties of gay cabaret performers. As well, Walrond introduced Van Vechten to African American women he may not have met otherwise, including Dorothy Peterson, A'Lelia Walker, Nora Holt, Nella Larsen, Ethel Ray Nance, and Regina Anderson. With and without them, Walrond and Van Vechten frequented cabarets where Van Vechten diligently recorded the names of waiters and dancers. Despite nursing what he called "a powerful hangover" one Wednesday in early 1925, he was delighted to have Walrond appear at his door accompanied by Jean Toomer, whom he had never met. They were joined by Cullen, Jackman, Gipsy Johnson, and Donald Angus, "who does the Charleston." Two nights later, Walrond returned to Van Vechten's for a dinner with an extensive interracial guest list. Hardly a night passed that a fascinating personage failed to lure Van Vechten out: "After dinner, about 10, we go to bed," he wrote in March. "But Tallulah Bankhead telephones & we go over to the Gotham to drink champagne with her & her maid."[108]

As Walrond introduced Van Vechten to Harlem he extended his own connections downtown. The transition was not without its attending anxieties. Walrond was proud, for example, that *The Independent* published his essay on Garvey but worried that Van Vechten would criticize it. "I hope you will not fail to recall that it was originally done for the Russian Bolshevik press and was later cut down and tightened up to suit the exigencies of local consumption."[109] This was the same letter in which he called himself a "pitiable object for a Freudian psychologist" and "a terrible searcher after things that are not always clear to me." Walrond's routine of working hard and playing harder was, it seems, a strategy for coping with the depression he could not dispel. Lamenting his "boorish" propensity for offending people, he worried about his "sorry condition."

> [I]t will probably mean that half of the people whom I care about most in the world will sooner or later pass me up entirely or graciously and charitably let it go at that . . . All of which is sometimes quite distressing to me. I have however managed to effect an escape in my work and the multitudinous things I am fond of, such as bumming around Harlem, sitting at the feet of women like Rose McClendon or absorbing the inimitable chatter flying about one in an unabashed Negro cabaret.

His experience was at odds with the effulgence of Van Vechten's accounts. One evening Walrond took him and Avery Hopwood to 580 ("a lot of girls and Winold Reiss") and on to A'Lelia Walker's ("more people but no drinks") where he parted ways with Van Vechten, who went to dance at the Bamville Nest until 4 a.m. But instead of returning home, he went "to join Eric at Small's."[110] From Van Vechten's account, it was another Roaring Twenties night on the town, but Walrond's letter the next day puts it in a desultory light.

I think it was exceedingly fine of you to leave your friends and come to Small's last night just to counsel with me. I am sure no man could wish for a diviner manifestation of interest and concern. Your words kept recurring to me so that I simply had to jot this off to you. You remember you once told me whenever I needed a firm hand-clasp (there is no attempt here to be literal) that I was at liberty to call on you? Well, here I am.[111]

He was desperate for reassurance. Van Vechten must have told him to avoid petty arguments and not fret about his impetuousness.

Yes, I realize if I am to get on that I've got to stop annoying people on grounds that are absolutely senseless. I really do not know why I should be this way. Outwardly I know I am incapable of perpetrating any injury on anyone; but inwardly or rather unconsciously I am beginning to suspect that I must be vicious or vituperative or something of the kind. All of which, of course, is unimportant as you so generously indicated to me last night. Of course all the items that have ever got me in Dutch with people have been of a decidedly perishable quality, but I did them either as exercises in certain forms of contemporary expression or as a means of keeping the wolf at bay.

The last assertion is especially perplexing. What "forms of contemporary expression" had caused offense? What "wolf" was he keeping at bay, and by what means? He felt like his own worst enemy, inadvertently sabotaging his self-presentation. The word "remorse" began appearing frequently in Van Vechten's journals too, notes Bruce Kellner, "always after a night of heavy drinking, although the context often suggests some other activity for which remorse might have been inevitable."[112] After staying out late with Walrond, Toomer, and Jackman at Small's and the Nest, Van Vechten arose "at 10 with a hangover and remorse." The high life was not easy for either man to sustain.

In a sense, this was a tremendous period for Walrond. "Kit Skyhead" ran in the same issue of *Vanity Fair* as Van Vechten's article on Gershwin;

his essay "The Negro Literati" appeared; and *The New Republic* published his review of Walter White's *Fire in the Flint*. *Opportunity* announced that his "Voodoo's Revenge" won a prize in its first fiction contest, and Crowninshield wanted more for *Vanity Fair*, "a series of Harlem personalities."[113] After a Paul Robeson concert in Greenwich Village, Walrond spoke to Waldo Frank, who had guided Toomer's *Cane* to Horace Liveright, and Frank said "to be sure and send him a batch of my stuff."[114] He suffered no lack of attention from women, some of whom—such as Louella Tucker, A'Lelia Walker, and Rita Romilly—may have been his lovers. Of Romilly, a white actress who taught at the American Academy of Dramatic Arts, Van Vechten wrote, "I think [she] is going to have an affair with Eric. She sees him at every conceivable moment."[115]

Moreover, he had become an ambassador for the younger generation. Locke relied on him to provide editorial assistance to *New Negro* contributors, and he issued invitations to guests of the Writers Guild.[116] But no one praised his ambassadorship more glowingly than Aaron Douglas, who arrived in 1925 and became one of the most celebrated visual artists of the Harlem Renaissance. Although he was broke and unemployed, Douglas wrote optimistically to his fiancée in Kansas City that Walrond and a friend of his, a retail store promoter, were "enthusiastic over my prospects." "Eric is a wonderful fellow," Douglas added, "I venture to say there isn't another fellow in town anywhere near his age with as wide an acquaintance."[117]

> Well, sweetheart, my two friends Emanuel Pomerantz and Eric Walrond have kept my head above water. They have been brothers to me in the truest sense of the word. They not only aided me, but would raise—with me for saying I had money when I didn't. I haven't yet ask[ed] either for a cent, but they never see me without placing some cash at my disposal. [. . .] Walrond's hot after a scholarship for me, and might get it.

Having met Douglas in Kansas City, Walrond sought to ease his transition and introduce him around. In fact, Locke felt Walrond overreached on Douglas's behalf. Told that Walrond was "handling" Douglas's work, placing it "in the hands of several editors, Vanity Fair and the Boston Transcript," Locke "appeared quite fussed. He told me in pretty good English that he could do more with my work than Walrond." Further illustrating his activity on behalf of emerging artists, Walrond helped secure Casper Holstein's financial support for the *Opportunity* contests.[118]

However, early 1925 took a severe toll on Walrond's mental health. One week after the *Opportunity* banquet that May, at which he was awarded third prize for fiction, he wrote Joseph Freeman, "I am particularly depressed these days, that is why I didn't write you before, and I am actually engaged in the absorbing process of counting the minutes of my existence—as if I were a condemned man."[119] Alarmed, Freeman replied, "The words in your letter which moved me most were the dark ones about counting minutes like a condemned man. I hurry to write: has the reprieve come yet? It does, sooner or later; even for us who so violently swing between heaven and hell." It is an exchange between people who understand themselves as depressives, suffering the "violent swings" of what today might be considered bipolar disorder. Walrond's behavior grew erratic, upsetting Van Vechten. When he stopped by Walrond's apartment, they walked to an antique bookstore and then dropped in on Hurston and Sol Johnson, finding neither. Returning to "Eric's room," he surprised Van Vechten by abruptly making "another engagement." Van Vechten stormed out "not very pleased," but the next morning Walrond called to apologize.[120] This was the day he wrote of feeling like "a condemned man."

Walrond's private expressions of pain are at striking odds with the litany of successes and festivities he enjoyed. Consider that the weekend before his "condemned man" note he attended the *Opportunity* awards dinner and Paul Robeson's performance, after which he made a promising pitch to Waldo Frank, then joined Fauset, White, Romilly, Jackman, the Van Dorens, and Hurston for a party at the home of Winold Reiss. And Nora Holt danced nude! Nowhere are the antinomies of Walrond's experience thrown into starker relief than in this first week of May 1925. Concerned for his friend's well-being, Freeman suggested Walrond contact

Roger Baldwin to see about finding him a job. Baldwin was the executive director of the ACLU and the son of the Urban League cofounder, Ruth Standish Baldwin. He was well connected in New York, and Walrond not only contacted him, he poured out his soul. "I told him everything," he wrote Freeman, "Just what I was up against, what I wanted to do, what I felt I could do, what I had done, whence I came and wither I ought to be bound . . . I told him that I felt I ought to be attached pretty soon to something definite—that if after the summer I didn't get what I wanted (or an approximation of that) I should go back to the sea and the easy death that comes with it."

But Walrond did not hear from Baldwin and asked Freeman to follow up. "I will soon," he replied, "to find out what he has done to save you from the sea."[121] That night, Walrond and Louella Tucker went to Small's, where they met Van Vechten and Lawrence Langner, founder of the Theatre Guild and the Washington Square Players. He and Tucker joined Van Vechten a week later to attend Regina Anderson's birthday party. Walrond and Van Vechten left there for the Bamville Nest, and this was the last anyone saw of Walrond for a long time. Two days later, A'Lelia Walker gave a benefit for Augusta Savage and, although many of his friends attended, Walrond was absent. The following weekend the regular crew made the usual rounds—Small's, the Nest—but without Walrond. He even missed Countée Cullen's college graduation party.[122]

That Walrond was not at peace is clear in his attenuated correspondence with Van Vechten. One attempt at reconciliation was a birthday telegram, a plaintive message. "I've exhausted half a dozen telegraph blanks trying to send you an appropriate birthday greeting and all I can get out of my sluggish bean is a gentle handclasp for you today. Tiger flowers and honeysuckle." He signed himself, "Your Harlem Buddy." The other was a letter that sounded newsy but betrayed evidence of its author's turmoil, continually calling attention to its own failures of expression. "This isn't the sort of letter I want to write you," it began, "But a bad beginning is better, I think, than no beginning at all."[123] The letter consists of thought fragments, and Walrond's failure to express himself satisfactorily is legible in its very structure, each incompleteness occasioning a postscript, which in turn occasioned another postscript. Each item he raised to impress or hearten Van Vechten or himself failed.

> Covarrubias has done a marvelous drawing to illustrate the Vanity Fair article and the other day when I was down there Mr. Crowninshield spoke to me about another article—a series of vignettes of Harlem personalities. I am, I think, to see either him or Miss Case further about it.
>
> While I am at it, I know you'd be interested to know that I took to Mr. Rose yesterday the article I did on "The Negro Literati" for "Brentano's Book Chat" and he said it was the best thing he'd had for the number.
>
> I've got a new story—a *story* this time—"Black Hawk" and I'm just itching for an opportunity to have you read it.
>
> Yours very sincerely,
> Eric
>
> p.s. Oh, never mind, but this is terrible. I intended adding, "When do I see you again?" E.
>
> p.s. #2 I got a note from Bob Littell of the "New Republic" the other day saying that my review of Walter White's book is scheduled to appear soon. Quoting from that letter, I find that, according to the review, "it sounds like a book I must read." So much for that . . .
>
> I had Roland Hayes on the telephone last night and he certainly relished the idea of coming to see you. He had a terrible cold and I am wondering how his concert came off tonight. He told me that he is leaving town immediately after the concert tonight and won't be back this way again before the 27th when he fills another engagement.
>
> In the meantime I am to communicate with him and if nothing untoward takes place he feels certain he'll be able, if it is convenient to you, to take advantage of your splendid interest.
>
> E.

I don't know whether this will interest you or not, but Monday, Jun. 19 there's going to be a performance of the National Ethiopian Theatre at the New Manhattan Casino . . .

I've got tickets for it and this morning one of the most charming ladies in the world called me up and asked me if I wouldn't be so nice as to sit in her box, etc. In that box, I assure you, will be some women like Mme. Walker whom it wouldn't be a bad thing for you to know . . .

But anyway, don't let me sell the idea to you. I promise if you can possibly make it that these girls will make it pretty interesting for you . . .

Eric

There are no fewer than four attempts to close the letter. In light of Walrond's precipitous decline and the birthday telegram sent the same day, it reads like a document of despair.

Locke was concerned about him now. Walrond had still not completed "The Mirrors of Harlem" and Locke met with him to discuss it. A few days later, Locke visited Van Vechten to discuss "Langston Hughes, Eric Walrond, Spirituals & other matters."[124] The next day, Walrond sounded chastened in sending Locke the revision: "I have tried my best to adhere to every suggestion you made while we went over it Sunday, and I hope I have succeeded in making it just as you want it." Though addressed lightheartedly to "My dear Lockus," the letter was signed formally, "With best regards, I beg to remain, Your devoted friend, Eric."[125] The self-reproach extended into the following month, when he apologized to Locke for being such a recluse and missing him "the innumerable times you called."[126] Walrond did not attend Van Vechten's "wild" forty-fifth birthday party, nor did he join Romilly and Van Vechten on the train two weeks later to visit A'Lelia Walker at her estate on the Hudson. He did not see Van Vechten again until the *Crisis* awards ceremony that summer, and thereafter their encounters were few and far between, always at public gatherings, and never discussed in Van Vechten's journal.[127] Walrond referred obliquely to the depression that consumed his spring and summer when he told Locke in August of "the chaotic state of affairs surrounding me."

These struggles had acquainted Walrond with what his Columbia writing teacher, Dorothy Scarborough, called "the night side of the soul," dimensions of himself that resisted rationality or conscious direction. In response, he had taken refuge in the night side of Harlem's soul, a libidinal subculture that mirrored in reverse the self-disciplined community of strivers projected by the proponents of racial uplift. But he had trouble sustaining it, and the drinking, dancing, carousing, arguing, and apologizing seem to have been palliative measures, failing to fulfill his ambition, which traveled the traditional channels of intellectual labor and publication. Nor did they express his ethnic difference, to which he clung despite his devotion to African American culture. Fortunately, two important developments in the summer of 1925 helped stabilize Walrond's mental health and impose order on "the chaotic state of affairs surrounding me."

One was the offer of a position as business manager at *Opportunity*, which he assumed in August. It is unclear precisely how the job came about, but Joseph Freeman was likely involved, given his relationship with Urban League officers. It helped that Walrond had published in *Opportunity*, won a fiction prize, secured Holstein's funding for the contests, and collaborated with Charles Johnson. Walrond's versatility made him a good fit, bridging *Opportunity*'s dual mission to cover "the social and economic problems affecting Negro life" and to promote "Negro authors, creative writers, and artists."[128] Walrond's time at *Opportunity* was brief, but it was a pivotal period for the journal, which nearly doubled its circulation.[129] His administrative savvy became instrumental as the journal expanded its contests and roster of artists. Two of Walrond's friends joined the staff: Gwendolyn Bennett wrote the column "The Ebony Flute" from 1926 to 1928 and Countée Cullen, who completed a master's degree at Harvard, returned to New York and wrote the column "The Dark Tower" until 1928.

The other stabilizing development in the summer of 1925 was literary. Walrond was writing new material and felt cautiously optimistic.

He told Locke in July, "I've been doing a lot of stuff since I last saw you, but much of it, I imagine, is a bit too esoteric for provincial consumption."[130] These were the stories that became *Tropic Death*, none of them set in the United States. This new fiction attempted at least two things without precedent in North America. He attended to "peasant" life in the Caribbean from an insider's perspective, rooting it in the experience of colonial subjectivity. And he enlisted in this effort an engagement with Caribbean folk speech that did not reduce it to mere dialect and was so intricate and extensive that it could not be heard as local color or narrative tourism.

We may be inured today to the strangeness of Walrond's project because Caribbean diaspora writers have developed sophisticated models for such an engagement. But one need only recall how recently Caribbean speech attained literary status to grasp the audacity of his effort in the 1920s. Even Claude McKay, who published Creole verse in Jamaica, was only persuaded to do it by an Englishman who believed somewhat fatuously that it was McKay's most natural voice. Stuart Hall suggests the audacity of Walrond's project in his remarks on Caribbean English.

> To encounter people who can speak to one another in exactly that transformation of Standard English which is patois, which is creole— the hundreds of different creole and semi-creole languages that cover the face of the Caribbean in one place or another—that these have become, as it were, the languages in which important things can be said, in which important aspirations and hopes can be formulated, in which an important grasp of the histories that have made these places can be written down, in which artists are willing, for the first time, the first generation, to practise, that is what I call a cultural revolution.[131]

Walrond wrote a generation before the revolution to which Hall refers. It was a quixotic choice to employ Caribbean English to formulate important hopes and aspirations, to say important things, and to record an important grasp of the histories that made these places. He risked being misread and, as we will see, he often was.

5

TROPIC DEATH

Tropic Death is a strange and brutal book, "a work of blistering imaginative power."[1] Written for a North American audience, it nevertheless refused to make the Caribbean easily accessible. Relying heavily on reported speech, it is an extended exercise in code switching, moving deftly between vernaculars and linguistic registers. A number of Caribbean dialects vie on the page with the narrator's Standard English, and Caribbean place names and practices are rarely explained. In this sense, it is a terrifically impertinent performance. Four stories are set in Barbados, one in British Guiana, one on a ship between Honduras and Jamaica, and four in Panama. Reading it was a bracing experience, even for those who had visited the region. One reviewer admitted, "To those of us who know the West Indies as a pleasant winter resort, [. . .] Eric Walrond's picture is like a stunning blow. One asks oneself, can it be true?"[2]

But Walrond was not just asserting an alternate truth about the Caribbean, he was revising the very terms of discussion. The book was primarily read for realism at the time, and although it often achieves a sort of verisimilitude, it frustrates realist expectations. Walrond abhorred what he felt was a tendency to disguise sociological tracts as novels and associated great fiction with the imaginative flights of romanticism, introducing supernatural elements into plausible plots. In one sense then,

Tropic Death delivered the "stunning blow" of an alternate Caribbean truth but, in another sense, it contested truth telling itself, presaging the Martinican writer Edouard Glissant's conception of the novel of the Americas: "Realism—that is, the logical and rational attitude toward the visible world—more than anywhere else would in our case betray the true meaning of things."[3] *Tropic Death* pursued this paradoxical project of depicting "the true meaning" of the Caribbean by discarding "the logical and rational attitude toward the visible world."

The book was eagerly anticipated in New York, where its publisher Horace Liveright was a minor celebrity. In her *Opportunity* column, Gwendolyn Bennett wrote, "I can scarcely wait for the book to be on the market. . . . Few of the Negro writers that are being heralded on all sides today can begin to create the color that fairly rolls itself from Mr. Walrond's facile pen. *Tropic Death* ought to have that ripe color that is usually the essence of Mr. Walrond's writing."[4] As he finished the manuscript, he hoped it would put him in contention for a coveted prize, the Harmon Award, given annually "for distinguished achievement among Negroes" in several fields. He would have to wait a year to win it but the endorsements he received indicated the expectations for his book—from the editor of *Forbes* magazine to the Urban League's executive director to Donald Friede of Boni & Liveright, who called *Tropic Death* "as fine as anything it has been my fortune to read in the last few years. I believe that Mr. Walrond has more real literary ability than all of the other negro writers put together." Although he did not prevail that year, Walrond's application drew attention to the book in advance of its publication.[5]

Walrond had long considered how to depict Caribbean life in fiction. At twenty-three, he wrote in *Negro World* about the Anglo-American tradition, which he called "literary sailoring."

One of the joys of literary sailoring is to picture the moral depravity of the black. The travel literature of Africa and the West Indies, and paradoxical as it may seem, of our own Dixie, is full of this sort of thing. A Boston adventurer, let us say, goes to Turkey, or Martinique, or to a

Spanish-American seaport. The first thing that attracts his attention is the awful lack of economic life, the free and unrestricted gratification of the sex instinct and the universal lowering of moral standards. He judges the native not by a local standard of things, but a far-fetched idealistic one. The art, morals, science, religion, and literature of a country [are] examined without regard to the country's history, geography, or anything else. [But] if one were to proceed on the basis of absolute equality in the human family an unprejudiced investigator may prove that all is not hopeless with the darker race. ("Morality" 4)

What would it mean to write "by a local standard of things," "to proceed on the basis of absolute equality in the human family"? To take account of the region's history, geography, and value systems? Models were few and far between. Beyond questions of authorial perspective stood questions of form. What would such a literature sound like? What shape would it take? After all, Caribbean poet Edward Kamau Brathwaite has said, "The hurricane does not roar in pentameters."[6]

Walrond felt compelled to write Caribbean fiction not only to correct a distorting tradition but for the affirmative reason that the region offered an untapped wealth of material. He asserted its "intrinsic artistic worth" in 1927.

In legends, folklore, and the primary essentials of a folk-literature, the islands abound. Rich in superstition, witchcraft, and Anancy tales, having in its cities and towns a social life quite as gay and abandoned as any to be met with in Venice or Milan; equipped with a climate that is designed to give color and ease to the pursuit of the native life, it is a bit disconcerting to find in the output of the native, with perhaps one or two ineffectual exceptions, none but the remotest idea of the intrinsic artistic worth of all this. Indeed, the poets and creative writers of the West Indies, who, it seems, are just beginning to get excited over the literary traditions of Europe and the British Isles, succeed usually in giving little more than a pretty continentalized version of the life of their exotic tropic heath. ("Color" 227)

Literary imitation of European models is disparaged for producing derivative, inferior work. But if Walrond wished to break with tradition, no obvious models existed. It would be seven years before McKay wrote *Banana Bottom*, ten before C. L. R. James wrote *Minty Alley*, and a whole generation before the Barbadian Brooklynite Paule Marshall wrote *Brown Girl, Brownstones*. "[W]riters of African American descent provided Walrond's fiction with no clear and direct models," notes Carl Wade, and the existing Caribbean fiction—"a handful of texts by white Jamaican writers"—was of limited utility.[7] *Tropic Death* was not *sui generis*, but the quality and force of its originality are stunning. Its relationship to available traditions is worth exploring, for Wade is right that it was at once their product and their rejection.[8]

Realism has a distinctive resonance in discussions of African American literature. Generally understood to mean verisimilitude in character and dialogue, probabilism at the plot level, and a repudiation of sentimentality, in its African American literary context realism meant a departure from the tradition of buffoonish or cloying "Negro" characters and a willingness to depict not only the virtuous and successful of the race but also its raffish and disreputable members. Realism was a contested term, a proxy for arguments about class, popular reading, and literature's relationship to journalism and photography. But even as Anglo-American modernists arrayed themselves against realism, African Americans tended to use realism and modernism interchangeably; to become modern meant discarding shopworn tropes and writing authentically about the race, showing things "as they are." Thus, the rhetorical divergence between realism and modernism in interwar Anglo-American writing was not mirrored in African American letters, despite the efforts of Toomer, Hughes, and Hurston to challenge realist constraints. Like much of their work, *Tropic Death* was excessive; it could pass for realism but announced its status as a linguistic performance, calling attention to its formal construction. It was difficult. Despite continued efforts to read it back into the domain of literary realism, and despite its engagement with material conditions in the Caribbean, it is a spectacular failure on realist grounds.

To be sure, geography and folk life appear in meticulous detail. Readers learn the differences among the lush verdure of the Guyanese coast, the marl roads of Barbados, and the tenements of Colón, between life above and below deck on a steamship plying Caribbean waters. Structures of class and race reveal themselves through dialogue and exposition rather than the didactic voice of an intrusive narrator. And in Walrond's greatest feat, speech is rendered with a careful ear for diction and pronunciation, a massive project in making the Caribbean audible. Thus, one could imagine it as realistic, a transcript of the author's observations. Finally, the book was averse to sentimentality, the realist's bête noire. Walrond's refusal to sugarcoat the squalor of his characters' lives, to dignify their motives, or to pull punches in resolving his storylines was the most consistent observation contemporary readers made. It was partly a question of plot; Walrond devised as many ways for his characters to perish as there were stories in the collection, each ending in a casualty. Three are murdered in cold blood, three fall prey to supernatural phenomena, and four die of ostensibly natural causes: disease, fire, malnutrition, and shark attack. But the book's antisentimentality was also a question of tone; the struggles and deaths are handled with clinical detachment.[9] Many take place offscreen, as it were, reported after the fact with ironic understatement. One hears in the ending of "Subjection"—a story about an insubordinate West Indian laborer who is chased off his Canal Zone worksite and shot by a marine—a precursor to Chinua Achebe's conclusion to *Things Fall Apart*. There, the death of the rebellious colonial Okonkwo is abstracted into a tally mark in a bureaucrat's ledger. "Subjection" ends similarly, "In the Canal Record, the QM at Toro Point took occasion to extol the virtues of the Department which kept the number of casualties in the recent native labor uprising down to one" (111). Walrond's tone suggested that the severity of Afro-Caribbean experience should be rendered with implacable directness. For this quality as much as his unhappy endings he was considered realistic.

The fact was, few North American readers could gainsay his representation of Caribbean folkways and speech, so a great deal of what passed for authentic was a projection. Readers hoping to find evidence of life as it was truly lived in the tropics were encouraged by Walrond's vivid evocations to feel satisfied. Certainly it was the promise Boni & Liveright made, calling the book "realistically drawn," its stories "a cross-section of tropical Negro experience." Happily for Boni & Liveright, what was "realistic" on Caribbean terms was extraordinary for others, conveniently fusing the book's realist and antirealist qualities.

> Only the exotic intermingling of races below the Gulf Stream could yield such a bountiful harvest. Culled from a varied and authentic experience, Eric Walrond's work is stark, brilliant, true. There is poetry, folk essence in it. [. . .] The people who come within the range of the author's vision are as colorful as a pheasant. They are British whites— buckra johnnies—and upstage blacks, senoritas and wordy West Indians, American marines and Latin seamen. It gives a cross-section of tropical life indeed.[10]

Framed as a survey, *Tropic Death* was offered as a distillation of "folk essence." Not poetry, though there was "poetry in it," another gesture reconciling objectivity and creative license, realism and lyricism. They went on to anoint Walrond as unique, but by negation: "With this book the least sentimental of Negro prose writers arrives." Publicity blurbs may tell us little about publishers' real opinions, but they say a lot about what they thought readers valued. The absence of sentimentality was emphasized, as was the novelty of the subject, for with Walrond's arrival "a region hitherto steeped in utter mist looms broodingly on the literary horizon." Boni & Liveright may have imagined African Americans among *Tropic Death*'s readers, but the target audience was mainly white readers who considered themselves cosmopolitan and progressive.[11]

The most significant statement may be one in which the copywriter hazarded a bit of literary history: "Stories by American negroes have busied themselves largely with problems of race either in the South or in our larger northern cities. Here, for the first time, are purely objective stories, devoid of prejudice, propaganda, or excessive race consciousness."[12] It is striking that Walrond is not distinguished from "American negroes," given the importance of his Caribbeanness to the book's publicity. More striking still are the terms in which Walrond's priority is established: the first to illuminate a "region hitherto steeped in utter mist"; the first "Negro" to write objectively, without "prejudice, propaganda, or excessive race consciousness." It is a willful misreading of the book, but revealing of the problematic as it stood at the time. Boni & Liveright similarly endorsed *There Is Confusion* as "a new sort of book about colored people" because of what it lacked: "no lynchings, no inferiority complexes, no *propaganda*."[13]

In fact, *Tropic Death* makes some of the most strident anticolonial statements in early-twentieth-century fiction and expresses a profound race consciousness. Only its lyricism and painterly quality obscure these commitments. "Once a day the Rums ate," Walrond writes of an impoverished Barbadian family in "Drought." "At dusk, curve of crimson gold in the sensuous tropic sky, they had tea. English to a degree, it was a rite absurdly regal. Pauperized native blacks clung to the utmost vestiges of the Crown" (31). The imagery and sibilance of the prose compete for attention with the substantive claim, the absurdity of "pauperized" islanders imitating their colonial rulers. Far from evading questions of imperial power, Walrond dramatizes them vividly, as in his approach to a shark attack—a tourist ship "came near. Huddled in thick European coats, the passengers viewed from their lofty estate the spectacle of two naked Negro boys peeping up at them from a wiggly *bateau*. 'Penny, mistah, penny mistah!' Somebody dropped a quarter. Ernest, like a shot, flew after it. Half a foot down he caught it as it twisted and turned in the gleaming sea" (80). When his brother dives into the shark-infested waters the crowd gasps, "Where has the nigger swimmer gone to?" (73). In another story, a West Indian mother explains to her "vagabond" son his stark options in Panama: "Yo' go to work, sah, an' besides, who is to feed me if yo' don't wuk? Who—answer me dat! Boy yo' bes' mek up yo' min' an' get under de heel o' de backra" (103). As her designation of the Canal Authority as "de backra" suggests, rule is rule whether English or American. This is also made plain in "Subjection," where a laborer provokes a U.S. foreman, who retorts, "I'll show you goddam niggers how to talk back to a white man" (111). The political dimension of these stories is barely concealed by their stylized surface, but style was critical to the book's presentation as "devoid of propaganda" and "excessive" race consciousness.

More important than its individual storylines, the collection traces the tumultuous process of migration and acculturation so many Caribbean residents experienced. Significantly, this is not represented as natural or inevitable but the result of contingent forces bound closely to capitalist development in the hemisphere. *Tropic Death* is a narrative of the entry of the Caribbean into industrial modernity, the transition of its inhabitants from estate labor and small farming to proletarianization. Tillers of the soil have become industrial workers, provincial estates are abandoned for markets, and the serfs and squatters of the old order now collect wages at the pay car. Culture provides continuity, linking back home through evangelical Christianity and familiar foods. Even the stories set outside Panama reveal its influence throughout the region as a labor market, a catalyst for disaggregating and reconfiguring communities.

Despite these concerns, the book passed as "objective" because its prose suggested a break with the politics of racial representation. It moved with the lapidary style and syntactic compression of much American modernism: "Blue cassava—unfit for cakes—about to be grated and pressed for starch; withering twigs, half-ripe turnips, *bolonjays* a languid flood of green and purple, a graveler—a watery corklike potato endwardly dangling; a greedy sow, tugging at a stake, a crusty, squib-smoked 'touch bam'" (116). Moreover, because it was set in the Caribbean, *Tropic Death*'s relationship to American race relations was equivocal. The impression the book gives of impartiality on the charged issue of race arises from a displacement. Walrond evoked the figure of the "Negro" only to conjure him away, still speaking eccentrically but now in new sounds. Locating *Tropic Death* in the Caribbean, he avoided the pitfalls of the two established literary traditions: the plantation tradition, suffused with sentimentality and stereotypes, and the protest tradition, often disparaged as artless. In fact, strong elements of both traditions persisted in *Tropic Death*, but its Caribbean location invited claims for its novelty.

Walrond challenged the North American tendency to see race first, ignoring intraracial differences. Mr. Poyer, recently returned to Barbados in the story "Panama Gold," runs a grocery that Ella Heath visits one afternoon. A kindly neighbor alerted her that Poyer lost a leg, "Got it cut off on de canal" (39). As Ella approaches, Poyer boasts to his friend, Bruin, of having forced the Canal Authority to pay damages by invoking his British citizenship.

> "Pay me," I says, "or I'll sick de British bulldog on all yo' Omericans!" [. . .] I let dem understand quick enough dat I wuz a Englishman and not a bleddy American nigger! A' Englishman—big distinction in dat, Bruing! And dat dey couldn't do as dey bleddy well please wit' a subject o' de King! Whuh? I carry on like a rattlesnake. Carry on like a true Bimshah. (44)

We may not be meant to take Poyer's bravado at face value, but the strategic use of the legal protections of the Crown did constitute an intervention in business as usual in Panama, and Walrond's strategic use of Poyer challenged prevalent assumptions about who built the canal and who was a "Negro." Poyer's refusal to be taken for "a bleddy American nigger," his claim to Englishness, reflects an important tension. Intraracial differences were not only cherished elements of cultural identity, they were matters of legal consequence.

Poyer's account was at odds with the Panama mythology Americans knew. In this respect, it exemplifies *Tropic Death*'s broader concern to articulate a counter-narrative about the region and about Panama in particular. This involved dramatizing a collision between West Indian life as elaborated under colonial rule and industrial modernity as administered by North Americans. It also involved changing the grammar of history, transposing Caribbean people into the subjects of the narrative not merely its objects. Finally, as important as the story were the voices, for as Walrond knew the voices were themselves the story.

AN EAR FOR THE TROPICS

Panama was central to the mythology of the United States' emergence on the global stage through ingenuity rather than force. It is "a tale enshrined in popular memory and innumerable histories and novels," notes historian Julie Greene, the United States becoming "a world leader at the very moment when World War I broke out and split the nations of Europe apart."[14] Despite adversity and against all odds, the Panama Canal succeeded through the Americans' steadfast resolve and native genius—so goes the popular narrative.[15] Starting with the French attempt in the 1880s, the U.S. popular press had been intrigued by the canal, but the U.S. revival of the project fired the public imagination, and periodicals sought to convey the grandeur of the project's scale and instill national pride.[16] Its completion occasioned public expositions, extolling the project as a triumph of the American character and suppressing the imperial dimension of the U.S. occupation and the role of West Indian labor.

Tropic Death exploited this popular fascination but challenged its premises. Instead of casting Panama as a testament to American ingenuity and civilization, Walrond wrote about its laborers, their families, and their communities. North Americans had been encouraged to imagine the area in touristic terms, "one of the world's greatest travel thrills." *My Trip Through the Panama Canal*, authorized by the U.S. Canal Administration, called itself "an accurate guide to the Panama Canal" without one reference to Panamanians. On its cover, smartly dressed tourists populate the deck of a steamship passing through the canal locks, parasols and bowler hats shading their eyes as they observe the lush forest and lounge on divans. "Not even the pyramids of Gizeh, for centuries counted the greatest of man-made wonders, can compare with the Panama Canal," it read, "The pyramids stand for the mystic past; the Canal is an imperishable tribute to the genius of the present."[17] The canal not only heralded the momentous entry of the United States into world affairs, it was also a gorgeous spectacle, replete with "flowers amidst the green along the shores," "waving foliage of banana plantations," "purple slopes of the mountains in the Continental Divide," and "red roofed military stations."

A feast for the senses and spur to the imagination, the canal was framed as pleasurable and picturesque.

Walrond wrote explicitly against the grain of this mythology, beginning "The Wharf Rats," a story set on the outskirts of Colón, with the labor behind the spectacle.

> Down in the Cut drifted hordes of Italians, Greeks, Chinese, Negroes—a hardy, sun-defying set of white, black, and yellow men. But the bulk of the actual brawn for the work was supplied by the dusky peons of those coral isles in the Caribbean ruled by Britain, France, and Holland. At the Atlantic end of the Canal the blacks were herded in boxcar huts buried in the jungles of Silver City; in the murky tenements perilously poised on the narrow banks of Faulke's River; in the low, smelting cabins of Coco Té. (67)

He affirmed the vivid pictorial quality associated with the region—its human mosaic—but restored a black presence and colonial history. He also introduced the Colón Man, around whom an entire mythology formed in the Caribbean.[18] The Colón Man was the prodigal son who returned to his island, resplendent in his new wealth, talking "Yankee" and acting proud. As *Tropic Death* indicates, he was regarded with a mix of envy and suspicion. Ella Heath, the Barbadian protagonist of "Panama Gold," smells arrogance on Poyer, the shopkeeper who lost his leg in Panama. "T'ink dat ev'y ooman is de same," she accuses him, "But yo' is a dam liar! Nutting can frighten me. All dem bag o' flour yo' a' got, an' dem silk shut, an' dem gold teets, an' dem Palama hats, yo' a spote round heah wid—dem don't frighten me. I is a woman what is usta t'ings" (47). Just as Poyer meets his death in a house fire in this story, others dramatize the plight of the Colón Man, both on the islands and the isthmus. Given this concern, it is striking that several of *Tropic Death*'s protagonists are women; six of its ten stories are devoted to women's experiences and the challenges of motherhood in particular.

Tropic Death also left no doubt that Panama was a new American frontier. "The Palm Porch," first published in *The New Negro*, was revised to amplify this critique. It originally began by introducing at length the owner of the brothel of the story's title. It proceeded to describe the surrounding area, transformed by dredges from a swamp into a habitable plain, but it cast the Americans as civilizers: "Before the Revolution it was a black, evil forest-swamp. Deer, lions, mongooses and tiger cats went prowling through it. Then the Americans came . . . came with saw and spear, tar and Lysol. About to rid it . . . molten city . . . of its cancer, fire swept it up on the bosom of the lagoon" ("Palm" 115). Not so in *Tropic Death*. The same story begins with the landscape's transformation, no longer a benign development. Blackness no longer signifies evil but the bodies of West Indian labor.

> Below, a rock engine was crushing stone, shooting up rivers of steam and signaling the frontier's rebirth. Opposite, there was proof, a noisy, swaggering sort of proof, of the gradual death and destruction of the frontier post. Black men behind wheelbarrows slowly ascended a rising made of spliced boards and emptied the sand rock into the maw of a mixing machine. More black men, a peg down, behind wheelbarrows, formed a line which caught the mortar pouring into the rear organ of the omnivorous monster. "All, all gone," cried Miss Buckner, and the girls at her side shuddered. All quietly felt the sterile menace of it. [. . .] "All of that," she sighed, "all of that was swamp when I came to the Isthmus. All." (85)

Miss Buckner's reminiscence deepens, painting an impressionistic history at odds with the original story's affirmation of the U.S. subjugation of savage wilderness. "Dark dense thicket; water paving it. Deer, lions, tigers bounding through it. Centuries, perhaps, of such pure, free rule. Then some khaki-clad, red-faced and scrawny-necked whites deserted the Zone and brought saws to the roots of palmetto, spears to the bush cats and jaguars, lysol to the mosquitoes and flies, and tar to the burning timber-swamp" (86). This is not salvation but the fall, a bucolic idyll slashed and burned. It is pursued with reckless abandon: "A wild racing to meet the Chagres [River] and explore the high reaches of the Panama jungle.

After the torch, ashes and ghosts—bare, black stalks, pegless stumps, flakes of charred leaves and half-burnt tree trunks" (86). This is a new world Waste Land, notes Michelle Stephens, the European nightmare of postwar impotence recast as the cataclysm of industrial modernity, a "sterile menace."[19]

Traditionally, the poetics of Caribbean representation were characterized by two dominant elements: a silencing or caricature of Afro-Caribbean voices and a "tropicalization" of the region through a discourse of the picturesque. Walrond's characters were not stock types splashing local color on the writer's canvas. Their voices expressed history in the stories they told and in the very shape of their sounds. Walrond dwells on exchanges such as the following between the Barbadian Ella Heath and her neighbor Lizzie Dalrimple, whose adolescent daughter has offended Ella.

"Hey, I ask de gal if she mahmie home an' Lizzie, yo' know what she tell ma, why de little rapscallion tu'n me she back side an' didn't even say ax yo' pardin."

"Come in heah, miss, come in heah an tu'n round. Ax Miss Heath pardin! Ax she! Yo' won't—yo' wretch! Vagabond! Take dat, an' dat, an' dat—shut up, I sez. Shut up, befo' I box ev'y one o' dem teets down yo' t'roat! Didn't I tell yo' not to be rude, shut up, yes—didn't I tell yo' not to be onmannerly to people, dat yo' must respect de neighbors? Like she ain't got no manners! Shut up, I sez, befo' I hamstring yo', yo' little whelp!"

"Dese gal picknees nowadays is 'nouf to send yo' to de madhouse! Hey, but Lizzie, what we gwine do wit' de chilrun, ni? Ev'y day dey is gittin' wussuh and wussuh." (36–37)

Passages such as this confront us with the conjunction of sound and sense. The literal matter could not be more ordinary: Capadosia's mother, furious at her irreverence, punishes her and laments the trials of motherhood. To say that Walrond was conveying something of the strictness of maternal discipline in Barbados would not be incorrect but it would be incomplete, for what is also communicated is the particularity of the women's voices. Standard English orthography is violated so consistently that we are compelled to read differently, to shape the sounds in our mind's ear, to aspirate differently and mind our glottal stops. This is not a question of translation, of substituting one lexicon for another. The daring is in the orality and the orthography: the dramatic compression of *He gwine beat she fo' true*, the transcription of *wussah* for worse. A non-Caribbean reader can infer meaning from context, but the real labor—and real pleasure—of *Tropic Death* is its injunction to sound.

Comparisons may be drawn to Walrond's Harlem contemporaries, who rendered folk speech on the page, liberating it from caricature by suggesting its ingenuity and integrity. But *Tropic Death* did something different. Unlike Hurston and Hughes, who worked principally with African American speech, Walrond addressed what linguists call the creole continuum, the range of influence by and divergence from English and other colonial languages. He not only attempted a variety of Caribbean dialects, from Barbadian English to Panamanian Spanglish, he mediated them with his own English, itself a North American inflection of the King's English he acquired as a child. It was not until a generation later, during the era of Caribbean nationalism, that such an undertaking was really theorized. Glissant referred to his own writing as a "synthesis of written syntax and spoken rhythms, of 'acquired' writing and oral 'reflex,' of the solitude of writing and the solidarity of the collective voice."[20] Walrond aspired to a comparable synthesis, recognizing that this was a transformative activity, not an unmediated transcript of Caribbean speech "itself."

Edward Kamau Brathwaite would express reservations about dialect during the nationalist era, distinguishing it from "nation language." The challenge, he felt, was to represent creolized languages not as inferior, "broken," but as repositories of a repressed history and consciousness. "It may be in English," he wrote, "but often it is in an English which is like a howl, or a shout or a machine-gun or the wind or a wave."[21] Thus, as Walrond's Ella Heath walks the marl road to Poyer's shop she mutters, "Sh, carrion crow, me no dead yet," repeating it again and again. "The evergreen leaves, caressing her face, brought it vividly to her," he writes, "Sh, carrion crow, me no dead yet."

> An old Dutch Guianese had uttered the ghastly words. Black Portuguese legend . . . For sticking his hand in a pork barrel in a Portuguese grocer's shop, a Negro had been caught and whisked off to a dark spot in the woods. His hands had been cut off and he had been buried alive, with only his head sticking out of the ground. That had happened at night. In the morning the crows had come to gouge the eyes out of his head. "Sh, carrion crow, me no dead yet. . . ." Evergreen leaves on Ella's face . . . crows swirling around the head of a body buried on the Guiana mound. (43)

In this way "me no dead yet" figures colonial trauma, the folk expression of violence and resistance. His characters do not speak "broken" English, they occupy a range of positions in the creole continuum and evince a linguistic awareness. Shondel Nero describes Walrond's extraordinary linguistic undertaking.

> In trying to capture the range, cadences, and texture of Caribbean speech, Walrond undertook a monumental task. Not only are his characters as diverse as their language, but their experiences reach beyond the anglophone Caribbean into the francophone islands and Spanish-speaking Panama; hence the need to include the language of those territories. Add to this the fact that Walrond was writing at a time when very few writers dared to put Caribbean folk speech—a language with no standard orthography—into the written form. Yet Walrond, living outside of the Caribbean, captures the colorfulness of Caribbean speech with remarkable accuracy.[22]

Stuart Hall praised the linguistic "revolution" of a later generation, rendering Caribbean "languages in which important things can be said, in which important aspirations and hopes can be formulated, in which artists are willing, for the first time [. . .] to practice."[23] But that revolution may be traced to *Tropic Death*.

I have been suggesting that *Tropic Death* is as much about its sound as its sense, that sound *is* its sense. This sonic quality is all the more striking given the priority accorded the visual in representations of the Caribbean during this period. Extensive public relations campaigns orchestrated by travel agencies, governments, and development boards made the region appear safe and attractive by rendering it *picturesque*. Postcards, images, and icons constructed the Caribbean *as* a picture, an emotionally stirring but safe sensory experience. These campaigns bolstered the tourist industry that was thought vital to the region's modernization and enhanced the effort of corporations such as United Fruit and Kodak to reorient the region's "imaginative geography." Outsiders are used to envisioning the Caribbean as a tropical paradise, but this was not the prevailing view a century ago.

Despite the availability of preventative medicines for "tropical" diseases in the 1880s, tourism promoters had to dispel the fear of the islands, which haunted the imaginations of potential tourism clienteles in Britain and North America. They had to radically transform the islands' much maligned landscapes into spaces of touristic desire for British and North American traveling publics. Photographic images played a constitutive role in this process.[24]

The imagery was pastoral: "exotic, strange, or grandiose forms" of flora and fauna abounded, but they were made to appear "cultivated or perfectly manicured into orderly displays." If people appeared, they "joined the parade of the picturesque," cast as "loyal, disciplined, and clean" colonial subjects. As the image industry expanded during the period in which *Tropic Death* appeared, promoters focused "on the islands' seascape as a repository of their 'tropicalness.' At this time representations of the coral reefs, surrounding marine life, and later the beach became increasingly popular. Images of the islands' transparent waters emphasized another tamed aspect of nature in the Anglophone Caribbean, in this instance, the ocean."[25]

The "tropicalization" campaign implied that colonial rule was effective and normalized the established social order, prompting Garvey's Universal Negro Improvement Association (UNIA) to cite the role of postcards in sanitizing oppressive conditions.[26] In 1958, Guyanese novelist

Edgar Mittelholzer would register his objection to the "deliberately falsi-fied" photographs trained exclusively on "grass-roofed huts and palms and jungle trees" because they justified "a refusal to see the islands as intrinsically a part of the modern world."[27] Mittelholzer's remark raises a crucial element in *Tropic Death*, for it is above all an effort to disrupt the prevailing visual economy of tropicality, which denied a place for the Caribbean in modernity. The book is relentlessly counter-pastoral, propelling the Caribbean into the twentieth century. Walrond trafficked in visual imagery as obsessively as did the "tropicalization" campaign against which he wrote. But his word-images functioned differently from the imagery constructing the Caribbean picturesque. As the prevailing discourse of tropicality worked to make the Caribbean suitable for con-sumption, Walrond's Caribbean voices literally stuck in one's throat, and his imagery saturated his pages with an equal and opposite intensity.[28]

As if to figure this narrative strategy, the blood of Walrond's injured protagonist drips vivid red on the blank white road of Barbadian marl in the book's first story. Returning from the quarry under a blazing mid-day sun, Coggins Rum, a shoeless laborer, stubs his toe on a rock jut-ting through the marl. "Pree-pree-pree. As if it were frying. Frying flesh. The nail jerked out of place, hot, bright blood began to stream from it. Around the spot white marl dust clung in grainy cakes. Now, red new blood squirted—spread over the whole toe—and the dust became crim-son" (24). His injury presages the death of his daughter, but the vividness of its rendering is an apt figure for the furious image production Walrond performed in his writing, which is like nothing so much as hemorrhaging. It was as though the author, foundering to the point of suicidal despair in 1925, had instead opened a vein upon the page.

AN EYE FOR THE TROPICS

Tropic Death begins and ends with the sun, with light and heat. It is a fitting motif given the play of light in representations of this region. "In the Caribbean world-view the sun is a dialectical entity," Jan Carew observed, "it is creative and destructive, it gives life and takes it away."²⁹ Or as Walrond put it, the sun both "burned and kissed things" (164). On one hand, "It wrung toll of the earth."

> The sun had robbed the land of its juice, squeezed it dry. Star apples, sugar apples, husks, transparent on the dry sleepy trees. Savagely prowling through the orchards blackbirds stopped at nothing. . . . Turtle doves rifled the pods of green peas and purple beans and even the indigestible Brazilian *bonavis*. Potato vines, yellow as the leaves of autumn, severed from their roots by the pressure of the sun, stood on the ground, the wind's eager prey. Undug, stemless—peanuts, carrots—seeking balm, relief, the caress of a passing wind, shot dead unlustered eyes up through sun-etched cracks in the hard, brittle soil. The sugar corn went to the birds. (26)

On the other hand, the sun helps coax another *Tropic Death* landscape into fertility.

> Once more the peewits sang. [. . .] Scudding popcorn—white, yellow, crimson pink guava buds blew upon the ground. Forwards and backwards the wind tossed the guava tree. It shook buds and blossoms on the ground—moist, unforked, ground—on Ella Heath's lap, in her black, plenteous hair, in the water she was drawing from the well. [. . .] All of nature gave flavor to Ella, wrought a magic color in Ella's life. (39)

Ella's association with nature is clear, but more than a feature of the landscape, she transforms it. "[E]xperimenting with the green froth of the earth," she grafts a pine to a breadfruit, cultivates tamarind, star apple, and almond trees, mates pigeons and ground doves (41). In contrast to her own condition, partnerless and without progeny, Ella encourages promiscuity, setting rabbits "in the thick sparrow grass [. . .] to play and frolic," ensuring that her "sows fared prodigiously" and her "boars grew tusks of flint-like ivory," while her cow "streamed milk from fat luscious udders" (40). This bounteous yield is Ella's genius, nature's response "under her tutelage" (42).

Other examples of Walrond's painterly sensibility abound, but it is most pronounced in depictions of the landscape. In "The White Snake," an intense eroticism repressed from the level of the plot returns in narrative imagery.

> Coral earth paved the one flake of road in Waakenam. Gathering depth
> and moss, the water in the gutters beside it was a metallic black. It was
> a perfumed dawn—the strong odor of turpentine and fruit flavoring it.
> For it was high up on the Guiana coast, and the wind blew music on the
> river. Vivid flame it blew on the lips of grape and melon, and ripened,
> like the lust of a heated love, the udders of spiced mangoes and pears
> peeping through the luscious grove. (134)

The fecundity of the land is evoked through image and sound, the consonance of peeping pears and gutter water, lust and luscious, love and grove occupying our ears and arresting the narrative. In this way we are invited to read as though scanning an image.

Rendering the sun's wrath involved similar techniques. In the title story, the sun rises on Sunday, subjecting a pious woman and her son to unrelenting heat on their voyage from Bridgetown to Panama.

> The sun baptized the sea. O tireless, sleepless sun! It burned and kissed
> things. It baked the ship into a loose, disjointed state. Only the brave
> hoarse breezes at dusk prevented it from leaving her so. It refused to
> keep things glued. It fried sores and baked bunions, browned and black-
> ened faces, reddened and blistered eyes. It lured to the breast of the sea
> sleepy sharks ready to pounce upon prey. (164)

Again the inventory technique is employed, the sun figuring a litany of depredations, dissolving the glue of syntax no less than the joints of the ship. *Tropic Death* thus establishes a counter-pastoral practice of landscaping and seascaping in which the sun figures centrally but equivocally. It resonates with the Caribbean worldview proposed by Carew, the sun as creator-destroyer, with the counter-pastoral sensibility of Winslow

Homer's painting *Gulf Stream*, which disturbed viewers accustomed to Caribbean "tropicality" by modulating the play of light on a shark-filled sea, and with Aimé Cesaire's designation of Caribbean colonialism as "the most putrid carrion that ever rotted under the sun."[30]

Focusing on the first term of *Tropic Death*'s title allows us to see how Walrond troped tropicality, bending it toward the sun, rendering the Caribbean a more fraught object of knowledge and consumption, and affiliating it with death, the title's second term. But death pervades the book to such a degree that it warrants separate discussion. The fact of death, the threat of death—these give the book its gothic quality.

TROPING DEATH

The preponderance of death and disease provoked speculation about Walrond's morbidity, his "fevered imagination." But there are additional reasons, historical and poetic, that a West Indian from Panama would feature death so emphatically. Nor was it simply an obsession with the return of repressed desire or trauma that led him to the gothic, for Caribbean folklore furnished its own expressive tradition—Anancy tales and legends of obeah, duppies, and *brujería*—that informed his reading of Poe, Hawthorne, Lafcadio Hearn, and Pierre Lotí. The cemetery at Colón's Monkey Hill appears regularly in his Panama stories because he played there as a teenager, but in fact he saw *all* of the Canal Zone, perhaps the whole Caribbean basin, as sepulchral, a tomb whose dead were silenced by history. The fresh graves in and around Colón, the hospitals, quarantine quarters, and fumigation crews—all were reminders that death held a peculiar significance in this region, one whose entrance into modernity involved death integrally and on a massive scale.

This observation is made so consistently in Caribbean literature, especially on Panama, as to constitute a trope itself. Mary Seacole, a Jamaican military nurse who wrote the first Caribbean autobiography, characterized Panama as a mass grave well before the canal's advent. Her *Wonderful Adventures* (1857) recalls a trip up the Chagres River, "as capital a nursery for ague and fever as Death could hit upon anywhere."[31] Work songs and testimonials of canal laborers document their peril, the myriad ways in which they were wounded, grievously if not fatally. When the Isthmian Historical Society solicited the "best true stories" of the canal construction era, submissions arrived from across the Caribbean, and many spoke frankly of the carnage. Death was so common it was discussed casually. A boiler man wrote, "Man die get blow up get kill or get drown during the time someone would asked where is Brown he died last night and burry where is Jerry he dead a little before dinner and buried so on and so on all the time." Another said, "It was nothing unusual to be walking on Front Street and suddenly you secs a yard engine with one ICC [Isthmian Canal Commission] flat car attached with dead men stretched out."[32] Estimates put the fatality rate of West Indian workers at roughly one in ten, or 15,000 men.[33] Caribbean families dreaded the postman's delivery of the black-bordered ICC envelope, announcing that a family member had perished.[34]

In this context, Walrond's obsession with death assumes a different cast. The severed limb of his cork-legged grocer, Poyer, seems less a lugubrious gothic device than a materialist critique of labor conditions. The murder of a young Barbadian at the hands of a vengeful marine sounds less like hard-boiled melodrama than a meditation on the vulnerability of workers who stepped out of line or organized. Indeed, the most chilling moment in "Subjection" is not Ballet's murder, which is foretold in the first paragraphs, but an exchange in which he tries to persuade his coworkers to use their collective strength to protect a fallen man from the capricious abuse of their white boss.

"Hey, you!" shouted Ballet at last loud enough for the Marine to hear, "Why—wha' you doin'? Yo' don' know yo' killin' dat boy, ni'?"

"Le' all we giv' he a han' boys—"

"Ah know I ain't gwine tetch he."

"Nor me."

"Nor me needah."

"Who gwine giv' me a han', ni'?"

"Ain't gwine get myself in no trouble. Go mixin' myself in de backra dem business—"

"Hey, Ballet, if yo' know wha' is good fo' yo'self, yo' bess min' yo' own business, yo' hear wha' me tell yo' yah."

"Wha' yo' got fi' do wit' it? De boy ain't got no business talkin' back to de marinah man—"

"Now he mek up he bed, let 'im lie down in it." (100–101)

Despite Ballet's exhortation, they are too intimidated to defend their coworker from being beaten near death. Their justifications—the caution not to bite the hand that feeds, the aversion to mixing in the "backra" business—suggest the ICC's effectiveness at dividing and conquering, ensuring compliance, a "cowed obedient retinue limping to the boats," Walrond wrote (109). He linked the U.S. occupation to previous colonial regimes, the overseer replaced by the marine, "the noisy rhythm of picks swung by gnarled black hands" echoing the rhythm of machetes in the old canebrakes.

In addition to *Tropic Death*'s laborers, its children, raised by doting but vulnerable West Indian mothers, are at considerable risk. Coggins Rum and his wife struggle to keep their children fed in "Drought," and five other stories hinge on an anxious mother's protection of her children. Even "Subjection" includes a pivotal scene in which Ballet's mother chides him for becoming a "wuthliss vagybond," carousing in "Spanishtown eva night"; "tek heed, ni, tek heed, yo' heah," she warns, brandishing her Bible (102). A Honduran mother in "The Yellow One" soothes her colicky infant during a sea voyage, but her husband refuses to go for hot water, prompting *la madurita* to go herself (57). Likewise in "The Black Pin," April Emptage struggles to raise four children alone, contending with their "ownwayish" tendencies and with Zink Diggs, a resentful neighbor woman. April challenges Zink, "Why yo' don' le' me an' me chirrun alone, ni?" to which Zink responds, "Tell dem de little watahmout' runts, not to come on my hedge-row an' pick an' mo' o' my tam'rin's. Oi'll set poison fo' dem, too. Why yo' don't feed dem? Why yo' don't giv' dem a good stiff ball o' cookoo so dat dey won't hav' to teef my tamarin's? Pack o' starved-out runts!" (119–20). Zink not only threatens to poison April's children, she steals their goat and sets fire to their house. The protagonist in "The White Snake" is as dutiful as these others in her maternal ministrations. She lives alone with her infant son in a hut on a remote Guyanese island, determined to be a good mother, to love him and raise him well despite his conception in what the residents of Georgetown called her lust and wickedness (130).

Miss Buckner, the owner of the Palm Porch brothel, is a less sympathetic mother figure; she prostitutes her own daughters. But even here Walrond illustrates the struggle of a single West Indian mother in a dangerous region. In Miss Buckner's view, the Palm Porch is a controlled environment in which she sets the rules and protects her daughters' interests, unlike the chaotic city of Colón. Their failure to appreciate their privilege provokes their mother's ire. When one daughter makes a casual joke about a man's erection—"wake up in de mawnin' time wid 'im marinah stiff out in front o' him"—Miss Buckner reminds her that this is their vocation: "Mek fun, an' be a dam set o' fools all yo' life" she warns (87). She needs them to attend at a party thrown by a Panamanian patron, and when her daughters resist, she admonishes them.

> "Well, yo' bess mek up unna mind—all 'o unna! Well, wha' a bunch o' lazy ongrateful bitches de whole carload of unna is, dough he?" Suddenly she broke off, anger seaming her brow. "Unna don't know me his hindebted to him, no? Unna don't know dat hif hit wasn't farrim a lot o' t'ings wha' go awn up yah, would be street property long ago—an' some o' we yo' see spo'tin roun' yah would be some way else, an' diffrant altogeddah." (88)

Even as she raises her children into prostitution, Miss Buckner believes she is saving them from becoming "street property." Protected by the cronyism that sustains the brothel, her daughters enjoy comforts—gowns, books, gifts, and a chef. They feel they "ain't owe nobody nothin'" but Miss Buckner replies, "Don't fool yourselves, children, there is more to make the mare go than you think" (88). Indeed, the death that resolves the plot is orchestrated by Miss Buckner and implicates one of her daughters, but because of her consummate professionalism, this murder never sees a courtroom.

The most anxious of all of *Tropic Death*'s mothers is fashioned after Walrond's own. Sarah Bright is a devout member of the Plymouth Brethren whose husband, a tailor named Lucian, has gone ahead of his family to Panama. The problem is that Lucian is undependable, "a wufless stinkin' good fuh nutton vergybin'" (172). The titular death of "Tropic Death" is Lucian's—he suffers from leprosy—but the story is of Sarah's efforts to keep her children out of harm's way. She appeals to her delinquent husband, who curses her for haranguing him with "the same old story." "Old?" she replies, "It will never be old! As long as I've got breath in my body—as long as I is got my boy child to shield from the worle—from de filth and disease of dis rotten, depraved place—as long as I got my fo' gal chirrun in B'bados in somebody else han'—um can't be a old story!" (184). As her husband's health declines, Sarah commits herself to protecting her son from the spiritual and physical depredations of Panama.

Whatever influence Walrond's depression exerted on *Tropic Death*, whatever gothicism he learned from Dorothy Scarborough, Lafcadio Hearn, or Pierre Loti, the tenuousness of life in Panama was also fresh in his memory. Despite his lyricism and painterly sensibility, the book conveyed what he called the "sepulchral" quality of the region, exhuming graves to create a genealogy of the diaspora.

RECEPTION

It was difficult for readers to hear the book's dissonant registers, its competing commitments to anger and entertain. Reviewers struggled to reconcile its critique of Caribbean social conditions with its florid prose. Reviews appeared in the black press, where Benjamin Brawley, W. E. B. Du Bois, Theophilus Louis, and J. A. Rogers discussed it, and in mainstream periodicals including *The New Yorker*, *The New Republic*, the *New York*

Times, and *The New York Herald Tribune*.[35] Some positively glowed, and admirers agreed that the book's virtue was the absence of overt propaganda or sentimentality. "There is nothing soft about this book," Langston Hughes wrote, it is "as unsentimental as blazing sun." "Unlike much American Negro prose and poetry," he added, "these pages are untainted by racial propaganda." Robert Herrick of *The New Republic* claimed Walrond "has no propaganda, raises no race question, nor is there in the writer's hand a mutinous background of controversy or resentment. He writes of this colored world as if practically it was the only world—as he should and as no other Negro so far as I remember has written." The *New York Times* said Walrond "recorded impartially" and within a single paragraph "terror and superstition and grim humor, oblivious tenderness and childlike sensuality and swift, brutal enmity." The review commended the suspension of sentimentality: "Coggins and his daughter are enough to break one's heart, yet Mr. Walrond offers no comment persuasive of commiseration. The story has been experienced rather than read." This distinction between *experiencing* and *reading* appeared consistently. "These West Indies [. . .] palpitate under his touch with light, heat, color," wrote Herrick. Rogers agreed, "Walrond's power in making his readers feel the milieu borders on the marvelous. One who has lived in the West Indies (as I have) will immediately recall the mannerisms of the peasants whom he portrays. It is as if the writer had almost transferred them alive on paper." The *New York Times* praised the book's "absorbingly interesting energy, as of life itself."[36]

This sense of immediacy, of experiencing not just reading, derived from Walrond's imagistic prose and his use of dialect. But the effectiveness of these techniques was debated. Even those who appreciated the writing found it eccentric. The *New York Times* called Walrond's "skill with words" "pleasingly bizarre." Another said, "The writing is not pretty, but it is well nigh indelible. [. . .] And though the diction throughout the book is irresistibly fresh and striking, the most tolerant welcomer of modernist vocabulary chokes occasionally when he is asked to swallow wholesale doses of alliterative splendor." Herrick noted, "His sense of color in words is remarkable, also the audacity of verbal manipulation.

It is all intensely nervous, impressionistic, syncopated, even disorderly."
Hughes called Walrond's prose "sometimes tangled and confused, yet
tough as the hanging vines from which monkeys leap and chatter." Others were put off, including V. F. Calverton, who called the stories "diffuse
in narration, tardy in climax, and often tedious in conclusion," and Mary
White Ovington, who found the style "vivid and often beautiful," but "at
times trying." She felt Walrond refused to meet his reader halfway: "His
milieu is unusual and if he wishes us really to see the pictures that flood
his mind, he must take a little more pains in presenting them." Nevertheless, much of the book's difficulty seems intentional, as though Walrond
set out to write a challenging book, both in its prose style and its counter-
pastoral vision.[37]

Two prominent African American scholars, Du Bois and Brawley, criticized the style, but both thought it among the most impressive achievements in "Negro" literature to date. "The book's impressionism, together
with its dialect, make it often hard reading and difficult to understand,"
wrote Du Bois, "But on the whole, it is a human document of deep significance and great promise." Because "our knowledge of the West Indies
has usually come from the words of English rulers and tourists and the
chance observations of white Americans," Du Bois thought *Tropic Death*
"a distinct contribution to Negro American literature in a field curiously
new."[38] Brawley was more effusive; despite some deficiencies, he felt Walrond's talent surpassed all other New Negro fiction writers, with the possible exceptions of Toomer and Walter White.

> In a purely literary way, it is the most important contribution made by
> a Negro to American letters since the appearance of Dunbar's "Lyrics
> of Lowly Life." Mr. Walrond differs from other writers in the freshness
> of his material, in the strength of his style, in his skillful use of words,
> in his compression—in short, in his understanding of what makes lit-
> erature and what does not. [. . .] The book is not always a pleasant one,
> nor is it a perfect one. [. . .] All told, however, the man who wrote this
> book knows something about writing; his style is becoming more and
> more chaste; and, in view of his firm grasp of his material and his clear

perception of what is worthwhile, we feel that there is nothing in fiction that is beyond his capabilities.[39]

Celebrating Walrond's "artistry," Brawley indexed the opposing terms of the polemic over representation. It was not that propagandistic or sentimental expression was without value, but they contaminated the "purely" literary. Thus in discussing White, Brawley said his "work preaches perhaps more than it expresses; accordingly, regarded purely from the standpoint of the artistic, it belongs to a different order of writing from that of Mr. Walrond."[40] Consistently recurring in reviews of *Tropic Death*, whether laudatory or critical, was this approval of the absence of an overt message.

Of course, works of fiction convey different meanings for different audiences, and *Tropic Death* suggests a number of messages that may not have been available to its initial audience. For example, Walrond's critique of European colonialism and North American neocolonialism is more pronounced than initial reviews indicated. Hughes wanted the book to stand on its literary merit alone: "*Tropic Death* is a book of short stories. Whether it is good Negro propaganda or not should be of no moment." So he downplayed the role of the white characters and the themes of racism and color prejudice. "The Vampire Bat" was for Hughes a story about "the son of an old colonial family killed on a devil-ridden island," not a meditation on social relations in the post-sugar plantation society. The shooting in "The Palm Porch" was an "incidental murder" arising from "some scraggy sailors drinking" at a brothel, a synopsis that, omitting the motive for the murder, obscures the story's shrewd staging of racial and colonial history. In the most egregious statement, Hughes called the marine who viciously beats one West Indian worker and shoots another "a moron military representative of a great government."[41] Perhaps Hughes was pulling his punches, but his willingness to soften *Tropic Death*'s social statements reveals the length to which reviewers went to expunge messages that threatened its status as literature.

Reflecting the polarized terms of debate, Hughes defended Walrond's many unflattering depictions of black people for precisely the reason

J. A. Rogers criticized him. Hughes welcomed Walrond's departure from the prevailing orthodoxy, an attitude of "O, see how nice and yet how mistreated we are." Rogers saw Walrond as stereotyping, pandering to an audience that preferred its "Negroes" exotic and primitive.

> The white public is not interested in the struggling, aspiring Negro— the one who is likely to be a competitor. What it demands is the bizarre, the exotic, the sexy, the cabaret side of Negro life. [. . .] The Negro is a fixed type in the white man's mind, including the white liberal and radical, and few will entertain any other. [. . .] The critics are loud in their praise of *Tropic Death*. One of them, colored, says the stories "are as impersonal as an epic of Homer." For my part I should say one of the defects of the book is that it is TOO darn impersonal—so impersonal that one would fancy it was some Negro-despising Englishman or Southerner, new to the tropics, that was speaking of these peasants. Not less than 20 times has the writer used such words as "nigger," "coon," "zigaboo," mark you, not as one of the characters speaking, which is permissible, but as the author, Walrond, himself a Negro. Speaking of one character he says: "Black as sin." The writer himself is a black man.[42]

It would be one thing, in other words, if Walrond put his slurs in the mouths of despicable characters, the problem is that they are his own, without mediating distance, tacitly endorsing them. Thus, Rogers could only conclude the book was "written particularly for the white market [. . .] because the interest of the vast masses of the white people, and those of the self-respecting Negro in this matter of literature are poles apart."[43]

But Rogers added a revealing codicil: "We are indebted to Mr. Walrond for much of the present vogue and interest in literature by and about Negroes, such as it is. His articles in numerous white magazines have done much to pave the way, as this reviewer, personally, knows." Such were the stakes of trafficking in stereotypes after *Nigger Heaven*. Suspicions abounded that Walrond, Hurston, McKay, Hughes, and Thurman, whose characters were often motivated by appetite rather than intellect, sought to exploit the Negro "vogue." These suspicions are understandable, but as they hardened into a litmus test they permitted little complexity or nuance. Already ambivalent about Walrond's contribution to "the present vogue," Rogers found his suspicions confirmed in *Tropic Death*. And although Hughes and Rogers disagreed about the book, they asked the same question of it: whether it was written for white people. As inevitable as the question was then, it foreclosed a number of others that have become more urgent since.

For one thing, if Walrond wrote *Tropic Death* with the preferences and prejudices of white North Americans in view, he did a poor job. To be sure, he used terms to describe nonwhite people that were derogatory then and now, terms such as "nigger," "coon," and "zigaboo," as well as "coolie" and "chink." In fact, given the opportunity to revise *Tropic Death* for republication in the 1960s, Walrond sought to redact many such words, substituting inoffensive alternatives. At the time, however, he was working at the intersection of two discursive formations that made it seem necessary. One was the movement in American modernism to ruffle the residual Victorian feathers of the middle class. Nowhere is this clearer than in the advertisement for *Tropic Death* in *The New Yorker*, where it was announced alongside Dreiser's *An American Tragedy*, *Gentlemen Prefer Blondes* by Anita Loos, and new books by Ezra Pound and Hart Crane. "There is a present here for everyone," they recommended in this Christmas issue, "and many a book that will remove the inhibitions of the dear old lady from Dubuque."[44] Walrond wanted to be part of this assault on propriety. The other reason he indulged in epithets and terms of disparagement was to distance himself from the high-toned, sanitized uplift rhetoric of the New Negro movement. As he had done in *Vanity Fair*, Walrond's willingness to use ethnic slurs was both a gesture of linguistic reclamation and a signal that "Negroes" could risk self-caricature. Their willingness to expose the race to ridicule marked a new self-assurance. It was a brash posture that reached its apotheosis in Hurston's "Characteristics of Negro Expression" (1937) and "A Story in Harlem Slang" (1942), accompanied by an extensive glossary and announcing itself as a tale "about this Zigaboo called Jelly."

Walrond's provocative language of race generated an unfortunate but perhaps inevitable critical impasse. Left aside were important questions about who, after all, were these "Negroes" to whom he sometimes referred in disparaging terms and how to square these terms with the characters themselves, whom he humanized and even dignified. Among the questions *Tropic Death* raised was the relationship between African Americans and West Indians. *Tropic Death* was a working out of the question of a racial "soul" in the multiethnic formation that was the turn-of-the-century Caribbean. His laborious project in Caribbean language is critically important—marked as speakers of dialect, his characters' speech resembled African Americans, whose vernacular was similarly marked. And because they were black, the specificity of their departure from a North American standard affiliated them not with the Irish in Joyce, with Faulkner's Mississippians, or with other vernacular speakers but with the characters in Hurston, Hughes, or Toomer. Reviewers tended to ignore the radical innovation of the book's polyvocality by construing it as regionalism. They disagreed about whether the book was "racial," whether it represented something uniquely black or spoke to universal concerns, but what got buried either way was the question of what difference it made to be West Indian.

Many reviewers simplified the matter by referring to "the tropical Negro," "the Negro of the American tropics," or as the *New York Times* put it, "these mystified, helpless blacks." Herrick finessed it by declaring that "the African temperament, modes of thought, have never been more exactly interpreted in language." Others bypassed the vexing questions of race and culture by observing that, after all, the book dealt in universals not in racial themes. "Like any book that deeply expresses the essence of any race," wrote John Dos Passos, *Tropic Death* "is much more human than it is racial." Devere Allen warned, "[T]o consider these stories of the lands bordering the Caribbean merely in terms of the output of any group would be an error. Here is a brilliance that will stand on its own feet against all comers."[45]

Of all the displacements *Tropic Death* occasioned, however, Waldo Frank's review in *Opportunity* was the oddest and most revealing of the critical climate. Frank was deeply impressed with the book, but he sided neither with the universalists, who saw it as "more human than racial," nor with those who praised its depiction of "the Negro character." For Frank, its significance lay in its language. Incongruously, however, the language he heard was "American." In a stunning gesture of linguistic assimilation, he subsumed the polyvocality of *Tropic Death* within U.S. cultural nationalism. Confessing that his "ultimate impression of the book is rather paradoxical," he wrote, "It seems to me that what stands in the way of the book, as a work of art, is its chief feature of interest and importance: to wit, its language." Although he found Walrond's prose overwrought, Frank hastened to add "that the deep aesthetic fault I find in it is the highest sort of promise," for Walrond's struggle was the struggle of all American writers to forge a national idiom, to break with European tradition. Informed by an opposition between European and American literatures, Frank perversely read *Tropic Death* as quintessentially American. "How can I make clear that the basis of this book—the very substance of its language—relates it to Poe, Melville, Thoreau even—and to their contemporary successors: excludes it radically, moreover, from the noble and long lineage of English literary prose?"[46]

Frank did not think Walrond was North American, but precisely for that reason he read *Tropic Death* as proof of the assimilative force of the United States.

> I suspect he comes from the West Indies: and in this case, his background is probably English. I find myself hoping that this is so. For if it is, my own claim about the true and whole America is strengthened. I should like to think that Mr. Walrond speaks English with a London accent, and that his grandfather was a British Squire who drank small beer at breakfast. For if this is so, the Americanism of Eric Walrond is all the more convincing: his profound affinity in language and in language-sense with the rest of us—whose background may be Scandinavian or Russian or Jewish or Spanish—becomes less possibly accidental, more certainly the result of an organic occurrence in our cultural world.[47]

In his eagerness to define American literature against English literature, Frank's voracious pluralism incorporates all cultural differences into one magnificent melting pot. Yet in rendering cultural difference the source and ground of America's distinctiveness, he ensures that there is no escape, no outside, no departure from the English tradition that resists incorporation as American. Scandinavian, Russian, Jew, Spaniard, and West Indian, all take their place on arrival as descendents of Whitman, Poe, Melville, and Thoreau.

It is ironic that a reviewer who is so insightful about the book's language, one who got the book right and refused to reduce it to "Negro literature," produced such a tone-deaf reading, for what is lost is the book's Caribbeanness, the fact that neither the setting nor the characters are American in the sense he means. It is precisely the alternate conceptions of "America" that Frank must forestall in order to read Walrond into a U.S. literary tradition. Other readers were all too willing to assume Walrond had been a Caribbean peasant just like his characters, but Frank erred in the other direction, claiming to "know nothing about Mr. Walrond's background" despite the appearance of his review in the journal at which Walrond was employed, and despite having spoken to him at some length.[48] Only in the 1920s could *Tropic Death* have been understood in so many conflicting ways: as taking its place in the American literary tradition, as New Negro literature, and as literature of "the tropical Negro."

Many observers called *Tropic Death* a literary first. As discussed, some felt it was the first work of fiction to treat the race so dispassionately, others the first to bring such technical virtuosity to bear in representing black people, and others the first to address Afro-Caribbeans. *Tropic Death* was indeed a first, though not principally for these reasons. What makes the book so elusively groundbreaking is that it was a new form of black transnational fiction, one attempted many times since but not before. Its settings are Caribbean, as are most of its characters, and the Caribbean literary tradition has a claim to the book, but it is also in an important sense—here Waldo Frank was partly right—a product of North America. The reasons it could only have been written in New York have less to do with the limited publishing options in the Caribbean than with the book's linguistic and discursive conditions of possibility. As the distance between the narrator's voice and the voices of his characters indicates, it is as much of the United States as it is of the Caribbean, which is to say it is fully neither. It will not do to say that it is the work of a colonial writer because the resources on which Walrond drew—his lexicon, idioms, and political and aesthetic sensibilities—are not those of an English colonial subject. He had spent eight years immersed in New York's linguistic cauldron, "a listening post, anchored in the middle of life's gurgling stream" ("Vignettes" 20). *Tropic Death* was the product of both his political radicalism and his disillusionment with politics, of the color-consciousness of U.S. race relations and the uplift agenda of the New Negro movement, of his studies at U.S. universities and his identification as "spiritually a native of Panama."

Walrond pursued a certain literary fashion—ostentatious in its technique, elliptical in its storytelling—yet he also confounded convention, turning the Caribbean picturesque on its head, or more precisely on its ear. *Tropic Death* took the first-person "I" that had traditionally yoked African American and immigrant literature to a sentimental discourse of personal experience and abstracted it into a narrative sensibility, a way of seeing and hearing rather than a disclosure of the author "himself." It was in this sense and above all else an extraordinary exercise in self-assertion and self-effacement. Langston Hughes had one real criticism of *Tropic Death*. "I wish some of the stories were longer," he wrote, "What else happens to these people?"[49] What else happens is the rest of black transnational fiction.

6

A PERSON OF DISTINCTION (1926–1929)

After *Tropic Death*, things went so well that one wonders why Walrond left the United States. Why desert the country whose acceptance he sought? Why abandon Harlem as it emerged into prominence? Surveying 1926, Charles Johnson observed that "more books on the Negro have appeared than any other year has yielded, Broadway has welcomed three Negro plays, and with Eric Walrond, another Negro writer has moved definitely into the ranks of American artists with his fiercely realistic Caribbean tales." His name appeared alongside Toomer, Hughes, and Cullen as writers of lasting import. "Eric Walrond automatically finds himself in this class," said the *Chicago Defender*, "His stories will live as long as stories live." There was no "discernible reason," Robert Herrick felt, "why the creator of *Tropic Death* should not go much farther in this field, which he has quite to himself."[1]

It had been an exhilarating year at *Opportunity*, which now rivaled *The Crisis* in featuring creative work. Johnson redoubled his efforts, developing networks among African American writers and white publishers and editors. The first *Opportunity* literary contest drew 732 submissions from around the country and enlisted eminent editors and writers as judges. The awards exemplified Johnson's care in cultivating a journal that was, after all, still in its infancy. More than 300 guests attended the inaugural *Opportunity* awards reception in 1925, and the crowds swelled over the next two years, filling the elegant Fifth Avenue Restaurant.² Johnson combined passion with pragmatism. His expertise lay in the systematic synthesis of hard data, which he saw as the basis of any firm and lasting public policy. But he recognized the vitality of the emerging artistic community, and *Opportunity*'s circulation nearly doubled between 1925 and 1927, concurrent with its embrace of the arts.³ Walrond's influence was vital. *Opportunity* had never had a steady business manager, and this one knew everyone. Having pitched to editors on both sides of the color line, he had extensive contacts and a measure of celebrity, moving among groups that did not always mix well. His heart and home were in Harlem, his office on 23rd Street, and his publisher in midtown. At the time of *Tropic Death*'s publication, Walrond's work appeared in six periodicals, none of which regularly featured "Negroes." He straddled the color line, interpreting developments in African American culture for white readers and providing a "Negro" perspective on white depictions of his race.

But what exactly was "his race"? Assuming the role of "Negro" spokesperson was an act of strategic identification. White editors may not have cared that he was from the Caribbean; they wanted someone with a command of African American cultural history and the experiential knowledge a black person inevitably acquired in the United States. However, among black New Yorkers, Walrond performed a different mediating role, bridging native- and foreign-born communities. He felt West Indian intellectuals could alleviate intraracial tensions and improve the ignorance among West Indians and African Americans of one another's history. Garvey's spectacular plight amplified the perception that West Indians were untrustworthy, perhaps un-American, an impression that their relatively low rate of naturalization did nothing to remove. The epithet "monkey chaser" was used, whether in jest or contempt, to disparage the uneducated, while the educated were accused of "putting on airs." Hostility toward West Indians was compounded by academic studies such as *The Fall of the Planter Class in the British Caribbean*, which said of the West Indian "Negro," "He stole, he lied, he was simple, suspicious, inefficient, irresponsible, lazy, superstitious, and loose in his sexual relations."⁴ That the American Historical Association awarded this study its

1926 dissertation prize, the year *Tropic Death* was published, indicates how much work was to be done.

A CARIBBEAN *OPPORTUNITY*

After submitting *Tropic Death*, Walrond spent the fall developing a special issue of *Opportunity* devoted to the Caribbean. This issue was unusual because the Urban League rarely pursued projects beyond U.S. borders; the organization's stated aim was to disseminate information about African American migrants relocating from the rural South. So extensive was this undertaking that Johnson, as director of the Department of Research and Investigations, seldom diverted his attention from migration. He was aware of immigration's scale, Harlem's foreign-born black population having increased tenfold in the first two decades of the century. But it did not register as distinctive in his work. In fact, when Johnson undertook a comparative migrations study in 1927, he examined the northward migration of African Americans in relation to European and Mexican immigration, omitting the Caribbean.[5] *Opportunity* took no fervent interest in the Caribbean or Africa, nor did it devote much space to intraracial dynamics.[6] Based on the progressive premise that "friendships usually follow the knowing of one's neighbors," the special Caribbean issue "aimed at an essential friendship," Johnson wrote, granting the West Indian a forum at a time when "the American Negro is constantly present in his newspapers and magazines." Walrond was indispensible for this project: "A native of British Guiana, who happens also to be the business manager of this journal," he selected the "special articles which appear in these pages." "We are indebted to his thorough acquaintance with the spokesmen of the Caribbean in this country."[7]

These included Arthur Schomburg, who contributed "West Indian Composers and Musicians"; Claude McKay, three of whose poems appeared; W. A. Domingo, who offered a history of the region; and Casper Holstein, whose history of the Virgin Islands dovetailed with another contribution, "Caribbean Fact and Fancy," by Virgin Islands chief justice, Lucius

SPECIAL CARIBBEAN ISSUE

NOVEMBER, 1926

6.1 Cover of special Caribbean issue of *Opportunity*, 1926.

Courtesy of the National Urban League, *Opportunity: Journal of Negro Life.*

Malmin. When Schomburg declined to write an article about prominent West Indians, Walrond solicited one from the editor of New York's *West Indian Statesman*.[8] Rounding out the issue were Waldo Frank's review of *Tropic Death*, an essay on Garvey by E. Franklin Frazier, and a "symposium" on West Indian-American relations between the Reverend Ethelred Brown of the Harlem Community Church and Eugene Kinckle Jones, the Urban League's executive secretary. The column "Our Bookshelf" was also Caribbeanized, addressing books about Surinam, Brazil, and Haiti.

An extraordinary document of the diaspora, the Caribbean issue is shot through with ambivalence about the United States, a reflection of its guest editor's own feelings. On one hand, it advanced the journal's pluralist premise that, equipped with better knowledge of one another, ethnic groups could coexist amicably and share prosperity in the United States. "A bond is being forged between [West Indian] and American Negroes," Domingo wrote, "Gradually they are realizing that their problems are in the main similar, and that their ultimate successful solution will depend on the intelligent cooperation of the two branches of Anglo-Saxonized Negroes." As "Anglo-Saxonized Negroes," West Indians and African Americans could surmount their differences, he suggested. The poems in the Caribbean issue, including Claude McKay's, offered universalizing gestures rather than matters particular to the Caribbean diaspora. On the other hand, the essays by Malmin, Holstein, and Domingo challenged U.S. foreign policy and inveighed against American racism. Malmin reflected on the crossroads in U.S. foreign policy, given the "clamor in the Philippines, certain dissatisfaction in Porto Rico, outspoken woe in Samoa and Guam, desperation in the Virgin Islands."[9] Holstein called the purchase of the Virgin Islands a pretext for subjugation, and joined Malmin in warning of imperial designs. Alarmed at the prospect of U.S. occupation of the Caribbean, he observed that the Navy ruled the Virgin Islands "with the transparent subterfuge that it is governed directly by the President of the United States," a ruse that "the inhabitants continue to protest."[10] Trepidation consumed all "informed and influential West Indians," said Domingo, at the prospect of exchanging British for American rule. The virulence of American racism was a factor: "They fear that under the hegemony of the United States they would be made to experience the social degradation to which Americans of color are subject."[11]

Despite the issue's emphasis on the "shared Negro blood" of West Indians and African Americans, it could not evade the discrepant circumstances in which they established self-understandings of race. "Unlike in the United States, the full-blooded Negro and his brother of mixed blood are not classified as one" in the Caribbean, Domingo noted, "The latter occupies a position midway between the two pure races and is regarded [. . .] as a link between white and black." Contributors acknowledged that tensions strained relations between West Indians and African Americans,

but the Caribbean issue maintained that conflicts arose from misappre-
hension. "The American Negro failed to discriminate between the different classes of West Indians, and thus mistakenly judged the best by the
worst," wrote Rev. Ethelred Brown.

> This mistaken judgment engendered a feeling of contemptuous superiority.
> Later when the more intellectual and more cultured West Indian compelled
> recognition, contempt gave way to jealousy. The West Indian on this part,
> especially the intellectual and cultured, also erred in this failure to discrimi-
> nate, and was on the whole much too self-assertive and in great measure by
> his words and conduct intensified the prevailing antagonism.[12]

Thus did Rev. Brown identify the "necessary misrecognitions" inherent in
efforts to forge racial solidarity across national borders.[13] The Caribbean
issue of *Opportunity* did not treat failures of transnational racial identification like the Universal Negro Improvement Association (UNIA) did, as
a conspiracy to keep "Negroes" disorganized. But it partook of a similar
utopian desire for a unified community, casting the impediments to harmony as individual deficiencies of apperception rather than as discrepan-
cies inherent in the translation of black experience. Intraracial differences
were important to acknowledge but only as a stage in their extinction.

The Caribbean issue of *Opportunity* was Walrond's effort to heal a
rift that threatened to divide black New Yorkers. Having lived in two
British colonies and a Latin American country under U.S. occupation,
he was alert to the paradoxes of black transnational cultures, which, as
Brent Edwards notes, "allow new and unforeseen alliances and interventions on a global stage" but also yield "unavoidable misapprehensions
and misreadings, persistent blindnesses and solipsisms, self-defeating and
abortive collaborations, [and] a failure to translate even a basic grammar
of blackness."[14] Having enlisted leading voices, Walrond brought *Opportunity* into an important new conversation. The Caribbean issue fulfilled
a pledge Walrond made in his earliest journalism: to demonstrate that the
distinctiveness of Harlem lay not in its concentrated blackness but in the
extraordinary diversity that blackness subsumed.

CULLEN AND MCKAY

The Caribbean *Opportunity* included an announcement that Countée Cullen had been hired as assistant editor. Having just completed a well-received first book and a master's degree at Harvard, Cullen's arrival was called "a step virtually decreed by the demands of that awakening generation to which this magazine [. . .] has consistently addressed itself."[15] He would contribute poems, editorial assistance, and a monthly column, showcasing his wit and analysis of race and culture. All had not been well, however, between Cullen and Walrond, for whom his friend's success was the source of mixed pride and envy. When he first saw *Color* in the fall of 1925, he fired off a congratulatory telegram, calling the book "gorgeous."[16] Within a week he wrote again, contrite, for he had overlooked Cullen's dedication of a poem to him. "I am sure it is well-nigh impossible for me to restore myself to your gracious graces. I am such a confirmed reprobate. I saw a copy of 'Color' and upon turning its pages I was entirely unprepared for the shock which I experienced upon seeing the dedication to 'Incident.' Now, is not that nice of you?"[17] Walrond lavished praise on the book.

> Your words are fraught with a high meaning; there is beauty and magnificence in the sentiments motivating them. You execute in your finished way the ideal which I have secretly held about Negro writing; utilizing material in its very essence virginal, the black poet or prose artist should fuse it into the drama via the avenue of the classical tradition. [. . .] I look to [you] for strength, power, endurance, beauty, distilled vision. [. . .] Endless emotions are orderly swept into the mosaic of your creations with an economy and compression.

He alerted Cullen, whom he affectionately called "kid," to his own recent publications and closed by asking, "How do you like Harvard?" He added plaintively, "Write me, Countee." But Cullen did not write, and Walrond despaired of their friendship. "With a telegram and a letter left unanswered I suppose we are quits," his next letter began, "But I do want to hear from you."[18]

Walrond did not realize Cullen was navigating personal travails of his own, circumstances he told Locke that same day. His companion, Llewellyn Ransom, was struggling with family obligations involving his marriage and now, with the holidays approaching, his vexations distressed Cullen.[19] Walrond's reconciliation with Cullen did not come easily. In response to his despairing letter, Cullen must have dashed off a quick message intended to mend things because Walrond's reply began accusingly, "Your horribly inadequate note came today." He added, "I am expecting you to be more generous with me when you come to town Thanksgiving."[20] Cullen restored himself to Walrond's favor, and within weeks they were again corresponding in breezy tones.

For Walrond, Cullen's *Color* was the realization of the terrible aesthetic potentiality of the Middle Passage and the creation of the New World Negro. "If, as some of us would have it, the presence of African slaves at Jamestown was ironically a fertilizing gesture of the Deity, Countee Cullen is the fulfillment of one of the pregnant promises of the New World" ("Poet" 179). Reviewing it for *The New Republic*, he refused to cast Cullen's accomplishment in narrowly national terms. "In this first book of verse by a Negro boy but twenty-two years old there is proof of many synthesized cultures. Spreading over a wide area are the roots of the poet's vision, incisive and unsentimental, fraught with objectives slightly imperceptible to him" ("Poet" 179). He felt the poems expressed "the Negro spirit"—"certainly the urge in that direction beckons strongest." Wary of puffery and public relations, he nevertheless hazarded superlatives: "Ordained is a pretty bloated word, but if there ever was a poet ordained by the stars to sing of the joys and sorrows attendant upon the experience of thwarted black folk placed in wretched juxtaposition to our Western civilization, that poet is Countee Cullen" ("Poet" 179).

As his friendship with Cullen revived, Walrond began losing patience with Claude McKay, who asked him to shepherd his work around New York while he wrote in self-imposed exile in Europe. Walrond was not alone in receiving McKay's entreaties; his correspondence with Louise Bryant and Nancy Cunard also conveyed exasperation with New York's capricious publishers and lamented his abject poverty. He was always down to his last *sou*, in ill health or ill temper, and in desperate need of a check, preferably made out in francs. His desperation became acute during his attempt to shop his novel, *Color Scheme*. By all accounts a flawed book, *Color Scheme* was never published and McKay discarded the manuscript. But he initially felt Walrond could help him place it. He showed one of McKay's letters to Lewis Baer in late 1925, who in turn contacted Locke, telling him McKay was "in Switzerland in dire distress. Eric wondered whether we could send him an advance on his share in 'the [New] Negro.' Even the smallest amount apparently would help him out."[21] Even as Walrond advocated, McKay found his efforts sluggish and asked Schomburg to prod him. Christmas Eve 1925 found Walrond defending himself to Schomburg: "I am sorry I had to give you cause to write me about McKay, but perhaps it is just as well as it forces me to do something which the rush of the holiday season had deprived me of the opportunity of doing." Explaining his efforts on McKay's behalf, he told of having read the novel and recommended it to two publishers despite his reservations and of attempting to obtain royalties from Harcourt Brace for poems they had anthologized. All the while McKay was writing "distressing letters" saying "he was terribly up against it" and enclosing poems for Walrond to "sell" if he would "consent to act as his agent." "I trust, by this letter, you will see that I haven't been asleep at the switch," he assured Schomburg.[22]

McKay contacted Walrond again a year later, asking his assistance with submissions to *Opportunity*. Walrond told him it was "foolhardy to try to sell MSS from such a distance without an agent acting in your behalf."

> Everybody here is so selfishly busy marketing or performing for the market wares of his own that it is a waste of time to try to butt in anywhere. If I were you I wouldn't bite my tongue when I write Johnson: tell him you are up against it and ask him what about the money he promised you for the stuff he has used. Bombard him to death; he's sure to quiver under continuous fire. I'd suggest that you write A & C Boni again [. . .] Du Bois is also offering upwards of $2,000 for literary prizes of all sorts and seems to be making an unexpectedly vigorous effort to get stuff by the younger men. I'd suggest that you re-establish relations with him.

McKay had asked Walrond about the status of *The New Masses*, which Walrond said was "going slowly to hell and is read by practically no one of consequence." There was also "a chap here who is constantly talking to me about you," an editor at the North American Newspaper Alliance, and he encouraged McKay to "drop him a line and tell him what you are trying to do." In short, he was constructive and solicitous: "Can't you try and get back to America? The world seems to have gone around a hundred times since you have been away."²³

McKay continued to rely on Walrond. It could take two weeks for letters between New York and Marseilles to arrive, and when they crossed paths consternation ensued. When Johnson rejected some work of McKay's, McKay pressed Walrond to exasperation. "I am taking this means of passing on to you the following from a letter which I have just received from Mr. Johnson." Walrond replied: "I am very sorry that Mr. Claude McKay has become exercised over the manuscripts which we had here in the office. However, I had written him saying that these stories about which he was very much concerned are to be returned, in fact, all of his manuscripts." "This was from a letter dated June 27, 1927," Walrond added peevishly, "I hope that this fully absolves me from the responsibility of having to jog Mr. Johnson's memory about your MSS again."²⁴

McKay denounced Walrond years later to Nancy Cunard. Cunard was gathering contributions for her *Negro* anthology, and their correspondence ranged across a number of subjects and acquaintances.

I dislike Eric Walrond. And he does me too. Think he is very pretentious light-weight. Knew him when I was on the Liberator with Max Eastman and he on the Negro World with Garvey, 1922. Garvey had given me hell and more in his paper (he always had a grudge about me for showing up the preposterous side of his movement in the Liberator) because the police had broken up a Liberator affair and beaten some guests on account of my dancing with a white woman—Crystal Eastman—and the NY papers had made quite a scandal of it. Eric came to see me and gave me some inside dope on Garvey's character for me to make a comeback attack—the crassest moral stuff and besides he was working for the man. Next time

I heard from him was 1925 in France *he wrote* asking me to send stories for a competition in the Negro magazine "Opportunity" for which he was assistant editor & offered to place some stuff for me. I was glad to do it for I was quite broke. The stories and poems I sent in did not take the prize, but because I was known a little the magazine proceeded to print them without paying me. And so I put my agent on them to collect.[25]

There may be something to McKay's account of the Garvey episode, but the *Opportunity* allegation does not comport with the evidence. Further, he wrote, "Walrond (in a widely reprinted article) said I had been invited to Russia by the Soviet Government and the impression was that I had become a Bolshevik agent. A lie." In fact, the article, a 1929 review of McKay's novel *Banjo*, was laudatory. Many reviewers skewered the book, not only for its licentiousness but also on technical grounds. Walrond's review, published in London's *Clarion* and Jamaica's *Gleaner*, expressed a high tolerance for *Banjo*'s formlessness, calling it "terribly illuminating" ("Negro Renaissance" 15). But he criticized McKay's dialogue, which undoubtedly provoked McKay's ire. "I have gone carefully through his stories," McKay said of Walrond, "and stripped of their futuristic verbiage they reveal nothing but the average white man's point of view towards Negroes."[26] The fallout between the two was protracted but final. Despite their professional ties and shared Caribbean background, Walrond and McKay were temperamentally unsuited for friendship. Island chauvinism may have been a factor—Jamaicans and Barbadians sometimes harbored mutual suspicions—but McKay's absence from Harlem during the period of the New Negro movement's literary efflorescence strained his relationship with Walrond, as with others.

A ROMANCE

Three revelers dropped by Alain Locke's New York apartment one evening in 1927, two contributors to *The New Negro* and a young woman, a recent University of Minnesota graduate, whom Du Bois had just hired at

The Crisis. Having missed Locke, they left a hastily scribbled note. "Eric Walrond, a beautiful lady, and I (no—Eric wasn't the "beautiful lady"!) found you out as usual. He is leaving tonight, despite the beautiful lady. *I'm not.* (Keep your mind in the right place, now!) Sorry we missed you. Marvel Jackson, Eric D. Walrond, R[udolph] F[isher]."[27] Marvel Jackson was often in Walrond's company in these years, and her absence from his extant papers is belied by the intensity of their attachment. They met while she was engaged to Roy Wilkins, who became executive secretary of the National Association for the Advancement of Colored People (NAACP), but Wilkins worked at *The Kansas City Call* and Jackson's move to New York opened her eyes to other possibilities. "I came to New York right at the tail end of the Negro Renaissance and I met such wonderful, much more exciting young men, I thought, than Roy," she recalled. "There was one that liked me very much; his name was Eric Walrond." "I really thought I was going to marry him. I was really in love with him, the first time I had cared deeply about someone of the opposite sex."[28] Jackson's reflections, recorded after an illustrious career in journalism and civil rights advocacy, offer a rare glimpse into Walrond's private life. They also underscore his abiding interest in West Indian experience in the United States.

Walrond met Jackson during a brief visit she made from Minneapolis in 1926. "If I examined it, I wouldn't be surprised if he weren't one of the reasons I really wanted to come to New York." Their relationship seems to have been the most durable of his attachments after his family's departure in 1923. Jackson later married a schoolteacher, Cecil Cooke, and wrote for *The Amsterdam News*, *The Compass*, and *The People's Voice.* She became a stalwart activist, organizing the Newspaper Guild, and a lifelong member of the Communist Party, refusing to name names during the McCarthy era and later serving as treasurer of the Angela Davis Defense Fund. Her story is fascinating in its own right, and it began when she moved to work at *The Crisis*, "a very thrilling experience for a little gal from Minnesota."[29]

Jackson was attracted to Walrond in part because of his captivating social milieu. Through him she met artists and writers with whom she formed lasting friendships: Hughes, Cullen, Robeson, Thurman,

Bontemps, and Aaron and Alta Douglas. She felt "lucky" to be there, dining at the invitation-only Civic Club with Jean Toomer, entering Lenox
Avenue nightspots in "a mixed group, half white, half black," and feeling "very safe" in doing so, accompanying Walrond to Robeson's sendoff
when the great baritone embarked to perform in London.[30] "It was a close-
knit group. They were talking about getting Guggenheim Fellowships. It
was really an inspiring group of young people to be involved with. [. . .]
Coming from where I did in Minnesota, to this very vibrant and alive
group of young people was wonderful." She moved into an apartment at
409 Edgecombe Avenue in Sugar Hill. "I can imagine almost any young
person just finishing college and getting into this sort of environment,
being excited about it." None of it would have been possible without
Walrond: "All my social life was built around him."[31]

Second, Walrond took Jackson seriously as an intellectual. Although
most of her work at *The Crisis* was clerical, she wrote the column "The
Browsing Reader" and was writing a novel about mixed-race children.
She and Walrond had a regular routine. "We spent every evening after
work at the Forty-second Street Library, where I wrote and he wrote. [. . .]
We would write until the library closed, and he would read what I had
written. [. . .] We'd go across to the Automat and he would go over the
stuff I wrote, and he expressed himself that he thought I had a lot of
ability. [. . .] I thought I was going to write the great American novel."
Jackson never completed her manuscript, but she kept writing and joined
workshops, including one in the 1930s that included a young Chicago
transplant, Richard Wright. "[H]e used to come by every Saturday night
to get some of my mother's hot rolls. I think I read that first chapter
of *Native Son* a million times. Every time he changed a comma in it, it
seemed to me he had me reading the thing." But "it wasn't just for the
writing" that Jackson valued Walrond, and "It wasn't just because of the
exciting people he introduced me to." "It was just that I liked Eric [. . .]
he was quite a nice companion." "I was really in love with him," she said,
"He was the first man that I had ever had any feeling for."[32]

For his part, Walrond would have been impressed by and drawn to
Jackson for a number of reasons, not least of which was her beauty. Three

years his junior, she had fair skin and flaxen hair, features she inherited from a grandmother she believed was the daughter of a white slave mistress. Politically astute and terrifically self-possessed, Jackson felt comfortable around white and black people alike. Her parents were middle class, her father a Pullman porter with a law degree, her mother a homemaker whose beauty as a young woman so impressed Du Bois that he worried for her welfare among the men for whose family she worked as a domestic servant. "From my father and mother we had a sense of pride and a sense of who we were, that we must work to make things better."[33] Marvel was the first black student in her elementary and high schools and one of five black women at her university, cultivating a mix of ambition, kindness, and dauntless determination that launched her career. These qualities, along with an incipient political militancy, undoubtedly attracted Walrond. And she was a formidable intellect, a shrewd analyst of the imbricated workings of gender, class, and race well before the term "intersectionality" was coined. She coauthored a prominent exposé, "The Bronx Slave Market," with Ella Baker.[34]

Jackson felt Walrond's pride in his West Indian heritage. One day they noticed the cover photo of *The Crisis* featuring a Syracuse University track star and Walrond declared, "He's West Indian." Jackson replied, "Anytime anyone seems to have accomplished anything, you say they're West Indian." In this case, his claim was substantiated by a personal connection; his younger sister had dated this sprinter in Panama. Ironically, it was also the man Marvel Jackson would later marry, Cecil Cooke. "I had not met Cecil at this time" of the photo, "I was going around with Eric." But later, when she started dating Cooke, she was certain Walrond had been wrong because "he talked very well" and without any "accent whatsoever that I could detect." "I thought to myself, 'Eric was certainly wrong about this one.'" But "after I had been going around with him about six weeks," an inadvertent Britishism gave him away.

> He said to me, "You like ice cream. You have never eaten any ice cream until you've had some Schroft's Ice Cream." We say "Schraft." I looked at him. I said, "Are you West Indian?" Well, there was great prejudice

then between West Indians and Americans. Americans didn't like West Indians, you know, and vice versa. [. . .] So I remember him saying to me, "Does it make any difference if I'm a West Indian?" And I said, "No" and I told him the story. "Eric said you were West Indian and I didn't [hear] any trace of accent." It turned out he was seven years old when his parents moved to Panama, and he grew up in the American sector.[35]

Jackson's recollection illustrates Walrond's abiding interest in the Caribbean. Cecil Cooke's all but complete linguistic assimilation concealed his Caribbeanness from his companion, perhaps unintentionally. Walrond did not object to assimilation, but as an index of anti-West Indian animus, and as a symptom of monolithic notions of blackness, it underscored the necessity for West Indians to assert their distinctiveness even as they made the adjustments immigrants make to new environments. Cecil Cooke's wayward vowel betrayed his ethnicity, compelling his future wife to admit, "It seems I was attracted to West Indians," though she gamely added, "I didn't know whether they were West Indian or not until I met them."[36] If her account of Walrond is to be credited, he later regretted their breakup.

COSMIC CONSCIOUSNESS

The community to which Walrond introduced Marvel Jackson had a more obscure component, a hidden transcript. In late 1925 he became involved in the work of the Institute for the Harmonious Development of Man. Based on the teachings of G. I. Gurdjieff, an Armenian spiritualist, the New York initiative was led by Jean Toomer and A. R. Orage, former editor of the English journal *The New Age*. Gurdjieff's philosophy was popularized in England in the early 1920s and, although it is unsurprising that it spread to New York given the trans-Atlantic traffic in avant-garde ideas, its foothold in Harlem was Toomer's doing. Walrond did not write directly about the Gurdjieff "work," but in this sense he was faithful to its teachings, which prized secrecy and kabalistic encryption. Several of

Walrond's friends were disciples while others were fellow-travelers, curious about Gurdjieff's "system" for heightening consciousness. Toomer's adaptation of Gurdjieff appealed to African American artists who felt confined by "Negro" identity. They sought full self-realization, something that the glacially slow shifts in race relations would not soon deliver but that Gurdjieff's teachings promised through transcendence of racial thinking. Other participants included Thurman, Larsen, Fisher, Hurston, Douglas, Dorothy Peterson, and George Schuyler. Given Walrond's relationships with them, his admiration of Toomer, and his desperate quest for psychological stability, it makes sense that he was drawn to this group. Beyond this circumstantial evidence, unmistakable traces of Gurdjieff's philosophy appeared in his writing.[37]

The Gurdjieff "system" was mystical and messianic. It posited an antagonism between "false personality," the insidious product of socialization, and one's true "essence." In Orage and Toomer's version, it reserved a particular place for art, which could—if practiced with "objectivity"—transform creator and audience alike. The practice entailed lectures, role-playing, and physical and mental exercises, participants proceeding from novice to advanced stages with a dual aim: to experience themselves authentically, yet also to appraise themselves objectively through the eyes of the "other," a technique called "self-observation and non-identification." Muriel Draper, a friend of Van Vechten's, convened meetings for Orage's lectures, while Toomer's group met in Harlem, Brooklyn, and Greenwich Village.[38] Hughes satirized it as a "cult," but he exaggerated when he said, "Nobody in Harlem could afford to pay for Gurdjieff. And very few there have evolved souls."[39] The group was active and large, notes George Hutchinson, "not, as often assumed, attractive only to white people with a large disposable income and plenty of spare time, although they ultimately depended on such."[40]

Toomer gave a presentation at the 135th Street library in April 1925 that Walrond would have attended. Entitled "Towards Reality," it praised the artistic renaissance and the Harlem issue of *Survey*, not as expressions of a racial inheritance but as evidence that "The Negro is in the process of discovering himself and being discovered," removing the "crust" of received ideas. Thus would "the Negro" arrive at "reality" and encounter "that strange thing called soul." But the "work" was not principally about race. As Aaron Douglas said, Toomer believed

> We all have the potentialities of intellectual, artistic giants if we could only get to the bottom of our real selves. He claims that back deep in our natures there is a mine of unused power, a source, a hitherto little known faculty which is neither body, emotion or intellect, but is the equal and combined power of all.[41]

This helps explain the idiosyncratic formulations in an essay Walrond published the month of Toomer's presentation. He referred to the emerging group of writers "utterly shorn" of a "negative manner of looking at life," an echo of Toomer's statement that "Because he was denied by others, the Negro denied them and necessarily denied himself. Forced to say nay to the white world, he was negative toward his own life."[42] Walrond said the younger generation refused to "put the Negro on a lofty pedestal" because "they don't think of the Negro as a distinct racial type at all. They only write about him because they know more about him than anyone else. His is closer to them. He is part of them. As such they see him" ("Negro Literati" 33). The notion that the "Negro" was "closer to" and "part of" these authors presupposed nonidentity, characteristic of Toomer's interpretation of Gurdjieff. When *Nigger Heaven* was published, Walrond was no longer close to Van Vechten, but his review of the novel referenced Gurdjieff explicitly. "[I]t prepares the way for examination of the fruits of a cultural flowering among the Negroes which is now about to emerge. And no colored man," he concluded, "adept as he might be at self-observation and non-identification, could have written it" ("Epic" 153). These last were Gurdjieff catchphrases, elements of the curriculum of Toomer and Orage.[43]

"Adventures in Misunderstanding," which Walrond published the same month, also made overt reference to Gurdjieff's system. The essay ranges across color prejudices in Panama and the United States. "I believe the dicta to restrict the creative impulses of the Negro to the experiences of the blacks will be tempered by a tolerance and even a wish for transcripts of life more cosmically felt and conceived" (112). The statement curiously decouples the terms "Negro" and "black," but Walrond meant that the expectation that "Negroes" confine themselves to the expression of racialization must be dismantled. His terminology sounded odd because it echoed Gurdjieff's formulation of the stage beyond "self-observation and non-identification," which was "cosmic consciousness," the precondition for being "fully human."[44] Esoteric mysticism thus emerged in Walrond's work, and for all its abstraction, it offered Walrond a way to negotiate something that had long troubled him: how to embrace his blackness without being considered, and considering himself, simply a "Negro." Jon Woodson notes, "Toomer's approach to the intricate problem was to paradoxically insist that African Americans had to disidentify themselves as African Americans, yet remain conscious that they were African Americans."[45] As a West Indian, Walrond had confronted this paradox well before the Gurdjieff group, if not on their "cosmic" plane.

The link between Walrond's Caribbeanness and Gurdjieff's principles was made in Wallace Thurman's novel *Infants of the Spring*. Toomer advised his audience in 1925 to "be receptive of [the Negro's] reality as it emerges, assured that in proportion as he discovers what is real within him, he will create, and by that act create at once himself and contribute his value to America."[46] The character Thurman based on Walrond, Cedric Williams, echoes this statement during a salon conversation. In response to claims by the Locke character and Cullen character that Negro writers succeed only by returning to "racial roots, and cultivating a healthy paganism based on African traditions," Cedric poses what Thurman describes as an intriguing question.

What does it matter what any of you do so long as you remain true to yourselves? There is no necessity for this movement to become standardized. There is ample room for everyone to follow his own individual track. Dr. Parkes wants us all to go back to Africa and resurrect our pagan heritage, become atavistic. In this he is supported by Mr. Clinton. Fenderson here wants us all to be propagandists and yell at the top of our lungs at every conceivable injustice. Madison wants us all to take a cue from Leninism and fight the capitalistic bogey. Well . . . why not let each young hopeful choose his own path? Only in that way will anything be achieved.[47]

The remark reflects Walrond's independent streak, but it clearly resonates with Toomer's teachings on Gurdjieff. It was a philosophy toward which his incomplete identification with African Americans predisposed him, but it also registered his increasing suspicion of collective social action. Instead he had placed his faith in individuals working out their own spiritual destinies.

A PERSON OF DISTINCTION

Alain Locke wrote before *Tropic Death*, "Eric Walrond has a tropical color and almost volcanic gush that are unique even after more than a generation of exotic word painting by master artists."[48] And after *Tropic Death* his fame grew. It outsold *Cane* nearly two to one in these years and was among the most requested books at the 135th Street library when it came out.[49] "One of the truly avant-garde literary experiments of the Harlem Renaissance," says David Levering Lewis, it was "a prism so strange and many-sided" that few readers missed "its iridescence."[50] Walrond's reputation was burnished by his association with Boni & Liveright, and Hughes and Cullen singled him out for public praise.[51] Thurman said Walrond was among the few who deserved acclaim amidst a generally fatuous celebration: "There is one more young Negro who will probably be classed with Mr. Hughes when he does commence to write about the American scene. So far this writer, Eric Walrond, has confined his talents to producing realistic prose pictures of the Caribbean region. If he ever turns on the American Negro as impersonally and as unsentimentally as he turned on West Indian folk in *Tropic Death*, he too will be blacklisted in polite colored circles."[52] In fact, Walrond had just "turned on" them in the story "City Love." A ribald tale of a young

Harlem couple's afternoon tryst, "City Love" was selected for the inaugural issue of *The American Caravan*. Edited by Van Wyck Brooks and Lewis Mumford, this was an annual compendium of modernist literature in which Walrond shared space with Hemingway, Williams, Stein, Dos Passos, and others. No longer a contestant, he now served as a judge for the *Opportunity* literary contest.

He still frequented Harlem's cabarets, but a Friday evening was as likely to find him at the Lafayette Theater on 132nd Street or at the Provincetown Playhouse in Greenwich Village. Many of his friends were performers, and he was an enthusiastic spectator, attending Roland Hayes concerts and Paul Robeson plays, watching with delight the lithe-limbed Florence Mills, and enjoying the syncopated exuberance of Fletcher Henderson's Rainbow Orchestra, the blues of Ethel Waters, and the stride piano of Willie "the Lion" Smith. He befriended the Trinidadian bandleader Sam Manning, who was Amy Ashwood Garvey's companion and creative collaborator. Dinner parties abounded, from the opulence of A'Lelia Walker's Italianate home in Sugar Hill to the modest apartments of Aaron Douglas on Edgecombe Avenue and of Dorothy Peterson in Brooklyn. Walrond threw parties too, though not every guest left contented; the Robesons attended a "little gathering" at Walrond's that Eslanda found "a beastly bore," just "some little insignificant talkative Negroes."[53] When the Fisk Jubilee Singers came to New York, Walrond joined Casper Holstein, who bought box seats at Town Hall.[54]

Certain functions were compulsory for an established writer who was also *Opportunity*'s business manager. In October 1926, Walrond joined dozens of Harlemites and a handful of white friends at the 135th Street YMCA for the Krigwa Players awards, a theater group started by Du Bois and colleagues.[55] That spring he attended the annual meeting of the National Urban League. Funded by the Carnegie Corporation, the Urban League proclaimed "inter-racial Good Will" and 100 attendees heard from the governor of New York and the lead organizer of the American Federation of Labor.[56] When the Comus Club, an elite group of black socialites, held its Christmas formal at the Savoy Ballroom, Walrond polished his spats and joined Cullen, Jackman, Bennett, Fisher, Walker, and

Du Bois. As "Negro" society columns such as the *Inter-State Tattler* suggest, there were more benefits, ceremonies, and concerts than one could possibly attend, a professional hazard for Walrond.

Two of the livelier engagements fell within ten days of each other in October 1927, when the black-owned cabaret Club Ebony opened in Harlem and A'Lelia Walker opened "The Dark Tower," an ostentatious tearoom overlooking the garden of her 136th Street home. Walrond arrived at Club Ebony with Marvel Jackson, meeting Aaron Douglas, whose murals adorned the club's walls depicting "tropical settings, African drummers and dancers, a banjo player, and a cakewalker."[57] Douglas should have been thrilled but had just been summoned from the scaffolding by Charlotte Osgood Mason and upbraided for accepting a fellowship in Philadelphia.[58] Walrond and Jackson also spoke to William Seabrook, a white novelist who would later write in support of a fellowship for Walrond. Equipped with a "spacious dance floor" and "large orchestra," Club Ebony celebrated Florence Mills as guest of honor, with socialites pouring in from Atlantic City, Greenwich Village, Washington, and Philadelphia to toast a club that promised to retain the profits of black entertainment within the community.[59]

Celebrity had not made Walrond rich, however, and he continued living in his 144th Street apartment and working at *Opportunity*, which kept him busy. He was tasked with marketing the magazine and maintaining contact with subscribers, supporters, and advertisers.[60] Sponsorship from Holstein expanded *Opportunity*'s awards program and their administration became a considerable undertaking. Advertising accounts required attention: Walrond wrote James Weldon Johnson to say he "had the distinction to prepare for the October *Opportunity* the advertising copy" for his *Book of American Negro Spirituals*.[61] He was suited for the job, task oriented, and familiar with editors and publishers. But Charles Johnson felt that his business manager was also one of the few "Negro writers who can, with complete justice, be styled intellectuals," and he sought a wider field for Walrond, nominating him for a Harmon Foundation Award in 1926.[62] The prizes associated with the award were not insubstantial—$400 to the winner, $100 to runners-up—but its real significance lay in the distinction.

Walrond did not stand a chance his first time out. The Harmon Awards, funded by a white philanthropist from Ohio, recognized "Distinguished Achievement by Negroes" in eight fields, including literature. To administer the award, the foundation partnered with the Federal Council of the Churches of Christ in America, whose Commission on the Church and Race Relations was led by George E. Haynes, cofounder of the National Urban League. The Urban League connection may have encouraged Johnson to submit Walrond's name, but he was outclassed. Nominees included Locke for *The New Negro*, Cullen for *Color*, Johnson for *The Book of American Negro Spirituals*, Du Bois and Charles Johnson for editorship of *The Crisis* and *Opportunity*, respectively, Hughes for *The Weary Blues*, and Charles Chesnutt, who was nominated for lifetime achievement. There was some question whether Walrond was eligible because *Tropic Death* was not due out until October.[63] But he rushed the page proofs to Haynes in early August, and references were solicited from the vice president of *Forbes*, Donald Friede of Boni & Liveright, and Eugene Kinckle Jones of the Urban League.[64] Awards committee chairman Joel Spingarn let it be known that he was not easily impressed. The younger generation's literary achievements "have been grossly exaggerated," he said. "A few minor poets and a few third-rate novelists are not a literature. The friends of the Negro, who have faith in his ability, would do him wrong if they were to give him a false impression of the literary work so far produced—not only a false impression but a false standard and a false hope."[65] The 1926 prizes went to Cullen and James Weldon Johnson.

Spingarn's colleagues the following year were no less exacting, but it was their inability to reach consensus that ultimately landed Walrond an award. Indeed, given the impact of this award on subsequent events it is no exaggeration to say that the messy deliberations of these combative judges decisively altered the course of Walrond's career. His selection was a compromise reached after a war of attrition over several weeks, phone calls, and telegrams. Surprisingly, *Tropic Death*'s staunchest advocate was the conservative critic and poet William Stanley Braithwaite. Joining Braithwaite and Spingarn among the judges were Henry Goddard Leach, editor of *The Forum*; Hamilton Holt, president of Rollins College; and

Albert Shaw, editor of *The American Review of Reviews*. Had Haynes anticipated the rancor they generated he may have advised the foundation to redirect its philanthropy. The judges' arguments remind one of the precariousness of events that over time acquire the appearance of inevitability. In order to win even the second prize of 1927 (first went to James Weldon Johnson for *God's Trombones*), Walrond had to beat Arthur Huff Fauset, Georgia Douglas Johnson, Benjamin Brawley, Willis Richardson, and Alain Locke, among others, and he had to overcome the objection of one judge who would do almost anything to prevent him from winning.

Charles Johnson jeopardized Walrond's candidacy by submitting his materials after the deadline, but the judges may have been persuaded to review the delinquent manuscripts upon reading the encomiums from his recommenders. Friede was the most knowledgeable and enthusiastic: "I have seen his first book of short stories, 'Tropic Death'; half of his book 'The Big Ditch,' his treatment of the construction of the Panama Canal; and part of a novel which he will finish after the publication of 'The Big Ditch'; besides various articles and short stories which have been published from time to time in periodicals." "I believe him to be the outstanding Negro prose writer of this country," he added, and "I believe that his work will in time place him among the important writers in America—both Negro and white." Friede's boss, Horace Liveright, also said he had known Walrond for two years and read *Tropic Death*, though it must be said that Liveright was notoriously inattentive to manuscripts, relying on the advice of established authors and contacts. He had read the first draft of *The Big Ditch*, he claimed, and praised "the beautiful style and excellent color which Mr. Walrond has employed in his writing, and the originality of his ideas." He added, "I believe his writing to be the finest now being produced by any member of the colored race." The novelist Joseph Hergesheimer said, "I have read *Tropic Death*, which seemed to me to be written with a fine sense of beauty and a respect for truth. [. . .] He can write extremely well; what is more important he writes with courage; I think he has the ability to see honestly." Asked why he endorsed the candidate, Hergesheimer said, "A sense of reality. The promise of dignity.

Freedom from any bitterness or prejudice."[66] In fact, no one was bitterer than Walrond, but the lyricism and Caribbean setting of *Tropic Death* inoculated it against that charge.

While the judges deliberated, Walrond had other irons in the fire. Determined to make it as an independent author, he renegotiated his contract for *The Big Ditch* and quit *Opportunity*. Under the new arrangement, Boni & Liveright would pay a $500 advance in installments of $40 per week. This was more than double the original amount, but the contract stipulated, "As you complete the various portions of the manuscript, you will submit them to us for examination and for possible placing with magazines."[67] Serialization proved difficult, and although Walrond continued to publish other work, he probably missed the steady *Opportunity* paycheck. Johnson threw him a fine sendoff. "We are having a little informal dinner party," he told Locke, "in the private dining room of Craig's on Thursday, February 3d, for Mr. Walrond, who has resigned from the staff of *Opportunity*. We should like very much if you could arrange to spend your dinner hour there. No speeches; no dress regalia—just a friendly little party."[68] *The Pittsburgh Courier* covered his resignation, Walrond assuring the reporter "that he has good prospects for making writing a paying career."[69] Johnson paid glowing tribute.

> In the resignation of Eric Walrond as Business Manager, *Opportunity* relinquishes from its staff one of the most brilliant of the younger generation of Negro writers. The duties of this department drew upon a skill less generally known to the public than his stories and essays, and it is a pleasing mark of well-rounded competence that artist and business man could be combined to the degree that he achieved. To his work, both in and out of the line of duty, *Opportunity* is indebted for new and valuable friends: he has been, perhaps longest of any of the younger writing group, successfully established in literary circles, although it was only last year that he offered a volume of stories to be published. [. . .] Here is a ready index to the prodigality of talent and material which are so unquestionably a personal resource with him. Mr. Walrond was one of the first to sense the new public spirit on Negro

aspirations and work, and contributed doubly, to a refinement of this public spirit and to the Negro aspirations. There are few young Negro writers in New York who do not associate some incident or personal discovery with his ceaseless, even if apparently unordered, activities. In withdrawing from the business department, there is the possibility and the hope that more time will be permitted for a field of writing in which he has already begun so magnificently to distinguish himself.[70]

Describing Walrond as a tireless organizer, an intellectual visionary, and a literary craftsman, Johnson stated his faith in Walrond. The Harmon Award would be a feather in the young writer's cap, but it would also be a feather in the nest Johnson made at *Opportunity*, which had been Walrond's refuge from the depression that two years earlier had him contemplating suicide.

The Harmon judging was muddled from the outset. Braithwaite put Walrond first and James Weldon Johnson second: "Walrond's book is far more native to his own individuality; more original, and the power of his substance, and the artistic excellence of his style is of his own intimate creation. He is emphatically my choice for the award."[71] Leach and Shaw wanted Benjamin Brawley first and James Weldon Johnson second. As the year's end approached, Spingarn attempted to forge consensus on this basis, but Braithwaite was obstinate. From a leafy suburb near Boston he wired the committee, "Cannot assent first award Brawley. [. . .] Insist upon minority decision. First award to Eric Walrond. Agree second award Johnson."[72] Recognizing the impasse, Spingarn called Braithwaite on what he quaintly termed "the long-distance telephone." The irrepressible Braithwaite persuaded Spingarn to his view, and Spingarn was compelled to write George Haynes, "We both agreed that Professor Brawley's work was highly creditable, and deserved some sort of recognition, but that to award it a prize over two such creative works as *God's Trombones* and *Tropic Death* would not cast credit on the Harmon Awards."[73] Thus, "after considerable discussion," it was agreed that Johnson would receive first prize, Walrond second, and honorable mention to Fauset and Brawley. Shaw lobbied successfully to have Locke added to the honorable mention list, and the matter seemed settled. But Holt was unappeased: "I still vote for Georgia Johnson for First Prize and Richardson for Second," or failing that, any combination "to prevent Brawley or Walrond from getting it. I would not vote for the two latter for anything."[74] Out of this tangle Spingarn somehow wove a compromise. Honorable mention went to Locke, Georgia Douglas Johnson, Brawley, and Fauset. Leach assented "under protest and only for the sake of arriving at a decision." They had worn Holt down: "As long as the mountain will not come to Mohammed, Mohammed will go to the mountain," he wired.[75] The next day, Haynes wrote to notify Walrond of his award, omitting reference to the battle of attrition behind it.

Skepticism pervaded the New Negro movement toward the proliferation of awards—the "ballyhoo brigade," Thurman derisively termed it. Walrond too felt white approval was not the goal, but he accepted the Harmon Award with unmitigated enthusiasm. "I cannot communicate to you the thrill I experienced on receiving your letter," he told Haynes, "And to be cited on the same 'ticket' with Mr. James Weldon Johnson was also a distinction which I should not hope to under-estimate, ever."[76] He was now expecting notice about another major award. The Pulitzer Prize–winning dramatist Zona Gale funded a scholarship to bring impecunious writers of promise to the University of Wisconsin, and Walrond applied. A longtime friend of *Opportunity*, Gale had judged its fiction contests and had attended the 1924 Civic Club dinner, and she championed women writers, especially Fauset, Angelina Weld Grimké, and Georgia Douglas Johnson.[77] She felt that the United States was tough on artists, and "if the artist is a Negro, his difficulties are needlessly greater in this country than in any other land of the civilized world."[78] She was moved by Walrond's fiction, so it thrilled her to learn that he received the scholarship in her name.[79] She pledged to have letters of introduction prepared for his arrival. Just three weeks after learning of the Harmon Award, in other words, Walrond decided to leave New York. The scholarship included a tuition waiver, "freedom in electing work in the University," and a monthly stipend of $25. A modest sum, but he could now resume his bachelor's degree and work with an esteemed faculty.

No record survives of Walrond's reaction to this turn of events but it constituted a tremendous upheaval. The day after receiving official word of the scholarship, a letter arrived asking him to rush a photo of himself to Du Bois at *The Crisis* "for his use in connection with an article on the Harmon Awards."[80] The next day he boarded a train to Madison. The haste with which he arranged his departure is reflected in the confusion about the ceremony at which he would receive his Harmon Award. "Can you by any chance arrange presentation in Chicago?" he wired Haynes en route to Wisconsin, "Profoundly regret inability to change present plans."[81] Haynes had no trouble securing a place for him on the program in Chicago, scheduled two weeks later at the historic Olivet Baptist Church. The whirlwind culminated in a dash to Chicago for the ceremony. "I went up on a six thirty train, took my award at eight, and flew back to Madison on the two o'clock sleeper." The event "went off splendidly," he felt, and the proceedings were "not too long but direct and to the point."[82] Reports reached Haynes that Olivet was filled to the rafters with 2,000 attendees, the ceremony coinciding with the annual "Interracial Sunday" convened by the Council of Churches. "Speeches were made" and "telegrams were received and read," including one from Countée Cullen.[83] Walrond reflected, "Everybody seemed to be immensely pleased."[84]

Little did he know how much more complicated things would soon become. Wisconsin faculty sought to identify "courses which will be directly related to [his] creative work" but this work was on Panama and required archival research. A novel manuscript was also in progress, but the Panama book was paramount. He had begun in earnest in January 1927, when he left *Opportunity* and renegotiated his Boni & Liveright contract. "On finding that I could not complete my researches in New York, I undertook, at the behest of the publishers, to make a trip to Panama early in the spring," a four-week sojourn.[85] The summer he devoted to writing, and in September, Bennett reported in *Opportunity*, "Who should I meet on the steps of the Forty-second Street Library the other day but Eric Walrond! He tells me that now that he has come back from Panama he is writing a book about that country . . . and I said how he surely ought to do just that!"[86] But Walrond rushed the project, anxious to meet the publisher's time line.

Returning to New York in April I was advised to prepare at once certain parts of the manuscript which might prove available for serialization. I prepared four or five chapters and sent them off to the agent. The narrative went the rounds of the editors but naturally did not "strike fire." I attribute this to no inherent weakness either in the plan or texture of the book, but to the unleisurely fashion in which the preliminary parts had been prepared.[87]

The month in Panama persuaded him that *The Big Ditch* required additional research and inspired other projects. He applied for a Guggenheim Foundation fellowship to fund a year of travel in Latin America and the Caribbean. Within weeks of accepting the Harmon Award and Zona Gale Scholarship and moving to Wisconsin, he got word that he would be moving again.

THE GUGGENHEIM FELLOWSHIP AND *THE BIG DITCH*

A young "Negro" with one book out had a lot of nerve applying for a Guggenheim Fellowship in 1927. Of the foundation's first 109 fellows, the vast majority had academic appointments and only three were African Americans.[88] In its second year, the foundation received 900 applications, of which just seven were selected in creative arts. That this number rose to eleven in the year prior to Walrond's application may have emboldened him, but he was a long shot. With a bequest of $3.5 million, the Guggenheim Foundation had ten times the budget of the Harmon Foundation and prestige of a different order. The selection committee included elite university administrators, and the director was Henry Allen Moe, who would become one of Walrond's most faithful correspondents.[89] The program's self-image was lofty: "By setting the standards of qualifications up to the highest possible point, the Foundation would necessarily designate its Fellows as being superior men and women," declared the first selection committee chairman.[90]

Walrond submitted a detailed research agenda and résumé, but he knew he needed impressive recommenders. He could not ask anyone like

Casper Holstein, who supported his Harmon nomination, and the list he furnished included no African Americans: Donald Friede of Boni & Liveright; Robert Herrick, the novelist and University of Chicago professor who reviewed for *The New Republic*; Zona Gale; and the adventure novelists William Seabrook and William McFee, the first of whom was a notorious scoundrel, the latter an early mentor of Walrond's who had managed within five years to forget him. Fortunately, Bob Davis of *Munsey's* came to his aid with a glowing endorsement. Walrond announced his publications: "I have already written one book of short stories dealing with native life in the West Indies" and his second book, due in spring 1928, was the "first human interest account of the canal from the arrival of the French on the Isthmus in 1880 down to the opening of the canal in 1914." The catalog copy read:

> The building of the Panama Canal, that gigantic triumph of engineering over the most stupendous physical difficulties, lends itself to vivid telling as a human interest story. Strangely enough, though other accounts of the feat have been written, Mr. Walrond is the first author to bring out the drama of this as yet unsung epic of human heroism. He tells of revolutionaries, riots and the stirrings of racial consciousness among the varied nationalities engaged in the work. He tells of the titanic achievements of science, of human labor, of engineering. He describes the life and death battle against disease and insect pests which in that tropical climate present a more formidable front than armies of mere men. In this book, as in *Tropic Death*, the atmospheric quality is enriched by the author's memories of his impressionable boyhood years spent on the Isthmus. *The Big Ditch* is a colorful and dramatic, yet careful and authentic work.[91]

Framed thus, *The Big Ditch* shared the "color" and "drama" of Walrond's fiction but came with an assurance of historical fact.

He proposed now to return to fiction and folk cultures. "My object is to write a series of novels and short stories of native life in the West Indies," emphasizing "the distinct racial and cultural composition of each island or group of islands."

I propose delineating the peculiar quality of life current in the islands of Barbados, Jamaica, Trinidad, Cuba, and Martinique. While I should be anxious to allow no phase of life in the seaport towns and cities of the West Indies to escape my notice, I, however, think my desire would be to concentrate on the life and ways of the more primitive classes further inland. As I see it now the bulk of the material accruing from this study would resolve itself in terms of fiction, but it would be my plan to weave into this imaginative pattern a considerable amount of the legends, folk tales, peasant songs and voodoo myths abounding in this region.

The objective was "to interpret native life in the West Indies for the edification of people in the United States and Europe," and as Herrick said in *The New Republic*, he had the field "quite to himself."[92]

Herrick and Gale recommended him on the strength of his writing, while Davis, Seabrook, and Friede addressed his character. Herrick was "impressed not only with the creative ability of his stories but also with the grasp Mr. Walrond had of his material."[93] Gale felt that his substantial talent was poised upon greatness. Reading his submissions to the first *Opportunity* contest, she felt he "stood far above any of those entering fiction, and abreast of writers quite outside his class."

His power was in the vigor, the clarity, the sweep of his style combined with amazing observation, and a certain accustomedness which seemed to belong to the Russians or the French. . . . But as I got into his manuscripts, I saw that he had not mastered his medium sufficiently to sustain a piece of fiction—he became powerless to direct his great gift, he lacked the knowledge and practice to find the flow of form. But all the time this great power over the minute, and this vigorous attack went on to the end. I recall that I said—though I could not vote for either of his stories for a prize—that if the contest had done nothing but to discover Eric Walrond, the effort and expenses were justified.[94]

Davis also suggested that racial background qualified Walrond for the proposed work but insisted that he offered something more: "Through education, application and a deep passion for self-expression in words he has come to understand the power of the English language and its interpretive value." Over seven years "I have watched his progress in letters, printed much of his literature and read his entire output."[95]

Donald Friede could only claim to have known Walrond half as long but was no less effusive.

> Tropic Death I consider a fine, faithful and beautiful picture of the life of the negroes of the West Indies, and such portions that I have seen of The Big Ditch lead me to feel sure that this too will be a very important and beautifully written book. I can say with assurance that Mr. Walrond's talents in this particular field are exceptional. I know of no one who can re-create life—in the regions he knows—as vividly as he can.[96]

Unlike the others, Friede and Seabrook sought to establish Walrond's personal integrity. "I know him to be temperate and painstakingly scrupulous," said Friede, "a diligent and conscientious worker who will leave no stone unturned to get the information that will make his material complete."[97]

There is some irony in Walrond's securing character testimony from Seabrook. An avowed proponent of the occult, he had purportedly eaten human flesh in Africa and had hosted Aleister Crowley, famous practitioner of "black magic," at his Georgia home for two months.[98] Having recently published a narrative of travels among Bedouin and Kurdish tribes, he would soon write books on the power of witchcraft, the zombie in Haitian vodou, and his own alcoholism, and he committed suicide by drug overdose in 1945. In recommending Walrond, he conceded that he may not be the finest judge of character.

> I have known and sincerely liked Eric Walrond for a number of years. My wife, on whose opinion of character I depend more than my own, liked him instinctively at first sight, and almost from our first acquaintance we have counted him as our friend. [W]e have known him under a great variety of circumstances, in our home, in his, occasionally in

the homes of mutual friends. He is one of the people, and I think there are many such, whom one seems to know intuitively is all right. I do not mean to imply that there is anything extraordinarily moralistic or saintly about him. I mean simply that he has a sort of fundamental integrity which is unmistakeable. I happen to like Eric Walrond very much—that of course is not necessarily connected with character; I like some people whom I wouldn't trust around the corner—but Walrond is the sort of man I would trust and know was all right even if I happened not to like him.[99]

Moreover, Seabrook declared him possessed of "a peculiar creative spark which may perhaps be defined as potential genius." "My feeling that he may go further and eventually become one of the truly great men of his race is shared by a considerable number of literary authorities who are not given to extravagant expression generally on such subjects."[100] The references had spoken; now there was the matter of the books themselves, which had not arrived at the foundation.

Walrond assured Henry Allen Moe that "a copy of *Tropic Death*, along with two scrap books containing comments and reviews concerning it, is being sent you today."[101] As to *The Big Ditch* he regretted "that the complete manuscript has not yet been delivered to the publishers." His haste in circulating it for serialization had hampered its development; but he told Moe, "Since that experience, the book has undergone careful planning, and the material relevant to it jealously selected." Moe had reason to wonder because *The Big Ditch* was publicized in Boni & Liveright's Fall 1927 catalog and was announced in *Opportunity* that November.[102] The book would never materialize, but the Guggenheim Fellowship did. Walrond got word from Moe a few short weeks after the Harmon ceremony in Chicago, his boxes still unpacked in Madison.[103] "It is with the profoundest joy that I acknowledge receipt of your letter of March 13, 1928, notifying me that I have been appointed to the Guggenheim Fellowship," he replied. "The opportunity is one that comes but once in a lifetime, and I assure you that I shall endeavor, by carrying out to the best of my ability the terms of this project, to merit the faith and confidence which have thus been reposed in me."[104] He presented himself to the Wisconsin General Hospital for physical examination. "A colored male, age 28, height 5 feet 10 inches, weight 138 pounds, whose general appearance is that of good health," he was deemed fit to travel.[105] Finishing the spring semester, he packed his things. Of the thirteen fellows in the creative arts, he was the only fiction writer and the only one not bound for France.[106] Ironically, his Caribbean journey would end there anyway.

7

THE CARIBBEAN AND FRANCE (1928–1931)

When news reached Zora Neale Hurston that Eric Walrond and Countée Cullen were leaving on Guggenheim Fellowships, she dashed off an indignant note to Langston Hughes. "What, I ask with my feet turned out, are Countee and Eric going abroad to study? A Negro goes to white land to learn his trade! Ha!"[1] Hurston could sniff, but unlike most Guggenheim Fellows, Walrond's journey took him throughout the Caribbean. His award was trumpeted in the African American press and beyond.[2] *The Times* of London noted that he was one of "three negroes" among the 75 fellowship recipients.[3] Shortly before Walrond left for Panama, his first destination, V. F. Calverton wrote W. E. B. Du Bois that he was compiling *The Anthology of American Negro Literature* and felt Walrond was self-evidently among the short-story writers to include.[4] *The American Caravan* also anthologized him, and *The Negro in Contemporary American Literature* credited him with having demonstrated "that the Negro may be judged as an artist with no special consideration because of race"[5] (51). When the *Encyclopedia Britannica* prepared a fourteenth edition in 1928, the editors invited him to submit the entry on Harlem. In subsequent years, he would present versions of this entry to audiences from Barbados and the Virgin Islands to Paris, Madrid, and London.[6]

Walrond's departure has been seen as the beginning of his end, an unraveling. It marked a decisive break from the exuberance of Harlem, and he would never be as prolific again. But he does not seem to have had misgivings, nor did he express regret later. Leaving the United States enabled a distinctive new sensibility, a critical cosmopolitanism. As he traveled, first in the Caribbean, then to France and England, his work came to exhibit a form of border thinking, an effort to articulate the disavowed links between modernity and coloniality.[7]

The seeds were sown before Walrond's departure for problems later attributed to his exile. Shortly after receiving the Guggenheim award, he wrote Boni & Liveright that he was "down to my last buck" awaiting his royalty check.[8] *Opportunity* reported that *The Big Ditch* was about to be published, but the announcement was premature; not only was the manuscript prepared too hastily, Boni & Liveright was beset with trouble.[9] Vice President Donald Friede was negotiating a buyout, and the firm was in dire financial condition. Horace Liveright and editorial director T. R. Smith had just been acquitted of obscenity charges for publishing a salacious Maxwell Bodenheim novel, but Friede still faced obscenity charges for selling a copy of Dreiser's *An American Tragedy* in Boston. Liveright's wife was suing for divorce, and he was badly injured in an inebriated fall from an open car.[10] The vice president for production and sales, Julian Messner, wanted to unload Walrond's book on Friede, who was forming a new company. Nothing suggests that Walrond was consulted or notified.

"Friede had me on the phone this morning," Messner wrote Liveright, "He is willing to take over 'The Big Ditch.'" Then Messner revealed something astonishing. "I rather think you will be for this, even though we have not yet seen the manuscript nor been able to judge its value." The book had been acquired, edited, and announced without review from the firm's highest officers. More than $200 had been dedicated to advertising and $1,000 advanced to the author. A month before Walrond embarked for the Caribbean, Liveright assented to the plan, stipulating that Friede must "give us cash down for what we have advanced, together with our expenses."[11] This arrangement would not be realized, however, and *The Big Ditch* would languish with a firm that no longer wanted it, its author laboring to improve it from abroad while clouds gathered for an economic collapse so catastrophic as to decimate the book business.[12]

AWESOME THERAPY

> The new returnee, as soon as he sets foot on the island, asserts himself; he answers only in French and often no longer understands Creole. A folktale provides us with an illustration of this. After having spent several months in France a young farmer returns home. On seeing a plow, he asks his father, an old don't-pull-that-sort-of-thing-on-me peasant: "What's that thing called?" By way of an answer his father drops the plow on his foot, and his amnesia vanishes. Awesome therapy.
>
> FRANTZ FANON, *BLACK SKIN, WHITE MASKS* (1952)

Walrond left New York in late September 1928 with two letters of introduction. One was from novelist William McFee, recommending him to H. G. De Lisser, the most important literary figure in Jamaica, a novelist and editor of *The Gleaner*. Another was a general letter from Henry Allen Moe of the Guggenheim Foundation recommending Walrond "to the estate, confidence, and friendly consideration of all persons."[13] His ship arrived at the Canal Zone six days later. What is known of Walrond's experiences during this period comes chiefly from letters to Moe. Some of the texture of his experience is therefore lost in the official cast of the correspondence. His trip took him from the Central American coast to the Windward and Leeward Islands of the Caribbean. He delivered a few presentations, and visits to Panama, Haiti, and Barbados germinated material for new projects. They would not come to fruition in book form, as he hoped, but they reflected his growing concern with a new form of imperialism in the service of U.S. corporate and military interests.

The canal had been open fourteen years, and although many West Indian laborers stayed after its completion, many more returned to the islands or headed north to the United States and Cuba. Those who remained faced tough conditions; by 1924, there were 20,000 unemployed

"Negroes" in the Canal Zone. The expansion of U.S. territory continued apace, with increasing militarization and the expropriation of more than 4,000 acres of land for canal defense and military posts. An average of 7,400 U.S. troops occupied the Canal Zone during these years.[14] Walrond had proposed "to concentrate on the life and ways of the more primitive classes further inland," but these new Panamanian conditions led him to reformulate his plan. Foul weather frustrated his goal of visiting the indigenous people displaced by the canal construction. As well, "disturbances" in the Chiriquí District near the Costa Rica border caught his interest. Social unrest had arisen, he said, from "the introduction of West Indian Negro laborers on the banana plantations of a subsidiary of the United Fruit Co."[15] Chiriquí was a United Fruit stronghold under watchful U.S. military protection. By 1913, the company held nearly a quarter of all private property in Panama, and by 1920, its holdings included 250 miles of railways and 46,000 acres of agricultural land.[16] The U.S. military presence grew in Chiriquí over the express objections of Panamanian officials. Conditions there and the fallout from the U.S. occupations in Haiti and the Dominican Republic forestalled any patriotic reverie in which the proud Guggenheim recipient may have indulged. There was also the matter of *The Big Ditch*, still incomplete. Part of his "quest" was to "verify in the Government Library at Balboa Heights certain researches which I had previously made into the history of the Panama Canal."[17] It is likely he did more than verify, for the holdings included *The Canal Record*, the published reports of the Isthmian Canal Commission (ICC), and local English- and Spanish-language periodicals. Having intended to stay through November, Walrond did not leave Panama until mid-December. It took four days for him to reach Haiti, and four thereafter to reach age thirty.

Cracks were forming in the U.S. occupation of Haiti, imposed in 1915, and a year after Walrond's visit the conflict would sharpen, compelling presidentially appointed U.S. investigative commissions to recommended withdrawal. "In the three months that I spent on the island I had exceptional opportunity to study the Occupation from both the American and the Haytian side," Walrond wrote, "Out of the curiosity that took me to

Hayti, I ultimately emerged with the material for two books." The first was to be a study of the aftermath of the Haitian revolution, which abolished slavery and effected independence from France, but not without tremendous loss of life and social upheaval. He felt that "the numerous revolutions that have taken place in the history of Hayti" could only be understood by "studying the underlying causes."[18] He proposed to title the book *The Struggle for Representative Government in Hayti from the Creation of the Black Republic in 1804 to the American Intervention in 1915.*

Walrond knew something few North Americans recognized at the time but many historians now grant: "The history of social revolution in the Western Hemisphere starts not with Lexington and Bunker Hill in 1775, but less auspiciously in the French tropical colony of Saint-Domingue in the Caribbean."[19] The intricate alliances and conflicts among the "small whites," the elite plantocracy, the French government, the enslaved, and the free people of color were, Walrond realized, as dramatic a tale of modernity as one could tell. Saint-Domingue slavery was as brutal as anyplace in the hemisphere, and the triumph of Toussaint L'Ouverture and the reversion to despotism under Jean-Jacques Dessalines and Henri Christophe were momentous events, the significance of which few North Americans appreciated. Having defeated one colonial regime, Haitians' quest for autonomy amid the competing claims of France, Germany, and the United States was a matter of considerable concern among African Americans. James Weldon Johnson, for example, was no radical, but he wrote penetrating critiques of U.S. policy in Haiti in *The Nation* in the early 1920s. Walrond was undoubtedly familiar with Johnson's account and possibly with Dantès Bellegarde, a Haitian intellectual who spoke against the U.S. occupation at the Fourth Pan-African Congress in New York.[20] But his most likely interlocutor on Haiti was Hubert Harrison, who wrote regularly on the subject when they worked together at *Negro World*. "Here is American imperialism in its stark, repulsive nakedness," Harrison bellowed, "And what are we going to do about it?"[21]

Walrond formulated his proposal to Moe, challenging the official narrative that justified the occupation.

I have decided, out of the welter of material I have acquired, to address myself to the *Revolt of the Cacos*. The *cacos* were supposed to be "professional bandits" who infested the hills of Hayti during the early years of the American Occupation, but there is concrete evidence to prove that on the contrary they were peaceful peasant farmers who were forced by the abuses perpetrated under the *corvée* to take up arms in defense of their dignity and integrity.[22]

Although the occupation improved Haiti's infrastructure, health care, and education system, staggering force was required to put down popular resistance. The corvée was a forced labor system, and the *gendarmerie*, supervised by U.S. officers, abused laborers, "forced them to march tied together by ropes, and made them work outside their own districts for weeks or even months. Haitians resented these practices, which recalled French slavery."[23] The conflict came to a head as the cacos, defeated in the U.S. invasion of 1915, regrouped, overthrew the gendarmerie in the northern highlands, and threatened Port-au-Prince. "From March 1919 to November 1920, the marines systematically destroyed the rebels, using, for the first time ever, airplanes to support combat troops," killing more than 3,000 Haitians.[24] With Haiti still occupied, Walrond sought to confront the prevailing view of the resistance as "professional bandits" and the Americans as a benign shield against European intrusion and internecine warfare.

From Port-au-Prince in January 1929, Walrond applied to the Guggenheim Foundation for a one-year extension "to carry out this program with a minimum of anxiety and the utmost independence."[25] By the time Moe replied, Walrond had left Haiti for the neighboring Dominican Republic. The foundation's response was not all bad, a six-month extension through spring 1930, but Walrond had overlooked a vital element in proposing to return to New York—appointments were for overseas projects only. Thus Moe stipulated something with fateful implications: "The grant made you is not available for work in the United States."[26] Making the extension conditional on Walrond's absence from the United States, the foundation kept him abroad during the country's worst financial crisis and in so doing propelled him to Europe.

Walrond's remaining months in the Caribbean entailed stops in Puerto Rico, St. Thomas, St. Kitts, and Barbados. At least twice, he was able to enjoy his celebrity, delivering speeches about his career in New York. He spoke in St. Thomas at an event reported in the *Chicago Defender* and in the Virgin Islands newspaper *The Emancipator*.[27] Walrond was asked "to put aside all modesty and to give a full account of himself and the obstacles with which he has had to contend in his climb to fame." His address was more sociological than literary. On moving to New York, he explained

> [It had been] necessary to maintain his individuality as a West Indian, as all his family were West Indians. Later, however, when he began to travel he found that he was different, both in thoughts and habits from the West Indian. He was an American in thoughts and acted like one. He could not adapt himself to the feudal system which still obtains in most West Indian Islands, and to which the inhabitants are accustomed.

It sounds as though Walrond may have been supercilious, evincing pride in his American identity and the American way of life, which he depicted as a color-blind meritocracy. "He recited the progress of the Colored race and the money accumulated by it. He told of colored bankers, orators, poets, musicians, authors, and so on, and how they did things, not as colored people, but as Americans, forgetting the color question entirely." Surely this overstated the contrast between West Indian "feudalism" and American egalitarianism, and it was a polite fiction to claim that African Americans were "forgetting the color question entirely." Perhaps he felt he was living the American Dream and thus trumpeted its democratic promise. But he may have meant to convey something more nuanced about the psychological distance he had traveled that was lost in translation between places. *The Emancipator* declared, "Personal contact with men such as Mr. Waldron [sic] will have the effect of setting us thinking and may eventually open to us the great possibilities that are ever before us."

A more developed literary community was forming in Barbados, where he arrived in April. The Forum Club, a new organization, invited him to speak on "Some Writers of the Negro Renaissance." Composed primarily of "educated professional black and coloured men, many of whom held or would assume leadership roles in the society," the Forum Club became an important venue for fostering a literary community in Barbados and beyond.[28] It launched a journal, *The Forum Quarterly*, in 1931 and hosted notable figures, including C. L. R. James, who spoke about crown colony government just before leaving for England in 1932. Barbadian scholar Carl Wade considers *The Forum Quarterly* a springboard for the better-known journal *Bim*, founded in 1942.[29] It is remarkable to consider Walrond's return to Bridgetown, his boyhood home, during this formative period.

En route to Barbados, Walrond had devised a plan to meet the terms of his fellowship. He would "wind up work in the West Indies" by late May, he said, then "journey on to Europe where I shall settle down to a siege of writing." The plan prevented him from accepting an invitation to deliver the keynote address at the Negro Progress Convention in British Guiana in July. An association with roots in the Garvey movement, the Negro Progress Convention hosted speakers from the Caribbean and North America, and although Walrond declined the invitation, he suggested in his place the Reverend F. G. Snelson, director of missionary work for the African Methodist Episcopal Church, whom he met on the boat to Barbados. When Snelson addressed the convention, he began by thanking Walrond, calling him "a wonderful little man [. . .] with athletic form and cultured brow" and praising his inquisitiveness. "He is a student, a young man of promise, and I declared to him that he owed it to South America when he finished his work to go back and found a University," a remark that elicited applause. Walrond had assured Snelson that "he had not forgotten the debt he owed to his native land."[30]

Despite the praise and attention, Walrond grew concerned as the end of his fellowship approached that the foundation might not be satisfied. He had not informed Moe of "the progress I have made in creative writing," he realized, because "most of my time has been spent in research and organization." Already a flicker of apprehension crept in. "It is with a full consciousness of the gap left to be filled in that I propose, unless it conflicts with the wishes of the Foundation, to proceed to Europe and devote myself entirely to developing the plans I have formulated for creative and other writing."[31] His difficulty with *The Big Ditch* was no secret among his friends in Harlem, though they did not understand it.[32] In a rant that was probably lubricated with gin, Wallace Thurman wrote Langston Hughes in 1929, prescribing cynical remedies for problems plaguing their peers, recommending that Jessie Fauset "be taken to Philadelphia and cremated," Countée Cullen "be castrated and taken to Persia as the Shah's eunuch," and "Eric ought to finish The Big Ditch or destroy it." (For himself he recommended suicide, which was sadly not far from his alcoholic fate.)[33] Finish it or destroy it: sound advice, but it went unheeded. For a number of reasons the project instead splintered into multiple versions and revisions. Not the least of them was an unsupportive publisher, a problem that worsened in subsequent months. One might also conjecture that the self-confidence Walrond had mustered to see *Tropic Death* into print was no longer available. But there is no evidence that severe depression returned until 1931. The problem with *The Big Ditch* was as much one of form as external circumstances.

The book was conceived as a project of cultural mediation, a Panamanian history for North American readers. "[T]hough other accounts of the feat have been written, Mr. Walrond is the first author to bring out the drama of this as yet unsung epic of human heroism," promised Boni & Liveright.

He tells of revolutionaries, riots and the stirrings of racial consciousness among the varied nationalities engaged in the work. He tells of the titanic achievements of science, of human labor, of engineering. He describes the life and death battle against disease and insect pests which in that tropical climate present a more formidable front than armies of mere men. In this book, as in *Tropic Death*, the atmospheric quality is enriched by the author's memories of his impressionable boyhood years spent on the Isthmus.[34]

Memory is a funny thing though, and a return to the Caribbean complicated the romance of "romantic history," challenging his intentions. Walrond's letters suggest new layers of feeling and awareness, an encounter
with U.S. imperialism shorn of the fig leaf of civilization.

If he had come to do some fact checking, visit the indigenous people,
and turn folklore into short stories, Walrond instead found a welter of
labor problems and militarization, democracy attenuated, and popular
resistance discredited as lawless banditry. In short, the fellowship that represented such comfort placed him onto the horns of the formal dilemma
of the colonial intellectual. Cosmopolitan projects emerge from the perspective of modernity, Walter Mignolo has said, while *critical* cosmopolitanism emerges from modernity's constitutive exterior, coloniality. Which
sort of book was *The Big Ditch*? How could a manuscript conceived in
the cosmopolitan tradition to delight and instruct be made to accommo-
date a sensibility "issuing forth from the colonial difference"?[35] In 1922,
Walrond had taken a therapeutic return trip to the islands, a prescription
filled by his voyage as the cook's helper aboard a United Fruit steamship.
But this subsequent Guggenheim journey had been "awesome therapy"
in Frantz Fanon's sense, as blunt a reminder of Caribbean conditions as
the plow dropped on the foot of the farmer's son returned from France.

FRANCE

He wrote me quite some long letters telling me about his experiences in
going to France and living on the Riviera, of accidents he had had, and
his life being very turbulent in through there. But for some reason he
was never very anxious to return to the United States.

ETHEL RAY NANCE (1970)

A generation later, London would have been the West Indian intellectual's
destination, but this was long before the Caribbean Artists Movement,
before the postwar *Windrush* generation. Black Britain was an oxymo-
ron in 1929; it was only comfortable to be a person of color in England

for entertainers, and even they felt uneasy once the curtain closed and the applause subsided.[36] J. A. Rogers, covering Europe for the *New York Amsterdam News*, called England "the only European country in which one is likely to find color prejudice."[37] France was known to tolerate social difference, and Paris had acquired such a fondness for African Americans that Ada "Bricktop" Smith, cabaret performer extraordinaire, called the phenomenon *la tumulte noir*. Friends told Walrond the city was enchanting. "There never was a more beautiful city," said Gwendolyn Bennett, who studied there in 1925, "On every hand are works of art and beautiful vistas . . . one has the impression of looking through at fairy-worlds as one sees gorgeous buildings, arches, and towers rising from among [the] trees."[38] Cullen, whom Arna Bontemps called "the greatest Francophile," was staying in Montparnasse, near the Latin Quarter.[39] Walrond knew musicians, singers, actors, and pugilists who had taken a turn in the Paris spotlight and reporters sent there on assignment, and although their opinions were not uniformly positive, the consensus was clear: "There you can be whatever you want to be," as Langston Hughes said, "Totally yourself."[40] When Walrond's ship from Barbados docked in London, he left immediately for Paris.[41]

A special legend had grown around Montmartre, a district in which many clubs and restaurants were operated by black owners, featured black entertainers, and served a predominantly black clientele. A steep tangle of cobblestone lanes near the Sacre Coeur cathedral, Montmartre was frequented by avant-garde modernists but was also hospitable to African Americans. When Hughes arrived in 1924, a sailor with seven dollars in his pocket, he was told "most of the American colored people [. . .] lived in Montmartre, and that they were musicians working in theaters and night clubs."[42] The cabaret where he washed dishes, the Grand Duc, was far from grand—"the size of a single booth at Connie's Inn"—but it became the cornerstone of Montmartre jazz.[43] In many ways, Montmartre was France's answer to Harlem. But as the decade wore on, "hot jazz" was popularized and venues like the Grand Duc became trendy destinations for white patrons—the avant-garde, bon vivants, and, more perniciously, Americans intent on curbing the association of white women with black men.[44] Black Montmartre also faced the "ten percent law," legislation aimed to keep French nationals employed, limiting the number of foreign musicians an establishment could hire. Thus, although it was Harlem's nearest equivalent, Montmartre was no longer the obvious destination for Walrond by 1929.

Instead he moved to Montparnasse, a choice that had less to do with its association with artists and intellectuals than the more practical consideration that Countée Cullen lived there. Cullen seems to have put him up until he found his own lodgings. Although Cullen was well known on the Left Bank, he preferred "the detachment of his studio out Montsouris way."[45] Montsouris, a park at the edge of Montparnasse, was a bucolic retreat from the grand boulevards and bustling cafés. Only one letter survives to document Walrond's residence there, but it is corroborated by a Paris *Tribune* column.[46]

> Eric Walrond, another Guggenheim scholar, is living with Countée Cullen. He is hard at work on his next novel, which we hope will be as interesting as *Tropic Death*, published a couple of years ago. Walrond [. . .] has traveled extensively but considers the Left Bank the bright spot of the cultural world. "Its traditions and literary associations," he says, "stimulate the best efforts in one. Here one can find variety or peace."[47]

Peace was the Parc Montsouris, where Hemingway sent his star-crossed lovers in *The Sun Also Rises*, a place whose "budding trees" Cullen "could see every morning from my window and whose leaves I could hear each night sighing and soughing in the wind."[48] Variety, on the other hand, was the social whorl, continually rejuvenated by fresh arrivals. "When Walrond isn't busy at work," a reporter noted, "he stops in, on occasion, at the Dôme, where he meets a number of his friends."[49] Meeting friends at Left Bank cafés was a time-honored ritual, and Walrond found no shortage of either friends or cafés.

He particularly enjoyed the Dôme and Café Capulade. With its "elaborate zinc bar, marble tables, leather banquettes, and mirrored walls," the Dôme was also a favorite of Henry Miller, Man Ray and Kiki, and

Hemingway. Walrond often met the painter Palmer Hayden, "tall, dark, and looking more like an English gentleman than like the proverbial painter," Cullen said, "shining out like a bit of ebony from among the other habitués of the Dome."⁵⁰ Invariably, Hayden's friend Hale Woodruff, a painter and recipient of a Harmon Award, accompanied them. Sequestered in a back room were the billiard and card tables this group preferred. "Eric Walrond . . . we used to play cards together all night in the cafés in Paris," Hayden recalled, "There's a part of the cafés there . . . set aside especially for people who want to play cards, not gambling but checkers and chess [. . .] so we'd hang out there, Countée, another West Indian, Dr. Dupré, all of them students."⁵¹ Hayden's watercolor *Nous Quatre à Paris* depicts their activity, and although they are not identified, the figures likely represent Hayden, Cullen, Walrond, and Woodruff. The cafés were also for catching friends up on the previous night's activities. After one evening of carousing and drinking with friends, Walrond got stuck with the tab, and when he could not persuade the owner to accept a personal check or even his watch in partial payment, he was thrown in jail for the night. Recounting the story to Harold Jackman at the café the next morning, Walrond was less amused than his friend, who replied wryly, "I didn't know anything new could happen to you."⁵²

Beyond its bohemian sophistication, Montparnasse had something else unrivaled in Paris, the Bal Nègre. Also known as the Bal Colonial, it was a little gem of a dance hall where Walrond's friends brought him the night he arrived, July 5, 1929. It had quickly become a preferred destination of the American "Negro colony," but its appeal lay in the diversity of its patrons. It was "probably the most cosmopolitan and democratic dance hall in Paris," Cullen said, "which may mean in the world."⁵³ No sooner had Walrond arrived than he was swept into a delirious week of festivities, punctuated by an Independence Day celebration and a night of carousing, including the Bal Nègre. The occasion was a birthday party for Louis Cole, the pianist at Bricktop's and a singer in the popular revue, *Blackbirds*. Hosted in a "magnificent mauve apartment near the Trocadéro," Cole's party featured torch songs from Zaidee Jackson and dancing by the Berry Brothers, costars in *Blackbirds*. Walrond may

7.1 Palmer Hayden, *Nous Quatre a Paris (We Four in Paris)*, watercolor and pencil on paper, c. 1930.

Courtesy of the Metropolitan Museum of Art, New York.

have been surprised to find his old friend Van Vechten among the revelers, who also included "two counts and a princess." He left with Cullen, J. A. Rogers, and a few others for Zaidee Jackson's apartment in the Champs-Élysées, then to the Bal Nègre "to complete the week of fun." "Our group can do a mean bout of ringing and twisting," wrote Rogers, "along with the Martiniquans doing their delightful dance—the beguine."[54] This was quite a welcome.

The reference to the Martiniquans and the *biguine* underscores another distinctive quality of black Paris, something the Bal Nègre crystallized: its heterogeneity. Stepping through its doors, Walrond would have experienced something uncanny, a bit like Harlem and a bit like the Caribbean yet more than the sum of its parts. Harlem's New Negroes were plentiful but émigrés from Guadeloupe, Martinique, and Haiti set the tone and the tempo. "As an American Negro we are somewhat startled to find that our dark complexion avails us nought among these kindredly tinted people," wrote Cullen, "Language must be the open sesame here, and it must be French."[55] Despite the awkwardness, Cullen enjoyed the Bal Nègre more, he once admitted, than his beloved opera. "The visitor who speaks only English had better take his interpreter with him," Rogers concurred, for "the majority of the Negroes come from the French West Indies or parts of Africa."[56] Eslanda Robeson became intrigued by the Pan-Africanist promise of black Paris as exemplified by the Bal Nègre, publishing a two-part essay in Dorothy West's journal *Challenge*. For Walrond, this milieu was familiar yet wonderfully strange: a community of "Negroes" that not only accommodated but affirmed intraracial differences. Unlike in New York, "Negro" was not synonymous with African American in Paris, and Montparnasse alone was home to nearly one thousand former Caribbean residents. Paris thus expanded and complicated African Americans' perspectives on race, introducing them to Antilleans and Africans, from the elites of Guadeloupe who strolled the Sorbonne speaking with Parisian accents, to Senegalese sailors who had joined France's military in World War I.[57] The confluence of people of African descent inspired more than dance hall meditations. The intellectual life of Pan-Africanism, galvanized by the 1919 Pan-African Congress, would soon flourish in Paris in the 1930s. Its most celebrated expression was the Negritude movement, led by Aimé Cesaire, Léopold Senghor, and Léon Damas, a movement that wed anticolonial politics with surrealism and Marxism.

But the seeds were sown for Negritude—and indeed for alternative modes of black transnationalism—during the period in which Walrond lived in Paris. In the 1920s, several African American intellectuals nurtured connections with French periodicals, engaging in translation and scholarship. The journals *Les Continents* and *La Depeche africaine* cultivated a transnational sensibility and artistic aspirations among France's black intellectuals. A brilliant Martinican student, Paulette Nardal, published regularly and hosted a salon with her sisters, Jane and Andrée, and their cousin Louis Achille. In 1931, she founded a bilingual journal, *La Revue du monde noir*, with the Haitian expatriate Léo Sajous. She was the most important connection between the U.S. New Negro movement and Negritude, an exceptionally gifted "intermediary." The Nardals shared so many contacts with Walrond as to make their meeting seem certain. Paulette introduced René Maran and Senghor to Claude McKay, Mercer Cook, and Carter Woodson, all of whom Walrond knew, and to his friends Cullen, Locke, and Woodruff. They were familiar with Walrond's work; Jane was a self-described "lectrice assidue" ("assiduous reader") of *Opportunity*, and she and Paulette translated *The New Negro*. The intervention they made would have been of great interest to Walrond: "Unlike the Francophone literature in the 1920s, *La Revue du monde noir* conceive[d] black culture as an autonomous and transnational tradition rather than a subset of colonial history." Paris salons are the stuff of legend, but these black intellectual spaces were distinct from the salons of "Lost Generation" modernists. They constituted a different counterculture to modernity because theirs involved colonialism centrally.[58]

Walrond was not in Paris just to dance and attend salons, however; he had plans for a novel, other projects conceived in the Caribbean, and of course *The Big Ditch*. At the National Archives he reviewed records and press coverage of the failed French attempt at the canal. Count Mathieu de Lesseps, the youngest surviving son of the project director, granted him an interview. After Walrond's lunch with the count and his wife at their apartment near the Arc de Triomphe, de Lesseps spoke ruefully about "the Panama affair," which ruined his father emotionally and financially. The countess translated her husband's account for their visitor.[59] It was a tale of calumny and deception, the story of a bold patriot, renowned for his direction of the Suez Canal, brought low by corrupt officials and an unscrupulous press corps. "The Government had to find scapegoats in order to save itself and clear the real culprits," explained the younger de Lesseps. Walrond did not believe much of it, but on the basis of this narrative and his research in the National Archives he wrote an essay, "The Panama Scandal." It appeared in the Madrid journal *Ahora,* titled "Como de Hizo el Canal de Panama" ("How the Panama Canal Was Made").

André Levinson did Walrond a good turn by publishing a puff piece in the weekly *Les Nouvelles Littéraires* soon after his arrival in Paris. Levinson's discussion of *Tropic Death* appeared between remarks on McKay's *Banjo* and Toomer's *Cane.* He criticized McKay for overreliance on "standard literary devices" but called Walrond a "determined artist whose concise, condensed tales of repressed passion unravel tragic themes against a glowing background of tropical magic." Levinson found Walrond's dialect "charming in its mellowness, [a] flavorful and melodious mixture." Whereas *Cane* was "a collection completely amorphous" and *Banjo* a "boneless piece [with] the inconsistency of a mollusk," Levinson thought *Tropic Death* exhibited formal coherence. Walrond's "bitter impassiveness" made it "the blackest book (no pun intended) that American literature has produced since the *Devil's Dictionary* by Ambrose Bierce."[60] In keeping with this coverage, a drawing of Walrond accompanied the article despite being less famous than McKay and Toomer. He appears brooding, staring fixedly with brow knit under a receding hairline. The image contrasts markedly with a drawing of Walrond published two months earlier in *The Clarion,* a London monthly. This image, featuring a casual smile, a three-piece suit, and a kindly gaze at the viewer, accompanied Walrond's article, "The Negro Renaissance." The article and drawing were reprinted the following month in the *Jamaica Gleaner,* and one wonders whether Edith Cadogan had a shock that Saturday in August, opening the newspaper to find the genial visage of her estranged husband peering back.

Although it included an abbreviated history of the movement named in the title, "The Negro Renaissance" was really a review of *Banjo*. Walrond credited McKay with having sparked the "cultural rebirth" in Harlem but lamented McKay's long absence, the result of which was a tin ear for dialogue. Walrond appreciated the "cesspool of bums, coke sniffers, perverts, wharf rats, and jobless seamen" that McKay assembled, but the "results are not terribly illuminating."

> One learns that blacks are not especially wanted in Britain, that the equality they enjoy in France is but skin-deep and that after all the best place for the black man is America! One learns also that amongst the blacks there is violent inter-tribal feeling. The high-toned mulattoes of Martinique are scornful of associating with the Senegalese on the ground that they are savages; the Senegalese stand aghast at the impudent assumptions of these descendents of slave ancestors. The Arabs of North Africa despise the blacks of the Madagascar archipelago. ("Negro Renaissance" 15)

Though *Banjo* contained no revelations, Walrond recommended the novel. He felt it "must be rather bleak and sad" for McKay to realize the conflicts troubling a diaspora that he wished to envision in harmonious community. The fact that *Banjo* came "from the pen of a man hipped on the universalization of the Negroes" made the challenges to community more poignant. This, "if for no other reason, ought to commend his book" (15). An odd concession, but it is worth noting that *Banjo* was until recently consigned to the dustbin of literary history, and the terms in which Walrond redeemed it prefigure those articulated by black Atlantic scholars, for whom *Banjo* indexes in form and content the tensions attending the diaspora.[61]

The journal in which his review appeared, *The Clarion*, was an "Independent Socialist Review" whose editorial board included Winifred

Holtby, a friend of Robeson and Cullen. Holtby took a keen interest in colonial independence, and when Walrond moved to London in the mid-1930s he would attend her salons. *The Clarion* was one of the few places his work appeared during his time in France. He reviewed books by Cullen and Paul Morand, and Eslanda Robeson's biography of her husband. But he did not place much work and lost touch with New Yorkers, including the Guggenheim Foundation, whose support ended in March 1930.[62] Efforts were made to burnish his status in France as "un écrivain noir de grande classe."[63] Mathilde Camhi was engaged to translate *Tropic Death* and may have served as his literary agent.[64] But the only translations to see print were a short story, "Sur Les Chantiers du Panama," and a sensational essay, "Harlem," both of which were published in *Lectures du Soir* in Brussels, which also ran an interview. "Chantiers" translates roughly as barracks, and the story dramatizes a conflict between a Spanish merchant who runs a grocery in a small village in the Canal Zone and the West Indian residents. It reappeared later as "Inciting to Riot" in London's *Evening Standard*.

"Harlem" was a paradoxical piece of long-form reportage, pandering at times to a prurient French interest in "the Negro," subverting it at others. With the casual address of a tour guide, Walrond described Harlem as "the African epicenter of the New World, the black capital of the universe," beginning with a flaneur's stroll at the corner of 135th Street and Lenox Avenue. A long line of people "wearing loud colors and Sunday finery" assembled at the Lincoln Theater, where "maids, valets, porters, and elevator boys are free to seek their pleasure."[65] Pleasure is the essay's theme, and Walrond insisted that their laughter was distinctive—"that unique Negro laugh, like the cackling of a barnyard gone berserk—a sound that must be heard to understand the Negro soul." This characterization sounds essentialist, but Walrond contended that the laughter was a mask. "Beneath the brassy insolence of their humor lies an intense mockery. There is a deep skepticism of the hypocrisy and absurd pretentiousness of mankind, and an understanding that life must be taken lightly." If the laugh expressed "the Negro soul" it should not be mistaken for unbridled mirth, he suggested, for it was complicated and hard-won. This tension between the language of essentialism and materialism characterizes the article. As in New York, Walrond waded into the murky waters of stereotypes but stirred the pot. "Harlem" is a richly textured account, from the shoeshine stand and barbershop to the cabaret and Striver's Row. It exhibits narrative flair, as Walrond identifies Harlem's "most curious and whimsical incongruities." We learn of the traffic in stolen goods, orchestrated by an entrepreneur whose café was a front for illicit enterprises. However, "Harlem" is a perplexing document, interleaving ribald accounts of theft, prostitution, and vice with sober sociology.

> In America, blacks are the last hired and first fired; they occupy the bottom rung of the country's economic ladder. They pay higher rent than whites for comparable lodgings, and so, naturally, in an effort to build a comfortable life and acquire the same material possessions as white people, blacks often fall prey to installment buying. The American Way of "one dollar down, a dollar a week," traps them into buying all sorts of things at exorbitant prices.

Refusing to resolve the tension pervading the essay, Walrond ends with a question: "Harlem, African epicenter, black capital of the universe! Do your tumultuous streets contain more immorality than the city of luxury that surrounds you?" Readers led into Harlem's underworld are thus cautioned against passing invidious judgment on its residents. "Harlem" was an attempt to exploit *la tumulte noir* and to query its terms. Its double voice was a symptom of Walrond's own predicament as his Guggenheim support ended: He could not conceal what he knew about the material conditions in which Harlemites conducted their lives, but he also needed to sell stories.

To this end, Walrond was introduced to *Lectures du Soir* readers in a chatty interview conducted "under the crude light of electric lamps" at Café la Coupole. Jacques Lebar called him "one of the most representative and colorful contributors to Negro literature." They discussed French literature, Walrond expressing his high regard for Flaubert and Blaise Cendrars, and Lebar asked about U.S. and French race relations. "An important question," replied Walrond, "especially in the United States, where the persecution of Negroes shows no tendency to subside." The Great Depression was "exasperating Negroes, who are accused of taking work from whites." He diagnosed in "American Negroes a veritable psychological duality. On one hand, racial sentiment remains intact; on the other hand, there is a veneer of superficial Americanism." Things were different in France, he maintained, as "Negroes in your country assimilate more easily. Or we could say that they are French Negroes, while those in the United States are Negro Americans and claim to remain thus." The distinction he drew is complicated by translation; the interview was likely conducted in English, and Lebar uses the word *nègre* rather than *noir* in both its adjective and noun forms. But the assertion is clear—in neither country is the tension between race and nation resolved but the claims of each operate differently. Asked how prejudice could be combated, Walrond was circumspect. "Despite appearances a progressive mixing of the races exists and is growing in the United States, which will lead to a certain easing, even if it takes many years." In fact, Walrond said he was writing a novel about an African American family, their "relation to life in the United States, their reactions, their rebellions." He described his concerns in avowedly racial terms. "I have to tell you that white life does not much interest me. My work and my *raison d'être* are to depict my race's existence, its history, its suffering, its aspirations, and its rebellions. There is a rich source of emotion and pain there. It is there that I draw the elements of my work, and it is in the service of the black race that I devote my activity as a writer."

His resolute tone and nobility of sentiment concealed the precariousness of his circumstances. These publications were really too little too late. By the time the interview ran, Walrond had left Paris, fallen into poverty, and suffered an ignominious setback when Horace Liveright broke the contract for *The Big Ditch*. It is a story that would be lost to posterity except that the person in whom he confided, a talented music instructor in Baltimore, would later marry W. E. B. Du Bois, ensuring the archival preservation of his correspondence. Examining Walrond's relationship with Shirley Graham not only helps to clarify the mysterious disappearance of

The Big Ditch and document a previously unknown period of Walrond's career, it underscores the methodological challenge of black transnational history. The survival of these artifacts suggests, in its status as an accident, how much else has been lost or muted in the archive.

"THE ONLY REAL LINK I HAVE GOT": SHIRLEY GRAHAM AND THE DEMISE OF *THE BIG DITCH*

Shirley Graham and Eric Walrond may have met before the summer of 1930, when she studied at the Sorbonne, but they came to know each other in Paris. A Howard University graduate, Graham had a busy career teaching, directing the Morgan State College music program, and caring for two sons from a marriage that ended in divorce. She took summer classes in the late 1920s at Columbia, where mutual friends may have introduced her to Walrond.[66] He was among the first to greet her upon her arrival in Paris. She had a week to get situated, so she strolled the Luxembourg Gardens, imagining the royalty whose steps she traced, gazed from the balcony of her Rue des Écoles hotel at the towers of Notre Dame, and when the opportunity arose she boarded a plane to London to see Paul Robeson play Othello and attend a reopening ceremony for Saint Paul's Cathedral.[67] Unlike a lot of people who "boasted about how well they knew" him, said Graham, Walrond "really *did* know Paul Robeson," and gave her a letter of introduction.[68] Graham was struck by how little Robeson spoke of himself, since "practically everybody else talked about no one" but him.[69] Within a few weeks she wrote an article about him that Walrond submitted on her behalf to *Opportunity*.

Graham indulged in the legendary charms of Paris nightlife, which offered a great deal to the music enthusiast, but she felt lonely. "I wish for the hand of a dear friend to clasp as I walk these streets," she wrote to friends in her hometown of Portland, Oregon. She was taken with Walrond's looks, as "handsome as a Greek god, done in ebony," and with his talent: "Eric could write!" Their activity in Paris may be inferred from the subsequent correspondence, and while it does not confirm a romance,

7.2 Photograph of Shirley Graham Du Bois and Eric Walrond, Paris, 1930, photographer unknown.

it does not preclude one. Their friendship was intimate and genuine. "Everyone came to Paris that summer," she recalled, and Walrond "introduced her to the gang."[70] He implored her to set aside her "phonetics and harmonies and whatever else you're putting your eyes out with," and spend time with him, from sidewalk café tables, to the Hotel de la Sorbonne, where Graham borrowed his typewriter to meet a deadline, to the Palace of Versailles, on whose spectacular grounds two black and white photographs document their visit. Graham appears smartly dressed, her floral print dress a fanciful contrast to Walrond's dark suit and bowler. He appears distracted, glancing past her while she smiles demurely, her pumps tilting her slender frame in his direction. Their hands seem to touch, but closer inspection reveals that he holds a cigarette.

Graham made sacrifices for Walrond during her stay, or so thought her contrite correspondent a few months later. "I am glad to know that you are well and materially content" in Baltimore, Walrond wrote, "You do deserve some snug bourgeois comforts after the way you roughed it—and all on account of me—in Paris." Walrond took Graham into his confidence in Paris, which he later consolidated in his letters, calling her "the one person alive who really knows me inside and out."[71] Whatever romantic element their relationship may have had, their correspondence suggests an intellectual companionship—two gifted, black expatriates whose marriages had ended badly, thrown together in lively Montparnasse. Although Graham is remembered as Du Bois's wife, she was prodigiously talented, the first African American woman to compose an opera for a major professional organization, the author of plays and scores for the Works Progress Administration, and a prolific writer of biographies for young readers. An energetic political activist, she joined the Communist Party and advised Kwame Nkrumah, president of independent Ghana, where she and Du Bois moved in 1961. Her letters to Walrond were not preserved, but his make clear that he relied on Graham for affirmation, a sympathetic ear, and an encouraging word.

Graham returned to Baltimore in September 1930, and Walrond moved to the Riviera.[72] It was unglamorous, a fishing village near Toulon called Bandol. His reasons for moving are unclear, but straitened finances were likely a factor. The economic crisis had reached France, unemployment

7.3 Photograph of Eric Walrond, Toulon, France, c. 1930, photographer unknown.

Atlanta University Photographs, Robert W. Woodruff Library of the Atlanta University Center.

rose, and the dollar accelerated its fall from the empyrean heights that sustained American visits in the 1920s. Walrond may also have needed a break from the Paris expat scene: "Another boatload and Saint Michel might be mistaken for Seventh Avenue," he groused.[73] It was not uncommon for the Montparnasse crowd to flee to the Mediterranean, and Nancy Cunard or William Seabrook were probably responsible for suggesting Bandol. These two eccentrics despised each other, but Walrond knew them in Paris and both had houses nearby. Cunard, who was planning an anthology on "the Negro," was staying near Nice at the time Walrond left Paris, and they saw each other socially. Her partner, Henry Crowder, an African American musician whom Walrond likely knew from New York, stayed with Walrond in Bandol for ten days.[74]

Seabrook, a novelist who supported Walrond's Guggenheim application, spent the late 1920s drinking himself nearly to death in Paris before repairing to Toulon to continue his bender. He hosted Walrond on at least one occasion and probably more.[75] After committing himself to a mental hospital in 1933, he reflected on his alcoholism, and one wonders at the extent of Walrond's participation: "For nearly two years I had been drinking a quart to a quart and a half of whiskey, brandy, gin or Pernod daily. This had been in France, where liquor is good, plentiful, and not expensive."[76] Now "at the peak of his fame," Seabrook received a $30,000 advance to serialize his new book, a lurid tale of human sacrifice in Africa.[77] But he wrote almost nothing amid the telegrams, visits, and invitations to go tuna fishing, hunt wild boar, gamble at Cannes, and watch "the latest pornographic movies in the red-light district at Marseilles."[78] No account of Walrond's contact with Seabrook survives, but Walrond's intimacy with Cunard raised the eyebrows of her partner. "Nancy seemed very much interested in Eric," said Crowder, "He went to her house to dine but without my accompanying him."[79] Years later, Cunard would assist in Walrond's discharge from the hospital that treated him for depression.

Soon after Shirley Graham returned home and Walrond moved to Bandol he began writing her, addressing her as "Shirley Old Scout" and gossiping about Paris acquaintances. Walrond relied on her as a professional resource, promising to return the favor. His first letter asked her to send the Guggenheim Foundation annual report and "stray copies" of *The Crisis*, *Opportunity*, *The Baltimore Afro-American*, *The Nation*, or *The New Republic*. "I don't want much, do I?" he joked, "Don't forget this is a service which I should like to make reciprocal—if there is anything over here that you would like to get and it is in my power to get it for you don't hesitate to command me."[80] He came to rely on her financially, and she sent between ten and forty dollars on several occasions as his requests grew more plaintive. Graham was not wealthy—until 1928 she made just $35 per month as a music librarian at Howard University, and thereafter her salary as director of Morgan College's music department was hardly lavish—but she always had something to send him.[81]

At first he was reluctant to ask for money, promising to pay her back soon. During the winter of 1930, however, his tone changed to desperation and his mental health suffered as his wallet thinned and his hopes of publishing *The Big Ditch* faltered. He thanked her "multitudinously" for cabling funds, a "life-saver" without which he could not have paid the *pension* bill. "I can't begin to describe the ordeal I would have had to undergo," he said.

> Well, I'm out of that hole temporarily at least, but taking colour from optimistic you, I'm going to keep my faith sturdy and won't cross a bridge before I get to it—even if it is in sight! Your letter and cable have given me courage to stand firm. In spite of economic troubles and because of my isolated surroundings, I'm pounding away—steadily and without interruption. If I only had the assurance of a temporary subsidy while I labored on, I'm sure you'd have some reason to feel your interest in me were not without some justification. Let's see if we can't put *that* idea over the top!

If Walrond left Paris to find an inexpensive writer's retreat, he instead found loneliness and poverty. "It is a torture for me to write letters," he said. "But since the ocean separates us it shall henceforth be a pleasure. I'm anxious to hear all the news surrounding you; to get niggerati gossip, newspapers, etc. Unfortunately nothing of any outside consequence happens in Bandol; I'm the only *noir* in the village." Friends were unsure of his whereabouts.[82]

Exile from the black community was a paradoxical strategy for someone whose "work and *raison d'être* are to depict my race." The careers of other black writers caution against passing judgment, but in Walrond's case the strategy proved harmful, both here and again in the 1940s, when he lived in rural England. One letter to Graham contained the poignant admission, "You are the one person alive who really knows me inside and out. There may be something prophetic after all in our meeting."[83] He moved to a cheap hotel near the bay where the fishing boats moored and palm trees blew in the wind as they had in the Colón of his youth. "Since I've been here I haven't been able to go anywhere, or see anybody of the Paris gang or anyone remotely connected," he wrote after the new year, 1931. "Dear Shirley, write and dissipate the desert island feeling I have got all over me!"[84]

At such a distance, transatlantic communication eroded Walrond's connection with New York, and problems arose with his publisher. He confessed "financial worries" that left him "hanging on by the skin of my teeth" and feeling "bluer than I've been since before you left Paris."

> My position seems incapable of alleviation. To live down to the lowest margin I need about a thousand francs a month—roughly $40. This amount for the next three or four months I'd give my right arm to get. I can't concentrate or work on account of the beastly way things just drag along without a silver break to the clouds. I don't know when my book is coming out but you may rest content that the responsibility for that is now in the hands of the publishers.

Walrond sensed that all was not well, accusing Liveright of "heartlessness and lackadaisical efforts in regard to the book." Nevertheless, he professed an "abiding faith" that the book "will bring me a lot of undisputed and well-minted prestige." So firm was this conviction that "in spite of sleeplessness and the usual worries" he determined to write a sequel, a history of the United States in Panama. Research fueled his confidence.

"The material I have got to put into the new book will appeal to an even wider audience. It will be a gigantic undertaking though and will easily exceed 'The Big Ditch' in length, and that's a 100,000 word book." He swore Graham to secrecy: "All of this I relate to you in the utmost confidence as it never pays to let the world know what you are doing until it is actually done," a bitter lesson of the perpetual deferral of *The Big Ditch*.

Enlisting Graham, he appealed to her sense of probity. He felt "morally obligated to execute" the new book because the Guggenheim Foundation funded it. Although he had dedicated himself in Panama to "digging up data," much was left undone.

> There are some items I have yet to look up and here, young lady, is where you come in. I don't know how on Lord's earth it's going to be done, but I appeal to you with all the earnestness of which I'm possessed. (If you ever get me out of this fix I'll about owe you my life!) Is there anybody you know in Washington or N.Y. who has some means of leisure, a kindly heart and a philanthropic spirit whom you can persuade to spend a few hours a day either in the Congressional library or the 42nd St. library in N.Y. copying out data which I shall indicate from old magazines and newspapers and the U.S. Gov't documents? I grant you this is no easy task but with your influence and get up why I believe anything can be done! Were I in America I'd do the job myself or if I had money I'd employ some professional researcher to do it. But as I'm not in America and have no money I've got to exhaust every friendly possibility at my command even though the request may seem to you presumptuous and unreasonable.

However "presumptuous and unreasonable," his desperation led him to impose on any sympathetic soul. Marvel Jackson had spoken well of him, Graham reported, and although she was now married and they had no contact, Walrond asked Graham to press her into service.[85]

He also risked presumption because he felt he could offer Graham something in return, professional advice. As a recipient of a coveted fellowship, Walrond's insight into the Guggenheim process was valuable

currency, and Graham sought guidance as she prepared funding applications. Her proposal involved "the tracing of African influence in the
musical expression of Europe" and "the African ancestry of American
Negro folk music." Walrond assured her of the project's originality:
"You'll do much to establish the universality of the Negro genius in general and to modify and even revolutionize the prevailing conception of the
comparative merits of African and European music."[86] Graham solicited
references from prominent figures, but when she missed the fellowship
Walrond reproached her for "cramming your list of sponsors with niggers or negro uplift workers." He believed endorsements from avowed
friends of the race invited suspicion. Suggesting she reapply, he advised
her to "look for disinterested sponsors without personal or group axes
to grind—your subject is sufficiently scientific in character to merit the
endorsement of the best scholars and musicians. And don't let up working on your plan—revise and clarify it, and don't drag in Ras Tafari if
you can help it."[87] He was concerned, in short, that she not appear too
race-conscious.

An uncharitable response to Graham's rejection, but he was not feeling magnanimous. He had subsisted for months on little or no income.
Months of silence from Liveright had dimmed his hopes. "I don't really
despair ultimately of the outcome of my relations with them; only they
are so darned slow in giving me a decision and in confiding to me the
nature of their plans," he wrote, "I do still manage to work in spite of
them, but I'd work better and with greater confidence if I knew how matters stood."[88] He assured Graham he was "plugging away"; "I have a long
new work of fiction half-done and the plans of my Panama sequel laid."[89]
Neither the Panama sequel nor the work of fiction, "a novel of Negro life
in America," would see print.[90]

More than money, Walrond needed Graham's personal assurance as
his distress deepened. When his resolve faltered he lamented, "I can't concentrate or work on account of the beastly way things just drag along
without a silver break to the clouds," or "I'm working hard as the devil,
although a little irksome and impatient at the way things have of dragging
on," or "Nothing seems to terminate as I hope and plan."[91] He tried to

sound cheerful, encouraging Graham in her pursuits, "I'm proud of you already Shirley, and I am glad to know you are studying and taking care of yourself and planning to do big things."⁹² "I think of you often and marvel at your courage and high ideals. One of these days you are going to arrive in a very big way and then unless I'm all wrong you'll have a perfectly wonderful 'up from obscurity' story to tell."⁹³ He tried introducing levity by reporting Paris gossip, but he could not conceal his isolation and disappointment. He missed Graham's comforting presence.

> I think often of you and of your incredible kindness to me. Sometimes I, too, feel terribly nostalgic and wish you were around for me to tell my troubles to. But I'm looking forward to this summer when I hope [. . .] affairs may arrange themselves so that we may meet in Paris. As I look back on our days together in the Latin Quarter, I'm sure there was some Grand Design back of our meeting. Do you remember the day you came to the Hotel de la Sorbonne to type your travel sketch to London—every time I think of the result of that encounter, I marvel at the quality of unselfishness and discernment in you which I have found in no one else.⁹⁴

He became anxious and peevish when she failed to contact him during melancholic stretches. "What has become of you? Ill, ill-disposed, extremely busy? I feel out of touch and worried," he confessed. "Are you in no mood to write me oftener? Don't you know that you are the only real link I have got with the world across the Atlantic? I feel sadly neglected and lonesome."⁹⁵

Graham agreed to assist with the Panama project, Walrond assuring her that his financial recovery was imminent.

> I'm so grateful to you for promising to do what you can on my references. As it stands at present the new book presents but a skeleton of what is to come—I can't supply the flesh and blood until the research problem is out of the way. You are the only person I have taken into my confidence about it, because it is inadvisable to let cats out of the

bag prematurely. My plan is to submit the book as soon as I have got about half of it ready to a publishing house and unless I'm absolutely crazy I believe I'll be able to raise on it sufficient money to carry me indefinitely.[96]

The prediction proved overly optimistic, but what is striking is his injunction to confidence and secrecy, a consistent refrain. "You must have an air-tight 'plan of study,'" he cautioned her early in her fellowship process, "and you mustn't let too many niggers know what you're about!"[97] He presupposed a field of pitched competition in which leaking one's plans spelled certain defeat. By late February, with still no word about *The Big Ditch*, he grew despondent. "You have no idea how I loathe myself and curse the fates at this condition I find myself in," he told Graham.[98]

Finally, after spending months in ignorance of his publisher's plans, Walrond heard from them in early March 1931. Rather than resolving the matter outright, they deferred what he had come to believe was an inevitable letdown.

My publisher [said] there is no question but that I had done an able job in both my actual documentation and in my method of presenting the material in "The Big Ditch," but that the firm, owing to prevailing conditions in the book market, was unable to come to a decision on it and that I'd have to wait another week or two. It took them nearly five months to write me even as indefinitely as all that, meanwhile I tweedle my thumbs and bite my nails awaiting action. So you see the sort of *cochons* I have to deal with. They haven't the decency to come out openly and say they can't or won't publish my book but they keep it months and months without letting me know what they are going to do.

As a result, he said, "I'm still in doldrums. [. . .] I don't wish to be an eternal nuisance but the breaks are a long time coming my way."[99] He asked Graham for the largest sum yet, one thousand francs, "and I'm asking you if there is any way in the world for you to cable it to me as soon as you receive this letter." Although he had completed only a draft of his "novel of Negro life in America," he felt "sure as soon as I've got it in the shape I desire I'll get a very substantial advance on it." With this advance and the publication of his Panama books, he planned to "make adequate liquidation to you for all the money you have loaned me." He sought to end his exile, "to return to Paris and put the finishing touches to my novel."

Before Graham had the chance to respond, the final blow fell upon *The Big Ditch*, and it was even worse than expected. Boni & Liveright had broken the contract and dropped the book. Not because it was poorly executed but because the Depression wrought havoc on the industry, and Liveright, already leveraged beyond recovery, was hedging. If that was not bad enough, he had contrived to prevent Walrond from shopping the manuscript. Walrond's letter to Graham is worth quoting at length as it is the only extant account of the book's fate.

The "cost of manufacturing and exploitation is too high" they say and they don't believe there'd be enough returns to warrant the risk. I'm assured by the chief literary editor of the firm that "this is not an easy decision to arrive at because the scholarship shown in your work, your documentation in particular, and your skillful way of interpreting the story result in your having turned out an excellent piece of history." But now comes the rub. Liveright himself is afraid to risk publishing the book, and is willing to let me submit it to somebody else but before I'm permitted to do that I must agree to return to him half the money he advanced me on it. In other words, something in the neighborhood of $500. Can you beat that for calamity? I have written him refusing to abide by such [a] tyrannical stipulation. How in God's name can he reasonably refuse to publish the work and then expect to profit by its publication? In a pinch I suppose I shall have to resort to a lawyer and see what legality there is in Liveright's terms. If he'd only free this book I'm sure somebody else would take it and pay down an acceptance a minimum of $500. If I agreed to pay Liveright $500 and did succeed in getting another publisher where would I stand? I have executed my obligation to him; if he decides for his own reasons to reject the book it's no fault of mine. He ought to release the mss. free of all claims and I have written him to that effect.

In one way despite the blackness of the immediate outlook, I'm better off. Liveright has broken his contract with me and therefore all our engagements are off. The suspense is over and though I have the spectre of a $500 rebate hanging over me, I have hopes of connecting with a real publishing house that'll appreciate the sound value and permanent nature of the work I'm engaged on. Only there is the eternal problem of the interim—this business of carrying on until I bring matters to a head. In this connection you're the only pal I've got in the world. Once you said you trusted me even if you didn't always understand me. Remember? Shirley, I want you to trust me now more than you've ever trusted anyone before. To you and you alone I'm laying bare matters as they stand. I figure it'll take at most and also at least two months to bring Liveright to terms—to release my mss free of claims which would automatically give me the right to send it elsewhere. I estimate it'll take another month before I can get action on it. But I firmly believe it won't take much longer. And as I have told you time and time again I believe in the virtues—historical, literary, and social—of "The Big Ditch." I didn't need my publisher's opinion to confirm my faith in it. I have been conscious of its merits all along—not because I'm conceited for you know I'm not, but because I have laboured on it according to a set plan of perfection and because I have had nothing else but that book in my mind-motions for upward of three years. I wrote you nearly three weeks ago asking you to help me on a $40 proposition. I have heard no word from you so far but hope while this letter is on the way I'll do so. I have had to put up part of my personal belongings as security against a bill at the pension where I formerly stayed. In the meantime I have taken a room separately and take my meals *when I can* in a public restaurant. It's a terribly discouraging state to be in.

Now that you've got your Guggenheim application let's see if we can't work on my problem a little bit. Shirley I promise you this shall be no losing proposition as far as you are concerned. While I negotiate with my publisher for an "unencumbered rejection" I want to return to my novel of which I have written in my last letter. In the meantime I can't carry on without funds; my morale is at a nadir and there you are.

You're the only real pal I've got and you understand the situation thoroughly. It'd be terrible if I had to throw up the sponge just for the sake of a few months' expenses. Write me c/o Guaranty Trust and remember I'm praying that matters will arrange themselves we'll soon be able to see each other in Paris. Good luck and much love. Affectionately, Eric

Driven to despair by Liveright's extortionate terms, Walrond put his "pal" in an unenviable position. As the only person in whom he confided, Graham was tasked with forestalling his spiral into depression and starvation—a rotten thing to require of a thirty-five-year-old single mother who was in the process of moving from Baltimore to pursue advanced studies at Oberlin College, where she worked in a laundry to make ends meet.[100]

Walrond's final letter to Graham suggests that she complied, sending an undisclosed sum. He was relieved "to feel, despite the vicissitudes of the past two or three months, I've got a friend back there in America who hasn't forgotten me or the terrific fight I'm putting up."[101] Nevertheless, "In regards to my situation, I'm sure if I tried I couldn't exaggerate its gravity. At the moment I'm between two minds: whether to jump in the Mediterranean or sit quietly and expire. There seems precious little else to do." One could read this as gallows humor were it not for similar declarations during other depressive episodes. He could not produce the $500 Liveright demanded for the "unencumbered rejection," and he seems to have been too ashamed to ask anyone but Graham for assistance. Walrond would eventually see his way clear to contacting Moe, but not amidst his present humiliation.

I've sent the correspondence between me and Liveright to an attorney in America to get his advice on what procedure to follow. In the meantime I'm carrying on a verbal duel with Liveright trying to get him to say definitely whether he will or will not release the mss free of all claims. He hasn't committed himself so far. I secretly believe the old Jew is playing for this so that he'll starve me into a surrender. I will probably have to give in in the end but at the moment I'm as uncompromising as nails and do not hesitate to call a spade a spade. I'm not in this damned country for my health.[102]

In fact, Graham had suggested an alternative to jumping in the Mediterranean or sitting quietly and expiring: return to New York. "You are right about my needing to return to America. I'm homesick and lonely as hell," he admitted, "If I could get back to New York I could arrange a showdown with my publishers, sell my book to a decent firm and get enough advance money to pay off my debts and go ahead with the plans I've made for a Panama follow-up. The only damned question is how on earth am I going to get to America?"

HOME TO HARLEM, WITH A SHRUG

The summer of 1931 is a blank; no evidence survives of Walrond's activity. Edna Worthley Underwood, Walrond's sometime agent, said he was hospitalized "for a long time" in the American Hospital in Paris, and given his plummeting finances and mental health in 1931 and the absence of any prior reference to hospitalization, it may have been that summer.[103] Perhaps Shirley Graham helped him scrape together the fare to New York, where he arrived on September 5, three years after having left. The Amsterdam News interviewed him, published his photo, and called him a "changed man." Just how changed they could not know; Walrond played the interview close to the vest. He revealed none of his travails and pledged to return to France within two months. What he made clear was that he did not relish the occasion. "Eric Walrond, Back in City, Feels No Homecoming Thrill," read the headline. The reporter struggled to identify the ineffable something that distinguished the author from his younger self.

> Outwardly he is much the same person as the young short story writer whose volume of sketches on Caribbean life, "Tropic Death," was hailed by many critics as the flower of a new literary movement. But inwardly there is a difference. And so, when he returned to New York [on] Saturday [. . .] he experienced no thrill of homecoming.

Walrond conceded that he was "glad to see old faces again and to have the opportunity to talk with friends," but he shrugged his shoulders at the suggestion that it was nice to be "home." "[T]here's no particular thrill in being here again. Somehow, I feel different. There has been an inward change. Only urgent business brought me back to this country." Declining to elaborate, he extolled the virtues of France, an account jarringly at odds with his actual experience.

> The south of France is the ideal place for the artist and writer. In the solitude and quiet of that region one gets a perspective on the ultimate. He can see the intrinsic value of the thing he is doing. I wish more of the young Negro writers could do their work in that country. None of the difficulties and interruptions which infest Harlem are present there.

It was a public face to put on things, a vision of what could have been.[104]

As the article noted, Walrond was staying with his parents in Brooklyn. At a private home, he gave the only public presentation of his brief stay, an address to "The Students' Literary and Debating League."[105] He obtained an "unencumbered rejection" of *The Big Ditch* from Liveright, perhaps through the intervention of Moe, who within two weeks was shopping the manuscript on behalf of his beleaguered ex-fellow. Moe approached the Century Company, who acknowledged the inquiry, but that was all.[106] Walrond tried to remain optimistic. "As you may have seen in the papers, I'm back in little old New York," he wrote Graham in Ohio, "Are there any chances of seeing you before long? I don't know how long I shall be back in the city, having planned to return to France in case everything goes well with me."[107]

Walrond looked up his old flame, Marvel Jackson, who had since married Cecil Cooke, discovering she was in the hospital recovering from surgery. Years later she told an interviewer that Walrond mistakenly believed she and Cooke had separated, leading him to profess his love. Someone told her Countée Cullen had admonished Walrond while they were in France for not having married her when he had the chance. His words had sunk in, she claimed, by late 1931, when "I was in my hospital bed, and in walks Eric. I almost fell out of the bed. That was during a period when Cecil was in the south, finishing out a contract, and I was up here. He thought that we were separated, and he said, 'I really came back because I made a mistake.'"[108]

Wallace Thurman wrote an essay around this time in which he called Walrond "an unknown quantity" among Negro authors. An apt title for one who had acquired such esteem then receded into virtual silence. Thurman hoped Walrond would fulfill his immense potential.

> None is more ambitious than he, none more possessed of keener observation, poetic insight or intelligence. There is no place in his consciousness for sentimentality, hypocrisy or clichés. His prose demonstrates his struggles to escape from conventionalities and become an individual talent. But so far this struggle has not been crowned with any appreciable success. The will to power is there, etched in shadows beneath every word he writes, but it has not yet become completely tangible, visibly effective. [. . .] He knows what he wants to say, and how he wants to say it, but the thing remains partially articulated. Somewhere there is an obstruction and though the umbilical cord makes frequent contacts, it never achieves a complete connection. Thus he remains an unknown quantity, with his power and beauty being sensed rather than experienced. It is for this reason that his next volume is eagerly awaited. Will he or will he not cross the Rubicon? It is to be hoped that he will, for he is truly too talented, too sincere an individual and artist to die aborning.[109]

When he expressed hope that Walrond would "cross the Rubicon," Thurman implied two kinds of success: not only that his next book would "achieve a complete connection" between intentions and effects so that "his power and beauty" might be "experienced," but also that it would bring him recognition.

Walrond crossed the Rubicon in a very different sense. In late 1931, he again traversed the Atlantic, never to return. Among the manuscripts he carried with him was *The Big Ditch*, never published yet never far from his side. It would appear in truncated form, serialized in the journal of a psychiatric hospital in rural England in the 1950s. An ignoble fate, but it would be hasty to conclude that Walrond's failure to fulfill others' expectations was just that, a failure. It is unclear why he determined to avoid the United States after this return, nor do we know why his destination was England. "For some reason, he was never very anxious to return to the United States," said Ethel Ray Nance. He was too uncomfortable there to make it his home, she felt. "He could find fault with the United States. He could tell you in a very few words its shortcomings and they always made sense."[110] But there were other factors. Walrond was ashamed of having disappointed the Guggenheim Foundation and other supporters, and he was profoundly discouraged by the conflict with Liveright. Moreover, the Depression was ravaging Harlem and transforming New York, and the departure of friends and colleagues during his absence must have made the prospect of staying there less appealing. There was one place in the Caribbean diaspora that he had not tried, and that was England.

Despite his distinctive sensibility and résumé, Walrond was, like many others then and since, the child of middle-class Barbadian parents seeking opportunity in the "mother country." The winds of Caribbean migration had not subsided since Walrond's family left Barbados, but they had begun to shift. Arriving in London in late 1931, he found himself once again at the leading edge of one of the twentieth century's most decisive demographic transitions, an exodus from the Caribbean that hastened the demise of the British Empire and altered English cultural identity. He would take all the lumps and pay all the dues attending that transition. Not even a smartly dressed gentleman with a crisp accent reminiscent of Devonshire could avoid doing so if he was "coloured."

8

LONDON I (1931–1939)

> As they unpacked their bags, hawked their manuscripts around the little
> magazines of the capital, went on the stump agitating against injustices
> in far-off islands, they were improvising new lives for themselves, creat-
> ing new possibilities for those whom they encountered, and decolonis-
> ing the world about them.
>
> BILL SCHWARZ, *WEST INDIAN INTELLECTUALS IN BRITAIN* (2004)

What happened to Eric Walrond? The question had "been asked numerous times over the past several months by persons who remember the promising author," reported the *Baltimore Afro-American* in 1935, "No one seems able to answer except that Mr. Walrond left about two years ago for Mediterranean points, and has been gone ever since."[1] The "unknown quantity," as Wallace Thurman called him, had become still more reclusive. He had granted just one interview during his brief visit to New York, terse and guarded. "Rumors reached [Charles] Johnson from Europe that Walrond had squandered the [fellowship] stipends and written nothing."[2] Even his mother lost track of him, unable to answer the Guggenheim Foundation's inquiries into his whereabouts. Gregarious by nature, Walrond withdrew and became "very successful at dodging people he didn't want to know or that he didn't want to talk with or meet."[3] On moving to London in 1931, he rented a room near the Crystal Palace, a suburb near Brixton. One of his fellow lodgers, an Indian student, struck him as a ridiculous type of colonial subject, performing Englishness, "swallowing hook, line and sinker all the Pukka Sahib nonsense of the British Raj" ("On England" 47). But a subtle shift was under way in London against this mentality. Still relatively small in number, emigrants from the colonies were finding common cause, organizing, and promoting independence.

They also sought to end racial discrimination in Britain, the "colour bar." Most of the newcomers were students, seamen, and laborers, but by the 1930s professionals, artists, and intellectuals began swelling the ranks. Their collective activity and energetic publication program helped bring the empire to its knees and pave the way for future generations calling themselves black Britons. The reclusive Walrond would write his way into this community.

What he subsisted on in the early 1930s is unclear, but subsistence it must have been because the work he published—sketches and fugitive essays—could not have supported him. He got by, as a reporter for the *Afro-American* discovered in 1934.

> Eric Walrond, one of the better writers, has made London his temporary hunting ground. He has the energy of a dynamo; gets up at seven in the morning; drinks a cup of tea in bed, reads the daily papers, smokes at least five cigarettes and then settles down to work. Writes until noon and then for a hike in Hyde Park, back to his desk at two thirty and writes until six. Drinks gin and chews spearmint gum while typing. Claims that England is Virgin territory for young colored men and women of letters; intends to stop here until the field is properly explored.[4]

A portrait of English discipline, stimulants and all. But he struggled to place his work. London's mainstream periodicals, such as *The Spectator*, *The Star*, and *The Evening Standard*, picked up a few stories. His published journalism included two essays translated into Spanish, an article in London's *Sunday Referee*, and another—a brilliant sketch entitled "White Man, What Now?"—that *The Spectator* carried and *The Gleaner* reprinted in Jamaica. But without regular income, he foundered. Help came in the form of Amy Ashwood Garvey and her Trinidadian companion Sam Manning, who arrived from New York and opened a Caribbean nightclub near the British Museum. When Manning offered him a job as the publicity manager for his "negro musical revue" planning a UK tour, Walrond took it. That such a fate befell "one of the better writers" with "the energy of a dynamo" says as much about London's difference in the 1930s from 1920s New York as it says about Walrond himself.

The challenge West Indian authors faced in England in the early 1930s was formidable, and Walrond's difficulty was not unique. Publishing opportunities were few and far between until the 1950s, and periodicals treated West Indian authors, particularly those quarreling with imperialism, with circumspection. Many "had to be convinced on ideological, social, marketing, and sometimes racial grounds before dissenting authors could get their words into the public domain."[5] Peter Blackman, a Barbadian theology student and leader of London's leftist Negro Welfare League, explained the resistance: "The West Indian author who hopes to succeed as a novelist looks outside the islands for a market," he wrote in 1948. "In most cases his hopes are pinned on England. But the themes he touches, the questions he raises, cannot greatly interest, can often disquiet and embarrass Englishmen."[6] Despite this reticence, the 1930s generation succeeded in developing a periodical culture that was unprecedented in its anticolonial ambition and international reach. Scholars place a higher value on books than periodicals and rate fiction over journalism, but the fact is that the West Indian novel as we know it had not yet been invented. The real cultural action in 1930s England was in journalism, fostering independence activity and galvanizing Pan-Africanism, a movement that, by the end of World War II, linked Manchester to New York to Lagos to Port of Spain to Johannesburg.[7]

London was a critical site, as writers arrived during upheaval in the colonies and emerging fascism in Europe. Even George Padmore, the most prolific of these activists, struggled to publish in book form and was most effective in periodicals, both in Britain and its possessions and in the United States, where during World War II he had 575 bylines in the *Pittsburgh Courier* and *Chicago Defender* alone.[8] To label Walrond "the writer who ran away," one from whom nothing was heard after 1929, as scholars have done, is to miss his role in this burgeoning periodical culture.[9] Walrond's supposed decline is belied by his contribution to this signal achievement in twentieth-century black letters, and his disappointments are as vital to understanding this achievement as are the triumphs of others.

STARTING OVER

Whatever similarities obtained between white supremacist practices in England and the United States, a long history of African American political struggle and acculturation conditioned the possibility for the New Negro movement in the United States, while in 1930s England people of African descent were not only fewer in number but also lacked a national narrative authorizing their claims upon the nation. As colonial subjects, they could claim colonial citizenship and even Englishness but could not claim England itself. Walrond began writing about England's "colour bar" at home and colonialism abroad shortly after his arrival, insisting on their connection. His path to publication in London resembled the one he had pursued in New York. Facing an industry that was indifferent if not dismissive in New York, he published pulp stories and eventually found work with the journal of Garvey's Universal Negro Improvement Association (UNIA). Similarly, his first publications in London were the stuff of penny dreadfuls, when who should appear in late 1934 with plans to rejuvenate the UNIA but Garvey, bearing a job offer. Walrond had just published the stories "Tai Sing" in *The Spectator* and "Inciting to Riot" in *The Evening Standard*. Despite their sensationalism, the stories are not without merit or interest. Anticipating by several years the Caribbean "barracks tales" of C. L. R. James, Edgar Mittelholzer, and Victor Reid, they are among the first works of Caribbean fiction published in England.

Set in Panama, both stories dramatize a conflict between West Indian laborers and merchants there to seek their fortunes. They convey an atmosphere of frontier lawlessness and revel in the friction of crosscultural communication. "Tai Sing" is a Chinese shopkeeper straight from central casting. He speaks in demotic dialect ("Me tek," "Me like," "You pay Chinaman, else yo' no can have bag") and is thoroughly infantilized ("A small boy with a toy gun, or a monkey with a peanut, could hardly have been happier than was Tai Sing with the revolver" [25–26]).[10] Tai Sing discharges his weapon twice in the story, murdering West Indians both times. The first is just for the thrill of it; he "wanted, in a sudden impish upsurge, to hit something that could feel," and that something is a "Negro" pushing a cart "full of smoky blue chunks of stone and clotted earth" (27). The second is a Jamaican itinerant nicknamed 'Fo 'Day Morning, whose "bare feet and trouser legs were spattered with the brick-red clay" of the canal cut (25). 'Fo 'Day—whose name reflects his routine, rising before daybreak—refuses to pay Tai Sing for minding his valise, and Tai Sing, tired of mouthy West Indians, shoots him with the revolver to end the story.

"Inciting to Riot" stages a similar conflict between West Indians and an immigrant shopkeeper, this one a grocer from Spain. Juan Poveda harbors a deep animus toward the "*sacré negroes jamaicanos*" because of an assault he suffered while supervising a work crew. Harassment from his customers pushes him over the edge, provoking him to an "avenging passion" (35). "Inciting to Riot" contains wonderful dialect, as when a laborer yells at Poveda, "Is fight yo' want, fight? Tell me, is fight yo' want, fight?" (35). "Some people can teef an' got so much mout' besides," says a woman witnessing a neighbor steal from Poveda then defend herself (32). Two elements link this story with "Tai Sing" beyond their plots. One is the shadow presence of the French, who lurk in the background as the Canal Zone's occupying force. The other is the vulnerability of the West Indian community to violence and the near impunity of the perpetrators. In neither story is the murderer brought to justice; his behavior is merely reprimanded as inflammatory, liable to incite a retaliatory mob. The stories were likely based on folk legends, and although they indulged in the sensationalism and stereotypes of pulp fiction, they incisively depicted the precariousness of West Indian lives in Panama and the tense coexistence of multiethnic communities.

Between "Tai Sing" and "Inciting to Riot," two of Walrond's essays were translated into Spanish and published in Madrid, one concerning the Panama Canal construction, the other a somber meditation on Harlem's decline during the Depression. The Depression had "undermined profoundly the proud notions of self-sufficiency of the 'black belt' of New York" ("El Negro"). A remarkable community was ravaged, its residents often the last hired and first fired. For white Americans, Harlem had been little more than a playground, "a great center of extravagant and exotic diversions," but for African Americans it had deep material and symbolic significance, the attenuation of which was painful to behold. The fragmentation and dispersal Walrond identified with Depression-era Harlem had an unmistakable feel of autobiography: "In these days of misery, hunger, and uncertainty, the Negro cannot go running after empty ideals which don't satisfy his hunger and can't even pay his rent." "The self-sufficiency" of the Harlem "Negro" "was, in reality, no more than a mirage brought about by the quicksand of credit and excessive confidence based on speculation." He would have said the same of his own career, of his own self-sufficiency, after philanthropic foundations and speculators in the literary market had created for him—the mirage of a career, the quicksand in which he was mired. He could not write his way out of it with the occasional article, not in early-1930s London.

Conditions were terrible among black Britons and showed little sign of improvement until the end of the decade. After demonstrating their love of king and country during World War I, some of the fifteen thousand men in the British West Indian Regiment moved to Great Britain, and they, along with thousands of colonial seamen and laborers, became scapegoats when the Depression struck. Although the worst tensions flared in seaports such as Liverpool and Cardiff, where fifteen hundred "coloured" were unemployed, factory towns such as Manchester were rife with hostility, as was London. "Things were hard for we people," said one West Indian, "Them days John Bull will shoot you if he see you with him woman. They like their woman pass God self."[11] African, Asian, Caribbean, and Arab seamen were required by law to register with the police as resident aliens and threatened with deportation and imprisonment. Jamaican writer Una Marson "dreaded going out" when she arrived in London in 1933: "People stared at her, men were curious but their gaze insulted her, even small children with short dimpled legs called her 'Nigger,' put out their tongues at her. This was her first taste of street racism. She was a black foreigner seen only as strange, nasty, unwanted."[12] The press offered few avenues of redress. The African Progress Union and the West African Student Union (WASU) were established, but vigorous antiracist and anti-imperialist campaigns only gained ground in the

mid-1930s: with the arrival of Marson and C. L. R. James; the inception
of the League of Coloured Peoples journal, *The Keys*, in 1933; the arrival
the following year of George Padmore and Marcus Garvey; and the Italian
invasion of Ethiopia, which quickened anti-imperialist sentiment.

It was thus a blessing that in the summer of 1934 Ashwood and Manning arrived to save Walrond from his writing routine of cigarettes, gin,
and spearmint gum, for his prospects were dim. Manning hatched a plan
involving Walrond touring the UK with the "first British negro revue." A
great popularizer of calypso, Manning was responsible for seven of the
first nine calypso recordings in England. The "negro revue" drew from
calypso and a repertoire of numbers from the New York stage. Calling
themselves the Harlem Nightbirds, the group "featured singers and musicians from Britain's old Black communities of Liverpool and Cardiff,
supplemented by more recent Caribbean arrivals," a kind of goodwill
tour.[13] Manning was a savvy fundraiser, securing the support of wealthy
Londoner Clifford Sabey. After opening engagements at Queen's Theatre, the Nightbirds toured the UK with Walrond as publicity manager
in spring 1935, performing at the Blackpool Opera House in Lancashire
and in the cities of Birmingham, Manchester, Glasgow, Edinburgh, and
Belfast, among others. Walrond executed his task capably, with notices
appearing in London, in regional newspapers, and in the Trinidad *Guardian*, where an article bore the provocative title, "West Indian 'Night Birds'
in London: All Black and All-British."[14] The *Baltimore Afro-American*
learned of Walrond's activities and implied that the mighty had fallen. "It
is out now: Eric Walrond is touring the continent with a musical revue;
from writing for the sophisticated journals as one of the exponents of
the 'new renaissance,' he is now penning publicity about the travelling
vaudeville troupe."[15]

As the Harlem Nightbirds made their way from Birmingham to Wigan
on the tour's final leg, Walrond must have been gratified to see his essay,
bearing the confrontational title "White Man, What Now?" on news-
stands. The *Spectator* was not radical, and Walrond's essay is remarkable
for its restraint. He employed a double voice that muted its critique of
English racism and colonial paternalism. The irony of English prejudice

against West Indians, he argued, was that West Indians like himself had always considered themselves English.

> As a West Indian Negro, I was reared on the belief that England was the one country where the black man was sure of getting a square deal. A square deal from white folk has always seemed so important to us black folk. Our position in the West Indies, in virtue of the ideas instilled in us by our English education, has been one of extreme self-esteem. We were made to believe that in none of the other colonies were the blacks treated as nicely as we were. We developed an excessive regard for the English. We looked upon them as the most virtuous of the colonizing races. It was to us a source of pride and conceit to be attached to England. We became even a bit truculent about it (279).[16]

But Englishness exacted a price, he maintained, at home and abroad. "Our love of England and our wholehearted acceptance of English life and customs, at the expense of everything African, blinded us to many things. It has even made us seem a trifle absurd and ridiculous in the eyes of our neighbours" (279). Only in traveling, he said, did West Indians realize the "absurdity of our ostrich-like" stance. In Panama, residents harbored "a strong feeling of antipathy toward British Negroes," a disdain "engendered by our love of England" and expressed in epithets and "occasional armed incursions" into their communities (280). Conditions in the Dominican Republic were similar, though their "terms of endearment" were *cocolo* instead of *chombo*. In Haiti, he found a long-held "grudge" against the English that "loosely extended to Britain's black wards in the Caribbean" (280). In Harlem, the appearance of community concealed a rift along national lines, as the West Indian "was joked at on street corners, burlesqued on the stage and discriminated against in business and social life. His pride in his British heritage and lack of racial consciousness were contemptuously put down to 'airs'" (281).

Indelibly marked by their Englishness everywhere else, West Indians were dismayed to be poorly treated in England, where they arrived "in the spirit of chickens coming home to roost." "We possess the undying certainty that in England we shall be on the equivalent of native soil. Trained to believe 'there is nothing in race,' and that there is no difference between ourselves and white folk, we expect to be treated on that basis" (281). In a closing flourish, he raised the issue weighing heavily on black Britons with a marvelous irony: "We do not suspect the existence of a Colour Bar. And so thorough has been our British upbringing that if, in the event, we did find a Colour Bar, we would consider it 'bad form' openly to admit its existence" (281). It was an English way to end an essay asserting West Indians' Englishness, mordantly witty and delicate in suggesting a difference from the strident militancy of American activists.

Reprinted in the Jamaica *Gleaner*, Walrond's essay appeared at a critical juncture in British race relations, sharpened by events in the Caribbean and Africa. At home, the League of Coloured Peoples conducted an extensive study of dire conditions in Cardiff's "coloured" community; and although the circulation of its journal, *The Keys*, was a modest two thousand, the League's director, Harold Moody, was the most influential black voice in domestic politics, and the study appeared amid the furor provoked by Italy's invasion of Abyssinia (Ethiopia). New York's *Amsterdam News* reported that Walrond was "returning from London soon with two manuscripts," but in fact his imagination was captured by the volatile transition England had entered. On occasion he wrote about Harlem, publishing a review of new books by Hughes and Hurston in *The Keys* and a story in *The Star* entitled "Harlem Nights." But by 1935, James's *The Case for West Indian Self-Government*, published by Hogarth Press, was the subject of vigorous discussion, as was Padmore's *How Britain Rules Africa*.[17] Mussolini's invasion of Ethiopia provoked Pan-African and antifascist sentiment. Padmore and James joined Amy Ashwood Garvey, Paul Robeson, and Ras Makonnen to form the International African Friends of Abysinnia, soon renamed the International African Service Bureau (IASB), a more radical organization than the League of Coloured Peoples (LCP), led by Moody and Marson. Along with WASU, these organizations were consistently publishing work of high quality, cultivating a periodical culture with an international reach.[18]

8.1 Photograph of Paul Robeson, 1932, by Carl Van Vechten.

8.2 Photograph of Amy Ashwood Garvey, date and photographer unknown.

Courtesy of the Lionel Yard Collection, Brooklyn, New York.

Walrond felt the Ethiopian invasion was a threshold event. In an article reprinted in *The Pittsburgh Courier* and *The California Eagle*, he urged intervention on behalf of the Ethiopians and the rest of "the world's two hundred million Negroes." Since one-fourth of these were her own subjects, Great Britain had a special responsibility, he argued. "Walrond points out Ethiopia is a symbol of the destiny of the world's Negro millions," reported the *Eagle*. "The attack on Abyssinia is not a colonial venture; it is a trial to prove whether the most advanced mind and conscience of the white people can remain satisfied by a new relation which will confirm the hideous slavery of the past" ("Writer" A2). Walrond cast Mussolini's invasion as a threat to British colonial relations. "If given a free hand in Africa he will stand a chance of kindling a violent war between the black and white races, which can only react disastrously on the position of the great Colonial Powers. Two hundred million people cannot forever watch with complacence their destiny torn by bayonets" ("Writer" A2). However, the invasion elicited a tepid response from British officials, even after Haile Selassie, Ethiopia's emperor, sought refuge and an audience in Whitehall. Walrond was among the growing number whose dashed hopes for a firm rejoinder to the fascists led to disillusionment with the Colonial Office and increased militancy.[19]

And it was not just black Britons; the movement was multiracial. Among the gatherings Walrond attended were those of Winifred Holtby, a white novelist and friend of Robeson's. With cohost Vera Brittain, a wealthy pacifist and writer, Holtby invited intellectuals and activists to their Russell Square salon. On one occasion, Walrond joined Holtby's cousin Daisy Pickering, the writer Odette Keun, and Una Marson of the LCP.[20] Marson's interest in the New Negro movement led her to consult Walrond about his peers in the States and solicit his review of Hughes and Hurston for *The Keys*, but he did not become a regular contributor. Instead he took a job with Marcus Garvey's *The Black Man*, the journal of the revived UNIA in London. The deciding factor seems to have been money—Walrond received a small retainer to work in the office and to contribute his writing—but the affiliation produced some of his best writing in England, seven articles and a story. He was among a handful of writers alert to the political and cultural potentialities of the diaspora, committed to articulating the jarring experience of black Britain in its formation.

THE BLACK MAN

Marcus Garvey tried to put a brave face on a relocation that was really an act of desperation. Although the UNIA remained in operation after Garvey's deportation in late 1927, the organization was bankrupt and in disarray.[21] Adversity never diminished Garvey's bravado, however, and he announced a ten-year, six-hundred-million-dollar program in 1928 "for the development of the Negro," established a new UNIA headquarters in Kingston, and ran for public office. But when he criticized "corrupt" judges, he was indicted, imprisoned, and soundly defeated in the election. From Jamaica, he could not control UNIA operations in the United States, where dissent increased, and as early as 1931 he expressed a desire to start afresh in London. Arriving there in 1935, he kept a modest UNIA office in West Kensington and sparred regularly with Hyde Park's polemicists at Speaker's Corner.[22] It was a far cry from the massive rallies of the early 1920s, and his diminished status likely contributed to his willingness to reach out to Walrond, with whom he had fallen out ten years earlier.

The relocation failed to restore the UNIA to its former glory, nor was *The Black Man* as important as other periodicals in the movement, but its twenty-four issues fanned the flames of anticolonialism and Pan-Africanism, transforming local initiatives into a broader, concerted campaign. *The Black Man* printed Garvey's final addresses—speeches delivered in Canada and the West Indies—including the principles of "The School of African Philosophy." Despite what Robert Hill calls "the sheer monopoly Garvey exercised over editorial matters," Walrond's contributions departed from the UNIA party line as often as not. He embraced historical materialism, a Marxist viewpoint at odds with Garvey's "increasingly idealistic conservative ideology."[23] Moreover, Walrond recognized the potentiality of black Britain in a way Garvey did not, for Garvey loathed his "competitors" in London and continued to see African Americans as the political vanguard.[24] *The Black Man* made "no direct mention of any of the important political initiatives or essential welfare functions which [London's] remarkably diverse and talented group of individuals and organizations undertook."[25] Their influence registers in Walrond's articles, however. He quoted Padmore approvingly, for example, but did not mention Garvey or exhort readers to join the UNIA. What *The Black Man* provided Walrond, in short, was a platform for a more militant critique of British conduct at home and abroad than mainstream periodicals permitted.

The kid gloves came off immediately in "The Negro in London," a 1936 essay that dispensed with the restraint he had shown in "White Man, What Now?"

Viewing the "Mother Country" with an adoring eye, the Negro in the British overseas colonies is obviously at the mercy of the rainbow. He sees England through a romantic and illusive veil. What he so affectionately imagines he sees does not always "square" with the facts. This deception, common to the virgin gaze of African and West Indian alike, is partly a case of "distance lends enchantment," partly a by-product of the black man's extraordinary loyalty to the Crown. On coming to England the first impression the black man gets is that of utter loneliness. [. . .] The Negro is made to feel as some species of exotic humanity from another planet, and this despite the 50,000,000 negroes in the British Empire (282).[26]

Walrond was mapping out a contradiction few writers at the time articulated. A generation later, the central trope of an emergent body of literature would be the jarring "moment when the emigrant came face to face with the lived realities of the civilisation in whose name he or she had been educated into adulthood, as distant subjects of the Crown."[27] But in the 1930s, Walrond was among the few with the comparative perspective from which to formulate black Britons' "discrepant reality" and the temerity to express it.[28] Having lived in British colonies, a Latin American country under U.S. occupation, and in New York and Paris, he was uniquely situated to address England's distinctiveness.

And he did find it distinctive. There is "a peculiar Negro problem" in Britain, he claimed, "despite so little one hears about it." It was not that treatment was uniformly bad, though in several cities segregation prevailed and "the feeling among whites is one of subtle antagonism" (283). It was that English racial attitudes were inconsistent and inscrutable. Outside London, the "keen competition for jobs" and the observance of a colour bar in employment and housing compelled black Britons to "fall back on the dole or eke out a miserable existence in some shady precarious undertaking" (283). "The problem of the Negro in London," however, was "much more complex and varied." In the East End, the high concentration of "discharged seamen from the farthest corners of the Empire" made conditions as desperate as in "the distressed areas of the North of England." Elsewhere, they were "enmeshed in a maze of bewildering subtleties and paradoxes." They might be rented a room or denied one, merchants might greet them with warmth or contempt, and students were invited from the colonies to study, while professionals and artisans were unwelcome, so "the educated Negro who is neither a doctor or a lawyer is of necessity a 'bird of passage,'" and students completing their degrees are "subtly discouraged from settling in England." In short, "the black man never knows just how the Englishman is going to take him" (284).

The most unnerving paradox was the English pride in their empire and their ignorance about its residents; they "lump them all together, and [are] invariably astonished to find them in command of the English language" (284). It was vexing, he concluded, "that London, the capital of the largest Negro Empire in the world—the cradle of English liberty, justice and fair-play—the city to which Frederick Douglass fled as a fugitive from slavery—should be so extremely inexpert in the matter of interracial relations." But his prior experience offered some comfort, for "in this respect, [. . .] London may be easily compared with New York twenty years before the big migration which resulted in the establishment of Harlem" (285). His prediction was accurate; twenty years later, George Lamming, Sam Selvon, V. S. Naipaul, Andrew Salkey, and Roger Mais were forging a place for West Indian fiction in England; Una Marson and Henry Swanzy brought *Caribbean Voices* to BBC Radio; and Claudia Jones, Trinidadian by way of New York, fled McCarthy's persecution and started the *West Indian Gazette*. Their work would not have been possible without their 1930s predecessors, who faced a British public that was indifferent if not hostile.

Having participated in the New Negro movement, Walrond could not conceal his impatience with conditions in London. Other West Indian writers were more circumspect, some advising immigrants and visitors to be deferential and know their place. Walrond chafed under this paternalism, recalling the assertiveness of black New York and the freedoms of Paris ("On England" 289).[29] He wrote withering critiques of imperialism in *The Black Man*, calling England's pretense of democracy a "farce."

He conceded that the monarchy was not absolute, but it excluded voices outside Great Britain.

> [T]he Empire is not confined to the British Isles; it sprawls over vast territories halfway round the globe and includes among its citizens millions of black, brown and yellow men, women and children in Africa, India, the Far and Near East and the Caribbean area. But these millions of citizens have no voice in the government of the Empire. There is no one at Whitehall or Westminster to plead their case. ("On England" 291)

The essay pursued the argument to the tremendous labor unrest that had provoked strikes and retaliatory crackdowns throughout the Caribbean.

> If as workers they find themselves in conflict with the sugar interests of Jamaica or the oil field owners of Trinidad, there is nothing they can do but submit to the repressive acts of the Colonial Office. They are a crushed, unorganized and completely voiceless mass. Unlike the coloured natives of the French Colonies, who send their own men to represent them in the Chamber of Deputies in Paris, they are utterly at the mercy of a system which even refuses to give them a hearing. Under such conditions can anybody seriously call England a democracy? ("On England" 291)

It was a rebuke the mainstream press would never have printed, an illustration of the critical function London's black periodicals performed.

Despite his radical affiliations, Walrond was invited to a coronation party in May 1937 for King George VI. Prominent figures from across the empire and luminaries from the United States descended on Aggrey House, a hall the British Colonial Office furnished for colonial students. The attendees included prominent African Americans such as Ralph Bunche and Ethel Waters; Caribbean visitors such as Audrey Jeffers, the first female councilmember in Port of Spain, Trinidad; and African elites such as the Alake of Abeokuta ("paramount chief of Nigeria"). These were respectable guests whose presence the Colonial Office could endorse, but their respectability did not preclude revelry, and they took their cue from Harlem's latest dance sensation: truckin'.[30] Walrond must have enjoyed the scene of the assembled giving truckin' a disaporic twist. "All night while the King and His men were pitching a ball at Buckingham Palace, the Africans from the motherland and those from the U.S.A. broke it down in Aggrey House. One of the West Indian boys told" *California Eagle* editor Fay Jackson "that the Chieftains and the high powered barristers put on the dog before the ofays but they can be really human among 'their own.'"[31] The notion that the colonial elite dissembled to impress the British struck Jackson as delightfully subversive, and she relished the irony of the segregated celebrations conducted "while the British were crowing over their One Big Happy Family Empire." Coronation festivities also furnished an opportunity for Walrond to report on the "colour bar." Discovering that white women were banned from a coronation reception in Brighton for Indian servicemen, he wrote an article for *The Pittsburgh Courier* alleging miscegenation anxiety. He cast the episode, which involved an invitation Brighton's mayor issued to 450 Indian troops, as a tempest in the brittle English teapot of race prejudice ("Ban" 7). The length to which Britons went to prevent socializing between white women and nonwhite men was a subject to which Walrond's reporting would return.

The Black Man was a platform for the militancy Walrond could not have expressed elsewhere, but his increasingly Marxist views were at odds with Garvey's conservatism. It is unlikely that he joined the Communist Party, but a number of factors made Marxism compelling. These included the Depression, the Scottsboro trial, in which the Communist Party USA led the defense, and closer to home, the rise of Sir Oswald Mosley's British Union of Fascists, against which Communists led the opposition.[32] The Marxists Walrond knew, such as Padmore, James, Robeson, and Ashwood Garvey, had complicated relationships to Communism, but their opposition to fascism and their class analysis appealed to him.[33] Adopting Marxist categories in *The Black Man*, he cast colonialism as a ruthless competition among advanced capitalist states for labor and markets. This analysis is all the more striking in light of the strenuous anti-Communism of Garvey, who devoted a whole chapter of this period's

"Lessons from the School of African Philosophy" to the perils of Communism. His contempt extended to Robeson, whose films he attacked for misrepresenting the race, and Padmore and the IASB, whom he blamed for the violence attending labor disputes in the Caribbean.[34]

Walrond's Marxist turn was sharpened by what he saw as the repellent "class basis of British society." The figure of the English gentleman provoked his ire, a creature whose vices and invidious social role were concealed by an appearance of gentility. "Any person of gentle birth, any unborn candidate for the playing fields of Eton, any suave, gilt-edged rascal may be a gentleman," he wrote. "He may be a jewel thief, a blackmailer or one who lives by his wits, and yet be one" ("On England" 290). He launched a searing class critique.

> "Gentleman" is nothing but a catch-word; but a catch-word that serves a deadly purpose. It is used to bolster up the social and economic division between the upper and lower classes. It puts a premium on the well-born and serves notice on the under-dog that the line which separates him from his "superiors" is an ineradicable one. [. . .] It has nothing to do with morality in the abstract. No bloke of a Cockney, however decent or upright, may aspire to that lofty estate. Purity of mind or heart is not enough. If he manages by sheer merit to emerge from the ruck and carve out a career for himself [. . .] he is looked upon at best as a curiosity. ("On England" 290)

Social conditions were once again changing Walrond's analysis and his sense of the relationship between art and politics. "If [the Negro] aspires to rise and move on to a high destiny, and not just be a helpless pawn in the game of Power Politics, he may have to alter his whole outlook on the world he lives in." Walrond seemed to be exhorting himself as much as his readers: "He cannot afford to be a stick in the mud. He may even have to revise his scale of values. He must be resilient and adaptable, and not be a romantic—out of step with the rhythm of the times" ("Negro Before" 286). It may have suited the New Negro to craft fine literature, he suggested, but times had changed, as had his location.

Employing a Marxist lexicon of value and private property and a model of history propelled by class conflict, Walrond explained the African diaspora as the underside of capitalist expansion. Africa was "the source of intense rivalry among the colonial powers," he wrote, and the African, whom he figured as a male threatened with emasculation, had struggled for centuries for sovereignty. If the Ethiopian crisis—African swords succumbing to Italian ballistics—was a source of humiliation and outrage, the displaced New World African had fared little better, "sold like cattle in the slave markets," "wincing under the slave-driver's lash" for three hundred years. "His lot was no better than oxen and sheep—with which he ranked in the white man's scale of property values" ("Negro Before" 287). By this account, it was political economy, not prejudice, that determined relations between races. The end of slavery had not ended "Negro" subjugation because the underlying economic system remained intact. "When, after the reading of the Emancipation acts, 'freedom' was revealed in all its emptiness, the powers that be contrived by their system of economy to re-enslave the Negro." The system to which the "Negro" was "yoked" had one objective: "to enrich and confer power upon a small governing class."

In its thrust the argument was classically Marxist, but in its particulars, drawn from the Caribbean and the United States, it invoked a *black* proletariat.

The men wielding the whip-lash—the sugar barons and the cotton kings, the factory owners and the absentee landlords [. . .] were not going to let a little thing like abolition thwart them in their desire to perpetuate themselves and their class in power. By exercising a monopoly on capital, they were able to exploit the black man, thrown penniless on a hostile world, just as easily as when he was a chattel slave. ("Negro Before" 288)

His confidence eroded by "years of bodily and mental enslavement," the "Negro" considered Africanness a source of shame, the mark of an "inferior being—without a past or a future, a heritage or a destiny—ordained by God to occupy the lowest rung of the human ladder." The tragedy lay in this mystification, compelling "Negroes" to misperceive their collective self-interest. "To escape from the blind alley up which he was being pressed, the black man, instead of opposing the system that oppressed him, set out, curiously, to build his hopes and ideals around it" ("Negro Before" 288).

But a good dialectician identifies forces available for harnessing resistance, and Walrond noted promising conditions amid the "chaos." "Side by side with his enforced humility, the black man [. . .] has kept the spirit of independence alive. Who knows but that at a time not far distant the war-clouds over Europe may darken into night?" A second "Great War" seemed imminent by 1938, and Walrond envisioned a crisis of the entire architecture of colonial capitalism. "When, and if, that time ever comes (no one doubts but that it will mean the collapse of the capitalist systems in Europe) the white man's rule over Africa will be at an end" ("Negro Before" 287).[35] Given Garvey's avowed anti-Communism, the appearance of this article in *The Black Man* suggests either his editorial aloofness or the autonomy Walrond enjoyed. Its subversive thesis could not have been more plainly stated, that "there can be no salvation for the Negro until and unless he takes a firm stand against" capitalism and imperialism. This argument resonated with contemporary expressions of Pan-Africanism such as Padmore's *How Britain Rules Africa*, James's *History of Negro Revolt*, and Césaire's *Notebook of a Return to My Native Land*. It was at odds with Garvey's hierarchical vision of authority derived from his location in Europe's capital of finance, handing down "commands from this great city where men move and act in controlling the affairs of the world," as he enthused.[36]

On no issue did Garvey prove more woefully out of step with Walrond and other black radicals than the Ethiopian crisis. Initially, he expressed outrage that the world's powers stood idly by as Mussolini invaded a sovereign African nation. But he became critical of Selassie, blaming the emperor for the defeat of his people, a position that infuriated other Pan-Africanists. He dissociated himself from the Communists, for whom Selassie was a cause célèbre.[37] Walrond, by contrast, examined the circumstances of Ethiopia's collapse and published an investigative report, his longest article in *The Black Man*. "The End of Ras Nasibu" offered a detailed account of Ethiopian attitudes toward war and errors of military strategy. He conceded that Ethiopians had been naïve and Selassie had made "ill-advised" decisions, but he asserted that the League of Nations abdicated responsibility and that Ethiopia's defeat left many martyred "in the cause of Abyssinian, and Negro, independence" (15). Even the moderate LCP, mainly concerned with education, social welfare, and bussing children to the salubrious countryside, was radicalized by the Ethiopian crisis, leaving Garvey practically alone "clutching at the chimera of a movement whose historic moment had long since passed."[38]

As sabers rattled in preparation for war, Walrond became intrigued by the practices of recruiting and training colonial subjects. He was moved by the bitter recognition that soldiers of color had participated, sometimes on the front lines, in wars against people toward whom they harbored no enmity, often other people of color. These were intricate paradoxes to which he later returned, writing for British and American periodicals about Caribbean, African, and Indian soldiers in the Royal Air Force (RAF) and African American troops in England. "The Negro in the Armies of Europe" was his first foray, comparing imperial attitudes toward recruiting colonial servicemen. Although Britain had come to rely on colonial recruits, it was only "dire expediency" that occasioned "the induction of Negroes into the British army." "Only as cannon fodder or as an instrument in the fruitful Roman policy of 'divide and conquer' has the Negro been of interest to the English" ("Negro in the Armies" 9). Despite minor differences in attitude among the European powers, Walrond grimly contended that their practices were all meretricious and objectionable, even the French, who "too often used" black troops "to pull the white man's chestnuts out of the fire" ("Negro in the Armies" 9).

Not everything Walrond wrote for *The Black Man* departed from Garveyism. "A Fugitive from Dixie" was a 1936 sketch about a sharecropper who fled Arkansas for St. Louis, where a "contact man" from an organization resembling the UNIA records his life story, a tale of intimidation by white men out to seize his crops and livestock. It celebrates the sharecropper's indomitable spirit and the magnanimity of the organization, which finds him a job to support his family. Capably executed, the story exhibited Walrond's skill with African American vernacular but was essentially a tribute to Garveyite ideals of race pride and masculine individualism. Another contribution hewing closely to Garvey's principles was "Can the Negro Measure Up?," an essay about the Enlightenment figure Abbé Henri Gregoire, "one of the early champions of the cause of Negro liberty." It affirmed that "Negroes" could "measure up" to Gregoire's high expectations, but more interestingly, it illustrated Walrond's voracious historical imagination and contained some of his only recorded reflections on Haiti and Guadeloupe.

At this point, a pioneering volume of literary scholarship praising Walrond appeared in the United States. *The Negro Genius*, by Benjamin Brawley, claimed that he "excelled in the freshness of his material, in his clear perception of what has value, and in the strength of his style. [. . .] One can only regret that he has not produced more within recent years."[39] Walrond shared this regret but as the foregoing discussion indicates, Brawley was not looking in the right places. Walrond had moved on, and the African American tradition could no longer claim him, if it ever could. For that matter, he had not quit fiction writing. In addition to "Fugitive from Dixie," he published an exquisite story in *The Spectator* entitled "Consulate." It was the third in a series of stories for mainstream London periodicals to feature Caribbean merchants or clerks as protagonists. Walrond was drawn to the dramatic potential of quotidian commercial spaces, setting stories in bodegas, brothels, beauty parlors, groceries, and restaurants. In these Caribbean tales, a petty bourgeois clerk plays a small but critical role fulfilling the lowly offices of empire. Clerks were useful for exploring the complexities of coloniality because they were neither the oppressor nor the oppressed, exactly. Often colonial subjects, they were not indigenous and did not identify with the peasants and laborers who comprised their clientele nor did they quite belong to the ruling elite.

In "Consulate," a wry critique of empire is mediated by a sympathetic treatment of one of its middlemen, a consul's clerk named Leon Cabrol.

A "middle-aged man of color" from British Guiana, Cabrol suffered for two years in the "funereal climate" of Colón, leaving him "sallow, yellow-eyed, white-lipped" (305). Performing his duties processing ship manifests and the like, Cabrol is besieged by the demands of the diverse community. He accepts a cash deposit for a Jamaican bank account, records testimony from an eyewitness to an assault, signs the passport of a Chinese man returning home with his six children by a "tall willowy Negress." Finally, he refuses a woman's request to send her daughter back to Jamaica on account of insubordination. The mother storms out, "properly scandalised," dragging the girl by the arm, and the story ends with Cabrol calling "Next!" and "scanning the slowly diminishing throng" (309). Like the grocer in "Inciting to Riot," Cabrol is no innocent—he is implicated in the colonial project—but he is the story's only individuated character and his predicament is treated as just that, a predicament, not an instrument of domination. The opening line describes him as "the arbiter of life and death" for Colón's residents, but we are meant to understand the misery of adjudicating the messy, quotidian aspects of Empire as it is lived day to day. If empire does its worst damage to colonial subjects, he suggested, it also punishes its managers, on whom devolved empire's most banal functions of discipline and regulation. "Consulate" anticipates Orwell's "Shooting an Elephant," a story about another middleman's crisis of conscience, a "sub-divisional police officer" in Burma "hated by large numbers of people" who realizes in a terrible epiphany his complicity with oppression. But Walrond pulls up short of Orwell's contention that such virtuous men might derail the colonial misadventure and expose "the real motives for which despotic governments act."

The link to Orwell was more than thematic. A few months after "Consulate" appeared, "Shooting an Elephant" was published in the journal *New Writing*, and when Walrond sought to jumpstart his fiction career, he looked to that journal.[40] He may have been emboldened by its mission "to further the work of new and young authors, from colonial and foreign countries as well as the British Isles." From his flat near Tottenham Court Road, Walrond wrote editor John Lehman "to ask whether I may be permitted to send you a short story of about 3,500 words in length

which deals with life in the West Indian Negro slum quarter of Brooklyn N.Y." He rehearsed his credentials, conceding that "not much of my
stuff has appeared in this country" despite his prior success in New York.
Lehman showed Walrond's story to a friend at the Hogarth Press, who
recommended it for *New Writing*, noting, "I think this has a good deal
of merit and originality." But Lehman demurred: "Agreed it's interesting,
but it doesn't come to anything." Thus was Walrond's effort to revive his
fiction career on this side of the Atlantic thwarted again.[41]

THE KING V. ERIC DERWENT WALROND

Lehman's characterization of the story—"interesting" but did not "come
to anything"—also summarized the impression forming around Walrond
generally. He was eager to disprove it and felt he had disappointed many
people, but he was reluctant to seek help. His career was further destabi-
lized when he came to blows with a coworker at *The Black Man* office in
1938. Walrond stabbed the man, was charged with "maliciously inflicting
grievous bodily harm," and although he was acquitted, spent nearly a
month "detained on remand" awaiting trial. His arraignment was covered
in the *Westminster and Pimlico News*, his trial at the London Sessions
reported in *The Times*. It must have been a source of considerable distress.[42] Conditions at the office were strained because Garvey's wife, Amy
Jacques, and their two sons, one of whom was gravely ill, had joined him
in London, and his marriage deteriorated. Garvey described the office as
"fraught with tension" and complained of his "inability to hire capable
clerks."[43] In the summer of 1938, soon after his son was discharged from
the hospital, Garvey left for a conference in Canada, instructing his wife
to mind the office and the children. Their son's health took a turn for the
worse, and she hastily arranged passage back to Jamaica.[44] It was during
this tumultuous period, during an unseasonably hot week in early August,
that the fight erupted between Walrond and James McIntyre.

Walrond had upset Garvey by flirting with the female staff, leaving the
impression that he was "making love to all of them at one and the same

time."[45] The particulars of the conflict with McIntyre are unclear because the newspaper reported only the statements of the defendant and the lawyers. McIntyre's profession was given as a clerk, Walrond's as a journalist, and their acquaintance was said to have been four years. McIntyre claimed Walrond spread a false rumor that he wished to leave to work "for another magazine for coloured men." When McIntyre arrived one morning, Amy Jacques confronted him, at which point he stormed into Walrond's office. He said Walrond "had been making insinuations against him, and recalled another occasion when he had made to his employer statements that were intended to be injurious to him. He warned him this must stop." Walrond replied that he was "talking nonsense" and "came up to him in an aggressive manner," at which point, McIntyre said, "I closed in on him." In the ensuing struggle, Walrond fell and McIntyre claimed to have "waited until he got up." But Walrond allegedly "whipped a knife from his pocket, rushed at [McIntyre], and slashed him on the right arm." He inflicted a serious wound, the fight spilling into the hallway. "I closed in on him again," McIntyre testified, "And while we were locked together I felt a stab in my back at the region of my neck. He struck me, and I fell down. I got up and rushed at him again. We continued struggling, and then he rushed down the stairs" and outside.

McIntyre denied having instigated the fight, but Walrond's lawyer introduced doubt by asking about his other jobs, which relied on aggressiveness, strength, and intimidation. McIntyre admitted to having fought once as an "all-in wrestler," and he had worked the door of a nightclub but never as a bouncer, only a "receptionist." This nicety brought out the judge's humor: "That is quite the opposite," he quipped to the delight of the assembled. McIntyre's case did not hold up at trial. He admitted to being "very annoyed" upon learning that Walrond told Garvey he was planning to quit, punching him in the face and breaking his chair. He denied having yelled, "I'll teach you to carry tales about me," and "Don't fool around me, or I'll kill you," and denied further that Walrond only reached for the knife in self-defense. The fact that the weapon was a penknife, which Walrond said he carried for the professional task of clipping articles, helped exonerate him. His lawyer also maintained that McIntyre came at him "again and again, regardless of the fact that he was holding the knife" and was "mad with rage." If Amy Jacques Garvey had been available, she would have been called to the stand to answer Walrond's claim that she pulled McIntyre off him, but she was in Jamaica. He did not need her testimony and was acquitted on September 21, 1938. He did not contribute another article to *The Black Man*, which folded the following year, just before Garvey's death.

EVACUATION

Perhaps the trial reminded Walrond of life's precariousness, or he may simply have become desperate for income, but he swallowed his pride and in the spring of 1939 contacted Charles Johnson, now director of Fisk University's Department of Social Sciences. Although neither Walrond's letter nor the response survive, Johnson told Ethel Ray Nance he had finally heard from "the wandering one, after about twelve years." "He seems to have been avoiding contact with persons he knew more out of sensitiveness about not keeping up the promise of *Tropic Death* than any other conceit. A note from you might on a long chance revive a flickering spark and yield something worth the effort," Johnson suggested, giving Walrond's address as 16 Fitzroy Street W1, London.[46] The two conspired to assist him. Nance thought Walrond might get work as a foreign correspondent, but Johnson was not optimistic. Better to use his fiction to reconnect with American editors, he felt.

> Walrond should have a story or two out of the past few years of living in Europe. It would help tremendously if there were a manuscript that could find its way to publication. He has been silent for a long time and these fresheners will be extremely helpful in restoring contact with the publishers and writers.[47]

Johnson knew a young sociologist headed to London and told him to look Walrond up. Horace Cayton, a prolific scholar who had coauthored

Black Workers and the New Unions and would soon write *Black Metropolis* with St. Clair Drake, met Walrond twice, encouraging him to apply for a Rosenwald Fellowship.[48] This proved impossible, not only because the fellowships were restricted to "American Negroes living in the United States, and to southern whites," but also because Henry Allen Moe served on the Rosenwald selection committee, and as Johnson gently observed, "Eric did not quite come through as expected" on his Guggenheim.[49]

Nance coaxed an article from Walrond, likely an excerpt from *The Big Ditch*, and sent it to Johnson for circulation to his contacts, including *The Atlantic Monthly*, but it was not accepted. Thinking the editor's comments may "be of some value to Walrond if he should ever decide to do any further work on his manuscript," Johnson returned the article to Nance.[50] "I find myself speculating upon the effects of the recent unpleasantness in Europe," he added. He was referring, with characteristic understatement, to Germany's invasion of Poland and the consequent declaration of war by England and France. Johnson wondered whether this might be the thing to get him "home." "The prospect of war may prove for our errant litterateur something of a boon," he wrote, "A recent radio announcement from England mentioned our Ambassadors' and the Americans' Clubs' patriotic efforts to get back home Americans with insufficient funds for the trip." He stopped himself, realizing his assumption: "Or is Eric American yet?"[51] The West Indian immigrant who had never filed for naturalization could not avail himself of the provision. Nor did he follow the many West Indians returning to the Caribbean with the threat of war looming.

Walrond wondered whether evacuation was necessary and on September 1, as Germany invaded Poland, he wandered Bloomsbury, canvassing local opinion and reporting the results for the *Amsterdam News*. "I went to see about trains out of London" and "found that early in the morning orders had come through suspending all goods traffic on the railways." The ticket clerk gave a stern caution: "If you haven't anything to keep you in London, I'd advise you to take the 6:15 tonight. Tomorrow the Government is expected to take over the railways and all the train services will be curtailed." Walrond confessed alarm. At the gates to the British

Museum he spoke with an Indian friend, a novelist, asking how seriously to take the gathering war clouds. A Marxist, the novelist was skeptical: It was "all part of a grand show put on with the object of hoodwinking the working classes." Around the museum, Nazis had previously lurked undercover, Germans whose identity was an open secret among patrons, but they were no longer about. Nor was the "young German" whom "all the museum staff knew to be a Nazi spy" in his place in Reading Room 1. Even the "buxom, middle-aged, always well made-up Fraulein who was not averse to taking tea at the lodgings of any Negro engaged in the colonial struggle was not there, either" ("Noted" 1).

Leaving the museum, Walrond stopped to chat with two West Indians, neither of whom seemed alarmed. The Barbadian, a recent convert to Communism, felt sure Stalin had averted war by signing a nonaggression pact with Hitler, a view Walrond found unpersuasive. The Trinidadian was confused by the prevalent fear of Germany, having just returned from a teaching stint in Berlin, where the people were nicer than in England and "the girls, the girls . . ." Advancing through Bloomsbury, Walrond checked the window of a Guyanese friend, a pilot who, despite having trained at the same aviation school as Charles Lindbergh, was denied a position in the RAF. "Will he get his chance now?" he wondered, "Will he be able to pierce the colour line now that war was imminent?" ("Noted" 10). With these conjectures on his mind, Walrond decided not to leave himself to the tender mercies of the German girls his Trinidadian friend promised or the Luftwaffe that might precede them. He boarded the train, joining tens of thousands of Londoners whose exodus was being hastily prepared for in evacuation centers around the country, the safe havens during what would be a war of immense, protracted brutality, reducing to rubble much of what had been Walrond's hometown for eight years. By the time he returned eighteen years later, London would be transformed, not only by the war and its regimes of austerity and rationing but also by the decline of the empire and the arrival of West Indians in waves so massive as to make the 1930s seem like a trickle.

9

BRADFORD-ON-AVON (1939–1952)

To ride the train from Bath to Bradford-on-Avon, as Eric Walrond did after evacuating London, is to thread eight miles of a pastoral idyll. Sloping gently to the River Avon, the meadows south of the Cotswold Mountains are embroidered with low stone fences, and for long stretches sheep and cows seem to be Wiltshire County's only residents. If Bath is Jane Austen, Wiltshire is Thomas Hardy, all copses and closes. In Bradford-on-Avon, limestone buildings line the narrow lanes that meander up from the valley. It had a grittier, prosaic feel when Walrond arrived in 1939, but in many respects it has retained its appearance. From the station, he crossed a sturdy thirteenth-century bridge on the edge of which sat a stone oubliette, a suspended jail of sorts, added in the seventeenth century to detain drunkards. To the left was the venerable Swan Hotel, established in 1500 and named after the graceful creatures patrolling eddies under the bridge. To the right lay the commercial district known as the Shambles, a tumbling nest of shops. Lifting his gaze up the hill that led to his house, Walrond could see the spires of the churches of St. Mary Tory, of Holy Trinity, an eleventh-century Saxon church originally built by King Aethelred for the nuns of Shaftesbury, and on the hilltop in the distance, of Christ Church. Across from Christ Church was Ivy Terrace, where Walrond lived for twelve years.[1]

He was the only black person in a town of four thousand residents. Communities of color had formed in cities outside of London, particularly in the ports, but Bradford-on-Avon was classically English— beautiful but austere, a Saxon town. The tablets of Stonehenge lay a few miles to the west, and the most striking monument of all, a tremendous tithe barn, all 168 feet of it covered by a thatch roof, flanked the canal as it had since 1341. It would be an exaggeration to say that time stood still in Bradford, but in the 1940s history was palpably present. It was a far cry from New York, farther still from the Caribbean.

Bradford's strangeness was not just a matter of race; it was amplified by the absence of modern conveniences to which Londoners were accustomed. When electricity arrived in the 1920s it reliably reached only the commercial district. One could purchase groceries and household goods from the shops in town or from merchants who hawked goods from trucks, but Ivy Terrace residents relied on the produce of their gardens. Walrond's neighbors, the Cottles, packed a family of six in a two-room house. "We used to have a toilet down in the garden," a Bradford resident recalled, "perhaps one between two or three families."[2] Bradford was not without comforts, however; by the 1940s, the cinema showed three Hollywood features a week, sixteen pubs served the community, and trains to London and Bath were frequent and inexpensive, especially the "Woolworth's train," on which a return trip to Bath cost a mere 4½ pence on Saturday.[3] Walrond was not the only stranger in the village, as wartime evacuation continued apace: four thousand trains removed nearly 1.5 million people in the first four days of September alone. Bradford's relative safety made it a popular destination, receiving more than one thousand evacuees.[4]

Walrond was unusual, one of the few who stayed on after 1940, when most evacuees returned, and of course he was "coloured." His writing during his twelve years in Bradford is instructive in its treatment of race relations. Many of the difficulties he faced in London persisted, but Bradford lacked the simmering antagonism that characterized the cities and ports. In this respect, Walrond may have preferred village life to someplace with a black community. James Baldwin wrote incisively about this paradox in "Stranger in the Village." He was shocked to discover what

a spectacle his blackness became in his adopted hometown in the Alps
in the 1950s. Local children pointed and called him "*Neger*," but he was
reluctant to equate their name-calling with American racism. The paradox of the racial stranger for Baldwin was that although he would never
feel he belonged, he was spared the extreme indignities of places in which
tension and acrimony had been normalized.

This seems to have been the case with Walrond. He rented a room
in the last of a row of nine stone cottages from a couple named Porter.
"Of course, the unusual thing was that he was a black man," said his
neighbor Gerald Bodman, "That was very unusual for Bradford. [. . .]
In fact, he was the only black man in the area, really, and of course
people talk about that sort of thing, naturally enough, because it's most
unusual for a little country town."⁵ Walrond was friendly but less gregarious now, keeping so much to himself that some Ivy Terrace residents
did not know he was a writer, much less a writer of renown. They speculated that he was involved in the war effort. He was kind but reserved,
saying hello but not much more. "He was a very nice fellow, friendly,"
according to Bodman, though "to be honest," John Cottle added, "he
didn't talk a lot to anybody. He was a very private sort of guy."⁶ "As
next-door neighbors you mingle and chat over things," said Bodman,
"He may well have spoken of his life in America, [but] I can't recall any
detail about that. But I remember him as a jolly nice man indeed. Obviously very well educated." Mary Lane, a neighbor who was starting a
family, recalls talking with him in the street but "not a great deal." In her
case, the limited contact may have involved more than his reticence. "He
was coloured," she said, "Not black; he was coloured. Because they used
to pull my leg—my daughter had very dark skin. And they used to pull
my leg and say, because she had dark curly hair, and she had, not *dark*
skin but she wasn't fair-skinned." The miscegenation anxiety behind the
teasing was characteristic of the time, when interracial relationships and
mixed-race children were widely deplored.⁷

The Porters used the cottage mainly in summer, so Walrond often
had it to himself, and even when they were in residence Mr. Porter's job
kept him away for long stretches. This raised some eyebrows. "In itself,

that was a bit of a phenomenon in those days," recalled Cottle, "a black guy living with a white woman. Now when I say 'living with him,' we don't know what their domestic arrangements were." Gerald Bodman did not think the relationship was romantic. "I have no recollection of that ever even being considered, thought about. They both lived in the same house," but we "never had any thoughts whatsoever that it was anything but that." Neighbors called him Mr. Walrond and treated him respectfully. With children, he chatted and played on occasion with their rabbits and chickens. With the family of Gerald Bodman, ten years older than Cottle, Walrond "used to talk quite a bit." Bodman and Mary Lane knew he was a writer, though he did not discuss particulars. Nor did he assert his West Indianness. "He may well have mentioned it," Bodman said, "But we took him generally to be an American." They only knew "he was a journalist. He worked for a paper back in the States, and he would write articles for the paper and submit them weekly, or maybe monthly. And I think it was a paper read mainly by black people in the States."

FOREIGN CORRESPONDENT

During his time in Bradford, Walrond's writing consisted almost exclusively of work as a foreign correspondent or war correspondent for African American periodicals, publishing twenty-seven articles between 1940 and 1945 for *The New York Amsterdam News*, *The People's Voice* (a Harlem-based weekly), and *The Monthly Summary of Events and Trends in Race Relations*, issued by the Fisk University Social Science Institute. The writing is uneven but often extraordinary, and collectively it represents a significant contribution to transnational black periodical culture, articulating Pan-Africanism with antifascism during World War II. A recurring set of concerns animated his work. He did conventional war reporting and discussed military operations, but his greatest concerns were to expose the "colour bar" in Britain, identify efforts to ameliorate it, and examine the impact of nonwhite servicemen from the colonies and North America on British race relations.

Amsterdam News readers were introduced to Walrond through his
"inner glimpse of London as war clouds appeared," composed just prior
to his evacuation. Under the cryptic byline "Somewhere in England,"
he reported Britons' impatience with the Allies' progress on the western front and with the Americans, who had not yet entered the war. He
endeavored to depict his village, transformed by wartime events.

> In an old Flemish weaver's cottage, I sit and listen to the starlings and
> the grunts of pigs far down the terraced slope. The hum of aircraft
> is incessant. Sometimes they fly low or circle round and round before
> zooming off again. Above the green tops in the valley, smoke is issuing
> from the chimney of the town's one factory. Before the rearmament
> of Britain began, the factory was engaged in the production of ten-
> nis balls. Now, on a day and night shift, it is turning out munitions.
> ("Slowness" 10)

The evacuation confronted the townspeople with "a new set of problems," he said, "The evacuees are poor, ill-clad and slovenly. Almost all of
them come from the slums of the big cities. The women sit in the door-
ways, lumber up and down the pavements, throng the narrow streets and
alleys. At night they booze in the pubs and stay up till all hours. [. . .] All
these things the town frowns upon" ("Slowness" 10). Walrond reported
on strategy and diplomacy, assailing the Tories for failing to "care a tin-
ker's damn about the benefits of unity" with France "or even a victory
over Nazi Germany." Their "choleric dislike of frogs' legs and snails"
jeopardized the Allies' effort ("Tories" 4). He assessed Ireland's stance
to remain neutral in the conflict, a reminder "of the nettle lying on England's doorstep" ("Ireland" 6). But most of his articles engaged thorny
questions of race and empire that the war had given fresh urgency. He
hoped the wartime demand for soldiers of every color and creed would
erode prejudice in Britain, and that the Allies would awaken to the right
of all peoples to self-determination, even if they were not white, a category whose superiority was now less comfortably assumed with Hitler
its belligerent champion.

He highlighted the contributions to the war effort of two distinct but related populations: colonial subjects serving the "mother country" and the descendants of immigrants living in Britain. In "Black Britons on War Front," Walrond chronicled the "coloured men" of the British Expeditionary Force, fighting "side by side with the African and West Indian troops," hastening to note that they were not "natives of overseas territories, but English-born sons of Negro fathers and white mothers from the 'half-caste' communities of Britain" ("Black Britons" 1). This was a powerful argument for changing public opinion about a mixed-race segment of the population that was growing but widely reviled. He canvassed the Bristol docks, interviewing West Indians, including a Jamaican who professed his countrymen's loyalty: "When the news of the declaration of war came through, there were swarms of people 'round the news bulletins outside the newspaper offices, and everyone I met was anxious and impatient to help the Mother Country, starting to volunteer for service at once" ("Black Britons" 10). Walrond risked a provisional assessment: "So far as can be ascertained, the colour bar in the British Army has been jettisoned. Coloured men are [. . .] being given a chance to show their fighting qualities" ("Black Britons" 1). It proved premature, he soon realized.

He reported on six young Jamaicans whose "loyalty to king and empire" led them to stowaway on a steamship bound for London, only to be jailed upon arrival. They were given "four weeks imprisonment, each with hard labor," and several were labeled "stateless" and "recommended for deportation" despite their desire to "join the British Army and help finish off Hitler" ("Jail" 1). He also reported that a ban of "coloured men" from the Royal Air Force (RAF) had been extended from Africa and the West Indies to India. This was galling because "in the last war the people of India made to the Allied cause a staggering contribution of men and money," and Walrond hoped that Nehru's insurgent Congress Party would win its demands for dominion status, thus removing the "colour bar" from India ("Racial Bar Persists" 1). He praised the neighboring Burmese for having seized the opportunity the war presented to press their demands at Whitehall ("Ireland" 6). When reports reached him that a group of South African mineworkers had voluntarily pledged a portion of their meager salaries to purchase a battleship for the Allies, he recorded his skepticism. "Most of them are detribalized workers of poor physique from the more remote parts of the African bush" ("Ireland" 6). He found it hard to believe they "met together of their own accord," as reported, and decided "to donate a shilling or about 25 cents a month towards the cost" of a battleship; that was "stretching one's credulity a little too far." His optimism at the war's impact on race relations wavered.

By the spring of 1940, Walrond doubted British claims that their only aim in the war was to eradicate Nazism and restore Polish and Czech independence. We are told that "no selfish motives animate" Britain, he wrote, and that "the government is spending $30 million a day and is risking the lives of its citizens not for the acquisition of new markets or spheres of influence, not for redivision of the world" but to "end the recurrent fear of Nazi aggression." But "such nobility of sentiment was also a feature of Britain's war aims in 1914–1918," he observed, yet when that war ended the claims of Serbian independence from despotic rule were ignored and Britain happened to "emerge with 1,415,929 square miles of new territory in Africa, Egypt, Cyprus, Palestine, Mesopotamia, New Guinea, and Samoa, directly or indirectly under her control" ("War News" 13). Forgive me, he suggested, if I am skeptical of official statements of Britain's objectives. He did not publish another article about the war for more than four years.

Walrond's own mother did not know where to find him, so she could not direct the Guggenheim Foundation, which inquired in May 1940. "I was in correspondence with him, but since the war I haven't heard from him."[8] But Walrond contacted Ethel Ray Nance soon after the evacuation, suggesting she forward his new address "to C. S. J. or anyone else who may enquire."[9] Nance informed Charles Johnson and mailed Walrond the notes accompanying his rejection from The Atlantic.[10] Johnson and Nance brainstormed on his behalf, speculating that the Associated Negro Press "probably needs a good foreign reporter."[11] The extent to which Walrond had vanished from American view is illustrated in an exchange a Panamanian writer had with W. E. B. Du Bois in 1941. "Recently I began [. . .] a study of the Isthmian Negro scene," he wrote Du Bois, wondering whether North American publishers would be interested. Du Bois answered, "there is no doubt of the need" of such a study; "Eric Walrond once planned and partially finished a study called *The Big Ditch* which treated the Panama Canal and the various West Indian Negroes who worked upon it. [. . .] I have often wondered what became of that manuscript."[12] Walrond had the opportunity to apprise Du Bois when they met in London years later. For the moment, however, he remained the subject of speculation.

Henry Allen Moe managed to locate Walrond in 1940, and Walrond's reply reveals his shame at having disappointed him. He wished to assure Moe that he had not been idle, but the letter exudes insecurity.

> Under separate cover I am sending you copies of some of the things which I have published since I returned to Europe in 1932. If you find that the quality of the stuff is poor, or that the quantity is absurd, I beg of you not to judge me too harshly. No one feels more keenly than I do the inadequacy of my performance up to date. However, I wish to assure you, despite all the evidence to the contrary, that I have not lost sight of my responsibility to the Foundation. My obligation to you personally, to those who were good enough to act as my sponsors and to the community at large is ever before me. Unfortunately, as a depression casualty, I have had my ups and downs; my quest for security in a world in which nothing is stable led me astray. Yet even now (I think it was Robert Herrick who, after examining my project, said it was a "life-work") with everything more insecure than ever before, all my energies are being directed towards one end, namely to produce something which would in some small measure justify the confidence which the Foundation so generously reposed in me twelve years ago![13]

He still felt he needed to prove himself, a sensation he would never quite overcome.

The trail grows cold at this point—conspicuously so. He stopped writing for the *Amsterdam News*, which named Padmore its London correspondent in May 1940. Aside from a short story that appeared in the *West Indian Review*, Walrond published nothing until late 1944, when he resumed with the *Amsterdam News* and began contributing to *The People's Voice* and *The Monthly Summary*. John Cottle recalled him traveling to London and inferred it "was something to do with the Ministry of Defence." Nothing corroborates the supposition, but the front page of the *Chicago Defender* in April 1944 announced Walrond's disappearance and presumed death in an airstrike over Germany. The report of his death was, as Mark Twain said, an exaggeration, but the article raises questions about whether it was a case of mistaken identity or had some basis in fact. "Eric Waldron [sic], Novelist, Lost In German Air Raid," read the headline.

> Sgt. Eric Waldron, West Indian born novelist and journalist, has been reported missing during a Royal Air force attack over Germany. Before coming here, Waldron lived in New York's Harlem where he was well known in literary circles as a promising young writer. Sgt. Waldron was a wireless operator and air gunner of a Sterling bomber. He joined the RAF when England was desperately in need of airmen after the fall of France and took part in that decisive battle which saved Britain from Nazi invasion. While in America, the young writer was a frequent contributor to *Opportunity* magazine and was author of a novel entitled "Tropic Death." He also wrote a volume of short stories during the period of the Negro renaissance literary and artistic movement of the '20s under Dr. Alain Locke, author of "The New Negro." When Waldron came here, he took up journalistic work with the late Marcus Garvey.[14]

The report might be dismissed as a case of mistaken identity but for a few factors. The start of the four-year silence in Walrond's record corresponds with the French surrender to Germany in June 1940, two days after his letter to Moe. In 1942, having failed to contact Walrond, Moe again inquired with his mother, who was unable to locate him. "I haven't heard from him for at least a year, letters have been returned saying that he can't be found." The Ivy Terrace address was accurate up to 1940 and accurate again starting in 1944, so it is unclear why letters in the interim were returned. No other accounts of his military service exist, and Louis Parascandola's attempt to confirm the enlistment of an Eric Walrond (or Waldron) in the RAF came back negative, leading him to conclude "the report was unfounded."[15] Nevertheless, the specificity of the *Defender* article coupled with his neighbors' speculation about his role in the war effort and the lack of definitive evidence to the contrary leaves open the possibility that he served and was shot down but recovered after the *Defender* article appeared.

However unlikely, it would account for his four-year silence, and while this too may be a coincidence, when he resumed writing in 1944 it was about black servicemen. He covered two cases in which sexual relations between white Englishwomen and African American GIs were criminalized.[16] And he resumed coverage of English and colonial race relations. "White Airmen in England Protest Treatment of Negro Comrades" discussed the twelve hundred West Indians who volunteered when the RAF issued "an urgent appeal for ground-staff tradesmen." After several months in England, they were discouraged by the "colour bar": "seemingly trivial incidents have been mounting up and helping to make their lot [. . .] well nigh unbearable," including prohibitions against socializing with the Women's Auxiliary Air Force (16). Nevertheless, servicemen from the colonies persevered, developing skills and forging new roles for themselves and their people ("Britain Spurs" 6).

As "London Correspondent of the *People's Voice*," Walrond articulated positions far to the left of *The Amsterdam News*. He accused newly elected Labour Party leaders of maintaining status quo foreign policy as the war drew to a close ("Soapbox" 5). He reproached British fecklessness as Italy's "trail of terror" advanced in Ethiopia ("Italy" 22). And he inveighed against Britain's exploitation of colonial troops, accusing the "ruling class" of using Indians the same way the French had used the Senegalese, "to do Imperialism's dirty work" ("Indian Troops" 13). West Indians enlisting to make the world safe for democracy were instead deployed to suppress Burmese resistance ("West Indians" 9). But the most compelling *People's Voice* article was a look back at the U.S. occupation of the Dominican Republic during World War I. Dominicans had been lulled into a false sense of security, he suggested, "basking in the sunlight of the Monroe Doctrine" ("Men" 21). He depicted U.S. Marines in the same terms he had in *Tropic Death*: "Lean young men in khaki with thin red necks and a southern drawl swaggered about with big Colt revolvers dangling from thigh or hip" ("Men" 21). During his visit in 1929, five years after the marines withdrew, residents were perplexed by the occupation because "all classes in the community agreed" to leave "all hands off the Yankee sugar properties" ("Men" 21). Walrond believed the United States wished to destabilize the political field in order to install a puppet president. He observed that Trujillo, who soon ruled the country with exceptional venality, was permitted to wear his National Guard uniform during the occupation while in others this was an affront to the Americans ("Men" 21). Residents placed their faith in the peasants of the Cibao region, who organized a resistance movement that earned the Americans' contempt as "bandits," much like the *cacos* in Haiti.

Walrond's critique of U.S. designs on the Caribbean was characteristic of a fleeting but forceful alignment of antiracist and anticolonial journalism during World War II. The U.S. State Department cautioned in 1944 that African American periodicals across the political spectrum were advancing critiques of "white imperialism."[17] Until the Cold War, the African American press linked the civil rights struggle with the liberation of colonized people the world over, challenging not only "French and British imperialism but the role of the American government and U.S. corporations in the rapidly changing global political economy."[18] These were precisely the questions Walrond raised by revisiting the Dominican occupation: "Are [today's] peasant masses of Indo-China and Indonesia forged in the metal of the hardy hut-dwellers of Hispaniola?" he asked, "Are they destined to duplicate the epic stand of the men of the Cibao?" ("Men" 21).

As Walrond started writing for *The People's Voice*, Charles Johnson hired him to contribute to *The Monthly Summary of Events and Trends in Race Relations*. Established at Fisk University and sponsored by the Rosenwald Fund, *The Monthly Summary* was aimed at "persons interested in or working directly with the current problems of race in our American democracy," but in fact its scope was international. With a small stable of contributors, its bylines were generally omitted because subscribers, many of whom were policymakers, "are not in need of inspirational material and personal viewpoints." Its operative definition of race was broader than most African American periodicals, featuring articles on Japanese Americans, Jews, and many others, an illustration of the journal's alertness to the shifting terrain of race in the 1940s.[19] Walrond contributed seven articles, drawing extensively on formal research. This was Johnson's preference, and he called the "application of the social survey technique to the current scene" the "special feature" of the publication.[20] Some of Walrond's work dovetailed with his other writing, such as "Education and Training of Negroes and Indians in Britain" and analyses of conditions in Liverpool and Cardiff. But he went farther afield, monitoring the fraught negotiations over British policy in Africa as the war drew to a close. He shone a bright light on systemic racial bias in South Africa, Rhodesia, and Kenya, not typical fare for the American press.[21] By the end of 1946, *The Monthly Summary* circulation reached nearly ten thousand, with "reporting services" in thirty-eight cities.[22]

Colonial matters may have held interest for *Monthly Summary* readers, but the most intriguing reading about segregation was Walrond's writing about race relations in Britain. This dynamic was influenced by the deployment there of African American troops, segregated from their white counterparts. The enlistment of nonwhite colonial troops in the British military created a combustible situation, and Walrond treated Wiltshire as a case study in English racial attitudes. African American troops stationed in Westwood in 1942 used Bradford as their designated recreation site, while white American troops were sent to Trowbridge, three miles away. "It was the first time that many townsfolk had seen a non-white person," notes historian Margaret Dobson.[23] Walrond's neighbors remembered it vividly. Gerald Bodman was a civil engineer in a munitions factory, and he recalled having socialized with the visiting troops. Although there were virtually no other nonwhites in the area, he said the residents "generally didn't worry anything about" the African Americans "because we weren't, shall I say, overrun by them, there were comparatively few. The camp at Westwood was a comparatively small one. And obviously they couldn't all be away from camp at the same time." The town organized "parties for the G.I.s. [. . .] Impromptu concerts followed where the visitors sang lovely spirituals. The Americans were seen regularly swimming by the River Avon, and [. . .] dances were held at the old Town Hall."[24] The portrait of interracial harmony was confirmed by John Cottle, who recalled the black Americans fondly.

> There was no animosity. The Americans were different; they were more outgoing. The English have gotten more outgoing than they were at that time. We as kids used to sit out at the end of Ivy Terrace and as the troops used to go up and down, especially the black ones, they used to throw us chewing gum. We were only six or seven, and we had no sweets—only oranges, apples, things like that—so everything we could scotch off them was great.

Walrond was intrigued by the local response to black troops, American and West Indian alike. He recognized an eagerness among English officials to distance themselves from racial segregation, and he saw the war as a mechanism for compelling them to do so. But he also perceived a recalcitrant racism in the very fabric of English culture and believed local antiracist campaigns were necessary. As always, he cast these concerns in connection with daily life, writing at least three accounts of wartime Wiltshire, one a short story for *The Crisis* in 1948 and two nonfiction essays for *The Monthly Summary*.[25]

"Chippenham's Way" chronicled a Wiltshire town collectively overcoming racial prejudice after a brazen imposition of the "colour bar." It was a true story but had all the elements of melodrama: nationalist fervor, football, young men in uniform, young ladies at a dance, and the triumph of Christian fellowship. Walrond observed that Chippenham had seen armies come and go for centuries, but until World War II the troops had never been black.

> The spectacle of Negroes in jeeps, Negroes driving big U.S. Army lorries and now and then a Negro M.P. directing traffic along the route of a convoy was quite a new experience for Chippenham. In fact, it almost took the town's breath away. Negroes suddenly appeared in a dazzling new light. But as though to suggest a restriction of some sort, few if any Negroes paused to linger long in the town. As birds of passage they were always correctly on the go. So it was only after Jamaican Negro airmen began to trickle in from a nearby R.A.F. camp (thereby causing an unsavory spot of bother) that Chippenham had a chance to show where it stood on the vexed question of colour discrimination. ("Chippenham's Way" 101)

The trouble arose after a football match between Jamaican troops and Chippenham Town. The Jamaicans impressed everyone with their skill and sportsmanship. These "products of Wolmer's College in Jamaica were totally lacking in self-consciousness, possessed charming good looks, a quiet self-assured manner, and an unobtrusive love of the things of the intellect" (101). Having been welcomed warmly, the servicemen decided to attend a dance in town, but "the doorkeeper refused to let them in on the ground that he had orders not to admit 'blacks'" (101). When word got out, a public outcry ensued. "It is a bad show when these boys who are British Empire subjects give up their afternoon to entertain Chippenham people and then are snubbed in this way," said an RAF soldier who had accompanied the Jamaicans (102). A reporter heard the dance promoters say they were merely "acting on the instructions of the American Army authorities" (102). This was a common refrain when segregation was practiced in wartime Britain, deference to the Yanks. Sometimes this was demonstrably true, other times it was a convenient pretext for Britons to discriminate. When the Jamaicans heard it in Chippenham, one remarked, "It looks as though the Americans are being allowed to rule England" (102). Trade unionists and clergymen organized to right the wrong, and a groundswell of support issued forth for the soldiers, "the nicest lot of chaps anybody could wish to meet," said the football club secretary. Promptly, an invitation went out for another dance, and reports indicated "they spent a very enjoyable evening." Walrond concluded that "the heart of the town was unquestionably sound" and had "put paid to the colour bar" (103).

He recognized that the presence of a segregated U.S. military raised questions about how Britons would respond, both in civilian and military contexts, and conversely how English behavior would influence race relations among American troops. "Some American officers are apparently interested in bringing the segregated transportation system to England, at least for the [war's] duration," he wrote, citing a Cardiff-bound train on which "two coloured American soldiers" were instructed by white American officers to leave their car. The officers eventually relented, but on alighting one chastised the conductor, "You English are making it hard for us; when we get back to America we shall not be able to manage these fellows" ("Colour Bar" 229). Walrond covered other instances, including "restrictive covenants" in rentals and discrimination in restaurants and hotels. *The Crisis* ran his story suggesting that English reluctance to discriminate on the basis of race emboldened African American troops and constrained the behavior of white officers. Set at the Bradford-on-Avon bus station, it was not only Walrond's last publication in a prominent American periodical, it was likely the first literary text in the United States to feature black Britons and black Americans. Despite its flaws, "By the River Avon" is a fascinating meditation on the tension between distinctive racial formations—one American, one British. It turns on the significance of a military salute, a gesture whose simplicity is belied by its complex social function. The characters include an African American GI who flirts with his English sweetheart as the story opens, a mixed-race factory worker, two of his white colleagues, and two American servicemen, one white and one black, patrolling in a jeep. Times were changing, the story suggested, and despite lingering prejudices, Bradford sought to demonstrate liberality and gratitude toward African American troops. They were even welcomed at afternoon tea in Bradford's oldest tearoom, which made their white officers uneasy. The English were shifting the ground of race relations at home, Walrond indicated, and by extension among the Americans stationed there.

POOR GREAT

Occasional publication was not enough to make ends meet, so Walrond took a job at a rubber manufacturing plant. Employee records were destroyed in a fire, but Gerald Bodman recalled Walrond "saying he was having to work pretty hard. It was different for him; it was factory work."[26] Adding to his stress was wartime rationing and the fact that Bradford, although removed from the theater of war, was not immune to violence. Bristol, Bath, and Cardiff were key targets, and the nerves of Bradford residents were frayed by air raid sirens. The Germans "used to go over every night," said a Bradford man, on bombing runs to Cardiff, Avonmouth, Bristol, and Bath.[27] In April 1942, a German bomber chased from Bath by RAF planes jettisoned four bombs near Bradford, damaging buildings and the canal but sparing residents. Two years later, Ivy Terrace was shaken by a crash behind Christ Church, when a Canadian fighter-plane burst into flames, killing all but one crewmember. Even after the war's end life was difficult; residents coping with austerity and rationing through the early 1950s. Despite the jubilation when hostilities subsided, postwar life was far from easy.

Having published nothing in more than a year, Walrond contacted Gwendolyn Bennett in 1946. He was feeling every bit of his nearly forty-eight years, but he put a brave face on things. He could not quite bring himself to ask for help, but he would clearly have welcomed it. Calling her "Dear Gwennie," he claimed, "The young Negro boy about whom you once wrote a poem is, alas! no longer young, but he is still pretty sure of himself at times and his courage, even though a bit erratic, can still be quite phenomenal." He mentioned having submitted something to *The American Mercury* but "failed to see eye to eye" with its editors "on something which I spent a lot of time and energy on, about Negro

GIs in Britain." Before signing himself "Down, but definitely not out!" he added, "Don't forget, you are still the closest approximation to a favourite sister I have ever had!"²⁸ What is striking, however, is the number of people Walrond seems not to have contacted. No further correspondence with Charles Johnson, who became president of Fisk University in 1947. No apparent contact with Una Marson, who helped start the important BBC program *Caribbean Voices*. No reference to the 1945 Pan-African Congress in Manchester—a pivotal event—nor any contact, evidently, with old London friends. Arna Bontemps and Langston Hughes were developing a new anthology and "right off" thought "of Eric Walrond's pieces on Harlem," but he was not reachable.²⁹ British Guiana's first literary journal, *Kyk-over-Al*, was established in 1945, but there is no record of contact with editor A. J. Seymour. Nor is there any indication that Walrond was in touch with his daughter Lucille, who enrolled in 1945 at the University of London.³⁰ A gifted scholar who went on to teach at the University of the West Indies, Lucille eventually visited her father in 1953. Instead one finds a record of withdrawal, a postwar silence. It cannot have helped that Countée Cullen died in 1946, his brilliant career cut short by a cerebral hemorrhage at 43. Knowing what followed for Walrond, one explanation for his withdrawal may have been worsening depression. Turning inward was a coping mechanism he had tried in the past, and it may have seemed like the only available response to adversity.

However, he managed to get three pieces of journalism into print in the United States. The first told of Britain's plans to establish universities in Africa, Malaya, and the West Indies, appearing in the *Journal of Higher Education*. The second, an essay in Carter Woodson's *Negro History Bulletin*, chronicled the life of a nineteenth-century Barbadian physician who served France nobly in the Franco-Prussian War. Then in June 1948, three ships from the West Indies brought several hundred immigrants to England, capturing Walrond's attention and the attention of many others. It was the first wave of an influx that gathered momentum and soon began transforming British national identity. Beginning with fewer than one thousand arrivals per year, the generation of West Indian immigrants that took its name from the first of the ships, the SS *Empire Windrush*, swelled to 161,450 in the years between 1955 and 1960.[31] Among them were Sam Selvon and George Lamming, talented writers and ardent followers of *Caribbean Voices*, whose novels would give eloquent expression to their exile. Writing in 1948, Walrond was among the first to attend closely to the arrival of the *Windrush* for what it presaged for the future, publishing an investigative report in the *Christian Science Monitor*. Anxious about the newcomers' employment prospects, he spoke with a representative of the Colonial Welfare Office in London, and although the official conceded that some of the passengers were unemployed in Liverpool and Manchester, job placement on the whole was successful ("Negro Migrants" 9). Through interviews with laborers and personnel managers, Walrond determined that instances of discrimination on the basis of color and nationality were rare. When it came to unions, however, his report equivocated, suggesting that immigrant laborers were safe while jobs were plentiful but were otherwise vulnerable to layoffs. The questions Walrond asked gained urgency over the next decade as West Indians arrived in greater numbers.

Walrond contacted Robert Herring, editor of the London journal *Life and Letters*, perhaps because Herring was interested in Caribbean writing, traveling to Jamaica in 1948 and publishing two Caribbean-themed issues. This was an ideal contact, but all that came of it was a handful of book reviews.[32] Here was a figure for Walrond's marginality—relegated to reviewer in the same journal in which Lamming and Edgar Mittelholzer were introduced to UK readers. Walrond reviewed a novel by a Scotsman set in Trinidad and England, a novel by a Chinese author writing in English, and a "passing" novel about a mixed-race Alabama girl who flees Jim Crow for Europe but returns to join the civil rights struggle. But the reviews revealed little of his critical acumen, much less his writing talent. These were more evident in his reviews of the African Americans Richard Wright and Roi Ottley and the Jamaican Edna Manley. Ottley earned Walrond's praise for *Black Odyssey*, an expansive history of African American experience, and Manley he commended for having celebrated Jamaican writing since the early 1940s. This work recalled his New York writing, the erudition and energy of which he also demonstrated in reviewing Wright's *Twelve Million Black Voices*. Together, these reviews demonstrate what an asset Walrond could have been to an English journal, a reviewer of considerable versatility who had taken part in modernist movements on both sides of the Atlantic and cut his teeth on black liberation struggles in the Caribbean and in the United States. Moreover, Walrond's fiction would seem to be ideal for a journal pursuing a cultural pluralist vision that was new to England, but he never made it beyond the book reviews.

An observation he made reviewing Manley's anthology is significant in this regard: "The form which the writing of a subject people takes is often, of necessity, oblique." He was referring to stories in *Focus: Jamaica* that bore "no relation to Carib lore or to Anancy tales of African origin" but were "in reality allegories—poetical, lucid, chock-full of content" (177). This question of form was one that New Negro writers had negotiated with discernment and sophistication. Defending the oblique as a "necessity" in the writing of "subject people," he anticipated later arguments advanced by theorists of Caribbean poetics: that Caribbean writing, in devising its modes of expression, may not follow established conventions, that its signal formal feature might in fact be *opacity*. For Edouard Glissant in the 1970s, formal "failure" was inherent in the project of Caribbean writing, a symptom of its fraught relation to history. "Its advance will be marked by a polyphony of dramatic shocks, at the level of the conscious as well as the unconscious, between incongruous phenomena or "episodes" so disparate that no link can be discerned. Majestic harmony does not prevail here, but [. . .] an anxious and chaotic quest."[33] Walrond asserted something similar, justifying the formally oblique in Manley's selections. He was also referencing his own fiction, that impetuousness readers never failed to note. As he returned now to writing almost exclusively about the Caribbean in subsequent fiction, much of it flawed on conventional grounds, he was asserting the integrity of disintegrative work, insisting even the oblique could be "poetical, lucid, chock-full of content."

"Poor Great" (1950) was his first story published in England since 1936. It appeared in a London quarterly, *Arena*, bundled with two Sam

Selvon stories. "Poor Great" is about black middle-class childhood in Georgetown, specifically the community's uneasy reaction to a group of indigenous people who beg for handouts. Alarmed, the six-year-old protagonist is too young to grasp the broader context. He feels torn between the responses recommended by the housemaid, a Barbadian, and the servant, a Guyanese. The Barbadian empathizes, offering biscuits, while the Guyanese, fearful of "witchcraft," says "send them away, soul. Le' them go to the almshouse" (322).³⁴ The story reveals the narrator's relative privilege despite his family's modest means. This is one sense in which he is *poor great*, a common West Indian phrase. But *poor great* also means false grandeur—pride or pretension beyond one's station in life.³⁵ And here the story becomes more interesting, a meditation not only on Walrond's childhood but also, obliquely, on his advanced age in England. Everyone in Georgetown sold goods to make ends meet, from the sugar cakes and corn pone set at the front gate, to the women in "white calico skirts" hawking tamarind syrup (324). But one who does not even attempt self-sufficiency is an elderly mendicant. "He begged his daily bread," and "as he went doddering along in the sun, weaving across the road, his hat outstretched in his hand," he was greeted genially: "Housewife after housewife would lean over the garden gate or zinc paling and hand him the leavings of a meal which Mr. Underwood, with a 'God bless you!' or a nod of silent gratitude would seize and instantly devour" (325). Despite his acceptance, Mr. Underwood is derided by the churlish neighborhood boys, his artificial leg matched by a swollen and scaly natural one, his "bearded face, drooping lips and mournful eyes" expressing "humility and distress" (325). The boys cry, "Br'r Goat comin' down the road!" Scattering, they taunt him with a mischievous rhyme: "Who stole the goat?" "The man with the long coat?" "What smells so high?" "You mean like a Billy goat?" (325). When Mr. Underwood hobbles after them, the protagonist cowers under his porch. "Then from underneath the house I saw Mr. Underwood standing on the road directly in front of our gate. 'You little poor great vagabond!' he shouted, waving a stick at me, 'You wait till I catch all-yuh. It's all-yuh that smell!' Then he turned and, leaning heavily on the stick, limped back up the road" (326).

The story seems like little more than local color, bits of assembled nostalgia. It is a coming-of-age tale in which the protagonist has an epiphany about social stratification. But it takes on a different cast in relation to Walrond's life in Wiltshire in the 1940s. In a sense, Walrond was, at age fifty, still like that boy, cursed to be *poor great*. He may well have believed he was meant for something better, his wounded pride resenting his modest station in life. In another sense, he may no longer have seen himself in the boy but in old Mr. Underwood, a pitiful spectacle indulged by the kindly townspeople whose weirdness children ridiculed. This may have been Walrond's self-image, an apprehension of who he could become. Certainly he was *poor great* in the sense of feeling "too proud to accept charity or help that is really needed."[36] His neighbors were not aware of it, nor were friends and family, but Walrond's depression had become unmanageable. One can imagine how stress and alienation contributed to his deterioration. Things reached a breaking point in early 1952 and he sought treatment at a county psychiatric hospital.[37] We may never know exactly what drove him there, but his sporadic record of publication, his neglect of friends and supporters, and his exile in a rural, overwhelmingly white village must have aggravated his longstanding condition. He decided to check himself into the Roundway Psychiatric Hospital, a sprawling compound on the outskirts of a nearby town, in early May. Although he was a voluntary patient, he would remain there five years. Among the manuscripts he brought with him were a dozen unpublished Caribbean stories and the yellowing pages of his Panama history. In this unlikely place, he finally saw them into print.

10

ROUNDWAY HOSPITAL AND
THE SECOND BATTLE (1952–1957)

Eric Walrond admitted himself to the Roundway Psychiatric Hospital after an unseasonably snowy spring. "South England Blizzard Chaos" read the local headline, and Walrond's sun-drenched stories of Barbados, Guyana, and Panama accompanied him, unpublished, to his new home.[1] The hospital, a massive complex on forty acres of land, housed thirteen hundred patients, many of whom were voluntary, like him. Formerly the Wiltshire County Asylum, it had been in operation since the Lunatics Act of 1845. For Walrond to acknowledge that he could no longer manage his illness required a good deal of courage and perhaps desperation. Patient records from this period were destroyed, but Walrond's correspondence reveals the emotional stability and community he found there. Roundway was shabby and overcrowded but had practiced "a judicious combination of moral and therapeutic measures" since its inception.[2] At a time when mechanical restraints and blunt coercion were still commonplace, the progressive Roundway staff believed patients recovered "by kindliness and vigilance, by ingenious arts of diversion and occupation."[3] A working farm, commissary, and laundry were staffed by patients, and a variety of clubs and activities kept them occupied. Teams competed in badminton and cricket against other hospitals. Walrond helped start a literary magazine, *The Roundway Review*.

The inaugural issue coincided with his fifty-fourth birthday and included a reflection on his peripatetic life, "From British Guiana to Roundway." He praised Roundway warmly: "It is a far cry from British Guiana and Barbados, Colon and New York to Wiltshire. [. . .] The jump, for a 'depression casualty' in the years following the Wall Street crash of 1929, is almost frightening." What he found at Roundway was solace, "a compact, almost self-contained community set in surroundings of rare beauty," "astonishing examples of brotherliness and self-sacrifice." These remarks are more poignant when one considers the difficulties facing West Indians, who were arriving in England by the hundreds. The Guyanese politician Eric Huntley wrote to his wife of alienation and uncertainty, calling London "a lonely place for us colonials, not only from the point of view of our own senses but also as part of a cold and sophisticated environment." "Alarming" rates of unemployment left "scores of coloured people loitering around" the East End, "possessing

10.1 Postcard of Roundway Psychiatric Hospital, c. 1950, photographer unknown.

Courtesy of the Wiltshire & Swindon History Centre, Chippenham, UK.

an air of nothing to do."⁴ For Walrond, Roundway was a refuge and a form of asylum.

Every third Wednesday of the month from December 1952 through December 1958, *The Roundway Review* published articles, sketches, notices, and puzzles, all contrived to keep contributors diverted and readers entertained. A lofty mission statement declared its intent "to encourage free expression of ideas." The hospital's management committee exercised official oversight, appointing an editor from the staff, while Walrond served as assistant editor. He was its most active contributor, publishing regularly until his discharge in 1957. Early issues were amateur productions, typescript on sheets fastened with staples. Production values began improving a year later, when the hospital, persuaded of the journal's quality and salutary impact, funded typeset printing. Forty of the first fifty issues contained Walrond's byline.

A year in, he felt confident enough to contact Henry Allen Moe, alerting him to his publications and hoping Moe would publicize them in the Guggenheim Foundation annual report. He declined to explain the journal or his new residence, and Moe responded that it was good to hear from him but wondered whether Walrond lived at a hospital: "Will you be so good as to let us know if the address to which we are writing is your permanent address?" A delicate question delicately phrased. "I might say that until further notice I can be reached here," Walrond replied, "I might also say that since May of last year I have been a voluntary patient in this Hospital." He was encouraged to have renewed this correspondence and further cheered by a visit from his eldest daughter, who was visiting England from Jamaica with her husband.⁵ However, he contacted Moe only once more during his stay, listing additional work to "show that I am still endeavouring to adhere to the project which I submitted to you with my application for a Fellowship."⁶

Most of his *Roundway Review* publications were Caribbean stories written over the previous fifteen years. They were redolent with tropical scenery, urban and rural, and burst with polyphonic voices. Tracing his successive relocations, the first stories were set in British Guiana, the next in Barbados, followed by Panama stories, a tale about Caribbean

Brooklyn, and a handful set in England. Interspersed incongruously among them were his accounts of the hospital facilities, from the commissary to the laundry to the farm. These explanations of ironing and the baking of lardy cakes seem odd alongside his literary publications, but they reflect his affection for the place. Most incongruous of all, however, was *The Second Battle*, a detailed treatment of the French canal attempt in Panama that spanned fifteen issues. It is the only surviving remnant of *The Big Ditch*. Meticulously researched, *The Second Battle* constituted a formidable encounter for readers of *The Roundway Review*, its installments sandwiched between accounts of the pleasant outings staff and patients had enjoyed to a local dairy, library, or apple orchard. There is something at once wonderful and tragic about the juxtaposition in these pages of some of the earliest Caribbean stories published in England and a startling work of colonial history, alongside other patients' tributes to the hospital band and reminiscences about a favorite horse at a nearby farm.

IN SEARCH OF LOST TIME

Caribbean discourse is characterized by a relay, Edouard Glissant has argued, by *detour* and *return*. "Detour is not a useful ploy unless it is nourished by return: not a return to the dream of origin, to the immobile One of Being, but a return to the point of entanglement (*point d'intrication*), from which one was forcefully turned away; that is where it is ultimately necessary to set to work the elements of Relation, or perish."[7] Returning from his extensive detour to the point of entanglement, Walrond wrote a genealogy of the present, publishing thirteen stories in three years.[8] Their literary quality is uneven, but their flaws and eccentricities are symptomatic. Walrond's characters grapple with vexing questions about the cultural inheritance of multiply colonized peoples, marked irrevocably by the social and political upheaval of their communities. Their embodied knowledge is expressed through their accents and idioms, their injuries and desires. Woven through the stories is a theme of personal vulnerability and dependence on others. "There but for the grace of God go I," they seem to sigh, their author scarcely believing he had survived the events they recount.

Although they are framed as fiction, "The Servant Girl," "The Coolie's Wedding," and "A Piece of Hard Tack" depicted Walrond's own cloistered and pampered childhood in British Guiana. Their theme of innocence succumbing to experience is a universal one, but their setting is a distinctive society shot through with race and class differences, an assemblage of plantations, small farmers, and merchants populating the urban coastline, beyond which lay a vast interior. There are three versions of otherness in relation to which Walrond's character finds himself defined: South Asians, indigenous people, and "barracks" boys who share the narrator's nationality and complexion but not his temperament, a reticence augmented by class privilege. In each story, the protagonist strays beyond the home in which his mother and the maid coddle him. Perched high above the dank soil, the house is a feminine sphere, alternately comforting and constraining. At this remove he is safe from danger—street urchins, diseased vagrants, "heathen coolies," iguanas, eels, bats, and "duppies." But he is also prevented from maturing through contact with the adult world and socializing with other boys, insulated from their codes of incipient masculinity.

Beyond the front gate was a community seething with social difference. The space beneath the protagonist's house was a squatting ground for an elderly Indian, a "coolie" who had outlived his utility on the plantations. "Foot-loose vagabond!" the servant girl called him, "Stinkin' up the place" with cow-dung cooking fires ("Coolie" 22). He had a speck of white in his eye and chanted, "Akbar-la-la, Akbar-la-la, Mahaica is comin' down." Although the servant girl ridiculed him, Walrond's narrator felt the song reflected his acculturation: the Mahaica River flooded in the rainy season, and he speculated that the squatter's fear of its "overflow had already become part of his existence in Guiana." The child's interest in the acculturation of Indians becomes more evident when, later in the story, he encounters a wedding party, an Indian bride and groom on the way to a church ceremony. As their carriage advances, an accident occurs, the horses dumping the carriage and its passengers into a canal. A "crowd of Negro women" witness the spectacle, their "white calico skirts billowing out," but offer no assistance. "'Hey,' breathed a female onlooker as though recovering from a shock, 'Fancy Babus goin' to the Church of England and gettin' married! Whuh they think they is, nuh?' And as the landau rocked and rolled, sinking deeper in the mud, no one offered the bride and groom a helping hand" ("Coolie's" 23). Walrond declined to put too fine a point on it, but the irony is that the West Indians—themselves newcomers to British Guiana—show their neighbors such contempt. The story's appearance in England just as West Indians and South Asians began laying claim to English institutions lent further poignancy.

Walrond fictionalized his transition to Barbados in "Two Sisters," published in installments. It follows Henry, who moves with his mother back to her home island after several years in British Guiana. Although Walrond had siblings and Henry does not, the story otherwise reflects his life, from his house and school to the church where his mother worshiped. Henry's father "was not converted and he was not with her"; like William Walrond "he'd gone to Colon; so there would be much eyebrow raising" (i, 19). Unresolved animosity between the titular sisters drives the story's plot, but its force is the narrative voice itself, evoking the area of Jackman's Gap near Bridgetown with vigor and precision.

> The marl was restive, moving in billowing clouds to and fro, spiraling up and up and powdering as it lazily descended the blue sand, the sweet potato vines and the gaping mouths of myriads of soldier crabholes in the dune on the opposite side of the road. Further down the slope, blotting out the beach, the log cabins of Negro fisher folk appeared amidst the dark foliage of machineel trees; but in a clearing below the rum refinery the sea rolled in upon white and golden sand. Nets lay outspread in the sun between overturned fishing boats undergoing repairs. The tall, smokeless chimneys of the refinery loomed across the flickering green dome of the sea as though to dispute the passage of a flying fish fleet serenely tacking in the Bay.

> Lay, lay
> Bessie down
> For the sake of the pumpkin
> Bessie down ("Two Sisters" iii, 19).

The passage closes with a ring game, the girls' voices interrupting Henry's reverie.[9]

Two of the four Panama stories in *The Roundway Review* depict an adolescence like Walrond's in Colón, while the others cast a "Silver Man," a West Indian laborer, as the protagonist. Each demonstrates the volatility of intercultural contact there, indicating the destabilization of race and class. Anxieties about that destabilization were expressed in racial epithets and casual stereotyping, but it also made possible realignments of interest and association, including, for our young Bajan, the opportunity for a white-collar job. The Silver Man stories are at once celebrations of this figure, whose labor built the canal, and object lessons about what might have befallen the author had he not met with the kindness of strangers. Throughout, Panama is depicted as enigmatic—highly racialized yet complicated by associations among migrants, their contact mediated by the Jim Crow regime of the U.S. occupation but continually exceeding that frame.

West Indian acculturation is the subject of "The Iceman," whose protagonist was reduced to pushcart peddling after a leg injury cut short his career as a railroad brakeman. The story is not strictly autobiographical, but it takes place in Bottle Alley and meditates on what might have become of Walrond had he stuck around. The legend of the "Panama Man," his fine suit and hat gleaming brighter than his watch chain, had its counterpart in the laborer who stayed on after the canal opened. Those who survived were rarely unscathed. "The Iceman" features one amputee, Natty Boy, whose leg was crushed by a train, and another who lost a leg in a dynamite blast. Rather than blame the Isthmian Canal Commission (ICC) for imperiling canal workers, Walrond attributes Natty Boy's injury to his affinity for risk and an implacable desire to perform his job with flair. It was the challenge that gave the work pleasure,

and Natty Boy took pride in it, performing like a matador. As he anticipates his treacherous dash to the switch, laborers gather at the train car
windows to witness the spectacle. But Natty "was not putting off the
moment to impress anyone with his fearless courage. [...] Something else
of which Natty was but vaguely aware, something connected with the
mastery of a new craft, was involved" (24). But this time he took a risk
and missed; "with an ominous jangling of the couplings the train leapt
forward under a sudden burst of speed and shook him off. He stumbled
and fell on to the rail and the wheels of trucks Nos. 9 and 10 passed over
his right leg, shattering it just below the knee" (25). Intentionally or not,
Walrond had written a story about his own career, cast in a different
register. His fervent desire to "master a new craft" had propelled him to
propositions far riskier than he realized, and as he sat in the hospital, he
might have seen his protagonist's fate—chipping blocks of ice to hawk in
the blistering Panama sun, where once he accomplished feats of derring-
do—as a figure for his own diminished condition, peddling Caribbean
sketches in an indifferent land.

He recognized, of course, that he had enjoyed privileges that were
unavailable to Silver Men, and the other Panama stories acknowledged
his fortune. "Bliss" and "Wind in the Palms" each feature an adolescent
"chombo" who makes good on a combination of charisma and luck. The
conventional wisdom was that someone of his complexion had to pay his
dues and behave with unstinting deference toward his social superiors.
But these protagonists defy expectation simply by securing white-collar
jobs in the ICC, the first rung on a ladder of success seldom extended to
Panama's West Indians. Taken together, the stories trace his path from
circumscribed West Indian communities into a multiethnic mainstream,
each step a springboard to the next. Few readers of *The Roundway
Review* would have recognized the Caribbean diaspora memoir unfolding obliquely in its pages.

Of the *Roundway Review* stories set in England, two are almost inde-
cipherable and two are evocative but slight. "A Seat for Ned" and "Cardiff Bound," both set in subterranean poker rooms in Soho, are rich in
atmospherics but finally yield more heat than light. "The Lieutenant's

Vol. 4   No. 6

ROUNDWAY

REVIEW

News and Views from
Roundway Hospital and Old Park House, Devizes, Wiltshire

MAY, 1956

10.2 Cover of the *Roundway Review*, May 1956.

Courtesy of the Wiltshire Museum and Library, Devizes, UK.

Dilemma" and "Strange Incident" are parables set in Wiltshire during World War II, when residents encountered African American troops. All four stories are autobiographical; one is set, for example, in "a town on the Wiltshire Avon to which I'd moved from London on the evening of the day Hitler's ultimatum to Poland expired" ("Strange" 45). Walrond depicted life among colonial seamen kicking about London's West End awaiting assignment in the late 1930s in "A Seat for Ned" and "Cardiff Bound." He may have been the first to attempt their portrait, but the stories amount to little more than character studies haphazardly assembled at a poker table. Like McKay in *Banjo*, Walrond sought to portray a community and idiom largely hidden from middle-class readers, and he seems unsure what to make his characters do. They eat curry with rice, leering and gesticulating through various states of inebriation, all narrated in the clipped prose of hard-boiled fiction. A hint of concern is registered for what lies ahead in old age for these toughs, but thin storylines make it hard to read these tales of London's colonial underworld as more than nostalgie de la boue.

By contrast, "The Lieutenant's Dilemma" and "Strange Incident" lead unerringly to a polemical point. A white lieutenant's dilemma is precipitated by the decision of his African American soldiers to boycott a Wiltshire town modeled on Bradford-on-Avon. One soldier takes the narrator, Walrond's surrogate, into his confidence on the matter, discussing it at the pub.

> Gently inclining himself toward me the G.I. lowered his voice. "You know how it is with the people in this town," he said, rolling his eyes away from me and over in the direction of the five other people in the room. "'Hello, darkey,' 'Good morning, darkey,' 'Oh, mummy, look at the darkey soldier!' 'Have you got any chewing gum, darkey?'" He paused, sat upright and stared ahead of him. "Well, we'd had enough of that 'darkey' stuff. We went to the company commander and told him we weren't going to have any more of it. We wanted to be sent back to the States." (135)

The narrator sympathizes, but he discourages the soldier from reading malicious intent into the townspeople's behavior. The men soon realize that two white officers are watching them vigilantly. Their apprehensions subside, however, when the lieutenant strides casually to their table and buys the soldier a drink. The gesture suggests that the lieutenant is overcompensating for the soldier's feelings of discrimination, hoping to soften his militancy on the boycott.

"Strange Incident" locates color prejudice in the U.S. military, carefully keeping Wiltshire residents above reproach. It is an unimpressive sketch, but it illuminates Walrond's everyday life. A November 1943 afternoon running errands goes sour when white American officers accuse the narrator of stealing his own shoes from the U.S. military. Despite being one of the few nonwhite regulars in this town, the narrator had good relations with the locals. A clerk in the department store that fills his book orders is described as having "golden hair and an invariably polite smile" (44). He notices "a surprisingly large number of American military police," "conspicuous in their white helmets and white armbands," but does not give them a thought as he proceeds—a visit to the doctor, a stop at the reference library, and a cup of tea. However, two American officers accost him, demand his identity card, and ask, "Do you live around these parts?"

> "We've had a complaint that you are wearing U.S. Army shoes. Are you?"
>
> "I don't think so," I replied.
>
> I glanced down at my shoes. They were an old pair of brown utilities I had purchased from a well-known firm of boot and shoe dealers in a West Country town.
>
> "Who made the complaint?" I said.
>
> "The U.S. military police."
>
> "I see."
>
> "They said you sounded when you walked as though you were wearing U.S. Army shoes."
>
> For a moment I contemplated the shoes. What was it that I had done, or omitted to do to them that had made them sound on the wet, shining pavement in the darkness of an early November evening as though they did not belong to me? I looked up at the officer. It was plain from the expression on his face and in his eyes that he did not believe my story. (45–46)

The narrator is exonerated, but not before the humiliation of detainment by a young soldier with a blonde crew cut and an examination by his commanding officer. This mistreatment is sharply contrasted with the behavior of the Wiltshire locals, who remain quietly loyal: "How did you get on?" whispers the woman who served tea. "It was a case of mistaken identity," he says, to which she replies, "I thought so." When Walrond had submitted "Strange Incident" for *The Monthly Summary*, Charles Johnson declined to print it, probably because it is less a report than a narrative. But it is a provocative account of one unstable racial regime colliding with another, and it articulated something that was widely felt but seldom expressed by people of color in 1950s Britain: "What was it that I had done, or omitted to do to them?" (46). These sketches suggest that Walrond made his peace with Wiltshire County, but one wonders whether his precarious mental health faltered under the casual racism he identified in "The Lieutenant's Dilemma" or the sensation "Strange Incident" documents of being an intriguing "exotic."

So, why did he stay so long in Wiltshire? Why had he not returned to London, New York, or Paris, or moved elsewhere? One reason was dwindling resources. He lived on very little after the war and had no career prospects. One can imagine the resignation with which a depressive met these circumstances. The other reason, at least as urgent, was a profound sense of shame at having lost his way, disappointing friends, supporters, and himself. *The Monthly Summary* folded in 1948 when Johnson became the Fisk University president, and Walrond's 1950 story in *Arena* had not led to further publications. But there was one redemptive measure he could safely attempt from inside the hospital. Having published stories that traced his life from the Caribbean to England, he returned to the project on which he had worked fitfully for decades. *The Roundway Review* was not what he had in mind for *The Big Ditch* when he secured Liveright's "unencumbered rejection" in 1931, but any forum was preferable to letting it collect dust in the closet of a mental hospital.

What resulted was *The Second Battle*, an epic history of the French attempt at the Panama Canal and the plight of its director, Ferdinand De Lesseps. The narrative had a hero, a mixed-race Panamanian lawyer who led a populist rebellion as the French canal scandal exploded. It also had a villain in the charismatic but monomaniacal De Lesseps, who ruined small sharcholders in France; manipulated politicians, the media, and the Paris stock exchange; and subjected thousands of laborers to malaria and yellow fever. However, there was one respect in which Walrond resembled De Lesseps, and it could not have been lost on him as he sat in the hospital revising the manuscript. The title he chose referred to a pronouncement De Lesseps made after the Inter-Oceanic Canal Congress selected him to lead the Panama project. He had won acclaim by directing the Suez Canal operation, accruing wealth and public adulation. "When a general has won a battle," he said, "if someone proposes to him to win a second one, he never retreats."[10] Walrond knew the way this story ended, in abject failure. But he also knew the extraordinary resilience and resourcefulness De Lesseps showed in the face of adversity. He went down with the proverbial ship, and the fact that his second battle failed so spectacularly after his first triumph added to the pathos. The author whose first book was celebrated as a triumph of New Negro fiction had failed spectacularly at his widely anticipated second effort, but by publishing something of it now he would prove, to himself if no one else, that he too refused to retreat in the face of adversity.

THE SECOND BATTLE

Walrond's history of the French attempt at an interoceanic canal was like the project it chronicled: audacious, often magnificent, but structurally compromised. He knew that the U.S. success had eclipsed a story that was equally fascinating and complex. The independence movement that severed Panama from Colombia developed during the French project, rebellion flaring into open revolution. The role the United States played during this crisis allied the Panamanian elite with the "Yanks," in whose hands they placed their land and economic future. The catastrophe that befell the French was not just a case of hubris or mismanagement, nor was it simply a casualty of the pestilential scourges that beset the workforce. A volatile political climate, an influx of West Indian laborers, and a calculated display of U.S. military force conspired to undermine the French. Moreover, Walrond recognized in the Inter-Oceanic Canal Company an experiment in a new colonialism, an undertaking that hearkened back, in one sense, to European stockholding companies but anticipated the business imperialism of the twentieth century, when corporations called the shots and it was no longer expedient or necessary to occupy territory by force. This was a pivotal transition, he felt, a story that needed telling.

When he contracted for *The Big Ditch*, the market was clogged with books about the canal. He sought to write a different kind of history, drawing on his multilingualism and familiarity with the region. With the help of a capable editor he might have pulled it off. Its only remnant, *The Second Battle*, attests to Walrond's ambitious vision and prodigious research. He examined as few others could the peculiar confluence of developments in France, Colombia, and the United States that thrust Panama into modernity. But he had trouble seeing the forest for the trees. Bursting with data and quotations, *The Second Battle* is more narrative than argument, and the narrative is circuitous, inverting chronology. It begins with the demise of the project and the repatriation of thousands of Jamaicans in the late 1880s, steps back to the project's conception and funding scheme, then moves abruptly to the problems facing the French in the mid-1880s, as public mistrust mounted at home and turmoil erupted on the isthmus. Thereafter, Walrond trains his focus so narrowly on Panamanian politics and military maneuvers that one wonders what happened to De Lesseps and the Frenchmen he featured earlier. Because he was discharged from Roundway Hospital before publishing the manuscript's final installments, it is difficult to judge its overall coherence. What was published suffers from the absence of a steady editorial hand that could have realized its potential.

Readers expecting a frontal assault on the white man's incursion into Caribbean territory would be disappointed by *The Second Battle*. As in *Tropic Death*, Walrond was eager to distance himself from an explicit ideological agenda. Just as he felt the best case for the "Negro's" talent at fiction writing was to suppress overt propaganda and sentimentality, so in this project he pursued a standard sort of historiography. He tasked himself with investigating the machinations at the Paris *bourse* with the same punctiliousness as a French historian; he examined the anti-Semitism behind attacks on the canal project's management; he discussed the diplomatic efforts of U.S. secretaries of state; and his references to U.S. Marines omitted the sunburned necks, blonde crew cuts, and pistols that appear elsewhere with baleful frequency. In these ways, he inoculated his work against the appearance of provincialism and partisanship. Indeed, his stated theme strikes the keynote of liberal history, "the struggle between democracy and dictatorship which occasionally flared into violence" (ix, 41). He left implicit the subversive conclusion toward which his evidence pointed, that the 1880s political crisis "firmly established that the real power on the Isthmus was the U.S. military."[11]

However, in this effort to perform conventional liberal history, *The Second Battle* fails to conceal the traces of its author's radicalism. Much as Walrond sought to suspend his authorial voice above the fray, he saw in Panama an exploitative rivalry among imperial powers, a view that becomes evident in that most novelistic of devices: characterization. An unholy trinity of Colón residents—Pedro Prestán, George Davis, and Antoine Portuzal—commits what is ostensibly the worst atrocity in *The Second Battle*, the near total immolation of Colón. The fire, which reduced hundreds of homes and businesses to cinders, left ten thousand homeless, and destroyed a million dollars of Inter-Oceanic Canal Company property, is attributed to the rashness and bravado of these rebels. But they are without question the narrative's most compelling figures. They are intemperate but populist to their bones. They are virulently anti-American but only because their vision of Panama for Panamanians defies the clutches of any distant power, whether Bogotá or Washington. They represent the vibrant Pan-Caribbean society of the isthmus: Portuzal a Haitian "mulatto," Davis a Jamaican, and Prestán, the rebel leader, a lawyer and statesman of mixed Panamanian and West Indian ancestry. Is it any wonder that Walrond, advocate of self-determination for the world's people of color, fails to condemn them persuasively?

He waves in that direction, to be sure. The U.S. suppression of revolutionary forces is cast as a victory for law and order, a saving throw that prevented Panama from descending into an anarchy that opportunistic European powers would have exploited (xiv, 158). We are asked to imagine that the United States arrested an "almost unbelievably sinister trend," preserving Panama for delivery into the protection of Theodore Roosevelt, not France or Spain. The problem is that the revolutionary energy of the *Prestanistas* does not come off as "almost unbelievably sinister." They are overmatched but cunning, negotiating to advantage and refusing to surrender. They are nobody's puppets, while the troops that subdue them are reinforcements from Bogotá and the United States, not Panamanians. Their disdain for Colombian authorities is represented as reasonable, with President Nuñez having abrogated the 1863 constitution. Nor was the unrest confined to Panama, flaring also in Chiriqui and Santander. Prestán was acquitted of a murder charge in the early stages of the uprising, and when his release was delayed the Panama state legislature passed a resolution declaring "that all parties who have been interested in keeping Mr. Prestán in prison shall be tried and punished according to law" (viii, 280). If Prestán was a militant rebel, in other words, he enjoyed the widespread support of a rebellious citizenry.

Walrond calls Prestán many unflattering things—"the most controversial figure thrown up in the Colombian civil war"; fond of "gun play" and "notoriously quick on the draw"; "a destructive influence"—but he could not disguise his admiration for the man (viii, 275–79). He loved a trickster, and Prestán was as expert as they come. Hiding from the Colombians as a murder suspect, he "masqueraded as a Chinese fishmonger" (viii, 280). On the lam after the burning of Colón, he escaped by impersonating a woman. He was a shrewd negotiator, arranging for the delivery of a massive arms shipment from the United States, and a bold adversary, taking American officials hostage when the arms shipment was detained in the harbor. Moreover, Prestán advocated for the Jamaican laborers who came to Panama in increasing numbers. The Colonial Office put the migration of Jamaicans at 22,480 in 1884 alone, two thousand more than the entire population of Panama City (vii, 256). Peak migration from Jamaica coincided with the highest mortality rate among canal employees in the French era, Walrond notes, in excess of twelve hundred deaths that year. His research revealed massive layoffs and an increase in "idleness" and "discontent," "too many men chasing too few jobs" (vii, 257). If Prestán and his rebels were an unsavory, impetuous lot, as Walrond said, his account legitimated them by illustrating the conditions requiring their intervention. Walrond's Prestán elicits our identification despite the pretense to discredit him.[12] For this reason *The Second Battle* is at odds with itself, alternately disparaging the rebels and celebrating their resilience and popularity. They act decisively and with conviction, while the Loyalists in Bogotá dither and bang at the telegraph, waiting for the French or Americans to impose order.

There are few sympathetic figures in *The Second Battle*. Officers and engineers come and go, and Panamanians are maneuvered around the theater of war like chess pieces. Only when writing about Prestán and his comrades does Walrond use free indirect discourse, a novelistic device aimed at generating intimacy with a character. Its effect is produced by introducing a character's thought and speech patterns into third-person narration. In *The Second Battle*, "As the party turned out of Lagoon into Fifth Street, Prestán paled with anger at the sight before him. Instead of the merchant ship Colon the U.S. gunboat Galena lay beside the wharf! What was in the wind? When had the switch been made? Didn't anyone ever tell him anything? Everything seemed to be tumbling down on him at once" (ix, 44–45). The third person is not relinquished, nor is Prestán quoted, but rhetorically the passage follows his consciousness, the narrator throwing his voice. The only other figure with whom Walrond uses this device is George Davis, Prestán's lieutenant. Led to the gallows, he is stoic, dignified. Shouts of "Incendiary! Assassin!" rain down. "Had he not heard the words and sensed the undercurrent of hostility?" Walrond asks, "Had he not heard the click of a photographer's camera upon his appearance in the crowd, manacled, flanked by the rifles and bayonets of Colombian soldiery? Had he not been spat at? *He would show them that he knew how to die!*" (xiv, 160). No one believed Davis or Portuzal had set fire to Colón; it was understood that they were scapegoats. But as Walrond emphasizes, they met their executions stoically: "Having refused to have their eyes bandaged, the men stood looking into the setting sun as the nooses were carefully adjusted under the left ear of each" (xiv, 160). Such efforts at characterization, coupled with free indirect discourse, enhance our admiration and identification, superseding the narrative's claims about the illegitimacy of the *Prestanista* cause.

The Second Battle is thus a perplexing document in both its argument and its structure. What it seeks to demonstrate is the confluence of events that undermined the French effort, from the gross miscalculations of its director, to the epidemics of disease, to the Colombian crisis in which the project was mired. In that fatally weakened state, it could not advance independent of the French government, as was De Lesseps' fervent hope. He was compelled to "eat humble pie" and ask his government to issue lottery bond bills, a plan that failed miserably (v, 204). He died a broken man, convicted by an irate Paris tribunal, his family's good name tarnished and his fortune squandered on a disastrous effort to create a sea-level canal with private financing. But Walrond told a broader story than the De Lesseps tragedy. It attended to the tension between the activities of the Inter-Oceanic Canal Company as a private stockholding company and the affairs of the governments interested in the outcome. This was an important test of a modern form of imperialism, one shorn of territorial possession, occupation, and other established practices. Had it succeeded, De Lesseps' canal would have redounded to the immense credit and profit of France, of course, but it would also have vindicated this vision of world affairs orchestrated by finance capital. Although the French failed, the lessons were not lost on the United States, where many in the private and public sector were poised to pick up where they left off. Precisely in its wedding of finance capital to state and military interests, the U.S. initiative would avoid De Lesseps' costliest errors.

Although Walrond was discharged before publishing *The Second Battle* in its entirety, there is a kind of poetic justice in its truncated appearance. The fifteenth installment was devoted to the "Culebra massacre," a bloody confrontation during the drawdown of troops after the revolution was suppressed. Culebra, situated at the highest elevation, presented the most difficult challenge of the excavation and was subject to massive flooding. The French contractor was involved in "an industrial dispute" with its Jamaican workforce. Colombian troops were called in and, keyed up from their victory over Prestán, dealt aggressively with the laborers, killing eighteen and wounding twenty. "Owing to the sanguinary nature of the occurrence and the conflicting evidence of 'eyewitnesses' it was at first difficult to obtain a true account of what had happened," Walrond writes (xv, 182). But investigations of the British Colonial Office clarified where responsibility lay, calling the attack "unprovoked" and declaring "the lives of British subjects on the Isthmus insecure." The massacre of Jamaicans demonstrated "the absence of protection for life and property" in Panama, warned the Colonial Secretary (xv, 183–84). Colombia's Supreme Court soon convicted the commander who ordered the attack, Walrond adds. It was an apt way to end publication, addressing the plight of West Indian laborers. *The Second Battle* presents itself as a work of conventional liberal history and it almost succeeds. But it continually produces signs of what it suppresses, the sympathetic identification of its author with the dispossessed, the politically militant, and the Afro-Caribbean.

TREATMENT AND DISCHARGE

The process of what Roundway Hospital management called "modernisation" included new treatments such as prefrontal leucotomy, a surgical procedure used sparingly in cases of severe mental illness, and electroconvulsive therapy (ECT), which came into use for treatment of depression in the late 1940s. "The general results of ECT have been most satisfactory," wrote the superintendent, "and in some cases of great benefit."[13] It was used increasingly during Walrond's time at the hospital, and although it may seem cruel to have induced epileptic seizures in patients, it must be recalled that this was just prior to the advent of antipsychotic and antidepressant drugs. Whether Walrond's depression was severe or persistent enough to warrant ECT is unclear, but considering the superintendent's enthusiasm—"a most useful form of treatment for depressed patients," he called it "safe and effective"—it seems possible.[14] The muscle relaxant curare was administered in conjunction with ECT to minimize muscle spasms, and the grisly irony would not have been lost on Walrond that he had traveled all the way to Wiltshire to be injected with a Guyanese plant toxin. Psychotherapy, practiced extensively at Roundway, may have proven an adequate palliative, or he may have taken largactil, the hospital's first "tranquilising drug."[15] What is clear is that he felt best when active and intellectually engaged. A security officer provided the only firsthand recollection of Walrond's tenure: "I knew Eric very well during his stay. I always found him a very nice fellow. He was never confined to ward, he was very helpful in everyway and was well liked by his fellow patients and by all the staff."[16]

Because Walrond had neglected or estranged friends and colleagues, it was unlikely that anyone would revive his career, but that is what happened. Nancy Cunard had been upset that Walrond failed to deliver a promised essay for her *Negro* anthology, but in the twenty years since she had apparently forgiven him. When he wrote her in 1954, enclosing a copy of "Success Story," she thanked him, feeling struck "once again—how well you write" and impressed by its "fantastic overlays of the Antilles and U.S." But "what *can* you be doing in that hospital?" she wondered, "I wish I had known where to get in touch with you when I was in England all last winter."[17] He had reclaimed her favorable attention. She wrote again to reiterate her praise, expressing eagerness to meet in London.[18] The hospital's policy was to release him for short trips if he requested permission. "Please let me know when we shall meet," she wrote. Reflecting on the growing West Indian immigration to England, she proposed they write something collaborative on this "matter of national interest." "You, as usual, will know a great deal about all of it. I wonder if there would be grounds for some kind of 'open letter' on the subject in one of the weeklies? I mean, correspondence, or articles answering each other— IF there is enough interest, this might we do?"[19] Although the proposal did not come to fruition, Cunard was in earnest. "I want to hear more about your stories—or book!" On her next visit to London, she contacted him. "Where are you dear Eric?" she wrote from the Hotel Whitehall, "Please send a line here and come and lunch soon."[20]

Cunard's first letter mentioned that Harold Jackman had established the Countée Cullen Memorial Library at Atlanta University. Walrond

10.3 Photograph of Langston Hughes and Nancy Cunard, Paris, 1938.

James Weldon Johnson Collection, Beinecke Rare Book and Manuscript Library, Yale University.

wrote Jackman immediately: "I understand that you need material," "all of it Negro." He was moved by Jackman's initiative.

> I was very touched to hear about this proof of your loyalty to Countee whose death [. . .] came as a profound shock. It's a splendid thing you are doing to try to keep his memory alive and I should like to do something to further the effort. Unfortunately, my belongings are scattered all over the place (in New York and in Bradford-on-Avon where I have been living since 1939) and it will be sometime before I can send you anything.

Contact with Jackman reconnected Walrond with a world he had long since left behind. "Whatever became of Jean Toomer?" he wondered. "Did the death of his wife, Margaret Latimer, hit him so hard that he took a kind of Oriental vow of perpetual silence? Or has he moved so far across the colour line that he has become practically invisible?" He assured Jackman he was well despite his return address: "I have been in the hospital for over two years now but at present I'm fine and still writing. Under separate cover I'm sending you a story which has appeared in the hospital magazine. It's a yarn ('Success Story') in six parts. I hope you like it." He pledged to "keep in touch" and send "from time to time anything that may be of value to the Atlanta collection." He stayed in contact with Jackman until May 1959.[21]

Another of Cunard's contacts led to Walrond's discharge from the hospital. Out of the blue in May 1957, he received an inquiry from Erica Marx, director of the Hand and Flower Press. She asked Cunard for help with a "Negro poetry" performance she wished to stage in London, the first event of its kind in England, she said, and Cunard referred her to Walrond. "As you know, he is a *beautiful* writer (prose, mainly), coloured, from the West Indies—a practiced journalist, able—charming too, and probably in touch with Negro talent in England."[22] Marx informed Walrond that in addition to running the press, she directed an arts organization, the Company of Nine, promoting poetry and the arts "in places where they are not so often to be found." She asked if he "had any good ideas to offer on" a "Negro poetry programme" and whether he "thought it a good idea."[23] He could not have been more enthusiastic. "I do think your idea is a good one and I should be only too pleased to do whatever I can to help further it. It was very kind of Nancy Cunard to mention me to you." He explained that although there had been comparable efforts on the radio, it was high time for what Marx proposed.

> There have been discussions of Negro poetry and Negro poetry readings on the wireless, in particular during and immediately after the last war, but this was before coloured immigrants started coming into the United Kingdom in large numbers. Now that so many of them are here the venture which you have in mind would seem to fill a need and I can think of many places both in London and the provinces where a programme of Negro poetry with music would be sure to arouse enough

interest and draw sufficiently large audiences to make the venture a sound one from a financial point of view. The bulk of the immigrants are concentrated at present in the Brixton area and the East End of London, Birmingham, Manchester, Liverpool, and Cardiff, and these are the localities which, I believe, audience response would be greatest.

Walrond felt that "the best Negro poetry (and the best known) is American," but he believed the event ought to represent the African diaspora, especially because "the coloured immigrants in Great Britain are mostly West Indians and Africans." Best to avoid "stirring chauvinist feelings," he advised, and make the program "representative," "a judicious mixture of American, West Indian, and Bantu poetry." From the Caribbean, he suggested not only Anglophone verse but also "some of Nancy Cunard's and Langston Hughes' translations of Haytian and Cuban poetry." The inquiry had fired Walrond's imagination.[24]

He told Marx the idea was "not only a good one from an aesthetic point of view, but from the standpoint of race relations it is a highly commendable one." He still believed in the power of literature to bridge the chasm between races and felt it was at least as wide in England as it was in the United States of the 1920s. "Believe it or not," he told Jackman, "even the *concept* of Negro poetry is something that is disturbingly new to quite a lot of people I have met recently."[25] Nevertheless, he told Marx the target audience should not be white: "Am I thinking in terms of a mainly Negro audience to begin with? I'm afraid I am, and I assure you this won't be a case of 'carrying coals to New Castle.'"[26] Even for black Britons, in other words, such a presentation would be revelatory. Walrond's enthusiasm was matched by Marx, who thanked him "for replying so quickly and so lucidly and fully" to her inquiry. Before proceeding, however, she felt compelled to clarify a question provoked by his mailing address. "May I, at this point, ask you what your position in the hospital is? Somehow or other, I had taken it from Nancy Cunard's letter that you were not a patient, but on the other hand maybe you are, and perhaps you would let me know." She was impressed with his acumen; it was his sanity that concerned her.[27] He settled the question by replying that he was a patient, but a voluntary one, and could "leave the hospital whenever I choose." He mentioned his work in the community, perhaps to allay concerns about his fitness for work. He said, in effect, that he no longer needed hospitalization. "The interest which has been keeping me here is the work which I am at present doing on the 'Roundway Review.'" Enclosing a copy of the latest issue, featuring *The Second Battle*, he said he hoped "fairly soon now to apply for my discharge."[28]

He was right; within four months he moved to London, hopeful and content, thanks in part to the ameliorative effect of his work with Marx. But the London to which he returned had changed in his eighteen-year absence as much as he had. Despite the changes wrought by the *Windrush* generation, and despite some promising opportunities in the world of letters, Walrond would remain a struggling outsider through the end of his life there.

11

LONDON II (1957–1966)

Relieved to be self-sufficient again, Walrond thanked Nancy Cunard breathlessly for having introduced him to Erica Marx. "If you had not given her my name and address and if she had not got into touch with me, I would not be writing this letter now to thank you for having made it possible for me to make a clean break with the life I had known for so very long," signing himself "Yours in eternal gratitude."[1] Some of the gregariousness returned. Over lunch in Leicester Square, he discussed the proposed program with Marx and her Company of Nine partners.[2] Walrond's task, undertaken at the British Museum, was to research "Negro poetry" in all its historical manifestations, including music. From his findings, he was to select a representative sample for performance by black actors. Walrond began the work while still living at Roundway, arriving at Paddington Station and visiting the reading room. He executed the task with his customary assiduity: "The programme should be up to date and none of the significant new voices should be overlooked."[3] After his discharge in September 1957, he took a room near the museum in the Alliance Club on Bedford Place, throwing himself into research. It was a shame the reading room now closed at 5 p.m., he told Marx, as he had been accustomed before the war to staying until 9.[4]

For his initial two-week research trip from Wiltshire he received £25 ($70), but he was not really in it for the money.[5] Captivated by the idea of a spectacular performance, the first of its kind, he worked vigorously. He was thrilled to partner with Marx, eager that she know "how grateful I am for everything that you did to make my visit to London such a pleasant one."[6] The project rekindled his sense of involvement at the leading edge of a black cultural initiative, showcasing the race's extraordinary inheritance. Marx suggested to Walrond's delight that the proceedings should be published by Hand and Flower Press, an anthology to which he should contribute a scholarly introduction and bibliography.[7] Would this project become his path back to literary work after all? Astutely, Walrond thought to leverage it into identifying a publisher for his Panama history. Marx was not in a position to publish it because Hand and Flower specialized in contemporary poetry, but she was well connected in London and offered to help him place *The Second Battle*. "Finish the work that you are already engaged upon," she advised, "and in the meantime you should send me 13 chapters, which I will deal with and try to interest one or two publishers."[8]

Having reviewed the manuscript, Marx was candid in her assessment, which was that although "the story becomes more and more interesting, I do feel it would do very well possibly to write the beginning of it in a slightly different way." "It reads slightly like a statistical commentary," she continued, "and it seems to me to need an atmospheric opening into which you can incorporate the manifold facts which you have weeded out more or less unobtrusively. In fact, it would only probably need the first 2 or 3 chapters going over again."[9] Walrond thanked her for "such useful criticism and advice" and acknowledged that the first chapters were too "closely knit, cramped and taut." He agreed to "introduce a little air into them and enough of the story of M. de Lesseps' first battle at Suez and how he came to be fighting a second one, in order not to leave the reader in a quandary about anything that has gone before." He stated his purpose plainly: "I am passionately concerned to remove the cinders from the eyes of those more or less interested parties who continually assert and appear to like to believe for reasons of their own that the failure of M. de Lesseps in Panama was due to the decimation of his workers by yellow fever." Walrond did not intend to minimize these casualties but to demonstrate the decisive impact of political factors. However, to "remove the cinders" from anyone's eyes he would have to write accessibly. "If I do not succeed in giving the reader who knows nothing of the subject a clear and convincing account of what actually happened, without soft-pedaling any of the relevant facts, I will have failed signally in my task."[10]

Despite their talents, neither Walrond nor Marx was an ideal producer of a "Negro poetry programme." Marx did not live in London and, despite her extensive contacts, had no experience with "Negro" poetry. Walrond had not lived in London in years, so his sphere of activity was limited. They relied on each other, Marx drawing on Walrond's knowledge, he on her experience staging readings. It took more than a year to realize the plan. "Black and Unknown Bards" was performed at the Royal Court Theatre in Sloane Square on October 5, 1958.[11] They could not have anticipated it, but the performance occurred during one of the most acrimonious periods in British race relations. White-on-black violence and intimidation increased throughout 1958, fueled by Fascists exploiting white working class resentment and culminating on a bank holiday weekend in August, when a massive gang of "teddy boys" terrorized Notting Hill. Five black men were left unconscious in the streets, and the community attempted to defend itself. An atmosphere of hostility and mutual suspicion reigned. Claudia Jones—born in Trinidad, raised in New York, and deported to London during the McCarthy trials—responded to the violence with a cultural weapon, organizing the now legendary Carnival festival. Similarly, it was through culture that "Black and Unknown Bards" sought to foster black pride and understanding across Britain's fraught lines of race. When they conceived it, however, Marx and Walrond did not anticipate this dramatic escalation of tensions.

THE SHOW *MUST* GO ON

Poring over the British Museum holdings, Walrond was fascinated with eccentric instances of "Negro verse": a seventeenth-century Dutch chimney sweep composing in Latin; a protégé of the Duke of Montagu who studied at the University of Cambridge; "a simple milk-maid of Bristol" whose poetic gift captured the attention of Hannah More, the eighteenth-century playwright.[12] Walrond knew the value of such exercises from his Harlem days and, at this pivotal moment in British race relations, he hoped that the documentation and performance of superb talent would help erode racial prejudice, which was widespread despite the fact that half of white Britons "had never met a black person—and among those who had the acquaintance had mostly been casual." Many whites were averse to "contact or communication with black people [and] objected vehemently to mixed marriages."[13] A Jamaican adolescent said, "The English are kind of funny. They think if they're polite and pretend something isn't there it'll go away and they won't have to notice it."[14] But it was no longer possible to ignore the people of color arriving in increasing number, nor were they going away.

On a Wednesday in August 1957, Walrond left Roundway Hospital to catch the 10 a.m. train from Devizes and present a draft of the "Negro poetry programme" to the Company of Nine executive committee, hoping fervently for a positive reception. His discharge hinged on the outcome; if the project got a green light, he would submit his request. The committee received Walrond enthusiastically, and it was agreed that the Arts Council of Great Britain should be brought in, and the Trinidadian actor Errol John should be invited to perform and recruit actors. Marx and Walrond planned the companion anthology. There was talk of a promising West African poet, J. David Rubadiri, from whom contributions might be solicited. In short, the meeting was a smashing success and spirits soared. Marx wrote Walrond that she "was extremely pleased how the evening went, on an increasing, rising scale, as far as the appreciation was concerned. [. . .] It was very nice seeing you, and I am glad that the reactions of our friends were as they were." Walrond replied, "Personally, I enjoyed every moment of the time I spent with you. [. . .] I am glad that you felt after the meeting [. . .] that we had 'broken the back' of the task before us." The rest of the week found him in the British Museum, his step lightened by a £100 advance. The day before he moved to London, Marx sent a note: "I shall be very interested to hear how your life goes, and where you are going to live, and I am glad you feel you are starting off something worth while."[15] But tough sledding lay ahead.

Errol John was in Port of Spain, declining inquiries, and their producer's office was always "crowded out with visitors" whenever Walrond sought a meeting, "the queue extending halfway down the stairs."[16] Marx excised much of the material Walrond submitted for the program, and although he feigned indifference he later complained that so little of his research made its way into the final product.[17] When Errol John returned to London, Marx found him boorish and demanding: "As far as bigheads are concerned—he is one. I have never been so tired in my life as I was when I left him at 3 p.m., having, as I thought, achieved a little something in the end. Anyhow, the long and short of it is that his mind has changed, and he no longer wishes to do the programme, for which I must say I am deeply and profoundly grateful."[18] As they scrambled to identify a new lead actor, producer, and location, Walrond fended off despair and rallied Marx with the old saw, "The show *must* go on!"[19] Fortunate developments ensured that it would. Marx interested the Arts Council, a major national organization, meaning "We have blessings in high places."[20] From Harold Jackman, word arrived of an anthology of "Negro" poetry compiled by the Amsterdam publisher Paul Breman, who "kindly offered to share with me the information which he has about the younger Negro poets in the U.S.A."[21] Marx contacted the African American actor Gordon Heath, who had performed on London, Paris, and New York stages and in film, written for *Theatre Arts* magazine, and owned a Paris club where he had performed folk music since 1953. Walrond felt confident: "I think he will enter readily into the spirit of the thing and will doubtless regard the programme not merely as an opportunity to 'shine' personally but as an opportunity to render a service to the minority group in the theatre to which he belongs."[22] Heath recruited two accomplished performers: a young black Briton, Cleo Laine, and the African American actor Earle Hyman, a veteran of the American Shakespeare Festival. Soon poems arrived from Rubadiri of Nyasaland. "I think they will add considerably to the interest of the [project]," Walrond enthused, "His vision of Africa is so different from that of his congeners in the U.S.A. and the West Indies."[23]

The most intriguing development was the interest in the companion anthology plan shown by the Arts Council director, William Emrys Williams. A passionate champion of arts education, Williams headed Penguin Books UK, and like Horace Liveright, was accustomed to controversy. He met Walrond in November 1957 to discuss publishing *Black and Unknown Bards*. Working furiously to finalize the anthology, Walrond needed to find full-time employment but worried that it would disrupt his research.

> I am trying to wind up the research on it as quickly as I can, so that if for obvious reasons I am compelled to devote only my evenings and week-ends to the rest of the work still to be accomplished there won't be too much delay in doing it. I gathered, however, from the conversation I had with Sir William [. . .] that a delay of a few more months won't make all that much difference provided the anthology comes up to scratch—that the whole thing runs to about 300 pages in length, and is buttressed with bibliographic notes, a select bibliography, and an Introduction of not less than 10,000 words.[24]

Marx urged Walrond to deliver a finished proposal by the end of January 1958. But the arrangement with Penguin did not pan out, and nothing in the record suggests the reason. It may have been a business decision on Williams's part, but it may also have been connected with Walrond's performance. Things grew much harder for him that winter.

He was staying at a Bloomsbury student hotel and could not find work. It had been some time since he had looked for a job, and even longer since he had written a ten-thousand-word essay, his Penguin assignment. Between the false starts on the poetry program, unemployment, the writing task, and bills coming due with a frequency he had been spared the last five years, his resolve seems to have faltered. He may have relapsed into depression. In the new year, 1958, he and Marx ceased correspondence. It is unclear when Walrond completed his research or whether it was to her satisfaction, nor did they discuss *The Second Battle* after her initial offer of assistance; but they went eight months without contact, and all indications are that Walrond was impoverished. Having transcribed by hand twelve exercise books "full of stuff" for the anthology, he could not afford a typewriter.²⁵ Spring came and went. He wrote Jackman that the anthology was "in the hands of a publisher" but negotiations were "very complicated." He moved from Bloomsbury to Hornsey, a northern suburb, where Jackman mailed him copies of *Jet* magazine, which made him "feel sort of homesick!"²⁶

When he wrote Marx again it was to ask for money. She responded with a check, and he thanked her "for coming to my rescue in the nick of time."

> As regards looking for other work, I assure you I have been looking. [. . .] Only a few days ago I had a long interview with one of the senior officials at the Labour Exchange where I am registered. (I was out weeks ago to the exchange on Farringdon Road, off Fleet Street, and tried in vain to get on their register.) In the meantime I am pressing on with my writing. I have sent out two stories so far, and it is obvious from the reactions I have had that what I am up against is a "marketing problem."²⁷

He enclosed rejection letters to illustrate the "marketing problem," perhaps also to confirm that his pen was not dormant. Labour Exchanges were intended to rationalize job searches, matching employees with open positions, but West Indians found them susceptible in the 1950s to the same discrimination that plagued the open job market.²⁸ There was good news from Marx, however. The English Stage Company was interested in "Black and Unknown Bards," looking to stage it at the Royal Court Theatre in London's West End. But Walrond was clearly on the project's periphery by this point, Marx having brought in another coordinator that spring.

Rosey E. Pool, a Jewish scholar of Dutch descent who lived in London, dedicated her career to studying and promoting African American literature. It is unclear whether Pool came aboard to replace Walrond or was invited with his blessing, but he met with her and Marx in May for lunch at the Theatre Arts Club, and she won his trust and affection. A genuine radical, she advocated tirelessly for African American literature, publishing in several languages. She was a friend and avid correspondent of Hughes, Cullen, Bontemps, and Cunard, and a Holocaust survivor who linked the experience of African Americans to the oppression of Jews under Nazism. She knew Walrond's writing and had saved newspaper reviews of *Tropic Death*. Having worked with Paul Breman in Amsterdam and George Lamming and Henry Swanzy on BBC radio, she was a tremendous asset. "She could have been a professor of black studies in the 1940s," said Gordon Heath, "long before America decided it should know more about black history and achievement."[29] It may have been Pool's involvement that propelled "Black and Unknown Bards" out of limbo. She and Walrond received equal credit for selecting the material, but Heath's memoir omits any reference to Walrond, suggesting that Walrond was unable to execute his duties after the difficult winter of 1958.[30]

Staging a prominent "Negro poetry" performance in the wake of the Notting Hill riots was a dicey proposition, but the Royal Court Theatre was no stranger to controversy. Its artistic director invited work challenging comfortable pieties, including John Osborne's *Look Back in Anger*, which delivered the post-war "angry young man" to the English stage in 1956, and Samuel Beckett's *Krapp's Last Tape*, which opened three weeks after "Black and Unknown Bards." The theater press announced "Black and Unknown Bards" with anticipation. "Something of a novelty," the *Guardian* called it, while the *Sunday Times* hoped for "an interesting evening. I cannot recall ever having come across a collection of Negro Poetry on the stage—or for that matter in book form."[31] In interviews, Marx situated the performance in the context of England's deteriorating race relations: "I practically despaired of it ever coming off, on account of the number of difficulties that have been experienced. But maybe there is a useful side to all this, in that the programme will bring itself to the attention of the public at a very psychological moment, with the troubles that appear to be happening here and there."[32] The performance had not been conceived as a response to local circumstances, but intervening events ensured it would be received in this context.

An evasion of England's "troubles" was built into the program. Despite Walrond's extensive research on African and Caribbean poetry, "Black and Unknown Bards" contained only African American material. As Heath announced, it reflected "the continuity of Negro life in America: through slavery, plantation life, civil war, emancipation, education, urbanisation and the promise of full integration at all levels of American life."[33] From the spirituals and work songs to modern verse, the performers held the audience spellbound. The exclusive U.S. focus may have been expedient given time constraints and the abundance of African American material. However, when one considers the vexing matters of British race relations and the decline of the empire, the decision to delimit the scope may have been deliberate. Ghana had just declared independence, Britain's first African colony to do so, and independence movements stirred much of that continent and the Caribbean. Tensions from the race riots simmered, and the Fascists and "teddy boys" struck again, brutally murdering Antiguan immigrant Kelso Cochrane. A performance of African American poetry addressed present conditions, but obliquely.

The audience in the Royal Court Theatre made the link. The *News Chronicle* observed, "At a time when we should all feel disquiet at the racial riots of Notting Hill and elsewhere, it was fitting to hear the voices of three Negro artists expressing their longing, their bitterness, and hopes through the words of the American Negro poets, greater and lesser."[34] *The Daily Worker* said, "At a time when it is particularly necessary to draw attention to the talent, dignity, sufferings and aspirations of the coloured peoples, we have this excellent programme which does just that."[35] Whether "short and witty," "nostalgic," or "bitter," the "magnificent" poems represented "the Negro who has been ill-treated for centuries," resonating beyond U.S. borders.[36] Even those who were critical of the performance drew the parallel. In one reviewer's opinion, the performance "underlined the truism that humanity seldom sees the whole answer the whole way; we can only do our best, and that goes for white as well as coloured nationals." The implication was that the performance afforded only a partial view, and whites were "doing their best" under the circumstances. This reviewer preferred "a glancing ray of sunny humour" to "self-pity."[37] But the consensus was that the performance deserved wider circulation. It "should be repeated on TV for a nation-wide audience," wrote the *News Chronicle*, while *The Daily Worker* thought it far "too good for a single performance before the exotic sophisticates of the Royal Court. [. . .] It really should be given the widest presentation."[38,39] The performance would not be repeated, but among the reactions it inspired, none missed its relevance to conditions in Britain and her waning empire. From the "Black and Unknown Bards" performance came a companion anthology of the same title, published by Hand and Flower Press. Featuring an Africanist woodcut on the cover, it contained the work of twenty poets and the lyrics of a "slave song," a "chain gang song," and two "traditionals."[40] It was Walrond's final publication.

Race relations in England would get worse before they got better. Incremental gains came from initiatives such as the Notting Hill Carnival; the *West Indian Gazette*, which Claudia Jones published with Amy Ashwood Garvey; and community-based programs emerging from the violence of the late 1950s. They contributed to a nascent culture of postcoloniality in which both white and "coloured" residents participated.[41] But the atmosphere remained rancorous because many social ills were attributed to immigrants, by which was meant the "coloured." The Conservative Party, having previously endorsed a relaxed immigration policy, now pursued restriction aggressively, leading to the Commonwealth Immigrants Act. This was a devastating blow not only to those seeking to immigrate but also to black Britons, who were stigmatized and subject to deportation if convicted of an offense within five years of arrival. Immigrants flocked to Britain to beat the impending restrictions, nearly one hundred thousand arriving from the West Indies alone in the fifteen months before the law took effect.[42] Jamaican poet Louise Bennett gave the migration the clever designation "Colonization in Reverse." The newcomers would transform English race relations in ways that were unimaginable at the time. Among them were Stuart Hall, Edward Kamau Brathwaite, John La Rose, Jan Carew, Ivan Van Sertima, Orlando Patterson, and Wilson Harris. They collaborated with

Windrush generation writers to launch the Caribbean Artists Movement (CAM), a concerted expression of black British sensibility. Walrond was not involved in CAM, but its founders were aware of his work. One of them, Kenneth Ramchand, devoted a section of his dissertation at the University of Edinburgh to *Tropic Death*, and his presentation at CAM's first conference led to the publication of *The West Indian Novel and its Background*, the first such study by a Caribbean scholar.[43]

Walrond drifted from public view after *Black and Unknown Bards*. He spent his last several years working for an import-export firm near St. Paul's Cathedral and living modestly in north London. George Lamming saw him at the bar of a Jamaican nightclub where he was a regular. "He had very special hours; he'd go in and have a drink." Walrond told Lamming he had been a war correspondent after leaving the United States. "He was something of a picaresque character, moving about without a fixed boat, as it were. He had a very interesting ear for picking up the language of the people of Panama. He was a very strong writer. It's a pity that something happened."[44] Despite the stirrings of a robust black British culture that he took part in cultivating before the war, Walrond seems to have been quite alone in the diaspora.

"LET THE CHOIR SING A STORMY SONG"

Walrond had not succeeded at writing his way into literary London, as he hoped. He tried putting the *Black and Unknown Bards* anthology in the hands of those who might recognize its merits. Nancy Cunard requested seven copies of the book, and when Walrond learned that Arthur Spingarn of the National Association for the Advancement of Colored People (NAACP) was in London on a holiday, he stopped by his Russell Square hotel with a copy.[45] He mailed some to Jackman, requesting the addresses of Gwendolyn Bennett and Francis Parkes, a Ghanaian poet in London. He groused that the anthology "does not quite reflect the immense amount of labour" he put into it. Jackman felt it should be made available to New York booksellers.[46] Cunard was effusive

("I *love* 'Black and Unknown Bards'") and brimming with affection ("How good to see your acute, dear, astute self again!"). She was also receptive to a business proposition Walrond made, a collaboration. "I *would*, yes, like *us* to do 'a job of work' together, let me think a bit—on a stage, yes; something like *enacted* poems—a kind of Masque perhaps, not quite All-Spade, but nearly. Oh, it could be gorgeous—people (and poems) of America." Although she found the prospect tantalizing, it may have been merely a diversion. "I have been so *down* lately," she confided, "not a laugh in a year, not a smile."[47] Nothing materialized.

Immediately after the new year, 1959, Walrond moved again, evidently under duress. It was just a few blocks' distance, but Cunard wrote, "I trust you are much better now and that things will go well." "How awful for you to have to move. I know only too well the detestable nuisance all that can be."[48] He planned to attend the inaugural Caribbean Carnival that Claudia Jones had organized and invited Cunard to join him. A prior commitment prevented her, but she pledged to look up Marx and get them all together. It was not until April, however, that she wrote again, and then just a telegram.[49] This was the last time they were in touch, and although a more extensive relationship cannot be ruled out, it did not yield any projects. Cunard's health was deteriorating, and she suffered from the strain of several relocations and a tempestuous affair with a photographer half her age, fraying her fragile nerves.[50] Walrond was grasping at straws in an attempt to revive his career. He was reduced to the literary equivalent of odd jobs. An Italian scholar at work on an African art book hired Walrond to select photographs, consisting chiefly of images of sculpture in the British Museum and the Wallace Collection. He was excited and wrote admiringly of the Nigerian sculptors Lucky Wadiri and Ben Enwonwu. He felt that if he performed his task creditably more work might follow, and he implored Jackman to contact their mutual acquaintances: "Whatever help you can give, either personally or by passing the word on to Richard Barthe (or anyone else: Elizabeth Prophet, Augusta Savage, Meta Warwick Fuller . . . ?) would be greatly appreciated. Only, I am afraid, time is of the essence!"[51] An unmistakable sense of urgency, even desperation, had set in.

George Padmore died that September, and Walrond attended his funeral, where he met Richard Wright. Wright was friendly and solicitous, asking Walrond about his Panama history. When W. E. B. Du Bois visited London later that year, Rosey Pool graciously arranged a meeting with Walrond, and Du Bois also inquired about *The Big Ditch*. These conversations provoked a conflicted response. Their kindness gratified him, but he was ashamed of his performance. Upon receiving the Guggenheim Foundation's annual report, he unburdened himself to Henry Allen Moe. He was "greatly in need of help," suffering under a "crushing moral obligation."

I won't say I "almost wept with joy" at the sight of an envelope with the name and address of the Guggenheim Foundation on it. I will say this though: the pleasure which I have had from a perusal of the report would probably surprise you. It somehow made me feel less like an "exile", and almost as though I was in touch with things again. As you see, I am back in London; I was able to return in September 1957 (I would rather not talk about the Devizes interlude), and since then I have had one or two "ghost-writing" jobs; but now, although I am greatly in need of help, I am determined to try somehow and get on with some of my own, long-neglected work. Last October at the funeral of a mutual friend, I met Richard Wright for the first time. Later in the year Dr. W.E.B. Du Bois was passing through London, and through a mutual Dutch friend I had the pleasure of meeting him, also for the first time. The solicitude of both Richard Wright and Dr. Du Bois appeared early, and they both wanted to know in particular what had happened to "The Big Ditch." This was a reference to a project I have been under a crushing moral obligation to carry through to success, before I could begin to feel really "free" aesthetically within myself: that is, write the story of what happened to the French in Panama. I did not tell either Richard Wright or Dr. Du Bois that the initial effort, which I once inflicted upon you and for which I hope you have forgiven me, was poorly conceived, based upon inadequate research and hurriedly produced. I do not even know how good a story I told them, by way of mitigation. I do remember intimating, however, that I have only one thing to live for (there was a moment in Wiltshire when I must have forgotten this), and in spite of age and years of silence I have not lost sight of my objectives, or the high aims with which I set out as a Guggenheim Fellow such a long time ago. With thanks for your kindness in remembering me, I beg to remain, Yours faithfully, Eric D. Walrond[52]

Even as the letter professed his resolve, it testified to the burden of an unmet responsibility.

Walrond took a job at E. Hornsby & Sons, an "export packing" firm located near the ancient walls of the City of London. St. Paul's Cathedral stood a few blocks to the north, the Thames and the Tower Bridge just to the south. It is unclear in what capacity he worked for the firm, but he likely found the position through the Farringdon Road Labour Exchange he mentioned to Marx.[53] His sparse address book included a few London literary contacts: Rosey Pool, Claudia Jones, and Paul Breman.[54] It has been said that Walrond wrote a preface to Amy Ashwood Garvey's *Liberia: Land of Promise*, but that text is scarce enough to make corroboration difficult.[55]

Walrond developed health problems and in the summer of 1965 suffered the first of several heart attacks. Confronting his mortality, he renewed contact with his daughters—two in Jamaica, one in Connecticut—and he sent Lucille and Jean a copy of *Tropic Death* marked with editorial changes should the book ever be reissued. Little did he know that was precisely what Arthur Pell had been contemplating in the Liveright office in Manhattan. Pell had received inquiries about the book and its author and sought a publisher to whom he could sell the reprint rights. The civil rights movement had revived the curiosity of scholars and general readers alike in African American literature, leading to reconsiderations of the Harlem Renaissance, and officers at Liveright contemplated bundling *Cane* and *Tropic Death*. The problem was, no one knew where to find Walrond. Pell was resourceful, reaching out to Arna Bontemps, now director of university relations at Fisk, who told him that the novelist Jack Conroy, a friend and collaborator, was in London and would look into Walrond's whereabouts.[56] Somehow Conroy located him and "took a great liking to him immediately."[57] Three days later, Walrond wrote Bontemps to say he "had long wanted to cut, trim and re-work certain passages" in the book and was eager for the opportunity.

Before the year was out, Pell wrote with a proposal for the sale of the reprint rights to a paperback press, an advance of $150, and 50 percent of world reprint royalties. He assured Walrond that Toomer had the same arrangement. "I do not know if you remember me," Pell added, "but I was with Horace Liveright at the time we published *Tropic Death*."[58] Pell's letter went astray, and it took some initiative on Walrond's part to discover his plans for *Tropic Death*. Walrond wrote in March 1966, asking "if there is any substance in what has been conveyed to me" about "a new edition," and if so "perhaps you would be good enough to let me know whether a decision has been reached in the matter." He confessed that he had sent his copy to his daughter, "who has a job with the University of the West Indies" (Lucille Mair was by then a dean at Mary Seacole Hall and a pioneer in the field of women's studies in the Caribbean), but did not think "she would very much mind letting me have it back."[59] He restrained himself from observing the irony, which must have struck him forcefully, that the firm that dumped him during the Depression was approaching him again as the market for "Negro" literature expanded.

Pell reiterated the proposal and welcomed Walrond's editorial emendations, indicating that he would ask Bontemps to write an introduction.[60] Walrond immediately signed the agreement, pledged to "send word to Jamaica to have the 'worked over' copy of the book sent direct to you," and expressed enthusiasm about Bontemps, "as he is about the most competent person to undertake such a task that I know." Should Pell be interested, he had three stories that could be added to *Tropic Death*, one of which *The Spectator* published, and one he was about to complete. Under separate cover, he included a handwritten note, revealing in its penmanship the toll of old age but in its composition his charm and powers of recall.

> Your name not only rang a bell when Arna Bontemps mentioned you in his letter. I'm almost positive that I have had the pleasure of meeting you. Wasn't it you who, shortly after the publication of "Tropic Death," arranged a publicity interview for me in the B&L office with a lady journalist on a Cleveland newspaper? Or am I mistaken?[61]

Pell confirmed, "not only do I remember you, but your signature is the same. Yes, I did arrange a publicity interview for you at the B&L office. It was quite a place!"

The prospect of reissuing *Tropic Death* was a thrilling surprise for Walrond, who had been down on his luck for years and at age 67 suffered from declining physical and mental health. What cheered him most was something Pell mentioned in a March letter—that he hoped to sell the reprint rights to a firm with an established market "in the schools." Within a week of signing the agreement, Walrond deposited his $150 check and sent Pell the stories he wanted to add to the book, including "Consulate" and "Poor Great." He found the prospect of placing *Tropic Death* in schools "exceedingly interesting" and reflected on the serendipitous developments.

> It is really extraordinary that after so many years I should have at once connected you with the publicity interview (held "on a roof garden nook, filled with porch chairs and pillows, and attached to the lovely offices of Boni & Liveright"), and that you should have been able to recall the occasion as well. Is that not a good omen? I have persuaded myself that it cannot be anything else.[62]

Unfortunately, he did not live long enough to test his hunch. He corresponded with Pell sporadically, asking that the dedication of *Tropic Death* be changed from Casper Holstein, his Harlem Renaissance patron now deceased, to his three daughters, whom he had put on a steamship bound for Kingston forty-three years earlier.[63] Confirming the change, Pell indicated his ongoing efforts to secure a reprint firm but lamented, "These things take time."[64]

That was something Walrond did not have much of. On a Monday in early August, four months before his sixty-eighth birthday, a heart attack felled him in the street. He was pronounced dead on arrival at St. Bartholomew's Hospital in Southfield, not far from his workplace, and buried without ceremony in the sprawling Abney Park Cemetery in Stoke Newington, North London.[65] He did not live long enough to learn of the sale of *Tropic Death*'s reprint rights to Collier Books two years later.[66] But one cannot help but think that the prospect of its reissue was a kind of vindication. The summer before Walrond died, Bontemps visited London, and he and Conroy called on Walrond. "We found Eric suffering from a heart ailment," Conroy recalled. "But during a lively talk session in Soho pubs, we heard him tell of his esteem for Arna and his gratitude for Arna's rediscovering him." So great was Walrond's enthusiasm that he insisted on showing them around Paris to "tour his old haunts."[67] Clearly, renewing acquaintance with his New York contacts had inspired him.

When Langston Hughes learned that Bontemps had located Walrond, he sent a Christmas greeting and a gift of one of his recent books. As Walrond recognized, it was a lovely gesture from someone with whom he had fallen out of touch, one of the few from that time whose fame had not diminished. Walrond replied with a card bearing the image of the Tower Bridge: "Dear Langston, What a pleasant surprise, hearing from you! Ever since Arna Bontemps wrote that you were getting out an anthology of Negro short stories I've had you very much in my thoughts. Many thanks for sending 'Simple,' its treasured inscription, and the Christmas card."[68] On learning of Walrond's death, Bontemps wrote Hughes, "Have you heard that Eric Walrond died in England a couple of weeks ago? It was a heart attack (about his 5th) on a street in London. [. . .] So 'let the choir sing a stormy song.'"[69]

POSTSCRIPT

The archive on Eric Walrond is riddled with gaps and silences. Much of what enables us to reconstruct his career is absent and perhaps beyond recovery. And yet a narrative emerges from the fragments, tracing a jagged path through the Caribbean diaspora, illustrating the boldness of Walrond's work and its polyphony. He was not as prolific as some of his peers, but he was far more prolific after all than many realized. Despite his limitations, there is something poignant about the path he followed and something significant about the stories he told, the disquieting impression his work leaves on readers. For he lived as he wrote, without a safety net. He published just one book, but it burst with Caribbean sounds—the speech of peasants, folk songs, and work songs—a jarring counterpastoral lyric that was distinctive right down to its orthography. As uncompromising as its author, the book was a translation of the Caribbean that refused to fully translate, valuing narrative performance above accessibility.

But *Tropic Death* did not represent the totality of Walrond's career, the full range of which included denunciations of white supremacy and colonialist ideology, prescient reflections on migration, portraits of artists, stylized vernaculars, and clever cross-cultural masquerades. He was not the first West Indian in Panama, the first Caribbean arrival to New York, the first "Negro" in Paris, nor the first of London's "coloured" colonials. But he managed to compress these paradigmatic lines of flight into a single, extraordinary career, and the unusual perspective he acquired was necessarily comparative and transnational. To put it this way, however, may imply an advantage when this study demonstrates the persistent challenges attending Walrond's relocations, a caution against idealizing the cosmopolitan "Negro" intellectual. Despite his versatility, ambition, and occasional good fortune, Walrond enjoyed only a year or two in which his writing sustained him financially, and he endured long stretches of publishing very little. This is the sense in which his failures are symptomatic, for they were only partly a result of his limitations as an artist and his debilitating bouts of depression; they reflect the attenuated conditions of possibility for "New World Negro" writers.

One can see the ways in which Walrond's world—the struggles and communities in which he participated—was a precursor to our own; it is more difficult to grasp its difference, its inscrutability, the possibilities that sprang into being but have since been foreclosed. The historian Carlo Ginzburg observed in *The Cheese and the Worms*, his magisterial study of a sixteenth-century Italian miller, "That culture has been destroyed. To respect its residue of unintelligibility that resists any attempt at analysis [is to] take note of a historical mutilation of which, in a certain sense, we ourselves are the victims."[1] Even as we recognize in Eric Walrond incipient forms of familiar contemporary identities and communities, we should also consider the "historical mutilation" of the anticolonial struggles, transnational periodical formations, aesthetic movements, and political solidarities that animated Walrond's work. We are ourselves the victims of their truncation. It may defy comprehension that a celebrated Harlem author would leave the United States, sabotaging his career at the height of the New Negro movement. It may seem unintelligible for a cosmopolitan Caribbean intellectual to spend twelve years as the only "Negro" in an English village. It may be difficult to understand why, as Ethel Ray Nance told an interviewer in 1970, "It's been so hard to trace some of his things."[2] Her confusion might be answered by calling him a renegade, a picaresque figure, or an exile, but it would really require a different sort of archive than those we have to render a career like Walrond's fully intelligible.

The current owner of 9 Ivy Terrace, Walrond's house in Bradford-on-Avon, happens to direct the local historical society; yet out of no fault of his own, he was unaware of the former resident of his house and his significance to literary history. During a visit to Colón, Panama, my cab driver was a young man whose grandfather moved from Barbados to help dig the canal, but when I showed him my copy of *Tropic Death* and read some passages about Colón's West Indian community at that time, he was indifferent. Not only had he never heard of the book, he could not read it because although his parents spoke English at home, he had grown up speaking, reading, and writing Spanish. Eric Walrond is much less remote from us than Ginzburg's sixteenth century, but comparable efforts are required to overcome the erasures inherent in Caribbean diaspora history. "The archive dictates what can be said about the past," Saidiya Hartman insists, "and the kind of stories that can be told about the persons catalogued, embalmed, and sealed away in box files and folios."³ If this study helps restore Eric Walrond to a status he once held alongside Jean Toomer, Countée Cullen, Nella Larsen, Zora Neale Hurston, and other peers whose work and reputations have only been recovered through painstaking investigation, I hope it also suggests the incompleteness and fragility of the archive where transnational black writers are concerned, even when they are established intellectuals.

Walrond forged a precarious career by crossing borders, none of which he crossed completely. From the "West Indian Circles" column of Panama's *Star & Herald*, to his work on Garvey's journals in New York and London, to his Caribbean efforts at *Opportunity* and his Wiltshire essays about colonialism and the "colour bar," his journalism was, like his fiction, an exercise in cultural translation. But borders are rarely neutral. They often presuppose or enforce privilege, and Walrond's translations challenged the privileges attending the borders he crossed. Even within New York, the unofficial border he straddled between white and black Manhattan occasioned a Caribbean challenge to monolithic notions of Harlem's blackness and a "Cabaret School" challenge to the prevailing discourse of respectability and "Negro" uplift. He benefited from his mobility and suffered for it, too. The Caribbean youth underwent the brutal alchemy that made him a "Negro" in New York, and the loss that process required was the source of both his intolerable grief and his most penetrating and impressive writing. The Harlem Renaissance celebrity, newly anointed in the cafés of Montparnasse, found that crossing borders failed to protect him from the caprice of his New York publisher and the vagaries of American capitalism. The black Briton, dozens of tropical tales in his valise, published some of the first Caribbean stories in England but arrived a generation too soon, a cautionary tale to the postwar authors who met him, as George Lamming did, nursing palliative drinks at the bar. Many observers have wondered what went wrong with Eric Walrond, why he did not produce more. We might wonder instead at his persistence, and at the countless peripatetic West Indians whose voice, insight, and artistry are far more resistant to recovery.

NOTES

INTRODUCTION

1. Ethel Ray Nance, interview by Ann Allen Shockley, November 18 and December 23, 1970 (Charles S. Johnson Collection, Fisk University Library), 14.
2. Robert Bone, *Down Home: A History of Afro-American Short Fiction*, 202.
3. Robert Bone papers, private possession of Louis J. Parascandola.
4. Aaron Douglas to Alta Sawyer, undated, Aaron Douglas Papers, SCNYPL.
5. Nance, 15.
6. David Levering Lewis, *When Harlem Was in Vogue*, 128.
7. Johnson to Alain Locke, January 27, 1925, ALP, Box 164–40, Folder 25.
8. Charles Rowell, "'Let Me Be With Ole Jazzbo': An Interview with Sterling A. Brown," *Callaloo* 14 (1991): 811.
9. W. E. B. Du Bois, "Five Books," *Crisis* (January 1927): 152.
10. Donald Friede correspondence, August 31, 1927, Box 51, HFP.
11. Lewis, *Vogue*, 234.
12. Ibid., 233.

1. GUYANA AND BARBADOS (1898–1911)

1. Frank Sullivan interview with Walrond, *Footnotes of Good Books*, October 1926, WFP.
2. When Benjamin Prout died, he had $6,530 of working capital, which as Robert Bone observes was "a substantial, if not a magnificent sum" in those days (5).
3. Robert Bone, Unpublished biography of Eric Walrond, Private collection of Louis J. Parascandola, 5–6. Any account of Walrond's childhood must rely on the biography Professor Bone began drafting in the mid-1980s. Although he was unable to complete

the biography due to illness, Bone interviewed Walrond's grandson, his cousin, and other family in Barbados, conducting research in the Department of Archives, Black Rock, St. Michael. Bone's work is invaluable, but it raises problems of interpretation for subsequent studies. They are especially acute in connection with British Guiana, which Bone understood to be the origin of Walrond's inner conflicts and the animating source of his literary gift. For Bone, an avowed Freudian, British Guiana threw into stark relief the two competing domains of human existence that Walrond struggled to reconcile: civilization and barbarism. The present study rejects certain constructions Bone put on his research even as it relies on that research.

4. Ibid., 8.

5. Ibid., 10.

6. Sir George William Des Voeux, *My Colonial Service in British Guiana, St. Lucia, Trinidad, Newfoundland, and Hong Kong, Vol. I*, 115.

7. Walter Rodney, *A History of the Guyanese Working People, 1881–1905*, 240; Franklin W. Knight, *The Caribbean: The Genesis of a Fragmented Nationalism*, 3rd ed., 131.

8. Bone, Unpublished biography, 20.

9. Rodney, *A History*, 196.

10. Walrond's stories of Guyana, most of which he wrote in England, are highly autobiographical. These include "The Coolie's Wedding," "The Servant Girl," and "Two Sisters." However, I have avoided drawing on his fiction for particulars of his life when it does not otherwise comport with biographical fact, as in *Tropic Death*'s "The White Snake."

11. Rodney, *A History*, 225, 229; Knight, *The Caribbean*, 213.

12. Rodney, *A History*, 196.

13. Ibid., 233.

14. Hubert Critchlow, "History of the Labour Union Movement in British Guiana," 42.

15. Rodney, *A History*, 192.

16. The 1904 *British Guiana Directory & Almanack* lists a self-employed tailor named Walrond at 189 Church Street. Although the first initials do not match, it is possible that this was William's shop. If so, it was not far from the principal targets of looting and arson along Water Street.

17. To this day, an area called Proutes lies a half-mile north of Flat Rock, near Highway 3.

18. David Levering Lewis, *When Harlem Was in Vogue*, 128.

19. Bone, Unpublished biography, 21.

20. Knight, *The Caribbean*, 259–62; Eric Williams, *From Columbus to Castro: The History of the Caribbean, 1492–1969*, 366.

21. George Lamming, *In the Castle of My Skin*, 36–37, 57.

22. Another fictionalized account of the Walronds' move to Jackman's Gap appears in "The Black Pin."

23. Transcripts of interviews with Canal workers are compiled in Lancelot Lewis, *The West Indian in Panama*; and in Bonham Richardson, *Panama Money in Barbados* (Knoxville: University of Tennessee Press, 1985). George Westerman also conducted a number of interviews, transcripts of which are in the Schomburg Center for Research in Black Culture.

24. Lewis, *The West Indian in Panama*, 31–32.
25. Matthew Parker, *Panama Fever: The Epic Story of the Building of the Panama Canal*, 277.
26. On the "Colón Man" in Caribbean folk culture, see Rhonda Frederick, *Colón Man a Come: Mythographies of Panama Canal Migration* (Lanham, MD: Lexington, 2005).
27. Julie Greene, *The Canal Builders: Making America's Empire at the Panama Canal*, 30; Velma Newton, *The Silver Men: West Indian Labour Migration to Panama, 1850–1914*, 93.

2. PANAMA (1911-1918)

1. On the discourse of "tropicality" and its ambivalent investment in the Caribbean as either repulsive or attractive, see Krista A. Thompson, *An Eye for the Tropics: Tourism, Photography, and Framing the Caribbean Picturesque*, 4–24; J. Michael Dash, *The Other America: Caribbean Literature in a New World Context*, 21–42; Nancy Stepan, *Picturing Tropical Nature*, 36.
2. Hubert Howe Bancroft, *California Inter Pocula*, 160.
3. Robert Tomes, *Panama in 1855*, 56.
4. *Mestizaje* resulted from contact between Europeans, West Indians, and Latin Americans and the indigenous people. Aims McGuinness offers a nuanced account of Panama's history of interethnic contact in *Path of Empire: Panama and the California Gold Rush*, 22–25.
5. John Major, *Prize Possession: The United States Government and the Panama Canal, 1903–1979*, 63.
6. Eric Williams, *From Columbus to Castro: The History of the Caribbean, 1492–1969*, 422–23.
7. Max Salabarría Patiño, *La Ciudad de Colón en los Predios de Historia* (Panama: Litho Editorial Chen, 2002), 17.
8. Thomas Graham Grier, *On the Canal Zone*, 15–36; Máximo Ochy, "Vida Material en la Zona del Canal de Panamá" (2003), permanent exhibit of El Museo del Canal Interoceanico, Panama City.
9. George Westerman, "Historical Notes on West Indians on the Isthmus of Panama," *Phylon* 22 (1961): 342.
10. On Bottle Alley prostitution and gambling, see David McCullough, *The Path Between the Seas: The Creation of the Panama Canal, 1870–1914*, 147.
11. Westerman, "Historical Notes," 345.
12. On the violent nature of everyday life in the Canal Zone, see Lancelot Lewis, *The West Indian in Panama*; Julie Greene, *The Canal Builders: Making America's Empire at the Panama Canal*; and Velma Newton, *The Silver Men: West Indian Labour Migration to Panama, 1850–1914*.
13. Greene, *Canal Builders*, 136–37.
14. Lewis, *West Indian*, 45–77; Rhonda Frederick, *Colón Man a Come: Mythographies of Panama Canal Migration*, 19–90; Greene, *Canal Builders*, 133–58.

15. Westerman,"Historical Notes," 341–42.

16. WFP, undated.

17. Data on Panama schools are from *Schooling in the Panama Canal Zone, 1904–1979,* 101–106.

18. Ibid.

19. Colin Grant, *Negro with a Hat: The Rise and Fall of Marcus Garvey,* 146.

20. WFP, undated.

21. *A Trip—Panama Canal,* 165.

22. That "Wind in the Palms" may be read autobiographically is indicated in Walrond's essay "From British Guiana to Roundway," where he writes, "As a junior clerk, checking and filing the reports on the war to exterminate the mosquito, observing the comings and goings of the field staff, overhearing talk about the tenements unfit for human habitation and about the case of the Sanitary Inspector who had involved the Department in a lawsuit in his 'cleaning up' zeal over in Colon, I obtained a kind of 'bird's eye' view of the measures which had not only made the construction of the canal possible, but had made the Canal Zone one of the healthiest places in Latin America" (1).

23. Linguists call this *front focusing,* introducing the main verb or clause then repeating it in its standard syntactic place to create emphasis. See Shondel Nero, "Notes on Caribbean English" in *"Winds Can Wake Up the Dead": An Eric Walrond Reader,* ed. Louis Parascandola, 46.

24. Three other Colón stories Walrond wrote in England are discussed in chapter 10.

25. WFP, undated.

26. Albert V. McGeachy, *The History of the Panama* Star & Herald, 3.

27. "Sixty-Seven Years Old Today, a Retrospect," *Star & Herald* (February 28, 1916): 4.

28. *Star & Herald,* August 1, 1917; August 4, 1917.

29. Grant, *Negro with a Hat,* 147.

30. Robert Hill, *The Marcus Garvey and United Negro Improvement Association Papers, Vol. I,* 182.

31. Preface to "The Godless City"; "Adventures in Misunderstanding."

3. NEW YORK (1918–1923)

1. The ship's manifest for June 20, 1918, is available at www.ellisisland.org. His name is misspelled Wolrond.

2. The 1920 Federal Census records roughly nine thousand West Indian residents of Brooklyn and thirty-six thousand in Harlem out of ninety-six thousand total in the United States.

3. The immigration wave in which Walrond participated led to a five-fold increase in the number of foreign-born blacks in the United States in thirty years, from roughly twenty thousand at the turn of the century to nearly one hundred thousand in 1930. In New York City, the foreign-born black population more than tripled during the decade in

which Walrond arrived, the vast majority of whom were West Indian. See Philip Kasinitz, *Caribbean New York: Black Immigrants and the Politics of Race*, 25, 41.

4. "Harlem Happenings," *Chicago Defender* (August 24, 1918): 5.

5. Walrond's 1927 application to the Guggenheim Foundation included a detailed work history. He reported working a year and a half at the Broad Street Hospital. See also Walrond, "From British Guiana," 2.

6. "Additions to the New Broad Street Hospital," *New York Times* (Feb. 23, 1919).

7. Ira de Augustine Reid, *The Negro Immigrant: His Background, Characteristics, and Social Adjustment, 1899–1937*, 118–21; Winston James, *Holding Aloft the Banner of Ethiopia: Caribbean Radicalism in Early Twentieth Century America*, 80.

8. See, for example, "The Color of the Caribbean," *The World Tomorrow* (May 1927): 225–27.

9. Reid, *Negro Immigrant*, 68.

10. Winston James, *Holding Aloft the Banner of Ethiopia*, 85.

11. James, *Holding Aloft*, 85.

12. James Baldwin, *Notes of a Native Son*, 165–66.

13. James Weldon Johnson, *Black Manhattan*, 3, 147.

14. "Brine" (1924), WFP.

15. Tony Martin, *African Fundamentalism: A Literary and Cultural Anthology of Garvey's Harlem Renaissance*, 7–8.

16. Marcus Garvey, "Editorial," *Negro World* (Dec. 6, 1919): 1.

17. Marcus Garvey, *Message to the People: The Course of African Philosophy*, 5.

18. Bone, Unpublished biography, 2.

19. David Levering Lewis writes, "For Walrond, debonair and superior, to have flirted with Garveyism was a measure of the bitterness of those days" (*When Harlem Was in Vogue*, 128).

20. Johnson, *Black Manhattan*, 156.

21. Ibid., 256.

22. James, *Holding Aloft*, 111.

23. Robert Hill, *The Marcus Garvey and United Negro Improvement Association Papers, Vol. XI*, ccxli–ccccxlvii; Colin Grant, *Negro with a Hat: The Rise and Fall of Marcus Garvey*, 148.

24. Julie Greene, *The Canal Builders: Making America's Empire at the Panama Canal*, 368–69; Michael Conniff, *Black Labor on a White Canal: Panama, 1904–1981*, 29–52.

25. Grant, *Negro With a Hat*, 148.

26. Hill, *MG/UNIA Papers, Vol. II*, 181.

27. Tony Martin, *Literary Garveyism*, 168.

28. By early 1920, *Negro World*'s circulation was roughly ten thousand; the following year, under Harrison's guidance, it rose to fifty thousand. See Jeffrey Perry, *A Hubert Harrison Reader*, 441, fn 18.

29. Walrond appeared on the masthead as assistant to the editor on December 24, 1921; his title changed to associate editor on March 18, 1922.

30. Tony Martin charges Walrond with opportunism in *Literary Garveyism*. Robert Bone's characterization of the *Negro World* writing as dilettantism appears in chapter 2 of his unpublished Walrond biography.

31. Garvey was denounced in the pages of *The Crisis*, *Opportunity*, and *The Messenger*, the most influential black journals, as a "monumental monkey," an "unquestioned fool and ignoramus," and "the most dangerous enemy of the Negro race in America and in the world." See John Runcie, "Marcus Garvey and the Harlem Renaissance," *Afro-Americans in New York Life and History* 10:2 (July 1986): 10–11.

32. On *Batouala* in relation to anticolonial French literature, see Brent Hayes Edwards, *The Practice of Diaspora: Literature, Translation, and the Rise of Black Internationalism*, 69–98.

33. Lewis, *Vogue*, 92.

34. Martin, *African Fundamentalism*, 24–5.

35. Robert Hill, *Marcus Garvey: Life and Lessons*, 203.

36. Martin, *Literary Garveyism*, 128–9.

37. Hughes to Locke, May 1923. ALP, Box 164–38, Folder 5.

38. Walrond believed the silence about Pushkin's African ancestry indicated "a journalistic conspiracy to suppress every ennobling fact about the Negro" (Martin, *African Fundamentalism*, 134). He reviewed white authors, including Max Eastman, Harold Stearns, T. S. Stribling, and Lafcadio Hearn, but focused on people of African descent.

39. Martin, *African Fundamentalism*, 319.

40. Blanche Colton Williams, *How To Study "The Best Short Stories,"* vii.

41. City College transcript, GFP.

42. Andrew M. Fearnley, "Eclectic Club," 327.

43. Martin, *Literary Garveyism*, 36.

44. Claude McKay, *A Long Way from Home*, 93. *Tenue de rigueur* translates roughly as "formally dressed."

45. These included the Jamaicans Claude McKay, J. A. Rogers, Amy Ashwood, and W. A. Domingo; the Communists Cyril Briggs (Nevis), Grace Campbell (Jamaica/Georgia), and Otto Huiswoud (Dutch Guiana); Arthur Schomburg, Eulalie Spence (a classmate of Walrond's at City College and a Jamaican-born playwright), and the redoubtable Hubert Harrison (St. Croix).

46. Louis Chude-Sokei, *The Last "Darky": Bert Williams, Black-on-Black Minstrelsy, and the African Diaspora*, 5.

47. Despite the provincial sound of its name, the *Dearborn Independent*, published by Henry Ford, boasted a national circulation of more than a half million in the mid-1920s.

48. On the polyvocality of Bert Williams' performances and Walrond's commentary thereon, see Chude-Sokei, *The Last "Darky,"* 111–12.

49. Ibid., 111.

50. Ibid., 112.

51. Led by Attorney General Palmer, the U.S. Department of Justice sought to suppress black radicalism in print, issuing the report "Radicalism and Sedition among the Negroes as Reflected in Their Publications."

52. Perry, *A Hubert Harrison Reader*, 189.

53. Ibid., 192.

54. Ibid., 190.

55. Ibid., 184.

56. Martin, *Literary Garveyism*, 124–32.

57. Runcie, "Marcus Garvey and the Harlem Renaissance," 8.

58. Grant, *Negro With a Hat*, 337.

59. W. E. B. Du Bois, "Back to Africa," *Crisis* (Feb. 1923): 542.

60. W. E. B. Du Bois, "A Lunatic or a Traitor," *Crisis* (May 1924): 8.

61. Martin, *African Fundamentalism*, 91.

4. THE NEW NEGRO (1923-1926)

1. Frank E. L. Stewart, "Eric Walrond, *Tropic Death*, and the Predicament of the Colonial Expatriate Writer," *Hiroshima Shudo University Studies in the Humanities and Sciences* 38:2 (1997): 42–43.

2. Robert Bone and Louis J. Parascandola, "An Ellis Island of the Soul," *Afro-Americans in New York Life and History* 34:2 (July 2010): 48; Robert Bone, *Down Home: A History of Afro-American Short Fiction*, 185–94.

3. Edna Worthley Underwood, "West Indian Literature: Some Negro Poets of Panama," *West Indian Review* [Kingston] (March 1936): 37.

4. Eugene Gordon, "The Negro Press," *Annals of the American Academy of Political and Social Sciences* 140 (Nov. 1928): 252.

5. Carl Wade, Robert Bone, and Louis Parascandola, "Eric Walrond and the Dynamics of White Patronage," 151–57.

6. David Levering Lewis, *When Harlem Was in Vogue*, xvi.

7. September 15, 1922. Edna Worthley Underwood correspondence, Leonard Axe Library, Pittsburg State University, Kansas. The author wishes to thank Janette Mauk for providing copies.

8. Revised, these became "The Godless City," *Success Magazine* (1924); "The Voodoo's Revenge," *Opportunity* (1925); "The Wharf Rats," *Tropic Death* (1926); and "The Consulate," *The Spectator* [London] (1936).

9. "The Penitent Shows Alexander Pushkin, Russia's Great Negro Poet, Was Influenced By Shelley," *Negro World*, October 21, 1922. Two weeks later, Walrond's "Books" column included several titles by Underwood.

10. Nance, interview, 13.

11. See Bone and Parascandola, "An Ellis Island."

12. Tony Martin, *African Fundamentalism: A Literary and Cultural Anthology of Garvey's Harlem Renaissance*, 104.

13. Walrond's claims may sound overstated, but as Irma Watkins-Owens explains, Holstein's "preeminence in fraternal circles and crusade for Virgin Island citizenship were known

and respected, [and] his support of the movement for a civil government was believed to be a key factor in the removal of U.S. naval rule." *Blood Relations: Caribbean Immigrants and the Harlem Community, 1900–1930*, 145–46.

14. Tracing "the trope of the new negro," Henry Louis Gates identifies the period between 1895 and 1925 as crucial to the term's elaboration. Some credit Harrison with having popularized the term, others note the currency Garvey gave it before it was adopted by intellectuals and artists, while still others credit Booker T. Washington.

15. A. Philip Randolph and Chandler Owen, "The New Negro—What Is He?" *The Messenger* (August 1920): 73.

16. The United States purchased St. Croix, St. Thomas, and St. John from Denmark for $25 million in 1917.

17. Its mission was to present "authoritative and unbiased information from both hemispheres, and for interpreting this information from a world standpoint. The *Interpreter*'s purpose is to foster amity among the nations; cooperation between Capital and Labor; equal opportunity for all; and liberty under law and order." *International Interpreter* (May 26, 1923): 1.

18. Reprinted in Martin, *African Fundamentalism*, 283.

19. Ibid., 282.

20. "Since I have been in America, it has been my privilege to know some of the finest people in the world here. Unheralded, unsung, untrumpeted, I go into the most amazing of places" ("Godless" 33).

21. Michelle Stephens, "Eric Walrond's *Tropic Death* and the Discontents of American Modernity," 175.

22. Walrond to Bennett, May 22, 1946. Bennett's "Outline Toward a Memoir" suggests Walrond's early formative presence. Gwendolyn Bennett Papers, SCNYPL.

23. Ibid.

24. Lewis, *Vogue*, 128.

25. Nance, interview, 15.

26. Ibid., 16.

27. Lewis, *Vogue*, 129.

28. J. Saunders Redding, "Playing the Numbers," *North American Review* 236 (Dec. 1934): 533.

29. For the second edition of *Tropic Death*, Walrond rededicated the book to his daughters. It is likely that Holstein provided Walrond an apartment and a stipend.

30. Cullen to Jackman, July 1, 1923, Countee Cullen Papers, JWJ, Box 1, Folder 19.

31. Ibid., August 10, 1923.

32. Page numbers refer to Louis Parascandola, ed., *"Winds Can Wake Up the Dead": An Eric Walrond Reader*.

33. By *discourse of coloniality* I mean the modes of representing and apprehending that emerge from conditions of colonialism and the elaboration of colonial subjectivity, as distinct from *colonialist discourse*, the modes of representing and apprehending that developed among Western nations pursuing colonial projects.

34. Louis Chude-Sokei, *The Last "Darky": Bert Williams, Black-on-Black Minstrelsy, and the African Diaspora*, 5.

35. At its height in 1927 and 1928, *Opportunity*'s circulation was 11,000, roughly 12 percent of *The Crisis* peak circulation in 1919. See Patrick J. Gilpin, "Charles S. Johnson: Entrepreneur of the Harlem Renaissance," 297, fn 27; Abby Johnson and Ronald Johnson, *Propaganda and Aesthetics: The Literary Politics of Afro-American Magazines in the Twentieth Century*, 35.

36. Langston Hughes, *The Big Sea*, 218.

37. Zora Neale Hurston, *Dust Tracks on a Road: An Autobiography*, 168, 175.

38. Lewis, *Vogue*, 90.

39. Cullen to Locke, August 26, 1923, ALP, Box 164–22, Folder 36.

40. Locke to Cullen, undated, ALP, Box 164–22, Folder 36.

41. *Brooklyn Eagle*, February 10, 1924.

42. Walrond to Cullen, December 8, 1923, Eric Walrond Papers, ARC.

43. David Levering Lewis claims Johnson "was determined to exploit the fascination with Afro-America in order to launch an effort at racial breakthrough" (*Vogue* xx).

44. George Hutchinson, *The Harlem Renaissance in Black and White*, 176.

45. Johnson to Locke, February 29 and March 4, 1924, ALP, Box 164–40, Folder 36.

46. Hutchinson, *Harlem*, 390.

47. Arna Bontemps, "The Awakening: A Memoir," 10.

48. Hutchinson, *Harlem*, 389–93.

49. Nance, interview, 13.

50. Charles S. Johnson, "The New Generation," *Opportunity* 2 (March 1924): 68.

51. Johnson to Locke, March 15, 1924, ALP, Box 164–40, Folder 36.

52. "The Debut of the Younger School of Negro Writers," *Opportunity* (May 1924): 143–44.

53. Ibid.; Lewis, *Vogue*, 93–5.

54. Bontemps, "The Awakening," 11.

55. Lewis, *Vogue*, 95.

56. *New York Times Book Review*, April 13, 1924.

57. Walrond to Locke, March 26, 1924, ALP, Box 164–40, Folder 36.

58. Robert Philipson, "The Harlem Renaissance as Postcolonial Phenomenon," in *African American Review* 40 (Spring, 2006): 145.

59. "Debut of the Younger School," 145.

60. *The Messenger*, July 1922: 477. Irma Watkins-Owens's excellent analysis of the nativism of the "Garvey Must Go" campaign appears in *Blood Relations*, 112–35.

61. Alain Locke, "The New Negro," 4, 6, 11–12.

62. Chude-Sokei, *The Last "Darky,"* 112.

63. David Levering Lewis, *W. E. B. Du Bois: The Fight for Equality and the American Century, 1919–1936*, 173.

64. Walrond to Locke, April 23, 1924, ALP, Box 164–91, Folder 38.

65. Ibid., May 5, 1924.

66. Charlotte Billet to Locke, May 16, 1924, ALP, Box 164–40, Folder 25.

67. No manuscript of *Tiger Lilly* survives.

68. In the same note in which he chastised Cullen for denying his homosexuality, Locke bristled, "Yes, I will plead guilty when the bitter time comes 'to corrupting the youth'—but there they are—as Socrates would have said—my spiritual children—Jean Toomer—Langston Hughes, Countee Cullen, Lewis Alexander, Richard Bruce—Donald Hayes—Albert Dunham—there they are—can a bad tree bring forth good fruit?" Undated letter, ALP, Box 164–22, Folder 36.

69. Locke and Kellogg excluded Fauset from the Harlem issue of *Survey*, and *The New Negro* only included her essay "The Gift of Laughter" at Du Bois' insistence (Lewis, *Du Bois*, 162).

70. W. E. B. Du Bois, "Mrs. Fauset's Confusion," *The New Republic* (July 30, 1924): 274.

71. Cullen to Jackman, August 14, 1924, JWJ, MSS 7, Series 1.

72. Hughes to Cullen, undated, ARC.

73. Walrond to Locke, undated, ALP, Box 164–91, Folder 38.

74. Ibid., June 25, 1925.

75. Walrond to Van Vechten, February 16, 1925. Carl Van Vechten Papers, JWJ.

76. Dorothy Scarborough, *The Supernatural in Modern English Fiction*, 1–2.

77. Columbia University transcript, GFP.

78. Joseph Freeman, publicity director at the American Civil Liberties Union and former assistant editor at *The Liberator*, corresponded with Walrond about this work, July 9 and August 20, 1924, JFC, Box 40, Folder 14.

79. Pagination refers to Parascandola, ed., *Winds*.

80. Allison Davis, "Our Negro 'Intellectuals,'" *Crisis* 35 (August 1928): 269.

81. Countée Cullen, "The Dark Tower," *Opportunity* 6 (March 1928): 90.

82. Henry Louis Gates, Jr., "The Black Man's Burden," 233.

83. Gloria Hull, *Color Sex and Poetry*; A. B. Christa Schwarz, *Gay Voices of the Harlem Renaissance*; George Chauncey, *Gay New York: Gender, Urban Culture, and the Making of the Gay Male World, 1890–1940*; Eric Garber, "A Spectacle in Color," in Martin Duberman, ed., *Hidden From History: Reclaiming the Gay and Lesbian Past* (New York: Dutton, 1991): 318–33; Gary Holcomb, *Claude McKay, Code Name Sasha* (Gainesville: University Press of Florida, 2009); and James F. Wilson, *Bulldaggers, Pansies, and Chocolate Babies* (Ann Arbor: University of Michigan Press, 2011).

84. George Chauncey, *Gay New York*, 12–13.

85. Charles Molesworth discusses this issue with sensitivity and insight in his 2012 biography of Cullen, *And Bid Him Sing: a Biography of Countée Cullen*, 4, 50; and in his article "Countée Cullen's Reputation," *Transition* 107 (2012): 67–77.

86. Cullen to Jackman, August 14, 1924, JWJ, MSS 7, Series 1.

87. Cullen to Locke, September 20, 1924, ALP, Box 164–22, Folder 37.

88. Ibid., October 27, 1924.

89. Ibid., October 31 and November 1, 1924.

90. Shane Vogel, *The Scene of Harlem Cabaret: Race, Sexuality, Performance*, 4.

91. Ibid.

92. Ibid., 133; Lewis, *Vogue*, xix.

93. Charles Johnson kept radicals off the Civic Club guest list, and the Harlem issue of *Survey* omitted prominent radicals such as Harrison, Briggs, and Randolph.

94. Vogel, *Harlem Cabaret*,133.

95. Hubert Harrison, "The Cabaret School of Negro Literature and Art," 357.

96. Covarrubias had impressed Mexico City's artists by age eighteen. His preferred form, caricature, was "a vital national tradition," "a powerful forum for comment and expression," and his work was syndicated "from Cuba to Buenos Aires." Arriving in New York in 1923, Covarrubias took New York by storm and within a few years "knew everybody" in the arts and the major philanthropists. See Wendy Wick Reaves, *Celebrity Caricature in America*, 164, 170, 180.

97. Schwarz, *Gay Voices*, 141.

98. Kathleen Pfeiffer, introduction to Carl Van Vechten, *Nigger Heaven*, xviii.

99. Ibid., xx.

100. Ibid.

101. Van Vechten did favors for friends that he did not want publicized, including securing a substantial loan for the Robesons in 1925. See correspondence with Marinoff, June 3 and July 2, 1925, CVV. Emily Bernard's *Carl Van Vechten and the Harlem Renaissance* (New Haven: Yale University Press, 2012) includes illuminating accounts of these relationships.

102. Jackman to Van Vechten, February 14, 1925, Van Vechten Papers, JWJ.

103. Hughes to Van Vechten, May 17, 1925, Van Vechten Papers, JWJ.

104. Carl Van Vechten, *The Splendid Drunken Twenties: Selections from the Daybooks, 1922–1930*, 58.

105. Ibid.

106. Ibid., 60.

107. Arthur Pell to Agnes Jackson, July 14, 1965, LP.

108. Van Vechten, *Splendid*, 74–5.

109. Walrond to Van Vechten, February 16, 1925, Van Vechten Papers, JWJ.

110. Van Vechten, *Splendid*, 77.

111. Walrond to Van Vechten March 20, 1925, Van Vechten Papers, JWJ.

112. Van Vechten, *Splendid*, 79.

113. The proposed series became "Black Bohemia," November 1925.

114. Walrond to Freeman, May 8, 1925, JFC.

115. Van Vechten to Marinoff, May 8, 1925, CVV, Box 36.

116. Walrond to Locke, June 25, 1925, ALP, Box 164–91, Folder 38; Walrond to Schomburg, November 13, 1924, Arthur Schomburg Papers, SCNYPL, Box 7, Folder 55.

117. Undated (1925), Aaron Douglas Papers, SCNYPL.

118. *Opportunity*, October 1926: 318.

119. Walrond to Freeman, May 8, 1925, JFC.

120. Van Vechten, *Splendid*, 83.

121. Correspondence of May 8 and May 13, 1925, JFC.

122. Van Vechten, *Splendid*, 83–8.

123. Walrond to Van Vechten, June 16, 1925, Carl Van Vechten Papers, JWJ.

124. Van Vechten, *Splendid*, 89.

125. Walrond to Locke, June 25, 1925, ALP, Box 164–91, Folder 38.

126. Ibid., July 25, 1925.

127. Van Vechten, *Splendid*, 89–93, 117, 133, 256. After the 1926 *Opportunity* dinner, Walrond and Van Vechten seem not to have met again until a chance encounter in Paris in 1929.

128. "An Open Letter," *Opportunity* 27 (1949): 1.

129. Walrond's responsibilities at *Opportunity* are difficult to ascertain. The business manager secured advertising accounts, wrote copy, and conducted the correspondence related to the journal's production, circulation, and sponsored events. Walrond likely shared responsibility for dealing with the foundations funding the Department of Research and Investigations, under whose auspices *Opportunity* was published (Nancy J. Weiss, *The National Urban League: 1910–1940*, 156–57). On the obstacles to researching the Urban League's history see Weiss, *National Urban League*, vii, and Touré F. Reed, *Not Alms But Opportunity: The Urban League and the Politics of Racial Uplift, 1910–1950*, xiii.

130. Walrond to Locke, July 25, 1925, ALP, Box 164–91, Folder 38.

131. Stuart Hall, "Negotiating Caribbean Identities," 35–6.

5. *TROPIC DEATH*

1. Kenneth Ramchand, *The West Indian Novel and Its Background*, 240.

2. Mary White Ovington, "West India Tales," *The Chicago Defender* (Jan. 1, 1927): A1.

3. Edouard Glissant, *Caribbean Discourse: Selected Essays*, 145.

4. "The Ebony Flute," *Opportunity*, August 26, 1926: 260.

5. Awards Competition 1926, HFP.

6. Edward Kamau Braithwaite, *History of the Voice: The Development of Nation Language in Anglophone Caribbean Poetry*, 10.

7. Carl A. Wade, "African American Aesthetics and the Short Fiction of Eric Walrond," *CLA Journal* 42:4 (June 1999): 404.

8. Ibid., 406.

9. The *New York Times Book Review* said Walrond "maintains an almost Olympian detachment toward human affairs." "Eric Walrond's Tales and Other New Works of Fiction," *New York Times Book Review* (Oct. 17, 1926): 6.

10. Boni & Liveright Fall 1926 Catalogue, HFP.

11. George Hutchinson, *The Harlem Renaissance in Black and White*, 367–72; Charles Egleston, ed., *Dictionary of Literary Biography 288: The House of Boni & Liveright, 1917–1933*, 3–4.

12. Boni & Liveright Fall 1926 Catalogue, HFP.

13. Advertisement, *New York Times Book Review*, April 13, 1924. Claims about *Tropic Death*'s "objectivity" echoed through reviews and later scholarship. Hugh Gloster's

Negro Voices in American Fiction, written amidst the civil rights movement, exemplified this tendency: "Raising no issues and reaching no conclusions," wrote Gloster, Walrond "is content to picture objectively the economic and social disorganization of Negro life in the region" (181).

14. Julie Greene, *The Canal Builders: Making America's Empire at the Panama Canal*, 2.

15. As recently as 2005, David McCullough, author of the prizewinning history *The Path Between the Seas: The Creation of the Panama Canal*, attributed the American success to an exceptional "gift for improvisation," calling the Canal "an extraordinary work of civilization" (Greene, *Canal Builders*, 3).

16. *Scientific American* drew visual analogies, equating the excavation's volume with a ditch fifty-five feet wide and ten feet deep across the United States; The *New York Times* devoted a section of a 1912 issue to exquisitely detailed drawings, and popular histories appeared by the dozens.

17. *My Trip Through the Panama Canal*, Leonard Carpenter Collection, Digital Library of the Caribbean (http://dloc.com/results/?t=my trip through the panama canal).

18. See Rhonda Frederick, *Colón Man a Come: Mythographies of Panama Canal Migration*, 1–18.

19. Michelle Stephens, "Eric Walrond's *Tropic Death* and the Discontents of American Modernity," 175.

20. Glissant, *Caribbean Discourse*, 147.

21. Edward Kamau Brathwaite, *History of the Voice: The Development of Nation Language in Anglophone Caribbean Poetry*, 13.

22. Louis Parascandola, ed., *"Winds Can Wake Up the Dead": An Eric Walrond Reader*, 44–45.

23. Stuart Hall, "Negotiating Caribbean Identities," 35–36.

24. Krista A. Thompson, *An Eye for the Tropics: Tourism, Photography, and Framing the Caribbean Picturesque*, 4–5.

25. Ibid., 6–7.

26. Ibid., 23.

27. Ibid.

28. Art historian Richard J. Powell makes a similar claim about Walrond's strategy of subversion from within the discourse of tropicality in "The Picturesque, Miss Nottage, and the Caribbean Sublime," *Small Axe: A Caribbean Journal of Criticism* 12 (February 2008): 164.

29. Jan Carew, "The Caribbean Writer and Exile," *The Journal of Black Studies* 8 (June 1978): 464.

30. Aimé Césaire, *Discourse on Colonialism*, 52. Art historian Peter Wood argues that Homer's 1899 painting "deals in subtle and extended ways with slavery, U.S. imperialism in the Caribbean, southern race wars, and Jim Crow segregation." Homer allegedly altered the painting to make it more affirmative, adding a rescue ship on the horizon after a poor initial reception. *Weathering the Storm: Inside Winslow Homer's Gulf Stream*, 91.

31. Mary Seacole, *The Wonderful Adventures of Mrs. Seacole in Many Lands*, 11.

32. Greene, *Canal Builders*, 130.

33. Michael Conniff, *Black Labor on a White Canal: Panama, 1904–1981*, 30–31.

34. Greene, *Canal Builders*, 132.

35. John Bassett includes an extensive, though not comprehensive, list of reviews of *Tropic Death* in *Harlem in Review: Critical Reactions to Black American Writers, 1917–1939* (Selinsgrove, PA: Susquehanna University Press, 1992): 65–67.

36. Langston Hughes, "Marl Dust and West Indian Sun," *New York Herald Tribune* (Dec 5, 1926): 9; Robert Herrick, "Review of *Tropic Death*," *The New Republic* (November 10, 1926): 332; "Eric Walrond's Tales," 6; Joel A. Rogers, "Book Reviews," *Pittsburgh Courier* (March 5, 1927): 8.

37. "Eric Walrond's Tales," 6; Devere Allen, "Living Stories of Tropic Death," *The World Tomorrow* (November 1926); Herrick, "Review of *Tropic Death*," 332; Hughes, "Marl Dust," 9; V. F. Calverton, "Ground Swells in Fiction," *Survey* 57 (November 1, 1926): 160; Mary White Ovington, "West India Tales," *The Chicago Defender* (Jan. 1, 1927): A1.

38. "Five Books," *Crisis* (January 1927): 152.

39. Benjamin Brawley, "The Negro Literary Renaissance," *Southern Workman* 56 (April 1927): 179.

40. Ibid., 180.

41. Hughes, "Marl Dust," 6.

42. Rogers, "Book Reviews," *Pittsburgh Courier* (March 5, 1927): 8.

43. Ibid.

44. *The New Yorker* (December 4, 1926): 58–59.

45. "Eric Walrond's Tales," 6; Herrick, "Review," 332; Egleston, *Dictionary*, 406; Devere Allen, "Living Stories of *Tropic Death*."

46. Waldo Frank, "In Our Language," *Opportunity* (Nov. 1926): 352.

47. Ibid.

48. Walrond to Freeman, May 8, 1925, JFC.

49. Hughes, "Marl Dust," 6.

6. A PERSON OF DISTINCTION (1926–1929)

1. Charles Johnson, "Editorials," *Opportunity* 5 (January 1927): 3; Dewey R. Jones, "The Bookshelf," *Chicago Defender* (September 17, 1927): A1; Robert Herrick, "Review of *Tropic Death*," *The New Republic* (November 10, 1926): 332.

2. "Contest Awards," *Opportunity* 3 (May 1925): 142–43. Documents on literary awards appear in Cary Wintz, ed., *The Harlem Renaissance, 1920–1940, Vol. I: The Emergence of the Harlem Renaissance*.

3. Nancy J. Weiss, *The National Urban League: 1910–1940*, 216–33.

4. Lowell J. Ragatz, *The Fall of the Planter Class in the British Caribbean, 1763–1833*, 27.

5. "Some Economic Aspects of Negro Migrations," *Opportunity* 5 (Oct. 1927): 297. Johnson editorialized on West Indians in November 1924, and Domingo wrote that year

about the restrictive impact of the Johnson-Reed Act on the Caribbean. But *Opportunity*'s national orientation is evident.

6. Exceptions included occasional articles by Alain Locke and Albert Barnes on African art and a testy exchange between Locke and René Maran about French colonialism.

7. Charles S. Johnson, "Editorials," *Opportunity* 4 (November 1926): 334.

8. Walrond to Schomburg, September 22, 1926, Arthur Schomburg Papers, SCNYPL, Box 7, Folder 55.

9. Lucius J. M. Malmin, "A Caribbean Fact and Fancy," *Opportunity* (Nov. 1926): 343.

10. Casper Holstein, "The Virgin Islands: Past and Present," *Opportunity* (Nov. 1926): 345.

11. W. A. Domingo, "The West Indies," *Opportunity* (Nov. 1926): 341.

12. Ethelred Brown and Eugene Kinckle Jones, "West Indian-American Relations: A Symposium," *Opportunity* (Nov. 1926): 355.

13. Kenneth Warren, "Appeals for (Mis-)Recognition: Theorizing the Diaspora," 404.

14. Brent Hayes Edwards, *The Practice of Diaspora: Literature, Translation, and the Rise of Black Internationalism*, 5.

15. Charles S. Johnson, "Editorials," *Opportunity* 4 (November 1926): 337.

16. Walrond to Cullen, October 20, 1925, Countee Cullen Papers, ARC.

17. Ibid., October 26, 1925.

18. Ibid., November 19, 1925.

19. Cullen to Locke, May 27, November 19, and December 5, 1925, ALP, Box 164–22.

20. Walrond to Cullen, November 23, 1925, Countee Cullen Papers, ARC.

21. Baer to Locke, December 19, 1925, ALP, Box 164–10.

22. Walrond to Schomburg, December 24, 1925, Arthur Schomburg Papers, SCNYPL.

23. Walrond to McKay, February 14, 1927, Claude McKay Collection, Series I, JWJ.

24. Ibid., June 7 and June 28, 1927.

25. McKay to Cunard, September 18, 1932, Nancy Cunard Papers, HRHRC.

26. Ibid.

27. Undated correspondence, ALP, Box 164–91, Folder 38.

28. Kathleen Currie, "Interviews with Marvel Jackson Cooke," 45–46.

29. Ibid., 47. In addition to Kathleen Currie's interview, biographical information appears in Richard Pearson, "Marvel Cooke Dies at 99," *Washington Post*, December 2, 2000: B7; Barbara Ransby, *Ella Baker and the Black Freedom Movement*, 76–77; and Lashawn Harris, "Marvel Cooke: Investigative Journalist, Communist, and Black Radical Subject," *Journal for the Study of Radicalism* 6 (2012): 91–126.

30. Currie 45–64.

31. Ibid., 46–47, 61–62.

32. Ibid.

33. Ibid., 2–3, 7–8.

34. When their essay appeared in 1935 "the modern concept of feminism was still a foreign concept to most Americans, black and white," historian Barbara Ransby observes, "Yet the black feminist notion of intersecting systems of oppression as the cornerstone of

black women's collective experience was an observable reality, and in their article [Jackson] Cooke and Baker came close to articulating it as a theory" (*Ella Baker*, 77).

35. Ibid., 36.

36. Ibid.

37. Scholarship on Gurdjieff's influence in Harlem has been reductive, compounding the lack of clarity about Walrond's involvement. Jon Woodson's *To Make a New Race* documents the participation of New Negro artists and writers, but its reach exceeds its grasp. For a discussion of Gurdjieff and Harlem that avoids either dismissing him or credulously identifying his influence everywhere, see George Hutchinson, *In Search of Nella Larsen: A Biography of the Color Line*, 183–86.

38. Jon Woodson, *To Make a New Race: Gurdjieff, Toomer, and the Harlem Renaissance*, 6–7.

39. Langston Hughes, *The Big Sea*, 243.

40. Hutchinson, *In Search*, 185.

41. Douglas to Alta Sawyer, undated, Aaron Douglas Papers, Box 1, Folder 3, SCNYPL.

42. Hutchinson, *In Search*, 183.

43. Jon Woodson, *To Make a New Race*, 39.

44. Ibid., 40.

45. Ibid., 33.

46. From "The Negro Emergent," an unpublished manuscript that "was the basis of, or a version of" the talk Toomer gave at the 135th Street library (Hutchinson, *In Search*, 541, fn 26).

47. Wallace Thurman, *Infants of the Spring*, 145.

48. Alain Locke, "Negro Youth Speaks," 51.

49. Its first year in print, *Cane* sold 565 copies, then 1,200–1,500 copies per year immediately thereafter. *Tropic Death* sold 2,000–2,500 copies per year its first few years in print. W.W. Norton Papers, Series III, Butler Library, Columbia University. In *Opportunity*, Cullen reported in January 1927 that *Tropic Death* was the fourth most requested book at the Harlem branch.

50. David Levering Lewis, *When Harlem Was in Vogue*, 189.

51. "Survey of the Month," *Opportunity* 5 (January 1927): 30–31.

52. Wallace Thurman, "Negro Artists and the Negro," 37.

53. Martin Duberman, *Paul Robeson*, 74.

54. "Survey of the Month," *Opportunity* 5 (February 1927): 61.

55. "Side Lights on Society," *New York Amsterdam News* (October 27, 1926): 4.

56. NUL, Part I, Box J1.

57. Hutchinson, *In Search*, 262.

58. Amy H. Kirschke, *Aaron Douglas: Art, Race, and the Harlem Renaissance*, 36.

59. "Harlemites Open New Night Club," *New York Amsterdam News* (October 12, 1927): 7.

60. Executive Secretary Eugene Kinckle Jones enumerated the business manager's responsibilities: "To increase the circulation and the advertisements of the magazine, to make contacts with the younger Negro writers and to make contacts with literary contributors

of the past and to reach new persons." Executive Secretary Report, November 19, 1928, Part I, Box A1, NUL. No personnel file on Walrond survives in the Urban League's records.

61. Walrond to Johnson, September 23, 1925, JWJ, Series I, Box 22, Folder 522.
62. Johnson to Locke, January 27, 1925, ALP, Box 164–40.
63. Memo from Haynes, Dec. 28, 1925, HFP, Box 51.
64. Walrond to Olyve Jeter, August 11, 1926, HFP, Box 51.
65. Spingarn to Haynes, Oct 21, 1926, HFP, Box 51.
66. Recommendations from Friede, Liveright, and Hergesheimer, HFP, Box 51.
67. Friede to Walrond, January 27, 1927, LP.
68. Johnson to Locke, February 1, 1927, ALP, Box 164–40.
69. Floyd Calvin, "Eric D. Walrond Leaves 'Opportunity' to Devote Entire Time to Writing," *Pittsburgh Courier* (February 12, 1927): 2.
70. "Eric Walrond," *Opportunity* 5 (March 1927): 67.
71. Harmon Foundation Papers (HFP).
72. Ibid.
73. Ibid.
74. Ibid.
75. Ibid.
76. Walrond to Haynes, January 11, 1928, HFP, Box 51.
77. Gloria Hull, *Color, Sex, and Poetry: Three Women Writers of the Harlem Renaissance*, 134, 175.
78. George Hutchinson, *The Harlem Renaissance in Black and White*, 214.
79. Letters from Zona Gale and Professor O'Shea of the University of Wisconsin, GF.
80. Olyve Jeter to Walrond, January 30, 1928, HFP.
81. Walrond telegram to Haynes, January 31, 1928, HFP.
82. Walrond to Haynes, February 16, 1928, HFP.
83. Arthur to Haynes, February 14, 1928, HFP.
84. Walrond to Haynes, February 16, 1928, HFP.
85. Walrond to Moe, December 17, 1927, GFP.
86. Gwendolyn Bennett, "The Ebony Flute," *Opportunity* 5 (September 1927): 277.
87. Walrond to Moe, December 17, 1927, GFP.
88. These were the writer Walter White; Isaac Fisher, Fisk University journalism instructor; and Nicholas Ballanta, a composer and musicologist from Sierra Leone.
89. As abstemious as he was ambitious, Moe was a Rhodes Scholar and military veteran who at age thirty had passed the bar in England and was lecturing at Oxford when he was tapped to head the Foundation in New York.
90. G. Thomas Tanselle, "Chronology," 30.
91. Boni & Liveright catalogue, Fall 1927, LP: 22.
92. Eric Walrond File, Guggenheim Foundation Papers (GFP).
93. Ibid.
94. Ibid.

95. Ibid.

96. Ibid.

97. Ibid.

98. William Seabrook, *Witchcraft: Its Power in the World Today* (New York: Harcourt, Brace, 1940): 223–24. His memoirs were *Asylum* (1935) and *No Hiding Place* (1942).

99. Eric Walrond File, Guggenheim Foundation Papers (GFP).

100. Ibid.

101. Ibid.

102. Gwendolyn Bennett, "Ebony Flute," *Opportunity* 5 (November, 1927): 340.

103. The Harmon Award and Zona Gale Scholarship likely redounded to Walrond's credit in the eyes of the Guggenheim selection committee, as Moe's correspondence with Walrond in February 1928 indicates his keen interest in these developments.

104. Eric Walrond File, Guggenheim Foundation Papers (GFP).

105. Reuben Stiehm, Wisconsin General Hospital, to Moe, April 3, 1928, GFP.

106. The creative arts appointees in 1928 included three poets, four painters, a sculptor, two playwrights, and two composers. Walrond was the only one for whom France was not the primary destination.

7. THE CARIBBEAN AND FRANCE (1928-1931)

1. Robert Hemenway, *Zora Neale Hurston: A Literary Biography*, 51.

2. *Chicago Defender*, May 12, 1928: 1.

3. "Guggenheim Foundation Awards," *The Times* [London], March 21, 1928: 15.

4. Herbert Aptheker, ed., *The Correspondence of W. E. B. Du Bois, 1877–1934*, 377.

5. Elizabeth Lay Green, *The Negro in Contemporary American Literature*, 51.

6. "Harlem" was a sub-entry within the general entry "The American Negro."

7. Walter Mignolo, who calls coloniality the "hidden face of modernity and its very condition of possibility," argues that "most stories of modernity have been told from the perspective of modernity itself, including, of course, those told by its internal critics," and as a result only the "border thinking" of those marginalized or exploited by the hegemonic projects of globalization constitute a "critical cosmopolitanism" that challenges existing inequalities. See "The Many Faces of Cosmo-polis: Border Thinking and Critical Cosmopolitanism," *Public Culture* 12:3 (2000): 721–45; and *Local Histories/ Global Designs: Coloniality, Subaltern Knowledges, and Border Thinking*, 49–89.

8. Letter to Miss Gluck, March 14, 1928, W. W. Norton Papers.

9. Gwendolyn Bennett, "The Ebony Flute," *Opportunity* 6 (February 1928): 56.

10. Charles Egleston, ed., *Dictionary of Literary Biography 288: The House of Boni & Liveright, 1917–1933*, 16.

11. Expenses for *The Big Ditch*, which totaled $1,592.45, were enumerated in a memo to Friede, September 17, 1928, three days before Walrond sailed for Panama. W. W. Norton

Papers, Butler Library, Columbia University. Messner and Liveright correspondence, July 27 and August 9, 1928, Annenberg Library, University of Pennsylvania.

12. It is unclear why Friede did not agree to the proposed terms. No mention of the matter appears in his memoir, *The Mechanical Angel*, nor do the Liveright Corporation Papers contain documentation. What is clear is that Friede was an adept violator of all sorts of commitments; he had been expelled from Harvard, Yale, and Princeton and divorced five of the six women he married. Preface to the Donald Friede Papers, Library of Congress.

13. Eric Walrond file, GFP.

14. John Lindsay-Poland, *Emperors in the Jungle: The Hidden History of the U.S. in Panama*, 40–42.

15. Walrond to Moe, April 2, 1929, GFP. United Fruit, a massive Boston-based company, had a long, checkered history in the region. Among the disgruntled West Indian workers for "el pulpo" (the octopus), as locals called United Fruit, was a young Marcus Garvey (Colin Grant, *Negro With a Hat: The Rise and Fall of Marcus Garvey*, 26–30).

16. Walter LaFaber, *The Panama Canal: The Crisis in Historical Perspective*, 76–77.

17. Eric Walrond File, GFP.

18. Walrond to Moe, April 2, 1929, GFP.

19. Franklin W. Knight, *The Caribbean: The Genesis of a Fragmented Nationalism*, 139.

20. Walrond may not have met Bellegarde in New York in 1927, but if not there or in Port-au-Prince the following year, they likely met in Paris in 1930, when Bellegarde wrote about Haiti's occupation in *La Dépêche africaine*.

21. The quotation from Harrison is from "Hands Across the Sea," *Negro World* (September 10, 1921). Harrison's critiques of Haiti's occupation are reprinted in Jeffrey B. Perry, ed., *A Hubert Harrison Reader*, 234–39.

22. Walrond to Moe, April 2, 1929, GFP.

23. Jan Rogozinski, *A Brief History of the Caribbean*, 265.

24. Ibid.

25. Ibid., January 22, 1929.

26. Moe to Walrond, March 8, 1929, GFP.

27. Adolph Gereau, "With Eric Waldron [sic] at the Eureka," *The Emancipator* 8 (April 3, 1929): 1; "Eric Waldron [sic] Seeks Material In Islands," *Chicago Defender* (May 5, 1929): A1.

28. Carl A. Wade, "A Forgotten Forum: The *Forum Quarterly* and the Development of West Indian Literature," *Caribbean Quarterly* 50 (2004): 64.

29. Ibid.

30. "Negro Progress Convention: Reception of Rev. F. G. Snelson," *Daily Argosy* (Georgetown), July 30, 1929.

31. Walrond sent two letters from "Off St. Kitts, British West Indies," to Moe dated April 2, 1929, GFP.

32. "I can't remember what the thing was," Ethel Ray Nance said years later, "I can't imagine Eric ever falling down on an assignment" (Nance, interview, 14).

33. Thurman to Hughes, undated, reprinted in Cary Wintz, ed., *The Critics and the Harlem Renaissance, 1920–1940*, 345.

34. Boni & Liveright Fall 1928 Catalogue, 22, LP.

35. By exterior, Mignolo does "not mean something lying untouched beyond capitalism and modernity, but the outside that is required by the inside. Thus, exteriority is indeed the borderland seen from the perspective of those 'to be included,' as they have no other option" ("Many Faces" 724).

36. William Shack, *Harlem in Montmartre: A Paris Jazz Story Between the Great Wars*, 71–73.

37. Joel A. Rogers, "Brightest Side of My Trip," *New York Amsterdam News* (October 5, 1927): 14.

38. Diary entry, June 28, 1925, Gwendolyn Bennett Papers, SCNYPL.

39. Michel Fabre, *From Harlem to Paris: Black American Writers in France, 1840–1980*, 76. Cullen's poem "To France" illustrates his association of the country and the language with the sensation of freedom.

40. Quote in Paule Marshall, *Triangular Road: A Memoir*, 27.

41. Walrond to Moe, June 30, 1929, GFP.

42. Langston Hughes, *The Big Sea*, 145.

43. Shack, *Harlem*, 31.

44. On heightened tensions due to white American visitors, including a Klan-initiated campaign to "protect" white women from black men, see Shack, *Harlem*, 68–71.

45. Wambly Bald, *On the Left Bank 1929–1933*, 4.

46. Walrond to Moe, August 26, 1929, return address 4 Rue du Parc Montsouris, GFP. However, Cullen's biographer, Charles Molesworth, confirmed that Cullen made no mention of housing Walrond in Paris. E-mail communication with the author, June 29, 2012.

47. Bald, *Left Bank*, 4.

48. Countée Cullen, "Countée Cullen in England," *The Crisis* (August 1929): 270.

49. Bald, *Left Bank*, 4.

50. Countée Cullen, "The Dark Tower," *Opportunity* 5 (September 1928): 4.

51. Theresa Leininger-Miller, *New Negro Artists in Paris: African American Painters & Sculptors in the City of Light, 1922–1934*, 84.

52. Charles Molesworth, *And Bid Him Sing: A Biography of Countée Cullen*, 169.

53. Cullen, "Dark Tower," (September 1928): 4.

54. Fabre, *From Harlem to Paris*, 141.

55. Cullen, "The Dark Tower," (September 1928): 4.

56. Fabre, *From Harlem to Paris*, 81, 141.

57. Tyler Stovall, *Paris Noir: African Americans in the City of Light*, 97–99.

58. Brent Hayes Edwards, *The Practice of Diaspora: Literature, Translation, and the Rise of Black Internationalism*, 119–24, 129; Stovall, *Paris Noir*, 107.

59. Mme. de Lesseps' handwritten translation of "the Panama Affair," WFP.

60. André Levinson, "De Harlem à la Cannebiere," *Les Nouvelles Littéraires* (September 14, 1929).

61. See Michelle Stephens, *Black Empire: The Masculine Global Imaginary of Caribbean Intellectuals in the United States, 1914–1962*, 167–203; Edwards, *Diaspora*, 187–240;

Louis Chude-Sokei, *The Last "Darky": Bert Williams, Black-on-Black Minstrelsy, and the African Diaspora*, 207–247; Heather Hathaway, *Caribbean Waves: Relocating Claude McKay and Paule Marshall*, 63–74.

62. "Why don't you send us something?" wrote Elmer Carter, the new editor of *Opportunity*, "I am mighty glad to hear from you, since I did not know where you were except that I heard that you were in Europe." July 18, 1930, SGD, Series III, Box 15.7.

63. This was his sobriquet in the *Lectures du Soir* interview, which translates roughly as "a first-class black writer."

64. Fabre, *From Harlem to Paris*, 320. Walrond's reference to "my Paris agent" appears in a January 9, 1931, letter to Graham.

65. Debora Bone translated the essay into English. The author gratefully acknowledges Dorothy Bone and Louis Parascandola for access to the translation.

66. Gerald Horne, *Race Woman: The Lives of Shirley Graham Du Bois*, 54.

67. Scrapbook, SGD, Box 1, Folder 1.8.

68. Shirley Graham, *Paul Robeson: Citizen of the World*, 211.

69. "People in Books," SGD, Box 1, Folder 1.1.

70. Graham, *Robeson*, 209–10.

71. Walrond to Graham, November 1, 1930, SGD, Series III, Box 15.7.

72. Postcard from Graham to her brother, September 21, 1930, SGD, Series III, Box 11.

73. Graham, *Robeson*, 210.

74. Henry Crowder, *As Wonderful As All That? Henry Crowder's Memoir of His Affair with Nancy Cunard, 1928–1935*, 132.

75. George Hutchinson, *In Search of Nella Larsen: A Biography of the Color Line*, 388.

76. William Seabrook, *Asylum*, 33.

77. Hutchinson, *In Search*, 383.

78. William Seabrook, *No Hiding Place: An Autobiography*, 322.

79. Crowder, *As Wonderful*, 132.

80. Walrond to Graham, November 1, 1930, SGD, Series III, Box 15.7.

81. SGD, Series III, Box 15.7, Folder 15.16. As Gerald Horne writes, "She was barely scraping by" (54).

82. N. S. Russell to Graham, November 18, 1930, SGD, Series III, Box 15.7.

83. Walrond to Graham, November 1, 1930, SGD, Series III, Box 15.7. It is possible to read the postscript to suggest profound *manipulation* rather than profound loneliness.

84. Ibid., January 27, 1931.

85. Ibid., November 29, 1930.

86. Ibid., March 22, 1931.

87. Ibid.

88. Ibid., January 27, 1931.

89. Ibid., January 27, 1931, and February 18, 1931.

90. Ibid., March 9, 1931.

91. Ibid., November 29, 1930, January 9, 1931, and January 27, 1931.

92. Ibid., November 29, 1930.

93. Ibid., February 18, 1931.

94. Ibid.

95. Ibid., January 27, 1931.

96. Ibid., January 9, 1931.

97. Ibid., November 1, 1930.

98. Ibid.

99. Ibid., March 9, 1931.

100. Autobiographical sketch, SGD, Series III, Box 1, Folder 1.1.

101. Walrond to Graham, April 22, 1931, SGD, Series III, Box 15.7.

102. Ibid.

103. Edna Worthley Underwood, "West Indian Literature: Some Negro Poets of Panama," *West Indian Review* [Kingston], March 1936: 67. Louis Parascandola consulted the American Hospital administration but was informed that records were destroyed after thirty years. "It may well have been psychological turmoil exacerbated by alcoholism," Parascandola surmised (Hutchinson, *In Search*, xxvii).

104. *New York Amsterdam News*, September 9, 1931.

105. "Mr. Walrond cited the benefits he received while a member of the Writers' Guild" ("Walrond Praises Literary Groups at Club's Meeting," *The New York Amsterdam News*, October 28, 1931: 15).

106. Correspondence between Moe and Horace Hitchcock, September, 1931, GFP.

107. Walrond to Graham, October 19, 1931, SGD, Series III, Box 15.7.

108. Kathleen Currie, "Interviews with Marvel Jackson Cooke," 49.

109. Wallace Thurman, "This Negro Literary Renaissance," 240.

110. Nance, interview, 15.

8. LONDON I (1931-1939)

1. "Walrond, Harmon Winner, Travels with Troupe," *The Baltimore Afro-American*, April 27, 1935.

2. David Levering Lewis, *When Harlem Was in Vogue*, 233.

3. Nance, interview, 15.

4. "Bob Williams in London," *Baltimore Afro-American* (June 23, 1934): 9.

5. Carol Polsgrove, *Ending British Rule in Africa*, ix.

6. Peter Blackman, "Is There a West Indian Literature?" *Life and Letters* [London] 59 (November 1948): 101.

7. Polsgrove, *British Rule*, xi xv; Penny Von Eschen, *Race Against Empire: Black Americans and Anticolonialism, 1937–1957*, 7–8.

8. Polsgrove, *British Rule*, 54.

9. "The writer who ran away" was the title of Kenneth Ramchand's essay about Walrond in *Savacou* in 1970. The characterization of Walrond as silent after 1929 appears in Lewis, *Vogue*, 233.

10. Pagination for "Tai Sing" and "Inciting to Riot" refers to Louis Parascandola and Carl A. Wade, eds., *In Search of Asylum: The Later Writings of Eric Walrond*.

11. Edward Scobie, *Black Britannia: A History of Blacks in Britain*, 154–59.

12. Delia Jarrett-Macauley, *The Life of Una Marson*, 49–50.

13. Tony Martin, *Amy Ashwood Garvey: Pan-Africanist, Feminist, and Marcus Garvey Wife No. 1*, 137.

14. March 19, 1935: 11. Another article two days earlier was entitled "Calypsoes in London Revue." The author thanks John Cowley and Howard Rye for information about the Harlem Nightbirds.

15. "Walrond, Harmon Winner, Travels with Troupe," *Baltimore Afro-American*, April 27, 1935.

16. "White Man, What Now?" *Spectator* (April 5, 1935): 562–63. Pagination refers to Louis Parascandola, ed., *"Winds Can Wake Up the Dead": An Eric Walrond Reader*.

17. Polsgrove, *British Rule*, 18.

18. Von Eschen, *Race*, 16.

19. Minkah Makalani, "An International African Opinion: Amy Ashwood Garvey and C. L. R. James in Black Radical London," 84–89.

20. On Walrond's presence at Holtby's with Marson and others, see Delia Jarrett-Macauley, *The Life of Una Marson*, 81–92.

21. Robert Hill, ed., *The Black Man: A Monthly Journal of Negro Thought and Opinion, 1933–1939*, 3.

22. Ibid., 5; Colin Grant, *Negro With a Hat: the Rise and Fall of Marcus Garvey*, 429, 438.

23. Hill, *Black Man*, 15.

24. "The American Negroes are the best organized and the most conscious of all the Negroes in the world," Garvey wrote in 1935 (Robert Hill, *Marcus Garvey: Life and Lessons*, 156).

25. Hill, *Black Man*, 18.

26. Pagination refers to Parascandola, ed., *Winds*.

27. Bill Schwarz, introduction to *West Indian Intellectuals in Britain*, 8.

28. Ibid.

29. Pagination refers to Parascandola, ed., *Winds*.

30. Composed in 1935, "Truckin'" was recorded by Fats Waller and Duke Ellington.

31. Fay M. Jackson, "Coronation in Review: Truckin' at Aggrey," *California Eagle* (May 28, 1937): 1.

32. The conflict between Mosley's "Black Shirts" and the anti-Fascists came to a head during Walrond's tenure at *The Black Man* in 1936. When Mosely announced a march through London's East End (home to many Jews), the Communist Party, Jewish advocacy groups, and other activists came out 100,000 strong to block the streets. A police force of 6,000 met them, beating and harassing demonstrators in an effort to secure access for the Fascists, a confrontation known as the Battle of Cable Street.

33. No documentation survives of Walrond's relationship with Padmore, but a 1959 letter to Moe indicates that he attended Padmore's funeral in London and considered him a friend.

34. Grant, *Negro With a Hat*, 438.

35. Linking the anticolonial struggle to the overthrow of capitalism and envisioning Africa as the critical site of struggle, Walrond echoed C. L. R. James, whose encounters with Africans in 1930s London dramatically revised his view of a "backward" Africa and politically advanced Caribbean (Makalani, "An International African Opinion," 83–95).

36. Marcus Garvey, "The Removal!" *Black Man* (August 1935): 3.

37. Grant, *Negro With a Hat*, 440–43.

38. Hill, *Black Man*, 19.

39. Benjamin Brawley, *The Negro Genius*, 253.

40. Walrond corresponded with Orwell in 1944, when Orwell was literary editor for *The Tribune*. He wished to review Charles Johnson's book *Patterns of Negro Segregation*. He later sent Orwell a sketch about the collaboration between the British police and the U.S. military police. Although Orwell "read it with interest and with some surprise," he passed it on to "the political section of the paper, to which I think it belongs," adding "I rather doubt their using it, because of our chronic shortage of space." Correspondence of October 17, 19, 21, and 23, and November 28, 1944, WFP.

41. Correspondence of July 14 and August 8, 1939, WFP.

42. "Law Notices," *The Times* [London] (September 14, 1938): 4; "News in Brief," *The Times* [London] (September 22, 1938): 7; "Coloured Men's Quarrel: A Struggle at West Kensington," *Westminster and Pimlico News* (September 9, 1938): 6.

43. Ula Yvette Taylor, *The Veiled Garvey: The Life and Times of Amy Jacques Garvey*, 129.

44. Grant, *Negro With a Hat*, 444–45; Taylor, *Veiled Garvey*, 128–134.

45. Taylor, *Veiled Garvey*, 129.

46. Johnson to Nance, May 4, 1939, ERN.

47. Ibid., July 12, 1939.

48. Ibid., September 2, 1939.

49. Ibid., January 3, 1940.

50. Ibid., September 2, 5, and 28, 1939.

51. Ibid., September 2, 1939.

9. BRADFORD-ON-AVON (1939–1952)

1. In addition to the author's observations in 2009, this chapter draws on Harold Fassnidge and Roger Jones, *Bradford-on-Avon: Past and Present*, 2nd edition (Jersey, UK: Ex Libris, 2007); and Margaret Dobson, *Bradford Voices: A Study of Bradford on Avon Through the Twentieth Century*.

2. Dobson, *Bradford Voices*, 101–103.

3. Advertisements in *The Wiltshire Times and Trowbridge Advertiser*, Wiltshire-Swindon History Centre.

4. Dobson, *Bradford Voices*, 115–17.

5. Gerald Bodman, interviewed by the author, Atworth-near-Melksham, March 17, 2009. Subsequent quotations are from the same interview.

6. John Cottle, interviewed by the author, Bradford-on-Avon, March 14, 2009. Subsequent quotations are from the same interview.

7. Mary Lane, interviewed by the author, Trowbridge, March 14, 2009. Subsequent quotations are from the same interview.

8. Ruth Walrond to Moe, May 31, 1940, GFP.

9. Walrond to Nance, September 4, 1939, ERN.

10. Nance to Johnson, September 28, 1939, ERN.

11. Johnson to Nance, January 3, 1940, ERN.

12. Herbert Aptheker, ed., *The Correspondence of W. E. B. Du Bois, 1877–1934*, 308.

13. Walrond to Moe, June 20, 1940, GFP.

14. "Eric Waldron [sic], Novelist, Lost in German Air Raid," *Chicago Defender* (April 29, 1944): 1.

15. See Louis Parascandola and Carl A. Wade, eds., *In Search of Asylum: The Later Writings of Eric Walrond*, lvii. Walrond's neighbor Mary Lane told the author, "During the war, the police came once and asked, did I know anything about him. Which I didn't, really; I couldn't say a lot about the man."

16. "The Hanging in England That People Hated," *New York Amsterdam News*, July 29, 1944: 6; "English Woman Held for 'Delinquency' of Child," *New York Amsterdam News*, August 19, 1944: 1.

17. Penny Von Eschen, *Race Against Empire: Black Americans and Anticolonialism, 1937–1957*, 42.

18. Ibid., 35.

19. Walrond's first article was the only one explicitly attributed to him, but the journal's contents leave little doubt about which contributions were his.

20. Mission statement, *The Monthly Summary* 1:1 (August 1943); Marybeth Gasman and Patrick J. Gilpin, *Charles S. Johnson: Leadership Beyond the Veil in the Age of Jim Crow*, 176–78.

21. "British Colonial Policy in Africa," *The Monthly Summary*, February, 1945: 198–200; "The Doctrine of States Rights in Africa," *The Monthly Summary*, November, 1945: 113–115.

22. Ibid., November, 1946: 99.

23. Dobson, *Bradford Voices*, 136.

24. Ibid., 137.

25. The fourth account, a sketch entitled "Strange Incident," waited several years to see print.

26. Avon Rubber Company spokesperson Fiona Stewart, e-mail message to author, May 29, 2009.

27. Dobson, *Bradford Voices*, 130.

28. Walrond to Bennett, May 22, 1946, Gwendolyn Bennett Papers, SCNYPL.

29. Charles Nichols, ed., *The Arna Bontemps—Langston Hughes Letters*, 228.

30. Anne Walmsley, *The Caribbean Artists Movement, 1966–1972*, 4.

31. Muhammad Anwar, "Immigration," 219.

32. Delia Jarrett-Macauley, *The Life of Una Marson*, 177. Two 1948 issues of *Life and Letters* included writing by Victor Reid, Peter Blackman, George Lamming, Clifford Sealy, Vivian Virtue, Edgar Mittelholzer, and Roger Mais.

33. Edouard Glissant, *Caribbean Discourse: Selected Essays*, 106.

34. Pagination refers to Louis Parascandola, ed., *"Winds Can Wake Up the Dead": An Eric Walrond Reader*.

35. Richard Allsopp's *Dictionary of Caribbean English Usage* defines *poor-great* as "Poor but haughty in appearance or conduct; too proud to be seen or known to accept charity or help that is really needed; poor and snobbish" (448). The Jamaican variant is *poor-show-great*.

36. Ibid.

37. As it happens, mental illness among "Negro" men was for the first time theorized with force and eloquence at that very moment in Frantz Fanon's *Black Skin, White Masks* (1952) and Ralph Ellison's *Invisible Man* (1952). V. S. Naipaul, a fledgling writer in London, descended this same year into suicidal ideation, "a great depression verging on madness." Neither his Oxford degree nor his renunciation of his Caribbean background prevented English landladies from disdaining his brown skin, and Naipaul said of 1952, "I was mentally disturbed. I was very, very disturbed, very melancholy, I had a degree of clinical depression" (Patrick French, *The World Is What It Is: The Authorized Biography of V. S. Naipaul*, 94, 96). Finally, the same month Walrond checked into Roundway Hospital, Guyanese writer Edgar Mittelholzer received a Guggenheim Fellowship taking him from the West Indies to Montreal, but he soon became unhinged and alcoholic, returning to Barbados and later taking his own life in Surrey, England.

10. ROUNDWAY HOSPITAL AND *THE SECOND BATTLE* (1952–1957)

1. *Bath and Wilts Chronicle and Herald*, March 29, 1952: 1.

2. Philip Steele, *Down Pan's Lane: The History of Roundway Hospital*, 3.

3. Ibid., 2.

4. Correspondence of December 1956 and March and April 1957, Eric and Jessica Huntley Collection, London Metropolitan Archives.

5. Correspondence between Walrond and Moe, September 24, October 9 and 30, 1953, GFP.

6. Ibid., August 30, 1954.

7. From "The Known, the Uncertain," originally published in French in *Le Discours Antillais* (Paris: Les Editions de Seuils, 1981). In J. Michael Dash's translation (1989), he prefers the terms "diversion" and "reversion," but I have used a modified translation from Brent Edwards, *The Practice of Diaspora: Literature, Translation, and the Rise of Black Internationalism*, 24.

8. Eleven of the thirteen stories are reprinted in Louis Parascandola and Carl A. Wade, eds., *In Search of Asylum: The Later Writings of Eric Walrond*.

9. *Bessie down* (or *bésé-dong*) is a song accompanying a Caribbean ring-game (Richard Allsopp, *Dictionary of Caribbean English Usage*, 95).

10. On the context in which De Lesseps made this statement see Matthew Parker, *Panama Fever: The Epic Story of the Building of the Panama Canal*, 67.

11. Parker, *Panama Fever*, 154.

12. Panamanian novelist Gil Blas Tejeira portrayed Prestán sympathetically in *Pueblos Perdidos* (1962), a fictionalized account of the civil war, honoring "the fundamental historical facts." Tejeira's Prestán was "a passionate man representing Colón's Black community who was hated by foreign Whites for his skin color and by Colombian conservatives for his rebellion" (John Lindsay-Poland, *Emperors in the Jungle: The Hidden History of the U.S. in Panama*, 213). Similarly, historian Matthew Parker argues that Prestán probably did not commit the crime for which he was hanged, the arson that destroyed much of Colón (*Panama Fever*, 154). It is hard to imagine Walrond examining the record and arriving at a divergent interpretation.

13. John Leech, *Inside-Out: The View from the Asylum*, 83.

14. Ibid., 86.

15. Ibid., 87.

16. Reginald Turner to Robert Bone, September 15, 1987. The author thanks Louis Parascandola for access to the letter.

17. Cunard to Walrond, undated 1954, WFP.

18. Ibid., October 4, 1954.

19. Ibid., December 2, 1954.

20. Ibid., January 7, 1956.

21. Walrond to Jackman, September 24 and November 8, 1954, CJMC.

22. Cunard to Marx, April 4, 1957, WFP.

23. Marx to Walrond, May 6, 1957, HFC.

24. Walrond to Marx, May 8, 1957, HFC.

25. Walrond to Jackman, September 23, 1957, CJMC.

26. Walrond to Marx, May 8, 1957, HFC.

27. Marx to Walrond, May 10, 1957, HFC.

28. Walrond to Marx, May 20, 1957, HFC.

11. LONDON II (1957–1966)

1. Walrond to Cunard, April 7, 1958, Nancy Cunard Papers, HRHRC.

2. The principal activity of the Company of Nine, which Marx codirected with Rumer Godden and James Haynes-Dixon, had been "literary lunches" at Foyle's Bookstore in Charing Cross.

3. Walrond to Marx, July 5, 1957, HFC.

4. Ibid., July 22, 1957.

5. Ibid., July 5, 1957.

6. Ibid., June 11, 1957.

7. Ibid., June 28, 1957.

8. Marx to Walrond, June 7, 1957, HFC.

9. Ibid., June 25, 1957.

10. Walrond to Marx, June 28, 1957, HFC.

11. The title was taken from a 1908 poetry collection by James Weldon Johnson.

12. Walrond to Marx, July 29, 1957, HFC.

13. Peter Fryer, *Staying Power: The History of Black People in Britain*, 374–75.

14. Donald Hinds, *Journey to an Illusion: The West Indian in Britain*, xxii.

15. Correspondence between Walrond and Erica Marx of July 25, August 1, August 22, August 25, and September 4, 1957, HFC. Walrond wrote Marx on August 27 to say that he would "apply for my release" on the 29th. He was officially discharged one week later.

16. Walrond to Marx, October 9, 1957, HFC.

17. Ibid., September 2, 1957.

18. Marx to Walrond, November 4, 1957, HFC.

19. Ibid., October 9, 1957.

20. Ibid., September 9, 1957.

21. Walrond to Marx, October 9, 1957, HFC.

22. Ibid., December 14, 1957.

23. Ibid., November 19, 1957.

24. Ibid., December 4, 1957, HFC.

25. Ibid., December 14, 1957.

26. Walrond to Jackman, April 2, 1958, CJMC.

27. Labour Exchanges were job centers, established at the turn of the century to link employers to workers through a centralized clearinghouse as an alternative to individual efforts.

28. Hinds, *Illusion*, 60–74.

29. Gordon Heath, *Deep Are the Roots: Memoirs of a Black Expatriate*, 87.

30. RPP. No correspondence between Pool and Walrond has survived. After "Black and Unknown Bards," Pool published *Beyond the Blues: New Poems by American Negroes* with Marx's Hand and Flower Press.

31. "Black Verse," *Sunday Times*, September 7, 1958; "Poetic Enterprise," *Manchester Guardian*, September 9, 1958. RPP.

32. *Books and Bookmen*, October, 1958. RPP.

33. "A Negro Triumph," *The Daily Worker*, October 7, 1958. RPP.

34. Elizabeth Frank, "TV Should Take Up This Show," *News Chronicle*, October 6, 1958. RPP.

35. "A Negro Triumph," *Daily Worker*, October 9, 1958. RPP.

36. *Books and Bookmen*, November 1958. RPP.

37. "Negro Poetry," *Stage*, October 9, 1958. RPP.

38. Frank, "TV Should Take Up This Show."

39. "A Negro Triumph," *Daily Worker*, October 9, 1958. RPP.

40. The poets began with Frances E. W. Harper, included Dunbar, McKay, Hughes, Bennett, and Cullen, and concluded with Robert Hayden, Gwendolyn Brooks, and Margaret Walker.

41. Bill Schwarz, "Claudia Jones and the *West Indian Gazette*: Reflections on the Emergence of Post-Colonial Britain," *Twentieth Century British History* 14:3 (2003): 264–85.

42. Fryer, *Staying Power*, 382; Muhammad Anwar, "Immigration," 219.

43. Anne Walmsley, *The Caribbean Artists Movement, 1966–1972*, 104.

44. George Lamming, telephone conversation with the author, November 18, 2009.

45. Walrond to Spingarn, April 1959, WFP.

46. Walrond to Jackman, December 21, 1958, CJMC.

47. Cunard to Walrond, December 18, 1958, WFP.

48. Ibid., January 6 and January 28, 1959.

49. Ibid., April 25, 1959.

50. Lois Gordon, *Nancy Cunard: Heiress, Muse, Political Idealist*, 322–42.

51. Walrond to Jackman, May 4, 1959, CJMC. *Incontro con L'Arte Africana* (1959), by Boris de Rachelwitz, was translated into English in 1966.

52. Walrond to Moe, June 11, 1960. GFP.

53. The Farringdon exchange was near the office, and Walrond had its contact information in his last address book, WFP.

54. Address book, WFP.

55. Tony Martin, *Amy Ashwood Garvey: Pan-Africanist, Feminist, and Marcus Garvey Wife No. 1*, 279–80. Others claim that Sylvia Pankhurst wrote the introduction. See Ula Y. Taylor, "Street Strollers: Grounding the Theory of Black Women Intellectuals," *Afro-Americans in New York Life and History* 30.2 (2006): 153–71. *Liberia: Land of Promise* was a 32-page pamphlet published by the Liberian Information Service.

56. Bontemps to Pell, September 14, 1965, LP.

57. Nance, interview, 14.

58. Pell to Walrond, December 28, 1965, LP.

59. Walrond to Pell, March 3, 1966, LP.

60. Pell to Walrond, March 7, 1966, LP. Walrond's editorial emendations appear on a copy of *Tropic Death* currently in the LP. Although he made some corrections to errors introduced in the original, most of Walrond's emendations were stylistic, particularly aimed to soften racial language that may have sounded offensive in the 1960s. Neither the 1972 Collier Books reprint nor the 2013 reissue from Liveright/Norton incorporated these emendations.

61. Walrond to Pell, March 11, 1966, LP.

62. Ibid., March 21, 1966.

63. Ibid., April 18, 1966.

64. Pell to Walrond, April 20, 1966, LP.

65. Walrond's death certificate cites the hospital and cause of death, "recurrent coronary thrombosis." The author wishes to thank Louis Parascandola for providing a copy.

66. Pell's suggestion that Collier commission an introduction from Bontemps was not followed, much to the dismay of Walrond's daughters. Adding insult to injury, Collier's edition included errors in Walrond's birthplace and the year of his death.

67. Jack Conroy, "Memories of Arna Bontemps: Friend and Collaborator," *American Libraries* (December 1974): 604.

68. Walrond to Hughes, undated [1965], Langston Hughes Papers, Series I, Box 167, JWJ.

69. Bontemps to Hughes, September 1, 1966 (Nichols 474).

POSTSCRIPT

1. Carlo Ginzburg, *The Cheese and the Worms: The Cosmos of a Sixteenth-Century Miller*, xxvi.

2. Nance, interview, 13.

3. Saidiya Hartman, *Lose Your Mother: A Journey Along the Transatlantic Slave Route*, 17.

BIBLIOGRAPHY

Allen, Devere. "Living Stories of Tropic Death," *The World Tomorrow* 9 (November 1926).

Allsopp, Richard, ed. *Dictionary of Caribbean English Usage*. Kingston, Jamaica: University of the West Indies Press, 2003.

Anwar, Muhammad. "Immigration." In *The Oxford Companion to Black British History*, ed. David Dabydeen, John Gilmore, and Cecily Jones, 218–21. New York: Oxford University Press, 2008.

Aptheker, Herbert, ed. *The Correspondence of W. E. B. Du Bois, 1877–1934*. Amherst: University of Massachusetts Press, 1973.

A Trip—Panama Canal. New Orleans and Panama City: Avery & Garrison, 1911.

Bald, Wambly. *On the Left Bank 1929–1933*. Athens, Ohio: Ohio University Press, 1987.

Baldwin, James. *Notes of a Native Son*. Boston: Beacon, 1955.

Bancroft, Hubert Howe. *California Inter Pocula*. San Francisco: History, 1888.

Bascara, Victor. "Panama Money: Reading the Transition to U.S. Imperialism." In *Imagining Our Americas: Toward a Transnational Frame*, ed. Sandhya Shukla and Heidi Tinsman, 365–86. Durham, NC: Duke University Press, 2007.

Blackman, Peter. "Is There a West Indian Literature?" *Life and Letters* [London] 59 (November 1948): 96–102.

"Bob Williams in London," *Baltimore Afro-American* (June 23, 1934): 9.

Bone, Robert. *Down Home: A History of Afro-American Short Fiction*. New York: Putnam's, 1975.

——. Unpublished biography of Eric Walrond. Private collection of Louis J. Parascandola.

Bone, Robert, and Louis J. Parascandola. "An Ellis Island of the Soul," *Afro-Americans in New York Life and History* 34, 2 (July 2010): 34–53.

Bontemps, Arna. "The Awakening: A Memoir." In *The Harlem Renaissance Remembered*, ed. Arna Bontemps, 1–26. New York: Dodd, Mead, 1972.

Brathwaite, Edward Kamau. *History of the Voice: The Development of Nation Language in Anglophone Caribbean Poetry*. London and Port of Spain: New Beacon, 1984.

Brawley, Benjamin. *The Negro Genius*. New York: Dodd, Mead, 1937.

——. "The Negro Literary Renaissance," *Southern Workman* 56 (April 1927): 177–83.

Brown, Ethelred, and Eugene Kinckle Jones. "West Indian-American Relations: A Symposium," *Opportunity* 4 (November 1926): 355–56.

Calverton, V. F. "Ground Swells in Fiction," *Survey* 57 (November 1, 1926): 160.

Calvin, Floyd. "Eric D. Walrond Leaves 'Opportunity' to Devote Entire Time to Writing," *Pittsburgh Courier* (February 12, 1927): 2.

Carew, Jan. "The Caribbean Writer and Exile," *The Journal of Black Studies* 8 (June 1978): 453–475.

Césaire, Aimé. *Discourse on Colonialism*. Translated by Joan Pinkham. New York: Monthly Review, 2000.

Chauncey, George. *Gay New York: Gender, Urban Culture, and the Making of the Gay Male World, 1890–1940*. New York: Basic, 1994.

Chude-Sokei, Louis. *The Last "Darky": Bert Williams, Black-on-Black Minstrelsy, and the African Disapora*. Durham, NC: Duke University Press, 2006.

Conniff, Michael. *Black Labor on a White Canal: Panama, 1904–1981*. Pittsburgh: University of Pittsburgh Press, 1985.

Conroy, Jack. "Memories of Arna Bontemps: Friend and Collaborator," *American Libraries* 5 (December 1974): 602–06.

Critchlow, Hubert. "History of the Labour Union Movement in British Guiana." In *The Voice of Coloured Labour*, ed. George Padmore, 49–55. Manchester: Panaf, 1945.

Crowder, Henry. *As Wonderful As All That? Henry Crowder's Memoir of His Affair with Nancy Cunard, 1928–1935*. Navarro, CA: Wild Trees, 1987.

Cullen, Countée. "Countée Cullen in England," *The Crisis* 36 (August 1929): 270, 283.

——. "The Dark Tower," *Opportunity* 6 (March 1928): 90.

——. "The Dark Tower," *Opportunity* 6 (September 1928): 4.

Currie, Kathleen. "Interviews with Marvel Jackson Cooke." The Washington Press Club Foundation, Women in Journalism Oral History Project, 1990.

"The Curse of Exploitation," *Star & Herald* (August 6, 1917): 4.

Dash, J. Michael. *The Other America: Caribbean Literature in a New World Context*. Charlottesville: University of Virginia Press, 1998.

Davis, Allison. "Our Negro 'Intellectuals,'" *Crisis* 35 (August 1928): 268–69, 284–86.

Davis, Richard Harding. *Three Gringoes in Venezuela & Central America*. New York: Harper, 1896.

"The Debut of the Younger School of Negro Writers," *Opportunity* 2 (May 1924): 143–44.

Des Voeux, Sir George William. *My Colonial Service in British Guiana, St. Lucia, Trinidad, Newfoundland, and Hong Kong. Vol. I*. London: Murray, 1903.

Dobson, Margaret. *Bradford Voices: A Study of Bradford-on-Avon Through the Twentieth Century*. Wiltshire, UK: Ex Libris, 1997.

Domingo, W. A. "The West Indies," *Opportunity* 4 (November 1926): 339–42.

Duberman, Martin. *Paul Robeson*. New York: Knopf, 1988.

Du Bois, W. E. B. "Back to Africa," *Crisis* 26 (February 1923): 539–48.

——. "The Criteria of Negro Art," *Crisis* 32 (October 1926): 290–97.

——. "Five Books," *Crisis* 33 (January 1927): 152.

——. "A Lunatic or a Traitor," *Crisis* 27 (May 1924): 8–9.

——. "Mrs. Fauset's Confusion," *The New Republic* 39 (July 30, 1924): 274.

Du Bois, W. E. B., and Alain Locke, "The Younger Literary Movement," *Crisis* 27 (February 1924): 161–63.

Edwards, Brent Hayes. *The Practice of Diaspora: Literature, Translation, and the Rise of Black Internationalism*. Cambridge, MA: Harvard University Press, 2003.

Egleston, Charles, ed. *Dictionary of Literary Biography. Volume 288: The House of Boni & Liveright, 1917–1933*. Detroit: Gale, 2004.

"Eric Waldron [sic], Novelist, Lost in German Air Raid," *Chicago Defender* (April 29, 1944): 1.

"Eric Walrond's Tales and Other New Works of Fiction," *New York Times Book Review* (October 17, 1926): 6.

Fabre, Michel. *From Harlem to Paris: Black American Writers in France, 1840–1980*. Urbana: University of Illinois Press, 1991.

Fearnley, Andrew M. "Eclectic Club." In *Encyclopedia of the Harlem Renaissance, Vol. 1*, ed. Cary Wintz and Paul Finkelman, 327–28. New York: Routledge, 2004.

Firestone, Matthew, ed. *Lonely Planet: Panama*, 4th edition. London: Lonely Planet, 2007.

Foner, Nancy. *In a New Land: A Comparative View of Immigration*. New York: New York University Press, 2005.

Frank, Waldo. "In Our Language," *Opportunity* 4 (November 1926): 352.

Frederick, Rhonda D. *Colón Man a Come: Mythographies of Panama Canal Migration*. Lanham, MD: Lexington, 2005.

French, Patrick. *The World Is What It Is: The Authorized Biography of V. S. Naipaul*. New York: Knopf, 2008.

Fryer, Peter. *Staying Power: The History of Black People in Britain*. London: Pluto Press, 1984.

Garvey, Marcus. "Editorial," *Negro World* (December 6, 1919): 1.

——. *Message to the People: The Course of African Philosophy*. Dover, MA: Majority, 1986.

——. "The Removal!" *The Black Man* 1 (August 1935): 3.

Gates, Henry Louis, Jr. "The Black Man's Burden." In *Fear of a Queer Planet: Queer Social Theory*, ed. Michael Warner, 230–38. Minneapolis: University of Minnesota Press, 1993.

Gasman, Marybeth, and Patrick J. Gilpin. *Charles S. Johnson: Leadership Beyond the Veil in the Age of Jim Crow*. Albany: State University of New York Press, 2003.

Gereau, Adolph. "With Eric Waldron [sic] at the Eureka," *The Emancipator* 8 (April 3, 1929): 1.

Gilpin, Patrick J. "Charles S. Johnson: Entrepreneur of the Harlem Renaissance." In *The Harlem Renaissance Remembered*, ed. Arna Bontemps, 215–46. New York: Dodd, Mead, 1972.

Ginzburg, Carlo. *The Cheese and the Worms: The Cosmos of a Sixteenth-Century Miller*. Translated by John and Anne Tedeschi. Baltimore: Johns Hopkins University Press, 1992.

Glissant, Edouard. *Caribbean Discourse: Selected Essays*. Translated by J. Michael Dash. Charlottesville: University of Virginia Press, 1989.

Gloster, Hugh. *Negro Voices in American Fiction*. New York: Russell and Russell, 1965.

Gómez, Nicolás Wey. *The Tropics of Empire: Why Columbus Sailed South to the Indies*. Cambridge, MA: MIT Press, 2008.

Gordon, Eugene. "The Negro Press," *Annals of the American Academy of Political and Social Sciences* 140 (November 1928): 248–56.

Gordon, Lois. *Nancy Cunard: Heiress, Muse, Political Idealist*. New York: Columbia University Press, 2007.

Goudie, Sean X. "New Regionalisms: US-Caribbean Literary Relations." In *A Companion to American Literary Studies*, ed. Caroline Levander and Robert Levine, 310–24. Chichester, UK: Wiley-Blackwell, 2011.

Graham, Shirley. *Paul Robeson: Citizen of the World*. New York: Messner, 1946.

Grant, Colin. *Negro with a Hat: The Rise and Fall of Marcus Garvey*. New York: Oxford University Press, 2007.

Green, Elizabeth Lay. *The Negro in Contemporary American Literature*: An Outline for Individual and Group Study. Chapel Hill: University of North Carolina Press, 1928.

Greene, Julie. *The Canal Builders: Making America's Empire at the Panama Canal*. New York: Penguin, 2009.

Grier, Thomas Graham. *On the Canal Zone*. Chicago: Wagner & Hanson, 1908.

Hall, Stuart. "Negotiating Caribbean Identities." In *New Caribbean Thought: A Reader*, ed. Brian Meekes and Folke Lindhal, 24–39. Kingston, Jamaica: University of the West Indies Press, 2001.

Harrison, Hubert. "The Cabaret School of Negro Literature and Art." In *A Hubert Harrison Reader*, ed. Jeffrey B. Perry, 355–57. Middletown: Wesleyan University Press, 2001.

Hartman, Saidiya. *Lose Your Mother: A Journey Along the Transatlantic Slave Route*. New York: Farrar, Strauss, and Giroux, 2008.

Haskin, Frederic J. *The Panama Canal*. Garden City: Doubleday, 1913.

Hathaway, Heather. *Caribbean Waves: Relocating Claude McKay and Paule Marshall*. Bloomington: Indiana University Press, 1999.

Hearn, Lafcadio. "Two Years in the French West Indies" (1890). Reprinted in *American Writings*. New York: Library of America, 2009.

Heath, Gordon. *Deep Are the Roots: Memoirs of a Black Expatriate*. Amherst: University of Massachusetts Press, 1992.

Hemenway, Robert. *Zora Neale Hurston: A Literary Biography*. Urbana: University of Illinois Press, 1977.

Herrick, Robert. "Review of *Tropic Death*," *The New Republic* 41 (November 10, 1926): 332.

Herring, Robert. "Editorial," *Life and Letters* 12 (September 1935): 1.

Hill, Robert, ed. *The Black Man: A Monthly Journal of Negro Thought and Opinion, 1933 1939*. Millwood, NY: Kraus-Thomson, 1975.

——. *Marcus Garvey: Life and Lessons*. Berkeley: University of California Press, 1987.

——. *The Marcus Garvey and United Negro Improvement Association Papers, Vols. I–X*. Berkeley: University of California Press, 1983.

——. *The Marcus Garvey and United Negro Improvement Association Papers, Vol. XI*. Durham, NC: Duke University Press, 2011.

Hinds, Donald. *Journey to an Illusion: The West Indian in Britain.* London: Bogle L'Ouverture, 2001.

Holstein, Casper. "T. S. Stribling in St. Croix." In *African Fundamentalism,* ed. Tony Martin, 104–05. Dover, MA: Majority, 1991.

——. "The Virgin Islands: Past and Present" *Opportunity* 4 (November 1926): 344–45.

Horne, Gerald. *Race Woman: The Lives of Shirley Graham Du Bois.* New York University Press, 2000.

Hughes, Langston. *The Big Sea.* New York: Hill & Wang, 1993.

——. "Marl Dust and West Indian Sun," *New York Herald Tribune* (Dec. 5, 1926): 9.

Hull, Gloria. *Color, Sex, and Poetry: Three Women Writers of the Harlem Renaissance.* Bloomington: Indiana University Press, 1987.

Hurston, Zora Neale. *Dust Tracks on a Road: An Autobiography.* Philadelphia: J. B. Lippincott, 1971.

Hutchinson, George. *The Harlem Renaissance in Black and White.* Cambridge, MA: Harvard University Press, 1995.

——. *In Search of Nella Larsen: A Biography of the Color Line.* Cambridge, MA: Harvard University Press, 2006.

Ikonné, Chidi. *From Du Bois to Van Vechten: The Early New Negro Literature, 1903–1926.* Westport, CT: Greenwood, 1981.

Jackson, Fay M. "Coronation in Review: Truckin' at Aggrey," *California Eagle* (May 28, 1937): 1.

James, Winston. *Holding Aloft the Banner of Ethiopia: Caribbean Radicalism in Early Twentieth Century America.* London: Verso, 1999.

Jarrett-Macauley, Delia. *The Life of Una Marson.* Manchester, UK: Manchester University Press, 2010.

Johnson, Abby, and Ronald Johnson. *Propaganda and Aesthetics: The Literary Politics of Afro-American Magazines in the Twentieth Century.* Amherst: University of Massachusetts Press, 1979.

Johnson, Charles S. "Editorials," *Opportunity* 4 (August 1926): 1.

——. "Editorials," *Opportunity* 4 (November 1926): 334–37.

——. "Editorials," *Opportunity* 5 (January 1927): 3.

——. "Eric Walrond," *Opportunity* 5 (March 1927): 67.

——. "The New Generation," *Opportunity* 2 (March 1924): 68.

Johnson, James Weldon. *Black Manhattan.* New York: Knopf, 1930.

Jones, Dewey R. "The Bookshelf," *Chicago Defender* (September 17, 1927): A1.

Kasinitz, Philip. *Caribbean New York: Black Immigrants and the Politics of Race.* Ithaca, NY: Cornell University Press, 1992.

Kirschke, Amy H. *Aaron Douglas: Art, Race, and the Harlem Renaissance.* Jackson: University Press of Mississippi, 1995.

Knight, Franklin W. *The Caribbean: The Genesis of a Fragmented Nationalism.* 3rd edition. New York: Oxford University Press, 2012.

LaFaber, Walter. *The Panama Canal: The Crisis in Historical Perspective.* New York: Oxford University Press, 1990.

Lamming, George. *In the Castle of My Skin*. Ann Arbor: University of Michigan Press, 1991.

Lebar, Jacques. "Avec Eric Walrond," *Lectures du Soir* No. 56 (January 14, 1933).

Leech, John. *Inside-Out: The View from the Asylum*. Bradford-on-Avon: Ex Libris, 1995.

Leininger-Miller, Theresa. *New Negro Artists in Paris: African American Painters & Sculptors in the City of Light, 1922–1934*. New Brunswick: Rutgers University Press, 2001.

Levinson, André. "De Harlem à la Cannebiere," *Les Nouvelles Littéraires* (September 14, 1929).

Lewis, David Levering. *W. E. B. Du Bois: The Fight for Equality and the American Century, 1919–1936*. New York: Holt, 2000.

——. *When Harlem Was in Vogue*. New York: Penguin, 1979.

Lewis, Lancelot. *The West Indian in Panama*. Washington, DC: University Press of America, 1980.

Lindsay-Poland, John. *Emperors in the Jungle: The Hidden History of the U.S. in Panama*. Durham, NC: Duke University Press, 2003.

Locke, Alain. "Negro Youth Speaks" In *The New Negro*, ed. Alain Locke, 48–52. New York: Simon & Schuster, 1992.

——. "The New Negro." In *The New Negro*, ed. Alain Locke, 3–18. New York: Simon & Schuster, 1992.

Major, John. *Prize Possession: The United States Government and the Panama Canal, 1903–1979*. Cambridge, UK: Cambridge University Press, 2003.

Makalani, Minkah. "An International African Opinion: Amy Ashwood Garvey and C. L. R. James in Black Radical London." In *Escape From New York: The New Negro Renaissance Beyond Harlem*, ed. Davarian Baldwin and Minkah Makalani, 77–104. Minneapolis: University of Minnesota Press, 2013.

Malmin, Lucius J. M. "A Caribbean Fact and Fancy," *Opportunity* 4 (November 1926): 343.

Marshall, Paule. *Triangular Road: A Memoir*. New York: Basic Civitas, 2009.

Martin, Tony. *African Fundamentalism: A Literary and Cultural Anthology of Garvey's Harlem Renaissance*. Dover, MA: Majority, 1991.

——. *Amy Ashwood Garvey: Pan-Africanist, Feminist, and Marcus Garvey Wife No. 1*. Dover, MA: Majority, 2007.

——. *Literary Garveyism*. Dover, MA: Majority, 1983.

McCullough, David. *The Path Between the Seas: The Creation of the Panama Canal, 1870–1914*. New York: Simon & Schuster, 1978.

McGeachy, Albert V. *The History of the Panama* Star & Herald. Panama City: Canal Zone Library-Museum, 1972.

McGuiness, Aims. *Path of Empire: Panama and the California Gold Rush*. Ithaca, NY: Cornell University Press, 2008.

McKay, Claude. *A Long Way from Home*. New Brunswick, NJ: Rutgers University Press, 2007.

Mignolo, Walter. *Local Histories/Global Designs: Coloniality, Subaltern Knowledges, and Border Thinking*. Princeton, NJ: Princeton University Press, 2000.

——. "The Many Faces of Cosmo-polis: Border Thinking and Critical Cosmopolitanism," *Public Culture* 12, 3 (2000): 721–45.

Miller, Kelly. "Watchtower," *New York Amsterdam News* (September 15, 1934): 8.

My Trip Through the Panama Canal: From the Atlantic to the Pacific. New York: International Mercantile Marine, 1929.

Molesworth, Charles. *And Bid Him Sing: A Biography of Countée Cullen.* Chicago: University of Chicago Press, 2012.

——. "Countee Cullen's Reputation: The Forms of Desire," *Transition* 107 (2012): 67–77.

Naipaul, V. S. *The Enigma of Arrival.* New York: Vintage, 1987.

Nance, Ethel Ray. Interviewed by Ann Allen Shockley, November 18 and December 23, 1970. Charles S. Johnson Collection, Fisk University Library.

Newton, Velma. *The Silver Men: West Indian Labour Migration to Panama, 1850–1914.* Kingston, Jamaica: Randle, 2004.

Nichols, Charles, ed. *The Arna Bontemps—Langston Hughes Letters.* New York: Dodd, Mead, 1980.

Osofsky, Gilbert. *Harlem: The Making of a Ghetto, 1890–1930.* New York: Harper, 1966.

Ovington, Mary White. "West India Tales," *The Chicago Defender* (January 1, 1927): A1.

Parascandola, Louis, ed. *"Look For Me All Around You": Anglophone Caribbean Immigrants in the Harlem Renaissance.* Detroit: Wayne State University Press, 2005.

——. *"Winds Can Wake Up the Dead": An Eric Walrond Reader.* Detroit: Wayne State University Press, 1998.

Parascandola, Louis, and Carl A. Wade, ed. *In Search of Asylum: The Later Writings of Eric Walrond.* Gainesville: University Press of Florida, 2011.

Parker, Matthew. *Panama Fever: The Epic Story of the Building of the Panama Canal.* New York: Anchor, 2009.

Perry, Jeffrey B., ed. *A Hubert Harrison Reader.* Middletown, CT: Wesleyan University Press, 2001.

Philipson, Robert. "The Harlem Renaissance as Postcolonial Phenomenon," *African American Review* 40 (Spring 2006): 145–60.

Polsgrove, Carol. *Ending British Rule in Africa.* Manchester, UK: Manchester University Press: 2009.

Powell, Richard J. "The Picturesque, Miss Nottage, and the Caribbean Sublime," *Small Axe: A Caribbean Journal of Criticism* 12 (February 2008): 157, 159–68.

Ragatz, Lowell J. *The Fall of the Planter Class in the British Caribbean, 1763–1833.* New York: Century, 1928.

Ramchand, Kenneth. *The West Indian Novel and Its Background.* 2nd edition. London: Heinemann, 1983.

——. "The Writer Who Ran Away: Eric Walrond and Tropic Death" *Savacou* 2 (1970): 67–75.

Randolph, A. Philip, and Chandler Owen, "The New Negro—What Is He?" *The Messenger* 3 (August 1920): 73–74.

Ransby, Barbara. *Ella Baker and the Black Freedom Movement: A Radical Democratic Vision.* Chapel Hill: University of North Carolina Press, 2003.

Reaves, Wendy Wick. *Celebrity Caricature in America.* New Haven, CT: Yale University Press, 1998.

Redding, J. Saunders. "Playing the Numbers," *North American Review* 236 (December 1934): 533–42.

Reed, Touré F. *Not Alms But Opportunity: The Urban League and the Politics of Racial Uplift, 1910–1950*. Chapel Hill: University of North Carolina Press, 2008.

Reid, Ira de Augustine. *The Negro Immigrant: His Background, Characteristics, and Social Adjustment, 1899–1937*. New York: AMS, 1939.

Rodney, Walter. *A History of the Guyanese Working People, 1881–1905*. Baltimore: Johns Hopkins University Press, 1981.

Rogers, Joel A. "Book Reviews," *Pittsburgh Courier* (March 5, 1927): 8.

——. "Brightest Side of My Trip," *New York Amsterdam News* (October 5, 1927): 14.

Rogozinski, Jan. *A Brief History of the Caribbean*. New York: Plume, 2000.

Rowell, Charles. "'Let Me Be With Ole Jazzbo': An Interview with Sterling A. Brown," *Callaloo* 14 (1991): 795–815.

Runcie, John. "Marcus Garvey and the Harlem Renaissance," *Afro-Americans in New York Life and History* 10, 2 (July 1986): 7–22.

Salabarría Patiño, Max. *La Ciudad de Colón en los Predios de Historia*. Panama: Litho Editorial Chen, 2002.

Scarborough, Dorothy. *The Supernatural in Modern English Fiction*. New York: Putnam's, 1917.

Schooling in the Panama Canal Zone, 1904–1979. Panama Canal Zone: Phi Delta Kappa, 1980.

Schwarz, A. B. Christa. *Gay Voices of the Harlem Renaissance*. Bloomington: Indiana University Press, 2003.

Schwarz, Bill, ed. *West Indian Intellectuals in Britain*. Manchester, UK: Manchester University Press, 2003.

Scobie, Edward. *Black Britannia: A History of Blacks in Britain*. Chicago: Johnson, 1972.

Scott, David. "The Sovereignty of the Imagination: an Interview with George Lamming," *Small Axe* 6, 2 (2002): 72–200.

Seabrook, William. *Asylum*. New York: Dell, 1935.

——. *No Hiding Place: An Autobiography*. New York: Lippincott, 1942.

Seacole, Mary. *The Wonderful Adventures of Mrs. Seacole in Many Lands*. London: Blackwood, 1857.

Shack, William. *Harlem in Montmartre: A Paris Jazz Story Between the Great Wars*. Berkeley: University of California Press, 2001.

Steele, Philip. *Down Pan's Lane: The History of Roundway Hospital*. Bradford-on-Avon: Steele, 2000.

Stepan, Nancy L. *Picturing Tropical Nature*. Ithaca, NY: Cornell University Press, 2001.

Stephens, Michelle Ann. *Black Empire: The Masculine Global Imaginary of Caribbean Intellectuals in the United States, 1914–1962*. Durham, NC: Duke University Press, 2005.

——. "Eric Walrond's *Tropic Death* and the Discontents of American Modernity." In *Prospero's Isles: The Presence of the Caribbean in the American Imaginary*, ed. Diane Accaria-Zavala and Rodolfo Popelnik, 167–78. London: Macmillan Caribbean, 2004.

——. "What Is This *Black* in Black Diaspora?" *Small Axe* 29 (2009): 26–38.

Stewart, Frank E. L. "Eric Walrond, *Tropic Death*, and the Predicament of the Colonial Expatriate Writer," *Hiroshima Shudo University Studies in the Humanities and Sciences* 38, 2 (1997): 29–88.

Stovall, Tyler. *Paris Noir: African Americans in the City of Light*. New York: Houghton Mifflin, 1996.

Swan, Michael. *British Guiana, The Land of Six Peoples*. London: Her Majesty's Stationary Office, 1957.

Tanselle, G. Thomas. "Chronology." In *The John Simon Guggenheim Memorial Foundation, 1925–2000: A Seventy-Fifth Anniversary Record*, 28–75. New York: John Simon Guggenheim Memorial Foundation, 2000.

Taylor, Ula Yvette. *The Veiled Garvey: The Life and Times of Amy Jacques Garvey*. Chapel Hill: University of North Carolina Press, 2002.

Thompson, Krista A. *An Eye for the Tropics: Tourism, Photography, and Framing the Caribbean Picturesque*. Durham, NC: Duke University Press, 2006.

Thurman, Wallace. *Infants of the Spring*. Boston: Northeastern University Press, 1992.

——. "Negro Artists and the Negro," *The New Republic* 51 (August 31, 1927): 37.

——. "This Negro Literary Renaissance." In *The Collected Writings of Wallace Thurman*, ed. Amritjit Singh and Daniel M. Scott, 241–51. New Brunswick: Rutgers University Press, 2003.

Tomes, Robert. *Panama in 1855*. New York: Harper, 1855.

Underwood, Edna Worthley. "West Indian Literature: Some Negro Poets of Panama," *West Indian Review* (March 1936): 35–37, 57.

Van Vechten, Carl. *Nigger Heaven*. Urbana: University of Illinois Press, 2000.

——. *The Splendid Drunken Twenties: Selections from the Daybooks, 1922–1930*. Urbana: University of Illinois Press, 2003.

Vogel, Shane. *The Scene of Harlem Cabaret: Race, Sexuality, Performance*. Chicago: University of Chicago Press, 2009.

Von Eschen, Penny. *Race Against Empire: Black Americans and Anticolonialism, 1937–1957*. Ithaca, NY: Cornell University Press, 1997.

Wade, Carl A. "African American Aesthetics and the Short Fiction of Eric Walrond," *CLA Journal* 42, 4 (June 1999): 403–29.

——. "A Forgotten Forum: The *Forum Quarterly* and the Development of West Indian Literature," *Caribbean Quarterly* 50 (2004): 63–73.

Wade, Carl, Robert Bone, and Louis Parascandola. "Eric Walrond and the Dynamics of White Patronage." In *Eric Walrond: the Critical Heritage*, ed. Louis Parascandola and Carl Wade, 149–66. Kingston, Jamaica: University of the West Indies Press, 2012.

Walmsley, Anne. *The Caribbean Artists Movement, 1966–1972*. London: New Beacon, 1992.

"Walrond, Harmon Winner, Travels with Troupe," *Baltimore Afro-American* (April 27, 1935).

"Walrond Praises Literary Groups at Club's Meeting," *New York Amsterdam News* (October 28, 1931): 15.

Walter, John C., and Jill Louise Anseheles. "The Role of the Caribbean Immigrant in the Harlem Renaissance," *Journal of Afro-Americans in New York Life and History* 1 (1977): 49–64.

Warren, Kenneth. "Appeals for (Mis-)Recognition: Theorizing the Diaspora." In *Cultures of United States Imperialism*, ed. Amy Kaplan and Donald Pease, 392–406. Durham, NC: Duke University Press, 1993.

Waters, Mary. *Black Identities: West Indian Immigrant Dreams and American Realities*. Cambridge, MA: Harvard University Press, 2000.

Watkins-Owens, Irma. *Blood Relations: Caribbean Immigrants and the Harlem Community, 1900–1930.* Bloomington: Indiana University Press, 1996.

Watson, Sonja Stephenson. "Are Caribbeans of African Ancestry an Endangered Species? Critical Literary Debates on Panamanian Blackness," *Latin American and Caribbean Ethnic Studies* 4 (November 2009): 231–54.

Weiss, Nancy J. *The National Urban League: 1910–1940.* New York: Oxford University Press, 1974.

Westerman, George. "Historical Notes on West Indians on the Isthmus of Panama," *Phylon* 22 (1961): 340–50.

Williams, Blanche Colton. *How To Study "The Best Short Stories."* Boston: Small, Maynard, 1919.

Williams, Eric. *From Columbus to Castro: The History of the Caribbean, 1492–1969.* New York: Vintage, 1984.

Wintz, Cary. *Black Culture and the Harlem Renaissance.* College Station: Texas A&M University Press, 1996.

——, ed. *The Critics and the Harlem Renaissance, 1920–1940.* London: Routledge, 1996.

——, ed. *The Harlem Renaissance, 1920–1940: The Emergence of the Harlem Renaissance.* New York: Garland, 1996.

Wood, Peter. *Weathering the Storm: Inside Winslow Homer's Gulf Stream.* Athens: University of Georgia Press, 2004.

Woodson, Jon. *To Make a New Race: Gurdjieff, Toomer, and the Harlem Renaissance.* Jackson: University Press of Mississippi, 1999.

ERIC WALROND BIBLIOGRAPHY

*Anthologized in *"Winds Can Wake Up the Dead"*
**Anthologized in *In Search of Asylum*

"Adventures in Misunderstanding," *The World Tomorrow* 9 (April 1926): 110–12.
"The Adventures of Kit Skyhead and Mistah Beauty," *Vanity Fair* 24 (March 1925): 52, 100.*
"Art and Propaganda," *Negro World* (December 31, 1921): 4.*
"Autocracy in the Virgin Islands," *Current History* 31 (October 1923): 121–23.
"Ban English Women," *Pittsburgh Courier* (June 19, 1937): 7.
"Behind Scenes of British Ban," *New York Amsterdam News* (March 2, 1940): 2.
"Bert Williams Foundation Organized to Perpetuate Ideals of Celebrated Actor," *Negro World* (April 21, 1923): 4.*
"Between Two Mountains," *Negro World* (December 17, 1921): 4.
Black and Unknown Bards: A Collection of Negro Poetry. Aldington, Kent: Hand and Flower, 1958. [Co-edited with Rosey E. Pool.]
"Black Bohemia," *Vanity Fair* 25 (November 1925): 125.
"Black Britons on War Front," *New York Amsterdam News* (October 7, 1939): 1.

"The Black City," *The Messenger* 7 (January 1924): 13–14.

"A Black Virgin," *Negro World* (February 11, 1922): 4.*

"Bliss," *Roundway Review* 1 (July 1953): 19–23.**

Brine. Unpublished manuscript (1924). Walrond Family Papers.**

"Britain Spurs Training of Negroes and Indians," *People's Voice* (December 30, 1944): 6.

"British Colonial Policy in Africa," *Monthly Summary of Events & Trends in Race Relations* 3 (February 1945): 198–200.

"British Hail Black Hero: Britons Praise Algerian Hero," *New York Amsterdam News* (October 28, 1939): 1–2.

"By the River Avon," *Crisis* 54 (January 1947): 16–17.*

"Can the Negro Measure Up?" *The Black Man* 2 (August 1937): 9–10.

"Cardiff Bound," *Roundway Review* 3 (February 1955): 55–60.

"The Castle D'Or," *Negro World* (March 18, 1922): 6.

"Charleston, Hey! Hey!" *Vanity Fair* 26 (April 1926): 73, 116.

"Chippenham's Way," *Monthly Summary of Events & Trends in Race Relations* 2 (November 1944): 101–103.

"A Cholo Romance," *Opportunity* 2 (June 1924): 177–81.

"City Love." In *The American Caravan*, ed. Van Wyck Brooks and Lewis Mumford, 485–93. New York: Macaulay, 1927.*

"The Color of the Caribbean," *The World Tomorrow* 10 (May 1927): 225–27.*

"The 'Colour Bar' in Great Britain," *Monthly Summary of Events & Trends in Race Relations* 2 (March 1945): 229–30.

"Como de Hizo el Canal de Panama," *Ahora* (August 19, 1934).

"Consulate," *The Spectator* (March 20, 1936): 510–11.*

"The Coolie's Wedding," *Roundway Review* 1 (February 1953): 19–24.**

"Cynthia Goes to the Prom," *Opportunity* 1 (Nov. 1923): 342–43.

"A Desert Fantasy," *Negro World* (March 4, 1922): 4.

"Developed and Undeveloped Negro Literature," *Dearborn Independent* (May 13, 1922): 12.*

"The Dice of Destiny," *Negro World* (March 11, 1922): 4.*

"Discouraging the Negro," *Negro World* (December 10, 1921): 4.

"Education and Training of Negroes and Indians in Britain," *People's Voice* (December 15, 1945): 13.

"The End of Ras Nasibu," *The Black Man* 2 (January 1937): 13–15.

"Enter, the New Negro . . . Exit, the Colored Crooner," *Vanity Fair* 23 (December 1924): 60–61.

"The Failure of the Pan-African Congress," *Negro World* (December 3, 1921): 4.

"Fascism and the Negro," *The Black Man* 2 (March/April 1937): 3–5.

"Florida Girl Shows Amazing Gift for Sculpture," *Negro World* (December 6, 1922): 3.

"From British Guiana to Roundway," *Roundway Review* 1 (December 1952).**

"A Fugitive from Dixie," *The Black Man* 1 (May/June 1936): 13.**

"A Geisha Girl," *Negro World* (April 8, 1922): 4.

"The Godless City," *Success* 8 (January 1924): 32–33, 90, 104, 108, 111.*

"Harlem." In *Encyclopedia Britannica*, 14th edition (1929): 200–01.

"Harlem," *Lectures du Soir* No. 59 (February 4, 1933).**

"Harlem Nights," *Star* (September 26, 1935).**

"*Harlem Shadows*" [review], *Negro World* (May 6, 1922): 4.

"The Hebrews of the Black Race," *International Interpreter* (July 14, 1923): 468–69.

"Higher Education in Britain's Colonies," *Journal of Higher Education* 17 (April 1946): 211–14.

"The Iceman," *Roundway Review* 1 (August 1953): 21–26.**

"Imperator Africanus: Marcus Garvey, Menace or Promise?" *Independent* (January 3, 1925): 8–11.*

"Inciting to Riot," *Evening Standard* (July 26, 1934): 22.*

"Indian Troops Employed for British Dirty Work," *People's Voice* (December 15, 1945):13.

"Inter-racial Cooperation in the South," *International Interpreter* (March 29, 1924): 1652–54.

"Ireland Sets Up Its Right to Be Neutral," *New York Amsterdam News* (December 30, 1939): 1, 6.

"Italy Leaves Trail of Terror in Ethiopia," *People's Voice* (March 24, 1945): 22.

"Jail West Indian Stowaways," *New York Amsterdam News* (April 20, 1940): 1, 16.

"*Jonah's Gourd Vine* and *The Ways of White Folk*" [review], *The Keys* 2 (Jan/March 1935): 61.

"Junk," *Negro World* (December 30, 1922): 4.

"The Lieutenant's Dilemma," *Roundway Review* 3 (May 1955): 134–138.**

"The Loan," *Roundway Review* 1 (September 1953): 22–27.**

"Marcus Garvey—A Defense," *Negro World* (February 11, 1922): 4.*

"The Men of the Cibao," *People's Voice* (December 29, 1945): 21; (January 5, 1946): 21.**

"Miss Kenny's Marriage," *The Smart Set* 72 (September 1923): 73–80.*

"The Morality of White Folks," *Negro World* (February 25, 1922): 4

"Morning in Colon," *West Indian Review* (August 1940): 31–32.

"My Version of It," *Negro World* (March 31, 1923): 4.

"El Negro, Expulsado del Cabaret, Vuelve a Labrar la Tierra," *Ahora* (June 21, 1934).

"The Negro Before the World," *Black Man* 3 (March 1938): 4–5.

"Negro Folk-Song," *Saturday Review of Literature* (July 11, 1925): 891.

"The Negro in the Armies of Europe," *Black Man* 1 (September/October 1936): 8–9.

"The Negro in London," *Black Man* 1 (March 1936): 9–10.*

"The Negro Literati," *Brentano's Book Chat* (March/April 1925): 31–33.*

"Negro Migrants in Britain," *Christian Science Monitor* (September 17, 1948): 9.

"A Negro Novel" [review], *The New Republic* 42 (March 4, 1925): 48–49.

"The Negro Poet: *The Book of American Negro Poetry*" [review], *Negro World* (April 1, 1922): 4.

"The Negro Renaissance," *Clarion* 1 (July 1929): 15; reprinted in *Gleaner* (August 17, 1929): 26.**

"The New Negro Faces America," *Current History* 30 (February 1923): 786–88.*

"Noted Writer Reveals Inner Glimpse of London as War Clouds Appeared," *New York Amsterdam News* (September 23, 1939): 1, 10.

"On Being a Domestic," *Opportunity* 1 (Aug. 1923): 234.*

"On Being Black," *The New Republic* 32 (November 1, 1922): 244–46.*

"On England," *Black Man* 3 (July 1938): 18.*

"Our Bookshelf," *Opportunity* 2 (July 1924): 219–21.

"The Palm Porch." In *The New Negro*, ed. Alain Locke, 115–26. New York: Simon & Schuster, 1992 [1925].

"A Piece of Hard Tack," *Roundway Review* 1 (October 1953): 18–22.**

"A Poet for the Negro Race," *The New Republic* 46 (March 31, 1926): 179.

"Poor Great," *Arena* (September/October 1950): 40–44.*

"Portrait I—An Artist," *Negro World* (March 4, 1922): 4.

"Racial Bar Persists in England's R.A.F." *Amsterdam News* (November 4, 1939): 1.

"Recent Negro Literature," *The Clarion* 2 (January 1930).**

"Review of *Black Odyssey* by Roi Ottley," *Life and Letters* 65 (March 1950): 230–33.

"Review of *Focus: Jamaica* by Edna Manley," *Life and Letters* 63 (November 1949): 174–77.

"Review of *South Bound* by Barbara Anderson," *Life and Letters* 65 (April 1950): 70–72.

"Review of *Twelve Million Black Voices* by Richard Wright," *Life and Letters* 59 (November 1948): 176, 178, 180.*

"Romance of a Reporter," *Messenger* 7 (December 1924): 382–83.

"A Rose," *Negro World* (March 11, 1922): 5.

"Says Casper Holstein is Champion of Oppressed," *Chicago Defender* (March 15, 1927): part II, 1.

"A Seat for Ned," *Roundway Review* 3 (October 1955): 254–59.

The Second Battle (i–xv), *Roundway Review* 4–5 (April 1956–July 1957).**

"A Senator's Memoirs," *Negro World* (December 17, 1921): 6.*

"The Servant Girl," *Roundway Review* 1 (January 1953): 7–13.**

"The Silver King," *Argosy All-Story Weekly* (February 23, 1924): 291–97.

"Slowness of Western Front Offensive Palls," *New York Amsterdam News* (September 30, 1939): 1, 10.

"Soapbox in Washington," *People's Voice* (September 29, 1945): 5.

"The Stolen Necklace," *Argosy All-Story Weekly* (April 19, 1924): 628–34.

"The Stone Rebounds," *Opportunity* 1 (September 1923): 277–78.*

"Strange Incident," *Roundway Review* 4 (January 1956): 44–46.

"Stribling on the Women of Trinidad," *Negro World* (December 24, 1921): 4.

"Strut Miss Lizzie," *Negro World* (June 24, 1922): 4.

"Success Story," *Roundway Review* 2 (February–July 1954).**

"Tai Sing," *Spectator* (April 20, 1934): 615–16.**

"There Is Confusion" [review], *The New Republic* 39 (July 9, 1924): 192.*

"Tories Act to Hurt Britain," *New York Amsterdam News* (November 11, 1939): 4.

Tropic Death. New York: Liveright/Norton, 2013.

"Two Sisters," *Roundway Review* 1 (March 1953): 18–21; (April 1953): 21–26; (May 1953): 19–25.**

"Vignettes of the Dusk," *Opportunity* 2 (January 1924): 19–20.*

"A Vision," *Negro World* (February 18, 1922): 4.

"Visit to Arthur Schomburg's Library Brings out Wealth of Historical Information," *Negro World* (April 22, 1922): 6.*

"The Voodoo's Revenge," *Opportunity* 3 (July 1925): 209–13.*

"War News," *New York Amsterdam News* (March 30, 1940): 13.

"West Indian Labor," *International Interpreter* (May 26, 1923): 240–42.

"West Indians Fight in Burma," *People's Voice* (March 10, 1945): 9.

"White Airmen in England Protest Treatment of Negro Comrades," *People's Voice* (December 9, 1944): 16.

"White Man, What Now?" *Spectator* (April 5, 1935): 562–63.*

"Wind in the Palms," *Roundway Review* 2 (September 1954): 235–40.**

"The Word 'Nigger,'" *Negro World* (February 4, 1922): 4.

"Writer Says 200,000,000 Negroes Thank John Bull," *California Daily Eagle* (October 11, 1935).

"Young Dr. Davis of Barbados," *Negro History Bulletin* 10 (June 1947): 211–12.

INDEX

Tropic Death (Walrond) (*continued*)
discussion of, 239; linguistic revolution
as traced to, 169; meaning of title, 27;
morbidity of, 31; as narrative of entry
of Caribbean into industrial modernity,
162; as new form of black transnational
fiction, 186; opportunity to revise, 183;
as product of multiple influences, 187; as
proof of assimilative force of U.S., 185;
publication of, 4; reception of, 178–187;
reissue of, 350–352; on relationship
between African Americans and West
Indians, 184; relationship of to American
race relations, 162; role of sun in, 171–
174; sale of, 1; sales of, 207; supernatural
in, 129; target audience of as mainly
white, 160; as tracing migration and
acculturation, 162; translation of, 241;
as understood in conflicting ways, 186;
Waldron as eager to distance self from
explicit ideological agenda in, 326;
Walrond as not keeping up promise
of, 288
"The Tropics in New York" (McKay), 120
truckin,' 279
Tucker, Louella, 99, 148, 150
Twelve Million Black Voices (Wright), 309
23rd Street office, 190
"Two Sisters" (Walrond), 15, 18, 19, 20, 21,
318, 319

Underwood, Edna Worthley, 83, 84–86,
87, 258
Underwood, Mr. (fictional), 310, 311
Universal Negro Improvement Association
(UNIA), 3, 37, 53–60, 62, 65, 67, 70,
78–80, 81, 87, 89, 90, 103, 170, 194, 266,
274, 275, 283
University of Wisconsin, 214, 220–221
Urban League: *See* National Urban League
U.S. Bureau of Investigation, 78
U.S. citizenship, 94

Van Doren, Carl, 81, 114, 116, 117, 118, 149
Vanity Fair, 3, 87, 135, 136, 138, 141, 142,
147, 148, 183

Van Sertima, Ivan, 346
Van Vechten, Carl, 3, 43, 128, 134, 135–136,
143–147, **144**, 148, 149, 150, 151, 152,
237
vernacular, 36, 73, 106, 121, 122, 136, 142,
155, 184, 284, 355
"Vignettes of the Dusk" (Walrond), 77,
96–97, 187
Villaine, Nestor (fictional), 104
Villard, Oswald Garrison, 115
Virgin Islands, 88, 89, 91
Virgin Islands Congressional Council, 129
"A Vision" (Walrond), 65
"Visit to Arthur Schomburg's Library Brings
out Wealth of Historical Information"
(Walrond), 69
Vogel, Shane, 134
"The Voodoo's Revenge" (Walrond), 103,
105, 148
"Voodoo Vengeance" (Walrond), 86

Wade, Carl, 2, 158, 230
Wadiri, Lucky, 348
Walker, A'Lelia, 43, 143, 145, 146, 148, 150,
208, 209
Walmer Lodge, 21
Walrond, Annette (sister), 43
Walrond, Carol (brother), 43
Walrond, Claude (brother), 43
Walrond, Dorothy (daughter), 51
Walrond, Edith (wife), 51, 109
Walrond, Eric: acclaim for after *Tropic
Death*, 189–190, 207; adolescence of,
31–32; advance on second book, 4;
ambition of, 111–112; ancestors of,
13–14; apartment at 137th Street and
Seventh Avenue, Harlem, 50; arrival
in Bradford-on-Avon, 291; arrival in
Europe, 5; arrival in New York, 5, 11,
41; attraction of black nationalism
to, 54; birth of, 2, 14; as catalyst for
New Negro movement, 100; childhood
of, 13, 15–16, 18–19; children of, 51,
109; chronology, xv–xvii; college
education of, 63, 69–70, 129, 214–215;
as considering self a failure, 1; death